PORTRAIT OF THE SOVIET UNION

PORTRAIT OF THE
SOVIET UNION

Fitzroy Maclean

You cannot understand us or our actions,
unless you know our history.
MIKHAIL SERGEYEVICH GORBACHOV
December 1987

WEIDENFELD AND NICOLSON
LONDON

For Margaret Augusta

Copyright © 1988 by Fitzroy Maclean and Turner Broadcasting Services

Published by George Weidenfeld and Nicolson Limited
91 Clapham High Street, London SW4 7TA

ISBN 0–297–79384—5

British Library Cataloguing in Publication Data

Maclean, Fitzroy, *1911*–
   Portrait of the Soviet Union.
   1. Soviet Union
   I. Title
   947.085′4
ISBN 0–297–79384–5

Typeset and printed in Great Britain by
Butler & Tanner Limited, Frome and London

CONTENTS

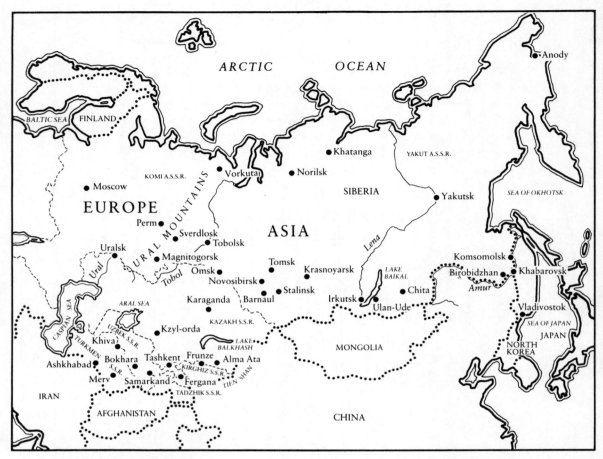

MAP ONE USSR; Central Asia

MAP TWO   USSR; European Russia

List of Illustrations

All the Russias

All the Russias, the land that has spread smoothly,
glidingly over half the globe.
GOGOL

When we speak of the Soviet Union, most of us are inclined to think of it as Russia and of its inhabitants as Russians. This does not take account of its immense diversity. More than half its territory lies in Asia and already the fast-growing non-Russian population is beginning to outnumber the ethnic Russians. Russia, though the largest and by far the most important, is only one of fifteen different Soviet Socialist Republics, many of them inhabited by people as different from European Russians as the people of Hong Kong or Bombay are from those of London or Edinburgh. In Turkestan, for example, the inhabitants are for the most part Turko-Tartars, speaking a language akin to Turkish. Others are closer to Mongols or Persians. The mosques are crowded with turbaned worshippers and the bazaars recall their counterparts in any other Islamic country. In the Caucasus you will find a jumble of races, languages and religions more varied than anywhere else in the world. Beyond the Caucasus, in Transcaucasia, the Georgians, unlike almost any other race in Europe or Asia, are not even Indo-Europeans, being, they will tell you, somehow akin to the Basques. The Armenians, again, are totally different. Each of these races has its own language, which, as often as not, is no more like Russian than Chinese is like French. And each has its own ancient civilization, reaching back for thousands of years to a period when Russia and the Russians, as such, did not exist and reflected in the entirely distinctive culture and way of life of its people. The same applies to the three Baltic Republics, conquered by Russia in the eighteenth century and between the First and Second World Wars briefly independent.

The historical reason for this is that in the sixteenth, seventeenth, eighteenth and nineteenth centuries, while other European nations were founding colonies overseas, the Russians were busy expanding at the expense of their immediate neighbours, conquering vast new territories and incorporating them and their inhabitants within the all-embracing frontiers of their Empire. Siberia, Transcaucasia, Central Asia, all went the same way. 'All the Russias', wrote Gogol, 'the land that has spread smoothly, glidingly over half the globe.' And the Tsar was called 'Tsar of all the Russias'.

Vital here was the plain – the limitless Russian plain – snow-covered in winter, muddy in spring and autumn, dusty and breathless in summer. The plain helped form the Russian character and shape the course of Russian history. To it can perhaps be attributed the autocratic character of successive Russian regimes. Historically, mountains have everywhere been the home of freedom and independence, while the dwellers in the plains have tended to fall under the rule of tyrants. If the Russians were to survive as a nation, a strong central authority was needed to keep them together and weld them into a homogeneous whole, into a nation which would over the years withstand the onrush of the Mongol and Tartar hordes that swept in from Asia and, in the north and north-west of the Poles, the Swedes, the Lithuanians and the Teutonic Knights.

The plain also had its effect psychologically. The flat expanse in which the Russians live is, I suspect, at least partly responsible for a number of their characteristics, for their explosiveness, their love of colour, their taste for drama and music and strong drink, for their moods and melancholy. They have a need to escape, from the weather and the cold and the bleak flatness stretching endlessly away under the grey dome of the sky. The plain, too, has surely contributed to the quality of which they are proudest, to the 'breadth' or generosity of their nature. Living in a plain that size, you might well not bother too much about details or distance or the passage of time.

In the long run it was the plain, spreading away for thousands of miles in every direction, that gave the Russians their urge to expand. It was the obvious thing for them to do, to expand at the expense of those same Tartar hordes who had come charging down on them out of Asia; to expand across Siberia and across the Bering Strait into America; to break through to the Baltic; to expand eastwards or westwards, northwards or southwards, wherever the opportunity offered.

Most people nowadays have (or think they have) a vague idea of what European Russia is like. When it comes to the non-Russian parts of the Soviet Union, they are on less familiar ground. If these areas are not inhabited by Russians, they ask themselves, then by whom are they inhabited? And what goes on there? What sort of life do the inhabitants have? Are they less Communist than the Russians or more so? Less or more civilized? Less or more prosperous? Have they any sort of autonomy or independence, or are they simply Russian colonies, governed from Moscow?

These are some of the questions that this book seeks to answer, as well as probing the far-reaching changes now taking place in Russia itself. For me, just half a century after my first arrival there, the Soviet Union is still one of the most exciting countries in the world, in many ways as different from the West as China, perhaps even more different. Leaving it after a two years' stay in the doom-laden spring of 1939, with the storm clouds fast gathering over Europe, I found it hard to imagine what the future might hold for the Soviet Union, then barely twenty years old. Half a century later, having watched with fascination, very often from close quarters, the developments of the intervening years, I find myself still seeking an answer to the same question: where is it going from here? Each time I return, which I do frequently, I come on something new and surprising. Since the advent of Mikhail Sergeyevich Gorbachov this has been particularly true. That big changes lie ahead is certain, though how far-reaching they will be, just what form they will take or how quickly they can be accomplished, is as yet less clear.

PART ONE

MOTHER RUSSIA

Russia is different.
F. I. TYUTCHEV
1866

You live here, walk about, talk and
forget that you are in a place which is quite unique
until some small sight or episode or phrase
brings home the fact to you and you say:
'This is Russia'.
MAURICE BARING
1906

1

Between Two Seas

The past is not a bad witness.
OLD RUSSIAN PROVERB

How, when and where did it all start?

For many centuries the great plain that is now European Russia served as a stamping-ground for a succession of savage nomad tribes mainly of Asian origin, Scythians, Sarmatians, Alans, Pechenegs, Goths, Khazars, Huns and Finno-Ugrians, whose public and private lives were, in Gibbon's telling phrase, 'neither softened by innocence nor refined by policy'. Not until the ninth century of our era are there signs of a more settled or more civilized population. It is at this point in time that most historians fix the beginnings of Russian history, the race or tribe who finally settled in the fertile plains of Southern Russia being the Slavs, attracted by a pattern of natural waterways and by the opportunities they offered for trade. Soon they had established a regular route from the Baltic to the Black Sea and on to Byzantium, its early trading posts becoming in time flourishing towns.

But the early Slav settlers still had to contend with fresh waves of invaders from the East and in due course the citizens of Novgorod, or New Town, in the north-west, feeling the need for support against these repeated encroachments, turned for help and protection to their northern neighbours, the better-organized and more effectual Varangians or Vikings. 'Our land,' they told them, 'is great and rich. But there is no order in it. Come and rule over us.' The Norsemen responded readily and soon the Varangian Prince Rurik had established himself in Novgorod, as founder of Russia's first ruling dynasty, the Rurikids, who, with time, became ever more closely assimilated to their East Slav, or, as they came to call them, Russian subjects.

On Rurik's death in 879, his brother-in-law Oleg assumed the regency. Like most Vikings, Oleg was a conqueror. Moving southwards from Novgorod, he seized Kiev on the Dnieper and made himself master of the considerable area which lay between them. It was now that Kiev, the Mother of Russian cities, became capital of a more or less unified Slav confederation, known as Russia or Rus. Russia, it has been said, was born between two seas, the Black Sea and the Baltic. Not unnaturally its new rulers' chief concern was to keep their trade routes open and each spring the prince in person would make his way southwards with a well-armed retinue known as a *druzhina* and a flotilla of cargo-vessels carrying furs, honey and slaves down the Dnieper and on across the Black Sea to Byzantium, the capital of the Eastern Empire.

Rurik's son Igor, who succeeded Oleg in 912, proved a weak ruler. On his death, power passed to his widow Olga, originally the girl who operated the ferry across the Velikaya at Pskov and a woman, it appears, of striking beauty and great strength of character, who now served as regent for her young son Svyatoslav. For some time already there had been contacts between pagan Kiev and Christian Byzantium. In 957, Olga came back from a visit to Byzantium a declared Christian, indeed a future saint. Olga's conversion to Christianity was, not unnaturally, an event of great significance.

Olga's son Svyatoslav, now the reigning prince, remained, it is true, resolutely pagan, brushing aside his mother's suggestion that he should follow her example on the grounds that it would make him a laughing-stock among his comrades in the *druzhina*. A warrior first and foremost, 'stepping lightly like a panther', Svyatoslav 'carried with him neither wagons nor kettles, but cut off small strips of horseflesh, or game, or beef and ate it after roasting it on the coals. Nor did he have a tent, but spread out a piece of saddle-cloth under him and set his saddle under his head.' By 967 he had brought the whole length of the Volga under Russian control.

But four years later Svyatoslav was ambushed and killed near the cataracts of the Dnieper by a band of Pecheneg marauders, who made a drinking cup of his skull. From the savage fratricidal struggle for power which followed his death, it was his third son Vladimir who emerged victorious, as anyone who knew him could quite easily have foretold. Vladimir was a man of outstanding ability and ruthless determination, who to Kievan Rus first gave the character of a true state. Moreover, marrying no less a person than Anna, sister of the co-emperors of Byzantium, he quickly embraced Christianity and, like his grandmother before him, was in due course canonized. Today in Kiev his statue, bearing a massive cross, looks thoughtfully out across the Dnieper.

In addition to its spiritual impact, Vladimir's conversion to Christianity, automatically followed by that of his subjects, duly baptized in droves in the muddy waters of the Dnieper, was to prove of great historical and geo-political importance. Vladimir, moreover, was not simply a saint. Known by his contemporaries as *fornicator immensus et crudelis*, he was a full-blooded and effective ruler with great zest for life and a harem of eight hundred concubines. Now closely and beneficently linked with Byzantium and increasingly exposed to its civilizing influence, Kievan Rus became an integral part of Christian Europe.

The year 1988, marking, as it does, the millennium of Russia's conversion to Christianity seems likely to be celebrated with due solemnity by all concerned even under a nominally atheistic Soviet regime. Already the ancient Danilovski Monastery in Moscow, at different times an electrical factory and a home for juvenile delinquents, has been returned to the Church reconsecrated amid moving religious ceremonies and lavishly refurbished as a fitting residence for the Patriarch – a further reminder that the history of Russia is in more ways than one the history of the Orthodox Church.

St Vladimir died in 1015. Following a further period of fratricidal strife, in the course of which one of his sons, Svyatopolk the Accursed, assassinated his two brothers, St Boris and St Gleb, before himself being eliminated, he was succeeded by his fourth son, Yaroslav the Wise, yet another strong and resourceful character, who, after decisively defeating the marauding Pechenegs, set about making Kiev a truly splendid capital city. It was he who built its great Cathedral Church of St Sophia and founded the famous Monastery of the Caves.

Powerful and civilized, Kievan Rus by this time possessed dynastic connections with many of the royal houses of Europe. Taken together, the reigns of Vladimir and Yaroslav marked the height of its cultural, economic and political development. But, though strong and effective rulers, neither father nor son governed as an absolute monarch. Under them Rus remained a confederation of principalities in which the nobles or boyars enjoyed considerable independence, while a *veche* or council of citizens retained the power to appoint or dismiss the ruling prince.

Yaroslav was the last Grand Prince to rule effectively over the whole of Kievan Rus. On his death in 1054, yet another fierce struggle broke out for the succession and the confederation over which he had so successfully presided quickly disintegrated. More nomad invaders now flooded into Russia. But, instead of uniting against them, the individual Russian princes quarrelled destructively among themselves, while their unfortunate subjects sought refuge as best they could in the woods and forests. In the north-west, meanwhile, new enemies were by now emerging, Teutonic Knights, Swedes and Lithuanians.

A last, not altogether unsuccessful attempt to reunify Russia was made by Yaroslav's clever grandson Vladimir Monomakh, a son-in-law of King Harold of England, who, ascending the throne in 1113, for a dozen years ruled over most of Kievan Rus and whose magnificently bejewelled hat of gold and sable you may to this day see carefully preserved in the Moscow Kremlin. But no sooner was Monomakh dead than fierce fighting broke out between his sons and grandsons, while fresh waves of invaders harassed Kievan territory.

After innumerable vicissitudes, present day Kiev, since 1934 capital of the Ukraine and now a city of over 3 million inhabitants, still recalls the dawn of Russian history. Approaching it on a fine summer's day, you catch sight, as you drive in from the airport, of the glittering golden spires and domes of Yaroslav the Wise's Monastery of the Caves, standing out against a background of bright green trees high above the River Dnieper. Through the centuries the Dnieper, a fine wide swift-flowing stream, was to remain a vital link in the trade route between north and south – 'from the Varangians', as the saying went, 'to the Greeks'. To Kiev came traders from the Baltic and the great fur-bearing forests of the north as well as from Arabia and Byzantium. Already a prosperous trading centre in Oleg's day, it was at the end of the tenth and beginning of the eleventh centuries that Kiev reached its zenith and became one of the most resplendent of European cities and an important focus of culture and civilization.

The site of the original town, built on the high ground overlooking the Dnieper, is not far from where the great Cathedral of Sophia now stands. Here the prince had his palace and here the nobles and other notables built their mansions. Here, too, stood the first stone church in Russia, *Desyatinaya Tserkov*, the Tithe Church or Church of One Tenth, founded by St Vladimir himself and dedicated by him to the Virgin Mary, but of this only the foundations now remain.

On the lower ground to the north of old Kiev in the area known as Podol dwelt the merchants, the craftsmen and the artisans. By now Lower Kiev was doing business with traders who, coming from all over the world, settled in the parts of the town specially allotted to them. Massive fortifications protected the city's riches against attack. In St Vladimir's time the Golden Gates, parts of which still survive, served as the principal entrance to the city, being adorned with doors of solid gold carried off as booty from the Chersonese. It was in 1037, on the very battlefield where he had defeated the Pechenegs, that Yaroslav the Wise built the great Cathedral of St Sophia, where he himself lies buried in a splendidly-carved marble sarcophagus.

As you enter the cathedral, you face a serenely beautiful eleventh-century mosaic of the Virgin, filling the whole of the central apse. The cathedral also contains some most unusual early frescoes, including an intriguing representation of Yaroslav the Wise and his family. On the walls of the turret stair leading to its upper gallery other secular subjects are depicted – hunting scenes, games and dances. High up in the roof of the great church was once a kind of periscope which gave a clear view of the countryside for miles around. Chancing to glance through this, it is said, a local maiden was rewarded with a close-up view of her absent lover dallying in some bushes with a Pecheneg damsel, which so enraged the poor girl that she smashed the whole contraption to pieces.

A mile or two to the south of St Sophia, strategically sited on the high ground above the river, is one of the oldest Russian monasteries in existence, the Monastery of the Caves or Pecherski Monastery, likewise founded by Yaroslav. Within its precincts are two little hills with a valley between them. Its name, Pecherski, derives from the underground cells of the early monks – caves carved out of the living rock and honeycombing the smaller and more northerly of the two hills known as the Hill of the Far Caves. Here stood the Church of the Assumption, built in the second half of the eleventh century, but reduced during the Second World War to a heap of rubble. The adjoining Church of St John the Baptist still survives. Later, more subterranean cells (known as the Near Caves) were dug in the valley between the two hills. Close to their entrance stands the seventeenth-century Church of the Holy Cross. Above the Monastery's main entrance is the single-domed Church of the Trinity, built in 1108, but largely rebuilt in the eighteenth century.

With the decline of Kiev, the Monastery of the Caves suffered a long period of neglect, but was lavishly restored towards the end of the seventeenth century when it acquired its present predominantly Baroque appearance. To feel yourself back in the Middle Ages, however, you need only spend an hour or two underground among the caves, where you come suddenly and somewhat unnervingly face to face with the mummies of the original inhabitants, notably with that of Nestor the Chronicler, to whom we owe a lively and not entirely unreliable account of early Russian history. Nestor's neighbour, John the Long-suffering, who, as a penance, had himself buried up to the neck with only his mitred head protruding from the earth and survived in this posture for no less than thirty years, I was unfortunately unable to find, though he was certainly still *in situ* as recently as 1914. Though the Monastery and its churches have not, in the Soviet phrase, been 'working' for half a century or more, the Caves are for believers still a popular place of pilgrimage, where camera-toting tourists rub shoulders with genuine worshippers.

Over the years, the Cathedral of St Sophia, like the Monastery of the Caves, fell into disrepair and was recast in its present Baroque mould at the end of the seventeenth century. Of the other buildings within the cathedral precincts, a refectory, the Metropolitan's palace, a seminary and the southern and western entrance gates to the precincts all date from the same period or later. It was not until the nineteenth century that Kiev, from a group of scattered monasteries and townships, grew to be a great modern city. Once a wooded valley, its principal street, the Kreshchatik, became a busy thoroughfare, leading from the heights above the Dnieper to the centre of the New Town. The chestnut trees which lined it gave it an agreeable greenness. Hitler's forces, who occupied Kiev from 1941 to 1943, left the city virtually in ruins. Once they were gone, the first thing the inhabitants did, they will tell you, was to replant the Kreshchatik and the other streets with chestnut trees, soon making it as green as ever it was.

With Kiev's decline in the twelfth century, power passed elsewhere. Fleeing before the invading hordes, large numbers of Russians moved into the forest regions of the north, hitherto inhabited by Lithuanians and Finno-Ugrians and known as the *Zalesye* or Land Beyond the Forests. By the beginning of the thirteenth century two powerful principalities had emerged in Northern Russia: Novgorod, where Rurik had held sway three centuries before, and, some hundreds of miles away to the south east, Rostov-Suzdal.

By this time Novgorod's dominions extended over an area greater than all the rest of Russia, while both Novgorod itself and Pskov, the second city of the principality, were larger than any other Russian city. From the north-west their merchants or *boyars* now ranged far and wide in pursuit of trade and in both cities a measure of democracy prevailed, power residing first and foremost with the veche or assembly, who themselves elected both prince and archbishop.

Bordering on Novgorod's territories to the east between the Oka and the Upper Volga was the principality of Rostov-Suzdal, likewise a land of forests, populated partly by indigenous Finnish tribes and partly by Russians fleeing before the ever-encroaching invaders. Independent by the end of the eleventh century, Rostov-Suzdal was bestowed by Vladimir Monomakh of Kiev on his enterprising and resourceful son Yuri Dolgoruki or Long-in-the-Arm, a grasping character, as his name indicates, who in his turn founded within the borders of his principality the new townships of Vladimir, Yaroslavl, Pereslavl Zalesski and Moscow, the last in those days no more than an isolated stronghold on a hill above the river of the same name, seized by Yuri from its rightful owner, the Boyar Kuchko.

On Yuri Dolgoruki's death in 1157 his son, Andrei of Bogolyubovo, declared himself Prince of Suzdal. Prince Andrei, who combined a warrior's energy and enterprise with the virtues and demeanour of a future saint, was, as it happened, also a man of considerable culture and admirable taste. Making the new town of Vladimir his capital, he summoned 'master craftsmen from all countries', endowed it with many fine churches built of the local white limestone and fortified it against all comers. Then, raising a powerful army, he sacked both Novgorod and Kiev and, returning to Vladimir laden with loot, assumed the title of Grand Prince.

Following his assassination in 1175 at the hands of some dissident boyars, acting in collusion with his wife Ulita, Andrei was succeeded as Prince of Suzdal-Vladimir and as Grand Prince by his brother Vsevolod, known by reason of his plentiful progeny as Big Nest. Like Andrei before him, Vsevolod dominated the Russian scene until his death in 1212 and in his turn greatly embellished the principality, their two reigns being marked by an exceptional flowering of Russian architecture and art. Suzdal now took Kiev's place as a religious centre, rivalling it by the beauty of its places of worship. On Vsevolod's death in 1212 a fresh dispute broke out over the succession, with unhappy results for what was left of Kievan Rus. More Russians now dispersed northwards, while others sought refuge in the south and south-west.

Meanwhile, two thousand miles farther east in Mongolia, a new and formidable phenomenon had arisen, which in a few years was destined to change the face of the known world. The year 1154 had seen the birth of a son to Yesugei Bagatur, a minor Mongol chieftain. At birth the child was found to be clutching in his tiny hand a clot of dried blood, boding ill for the future. For better or for worse he was given the name of Temujin, which he was in due course to exchange for the more resounding title of Jenghiz Khan or Ruler of the World. 'The greatest joy a man can know,' declared Jenghiz, on reaching what are sometimes called years of discretion, 'is to conquer his enemies and drive them before him. To ride their horses and plunder their goods. To see the faces of those dear to them bedewed with tears and to clasp their wives and daughters in his arms.' He lost no time in putting his theories into practice. Having first made himself master of Mongolia and Northern China, he next turned westwards and in 1223, eleven years after Vsevolod Big Nest's death, reached the frontiers of Russia at the head of an immensely formidable force of a quarter of a million well-trained nomad horsemen.

The sudden advent of the Mongols took the Russians completely by surprise. 'No one knows for certain', wrote a contemporary chronicler, 'who they are or whence they come or what their language is or race or faith. But they are called Tartars.' It was not long before the Russians discovered more about the invaders, with their 'broad flat faces and cruel looks, thin hair upon their upper lips and pit of their chins, light and nimble bodies with short legs, as though made for riding a horse'. 'Their speech', added the chronicler no less evocatively, 'is sudden and loud, coming, as it were, from a deep and hollowed throat.' In 1223 Russians and Mongols met for the first time in battle near the Sea of Azov. In the ensuing engagement the Russian army was annihilated and the Prince of Kiev crushed to death under the boards on which the triumphant Tartars spread their victory feast.

For the Mongols this first assault had been no more than a reconnaissance. Fourteen years later, while other Mongol armies launched offensives in other directions, Jenghiz's grandson, Batu or Baty Khan of the Golden Horde, set out in all seriousness to conquer Russia. Hurling his cavalry across the Volga in December 1237, he first attacked Riazan. Then Kolomna. Then Moscow. Next, pitching his camp at nearby Batyevo, as it has been called ever since, he sacked Vladimir and Suzdal. In the spring of 1238 his troops moved against Novgorod, but, checked by its marshy approaches, withdrew southwards to the country of the Lower Volga and the Don. A year later, the Mongols were back, ravaging the north-east. In 1240 they again turned south and, after a great battle, stormed ancient Kiev itself. 'We found', a passing traveller reported, 'countless heads and bones of dead people lying in the fields.' After that Batu continued his advance westwards, conquering Volhynia and Galicia, crossing the Carpathians, over-running Hungary and Poland. Soon the Mongol Empire reached from Peking to the gates of Vienna.

Then, early in 1242, came all of a sudden the news that the Great Khan of the Mongols was dead and, equally suddenly, Batu set out for Mongolia to elect a successor. Mongolia was a long way away. By the time he returned to Russia, his army's advance westwards had lost its impetus. Withdrawing to the Lower Volga, he set up his headquarters at Sarai, near the site of the future city of Stalingrad (or Volgograd, as it is now rather confusingly called).

For the next two centuries Sarai served as capital for the Golden Horde. Almost all European Russia was by this time under Mongol suzerainty. Mongol rule was absolute. The Mongols exacted heavy tribute and ruthlessly repressed any attempt at rebellion. Otherwise, they did little to disturb the Russian way of life, leaving the Russian princes to rule over their own principalities and collect their own taxes, always providing that they paid due tribute and did due homage to their Mongol masters. Needless to say, Russia's northern neighbours quickly took advantage of her misfortunes to encroach on her territories, the Swedes seizing what is now Finland, the Danes part of Estonia and the Teutonic Knights the country near the mouth of the Western Dvina and the Niemen.

With the years, the Russians came in practice to accept their new situation as vassals of the Mongols. In time Vsevolod's son Yaroslav, who had succeeded him in 1212, rebuilt the cities of Suzdal-Vladimir, while Yaroslav's son Alexander, who was soon to prove a consummate statesman as well as a great military commander, ruled over Novgorod. Though Novgorod was never conquered by the Mongols, Prince Alexander was wise enough to pay them tribute, which left him free to face the dangers now threatening his principality from the north and west. In 1240, on the River Neva, where it flows into the Gulf of Finland, he heavily defeated the Swedes, who had invaded Novgorod from Finland, thus winning for himself the title of Alexander Nevski. Two years later he inflicted a no less decisive defeat on the German Knights of the Sword, who had by that time established themselves in Livonia. Then, pushing on to Pskov, he again routed the Germans in a famous cavalry battle fought on the ice of Lake Peipus and immortalized in our own times by Eisenstein's memorable film. Finally, in 1245, Alexander fell on the Lithuanians and drove them, too, headlong out of his principality.

On his father Yaroslav's death in 1252, Alexander Nevski became in his turn Prince of

Vladimir and Grand Prince, titles in which he was duly confirmed by his Tartar suzerains. In 1263 he died and was buried at Vladimir. In a score of years he had become a Russian national hero and as such was in due course canonized by the Orthodox Church. Some seven centuries later, in 1942, Generalissimo Stalin, himself at the time hard pressed by the Germans, was to institute a high Soviet decoration in his honour.

With its massive fortifications and austere white churches, Novgorod, where Rurik once ruled and whence Alexander Nevski set out in 1240 to fight the Swedes and the Teutonic knights, still vividly recalls Russia's early struggle for nationhood, indeed for existence – a struggle resumed in our own times, when the city again became an outpost of embattled Slavdom.

Lord Novgorod the Great, as its inhabitants liked to call it, is divided into two halves by the River Volkhov. The west bank or Sophia Side is dominated by the golden-domed Cathedral of St Sophia, which stands within the walls of the Kremlin or *detinets*, built on a slight eminence above the river. A first wooden church with thirteen cupolas was built in 989 on the site of the present Cathedral by a certain Joachim, despatched from Kiev by St Vladimir to be the first Bishop of Novgorod. As in other mediaeval Russian towns, most of the buildings in Novgorod were made of wood, but in 1044 the Kremlin was given walls of stone and a year later work was begun on the present cathedral, an outstanding example of early Russian architecture.

On the east bank of the Volkhov, the so-called Market Side centres round the *Yaroslavovo Dvorishche* or Court of Yaroslav, which lies immediately across the river from the Kremlin and consists of a group of ancient churches, of which the oldest and most important is the Cathedral of St Nicholas. Right around both halves of the old town runs a line of crumbling earthworks dating back to the twelfth century.

In Novgorod's early days the reigning Prince's authority went undisputed and St Sophia served as his chapel royal. But by the twelfth century his powers had already been considerably reduced and he had been made responsible to the veche or assembly of boyars and leading citizens. Thereafter the princes of Novgorod moved out of the Kremlin and St Sophia ceased to be their personal place of worship. Establishing themselves in the *gorodishche* or fort, a mile or so south of the town on the east bank of the river, they built during the early part of the twelfth century a number of other churches, notably the Cathedral of St Nicholas in Yaroslav's Court and the Monastery and Cathedral of St George at Yurievo, a mile or two to the south of the town on the west bank of the Volkhov.

With time the princes' position deteriorated still further and in 1136 the prince of the day was driven out of Novgorod which became to all intents and purposes a republic. '*Koli Khud Knyaz, tak v gryaz!*' yelled the citizens. 'If the Prince is no good, into the mud with him!' Thereafter, during the twelfth and thirteenth centuries, much of the building in Novgorod was done by the boyars or rich merchants, notably the Stroganov family, merchant-adventurers and natives of the town, who were later to win fame and fortune in Siberia. It was a group of these same merchants who in 1207 built the remarkable Church of St Paraskeva on the Market Place.

Though never taken by the Mongols and firmly put back on the map by Alexander

Nevski, who in his own day firmly reasserted the Prince's authority, Novgorod did not altogether escape the blight of the Mongol invasion and for a time few new churches were built there. But the beginning of the fourteenth century things had begun to improve. Having established extensive trading connections with Western Europe and become a leading member of the Hanseatic League, Novgorod enjoyed greater prosperity than ever. In architecture and the arts, no less than politically, the people of Novgorod maintained their independence and their contacts with the outside world and went their own way. By the fifteenth century, however, Novgorod's independence had begun to be threatened by Moscow, now in its turn Russia's most powerful principality and already reluctant to tolerate any rivals. A staunch upholder of his city's rights against Muscovite encroachment was the city's archbishop, Euphymius, though, despite his efforts, Novgorod's days as an independent state were by now numbered.

With the glittering domes of St Sophia showing above its walls, the Kremlin or *detinets* still dominates Novgorod. Its massive late fifteenth-century towers and ramparts (roughly contemporary with those of the Moscow Kremlin) provide an impressive setting for the cathedral. On one of its walls an inscription recalls that it was from here that Alexander Nevski set out to do battle with the enemies of Russia in 1240 and 1242. It was in the Kremlin, too, that Novgorod's famous *veche* assembled when summoned by its bell and here that state business was carried on. Near St Sophia are the *Vladichni Dvor* or Archbishop's Residence, the *Granitovaya Palata* or Palace of the Facets and the clock tower built by the good archbishop Euphymius in the fifteenth century.

Facing St Sophia stands Novgorod's fantastic Millennary Monument, cast in solid bronze in 1863 to commemorate the first thousand glorious years of Russian history, from Rurik to Alexander II by way of Ivan the Terrible and Peter the Great. Deliberately defaced by the Germans in World War II, it has since been lovingly restored and is visited daily by troops of patriotic schoolchildren.

Latterly, one of the Kremlin's churches, the little white Church of the Intercession, has been converted in the Williamsburg manner into an Olde Russian Restaurant, serving a selection of ancient Russian delicacies. Happening to shelter there from a shower, I soon found myself seated at a massive mediaeval style table being served in the dim religious light with *Borshch Tsarski* (à la Tsar), eaten with lacquered wooden spoons, and *Pokrovski Kotlyeti* (Cutlets Intercession), washed down with Olde Russian mead which serves in moderation as an excellent chaser to a tot or two of modern Soviet vodka, when you can get it. From the Kremlin, a short walk over the bridge across the river brings you to the Market Side and to Yaroslav's Court and the Cathedral of St Nicholas. Nearby is the seventeenth-century gatehouse of what was once the Gostini Dvor or Market

A hundred and twenty miles to the west lies Lord Novgorod's 'younger brother', the old town of Pskov, most easily reached by train from Leningrad. Arriving there at three in the morning by the Baltic Express and doing my best not to disturb the young woman in a sky-blue nightdress with whom I was sharing my sleeping compartment, I stepped out on to the station platform in the pitch dark. It was here, I recalled, that in the Imperial Train, on the afternoon of 15 March 1917 the ill-fated Tsar Nicholas II had signed his abdication. As far as I could see, nothing much had changed since then. After two World Wars and a Revolution, the nineteenth-century station building was still standing, painted a soothing shade of green; at most there had been some adjustments to the station master's uniform. Collecting my bags, I took a cab to the Hotel October, a solid-looking product of the 1950s. At the cinema opposite, I noticed with pleasure, they were giving Agatha Christie's 'Murder on the Orient Express'.

Smaller than Novgorod, Pskov is planted in a commanding position at the junction of two rivers, the Velikaya and the Pskova. Towering above the massive battlements of the Kremlin stands the great square white Cathedral of the Trinity, first built on this site in the twelfth century in place of an earlier wooden church and largely rebuilt in 1699. It is still in use as a church and on Sundays and feast days is crowded with worshippers. Two great towers guard the point where the Pskova flows into the Velikaya. Near the tower on the far bank are the fifteenth-century Church of the Resurrection as well as a couple of robustly built seventeenth-century merchants' houses resembling miniature fortresses, a number of which still survive in the town, recalling the days when Pskov was at the peak of its prosperity and ready to defend itself against all comers.

In the Middle Ages, when Pskov, like Novgorod, was an independent republic, the Kremlin served as its military, religious and administrative centre. Within its walls the *veche* assembled and it was here that Alexander Nevski was acclaimed in 1242 after his victory over the German Knights of the Sword. In those days, the city's government was carried on in the Prikaznaya Palata, where busy bureaucrats are said even then to have got through no less than twenty buckets of ink in a week. Adjoining the Kremlin is the Dovmontov Gorod or town of Prince Dovmont, a thirteenth-century ruler who in his turn beat off the attacks of the Teutonic Knights and in due course was canonized. On the Kremlin wall hangs his sword, or, rather, a replica of it. Guarded by the great tower of St Basil, Vasilyevskaya Bashnya, this little settlement once contained no less than nineteen churches, of which now only the foundations remain. Not far from the Kremlin are the former Torg or Market Place, now renamed Lenin Square, and the fourteenth-century Church of the Archangel Michael. Further on, on October Street, are several more ancient churches. Though it had existed as a fortress for hundreds of years before that, the Kremlin's fortifications were only given their present form in the fifteenth century. Pskov also possesses an outer ring of fortifications built of local limestone, six miles in length and dating from the thirteenth century. Of these a good part still survives, notably several fine old towers. One of these, the Pokrovskaya Bashnya or Fortress of the Intercession, built in the fifteenth century, stands on the river bank at the far end of the town from the Kremlin. Inside its gate is the little double Church of the Nativity and Intercession with its twin domes and belfry. From here you look across the Velikaya to the Mirozhski Monastery, founded in the eleventh century. Also on the left bank a mile or so away is the thirteenth-century Church of St John the Baptist. Up and down the river oarsmen and oarswomen from the Pskov Rowing Club skim energetically past in their wherries and skiffs.

Due west from Pskov on the borders of Estonia two fortified monasteries, Izborsk and

Pechori, served as outposts of Slavdom and Orthodoxy in the low-lying marshlands of the north-west. Said to have been founded by Rurik's pagan brother Trevor or Truvor, whose gravestone, in the form of a massive cross, is still shown to gullible tourists in the nearby cemetery, Izborsk is strategically sited on a hilltop. Within its fortress walls which date from the early fourteenth century stands a church dedicated to St Nicholas.

As you approach Pechori, you catch sight of its golden domes shining brightly in the sunlight from among the encompassing greenery. Within its precincts numerous churches and shrines have been built over the years in a great variety of styles. The monastery and its churches are still very much in use. Heavily bearded monks are to be seen everywhere and lady visitors wearing trousers are firmly turned away. Exactly when the monastery was first founded is not certain, but it is said that an early hunter, wandering through the woods, was mystified to hear singing proceeding apparently from underground and, on investigating a little further, came on some holy men chanting in a cave. Around this cave, which you can still visit, the monastery was eventually built, remaining to this day an important religious centre. The fortress itself with its great stone walls and towers was given its present form in around 1560 and the towers and walls further strengthened a hundred and fifty years later at the time of Peter the Great's Northern Wars against the Swedes.

It was in the twelfth century, as we have seen, that with the gradual decline of Kiev, power passed to Novgorod in the north and to the cities of the Zalesye, the Land beyond the Forests, some four hundred miles away to the south-east – Pereslavl Zalesski, Rostov Veliki, Yaroslavl, Suzdal and Vladimir.

Here, more than anywhere, you get the true feel of mediaeval Russia. Approaching the Zalesye from Moscow, as most people do, you come, after driving for eighty or ninety miles in a north-easterly direction, to Pereslavl Zalesski, Pereslavl Beyond the Woods. Pereslavl had been a Slav outpost since as far back as the tenth century. But it was Yuri Dolgoruki who, as Prince of Rostov-Suzdal, rebuilt the town on its present site on the shores of Lake Pleshcheyevo, a sizeable sheet of water, reputedly rich in fish, two of which figure prominently beneath Vladimir's golden horn on the town's coat of arms. Having fortified Pereslavl and thrown a moat round it, Yuri began in 1152 to build the little white limestone Cathedral of the Transfiguration, which stands beneath the ramparts of his fortress and in its simple way provides as good an example as you will find of early Russian architecture. In front of it stands a Soviet-erected bust of St Alexander Nevski, who was born here and whose summer palace was sited on a neighbouring hill. Nearby are three ancient monasteries.

Leaving Lake Pleshcheyevo behind you and continuing north-eastwards through wooded country for another forty miles, you eventually reach Rostov, which stands on the shores of another considerable expanse of water known as Lake Nero. Rostov Veliki, Rostov the Great, the only Russian town besides Novgorod to bear this epithet, is over 1,000 years old. From 988 onwards, it was ruled over by Yaroslav the Wise, passing on his death to his son Vsevolod. Approaching it from Pereslavl, you first catch sight of it from six or seven miles away, with the white limestone walls and ten round towers of its Kremlin and half-a-dozen onion-domed churches dramatically reflected in the waters of the lake. Its oldest church, the Cathedral of the Assumption, originally built in 1162 by Andrei Bogolyubski, but rebuilt more than once in the intervening centuries, stands white and foursquare at the northern end of the Kremlin enclosure. Outwith the Kremlin walls are the Cathedral of St Gregory the Divine, built on the site of a much older monastery of the same name, the Church of the Saviour in the Market Place and that of St Isidore, dating from the sixteenth century. Some way along the shore of Lake Nero stands the thirteenth-century Church of the Saviour on the Sands.

Thirty miles beyond Rostov Veliki, where the River Kotorsl flows into the Volga, lies the ancient town of Yaroslavl, founded by Yaroslav the Wise in 1010 at a spot known as Bear's Corner, where he killed with his battleaxe a bear set on him by the local inhabitants who much resented his arrival. Though now a flourishing modern city, Yaroslavl, which still displays a bear on its municipal coat of arms, has retained a great deal of its original character. Approaching it from the south through the pleasantly wooded countryside of the Zalesye, you first catch sight of the white walls and towers of the Monastery of the Transfiguration, founded in the twelfth century, and of the shining golden domes of its cathedral, built four centuries later on the site of an earlier church. The bell-tower, holy gates and refectory were likewise built in the sixteenth century, the monastery walls and towers a hundred years later. Outside the monastery precincts stands the seventeenth-century Church of the Epiphany with its five green onion domes.

From Rostov Veliki, if you can get the necessary permission, it is likewise no more than a short drive along the valley of the River Nerl to Suzdal, the domes and spires and bastions of its innumerable churches and monasteries silhouetted against a background of green. Here, on the banks of the Kamenka, a tributary of the Nerl, Vladimir Monomakh built a church and a palace to go with it and in due course his son Yuri Dolgoruki made it his capital. Though now little more than a village, Suzdal, once the religious capital of Russia, can still boast any number of fine churches, convents and monasteries. With its palaces and churches, its fortified walls and towers, the Kremlin, situated in a loop of the Kamenka, formed the nucleus of the town, while another loop enclosed the merchants' quarter. Though little now remains of the Kremlin's fortifications, their line is still clearly enough marked. Of the buildings that survive, the oldest and most striking is the Cathedral of the Nativity of the Virgin, built early in the thirteenth century on the site of an even older church, but since more than once restored and rebuilt. The cathedral's five onion domes, star-spangled and supported by plain white drums, rise from a square white church. Its famous Golden Doors, dating from the early thirteenth century, are magnificent. Inside the church some of the original frescoes still remain. The belfry with its sugar-loaf spire was built toward the middle of the seventeenth century. The Bishop's Palace, a rambling white three-storied building, dates from a succession of different periods between the fifteenth and eighteenth centuries.

In and around Suzdal are no less than five ancient convents or monasteries, the largest of which, the fourteenth-century Spasski or Spaso-Yefimyevsi Monastery, stands to the north of the town in a commanding position on the left bank of the Kamenka. It is surrounded by a high fortified wall with twenty massive towers built in the sixteenth and seventeenth centuries. From the river bank beneath the monastery wall you look across the river to the fourteenth-century Convent of the Intercession (Pokrovski Monastir) lying amid the water-meadows that fringe the Kamenka and contained by a low white wall broken by occasional towers. Across the river from the Convent of the Intercession is the rather dilapidated Aleksandrovski Monastery, said to have been founded in the thirteenth century by Alexander Nevski. The Convent of the Deposition of the Virgin's Robes, dating from the sixteenth century, is nearer the centre of the town, where Lenin Street, as it is now called, joins the local Red Square. Besides its ancient convents and monasteries, Suzdal abounds in beautiful churches, built for the most part in the late seventeenth and eighteenth centuries. Many of these were built in pairs, a big, cool summer church and a small, cosy church, for use in winter.

A mile or so away from Suzdal, due east across the fields, lies the little village of Kideksha, strategically sited at the junction of the Nerl and the Kamenka, where Yuri Dolgoruki, on becoming Prince of Rostov-Suzdal, built himself a stronghold and a palace at a time when Suzdal scarcely existed as a town. Here, too, dwelt the martyr-princes Sts Boris and Gleb, sons of St Vladimir, murdered in early youth by their elder brother, Svyatopolk the Accursed, himself to be eliminated not long after by his quick-witted brother Yaroslav the Wise. Of Yuri's original palace nothing now remains, but it is still quite easy, if you know where to look, to trace the line of its ancient grass-covered fortifications beneath the beautiful white limestone cathedral, built in 1152, which by its name recalls the martyrdom of St Boris and St Gleb at their brother's bloodstained hands.

Of Suzdal's ancient treasures good care is being taken. At the town's Institute for Restoration the tasks of conservation and restoration are being tackled in a thoroughly professional manner at a cost of millions of roubles. Here icons and frescoes are carefully restored, while at the same time every effort is being made to keep the churches and monasteries from which they come in a good state of preservation. An important part in all this has been played by a remarkable *samorodok* or self-taught craftsman, Vyacheslav Ivanovich Basov, a notable local character in his own right. Under his expert guidance the city's ancient ironwork, its magnificent wrought-iron gates in particular, is being lovingly repaired and so skilfully restored as to be indistinguishable from the originals.

Russian through and through, Vyacheslav is immensely proud of his work and deeply conscious of the part he is playing in preserving Russia's ancient heritage. 'I believe man was made', he says, 'to create beauty. My trade is for me the most important thing in life. What I am doing is to rediscover ancient techniques and pass them on to my students .... We must preserve the beautiful things of the past, not just for ourselves, but for our children and their children too.' And he showed us some of the magnificent sword-blades he was making, comparable to the finest Damascus steel. Meanwhile, one of his brightest students, Sasha Bichkov, is usefully employed decorating Suzdal's latest *traktir* or hostelry with beautiful wrought-iron ornaments in the traditional Russian manner.

Now provided with an up-to-the-minute motel, complete with swimming-pool and sauna and a quite adequate restaurant, not to mention the refectory of one of its many monasteries well equipped to handle package tours, Suzdal is fast becoming one of the show places of the Soviet tourist industry, to which it can fairly be said to do credit. The well cooked and well presented lunch I ate in the refectory in company with a group of East or possibly West Germans would have met with the approval of the greediest monk.

Driving southwards from Suzdal through a pleasant landscape of woods and meadows, you come after twenty-five miles to Vladimir. Having once moved the capital of Rus to Vladimir, the city in which he had spent his youth and which he loved best of all, Andrei of Bogolyubovo did all he could to make it as magnificent and fortify it as strongly as the former capital, Kiev, which, as though to clinch matters, he promptly invaded and sacked. Just as Kiev is sited on a high bluff overlooking the Dnieper, so Vladimir occupies a dominating position on the lofty left bank of the Klyazma, once a far more considerable stream than it is today. Here, a hundred and fifty feet above the river, Vladimir Monomakh had built the Kremlin which his grandson Andrei now set out to strengthen and adorn. In 1160, soon after his accession to the throne, Andrei, with the help of the skilled craftsmen he had imported from abroad, started work on the Cathedral of the Assumption in which he himself lies buried. In it he installed the famous miracle-working icon which he had carried away with him from Kiev and which has been known ever since as the Virgin of Vladimir. First of the so-called Virgins of Tenderness, this extraordinary masterpiece, said to have been brought to Kiev from Byzantium and by some attributed, rather improbably, to St Luke, reflects both a new religious sense and a fresh artistic approach which, discarding virginal austerity for the warmer concept of motherhood, were with time to make the Mother of God the mother-image of all Russia. Twenty-five years after being built, the cathedral of the Assumption was badly damaged by fire, but quickly rebuilt, this time, it is proudly recorded, by native Russian builders and craftsmen, the single gold cupola of the original structure being now replaced by a group of five domes in accordance with later Orthodox practice.

Today, despite subsequent conflagrations and despite the flourishing industrial town which has grown up all around it, the white and gold cathedral, still standing on its hilltop, must look just as it did eight centuries ago. Its austerely beautiful western façade, divided into five tall arched panels, each containing a window and decorated with elegant limestone reliefs, in many ways recalls the contemporary churches of Georgia and Armenia beyond the Caucasus, countries with which Andrei had family connections, notably with Georgia whose great Queen Tamara was briefly and disastrously married to his deplorable younger son, Yuri. To this day the cathedral is still in use and is so popular that on Sundays and feast days a large and devout congregation regularly overflows into the park outside. ('Pay no attention to them. They are all *old*', an interfering middle-aged woman said to me irritably. 'A lot of them look a good deal younger than you', was the best retort I could think of at the time.) The famous Virgin of Vladimir, for its part, remained in the cathedral until 1395, when it was taken to Moscow to protect that city against Tamerlane's Tartar hordes (a task which it most effectively performed). It is now in the Tretyakov Gallery. A few fine frescoes by the famous painters Andrei Rublyov and Daniel Chorni still remain, but most of the icons which originally decorated its iconostasis have, like the Virgin of

Vladimir, by now found their way to the galleries of Moscow or Leningrad.

Only a few hundred yards from the Cathedral of the Assumption stands the Cathedral of St Dmitri, built by Russian masons in the reign of Andrei's successor, Vsevolod, whose chapel royal it became. A square building of white limestone with a single golden cupola, it is, like its neighbour, a magnificent example of the Suzdal-Vladimir style of architecture. In contrast to the more sober style of the Cathedral of the Assumption, its walls, each divided by tall slender pilasters into three arched compartments, are lavishly decorated with the liveliest possible carvings of saints, kings and prophets as well as a number of historical and mythological characters including Hercules at his Labours and Alexander the Great, who is shown being flown up to Heaven by a team of griffins.

In the pleasant park where these two ancient cathedrals now stand, looking out across the valley of the Klyazma, no trace remains of the original Kremlin built there by Vladimir Monomakh, though the commanding position clearly suggests the strategic reasons for his choice of site. Not far away is the Golden Gate, built by Andrei Bogolyubski as part of the town's defences, its white limestone arch flanked by circular bastions and surmounted by the golden dome of the little Gate-Church of the Rizopolozhenye.

For his own place of residence Andrei chose not Vladimir itself but the neighbouring village of Bogolyubovo, five or six miles away, from which he took his name. Here he planted his stronghold on a high bluff overlooking the Klyazma River and here in 1174, with the connivance of his beautiful wife Ulita, he was assassinated. Ulita, as it happened, was the daughter of the boyar Kuchko, whom Andrei's father, Yuri Dolgoruki, had murdered some years before in order to gain possession of the strategically sited wooden stockade on a hill above the river which in course of time was to become the Moscow Kremlin. She had, it appears, never liked her saintly and, some say, sanctimonious husband and for years had been waiting for an opportunity to get rid of him.

Of Andrei's original residence all that remains is part of a turret staircase now incorporated in a later building, but still easily identifiable. It was on this very staircase that on the night of 29 June 1174 his assassins came on him and, after killing him, threw his body to the dogs. They did not, however, escape the consequences of their crime, being in their turn caught and killed and their bodies consigned in specially tarred coffins to the swamps around Bogolyubovo. There, it is said, they have floated ever since, making the night hideous with their wailing.

Whether sanctimonious or not, Prince Andrei, subsequently canonized, must rank as one of the creators of Russia. Nor were the great churches of Vladimir all that he left to posterity. Barely a mile away from Bogolyubovo, across flowery meadows, is the little Church of the Intercession which he built in 1165 on the banks of the River Nerl in memory of his eldest son, killed in battle with the Bulgars. Standing among a group of elm trees on the edge of a small lake fringed with reeds and water-lilies, it is one of the supreme achievements of early Russian architecture: a single dome set on a slender drum, pierced by six lancet windows, springs from the graceful four-sided white limestone church. With its soaring piers and arches, the little church's interior is as simple and as perfectly proportioned as its exterior.

2

The Rise of Muscovy

Moscow is neither Europe nor Asia;
it is Russia — and it is the heart of Russia.

MARQUIS DE CUSTINE

1839

The Russians were to spend more than two and a half centuries under Mongol suzerainty. The effect on their subsequent development and national character was immense. Though they somehow preserved their nationhood, they were during this period inevitably cut off from the civilizing influences of the West and no less inevitably exposed to Mongol influences and ideas, notably to the concept of a centrally controlled and highly regimented autocracy.

An important result of these years of Mongol domination was the rise of the new town of Moscow to be the chief seat of power in Russia. Founded in 1147 by Yuri Dolgoruki, whose memory is celebrated by a fine bronze statue, erected in the city centre by a grateful Soviet Government just 800 years later, Moscow or Muscovy became a separate principality in the second half of the thirteenth century. Gradually the territories of the new principality grew in extent and importance until in 1328 Prince Ivan Kalita or John the Moneybag was formally recognized by the Mongols as Grand Prince of Muscovy, with the right and duty to collect tribute on their behalf. Soon Moscow had swallowed up the Principality of Vladimir, of which it had originally been part, and had become the seat of the Orthodox Metropolitan. Before long the official titles of both Grand Prince and Metropolitan came to include the phrase Vseva Rusi, 'of all Rus'.

Close cooperation between church and state were from the first fundamental to the Russian system of government and church leaders regularly played an important part in political affairs. During the reign of Ivan Kalita's weak son, Ivan the Red, and the minority of the latter's son Dmitri, St Aleksei, at that time Metropolitan, practically governed Muscovy, strongly supported by St Sergei of Radonezh, founder of the famous Monastery of the Trinity and St Sergei at Sergievo (now Zagorsk).

On coming of age, however, young Prince Dmitri Ivanovich, son of Ivan the Red, soon proved himself a strong ruler, vigorously asserting Moscow's ascendancy over the other Russian principalities. In their prayers, the Russian princes had long appealed to the Almighty to 'take away the Tartars', begging that 'the candle', in other words Russia's national spirit, 'should not be extinguished'. So long as the Tartars, as they called the Mongols, stayed strong and united, their prayer remained a pious hope and they continued to do their best to conciliate their Tartar suzerains. But now a struggle broke out between rival factions within the Golden Horde; the Russians took sides; and in 1377, after almost a century and a half of subjection, fighting once again broke out between Russians and Tartars. Soon this developed into a regular war and on 8 September 1380 Prince Dmitri, with St Sergei's blessing, actually managed to defeat the Khan of the Golden Horde at Kulikovo, the Field of the Snipe, an expanse of flat, marshy ground on the right bank of the River Don.

For the Russians, however, the cost of victory proved heavy. Nor had the Tartars as yet been 'taken away'. On the contrary, they were still very much there, waiting for a chance to avenge their defeat and reassert their authority. But, by his victory at Kulikovo, Dmitri, henceforth to be known as Donskoi, Prince of the Don, had undermined the legend of Tartar invincibility, rallied the Russians to his standard and effectively established Moscow's claim to the leadership of all Russia.

For the part he played in these critical times, St Sergei, who combined great spiritual gifts with remarkable strength of character, was to be known by subsequent generations as the Builder of Russia. Sergievo or Zagorsk, the great fortified monastery he founded some fifty miles to the north of Moscow which never fell to a foreign invader, is still to this day a most important centre of Orthodox Christianity.

The years that followed Kulikovo were difficult ones for the Russians. The Tartars continued to harass them and exact tribute from them and, following the dynastic union of Poland with Lithuania in 1385, they were seriously threatened by the emergence on their western borders of a powerful Polish-Lithuanian state, Roman Catholic by religion. But better times lay ahead. By now the power of the Tartars' Golden Horde had begun to decline and in 1488 the appointment of a Russian bishop as Metropolitan of All Russia marked the church's final break with Byzantium and its establishment as a Russian national church.

In 1462, Prince Ivan Vasilyevich succeeded his father as Ivan III of Muscovy. Able, ruthless, ambitious and of such striking appearance that excited women frequently swooned at the mere sight of him, Ivan was to earn himself the name of Ivan the Great. Early in his long reign he married the massive Zoe or Sophia Paleologue, niece of the last Emperor of Byzantium, at the same time boldly assuming as his arms the Imperial double-headed eagle of the Eastern Empire. Sophia weighed some twenty-five stone and it is said that on the night of her arrival in the Kremlin, her weight alone caused the great State Bed to disintegrate.

During his forty-three years as Grand Prince of Muscovy, Ivan III expanded his dominions to more than three times their size, mainly at the expense of his Russian neighbours. His first target was Novgorod, Lord Novgorod the Great, whose far-flung dominions now reached to the Arctic Ocean and beyond the Urals and effectively blocked Moscow's access to the Baltic. Attacking Novgorod, he overran its territories, massacred or deported a large number of its inhabitants and in the end annexed it. In due course Tver, Rostov, Yaroslavl, Riazan and Pskov went the same way. Soon Ivan was lord of most of northern Russia. The Tartar Khans he played off against each other and, without ever fighting a battle, effectively freed Muscovy from the Tartar yoke.

In a score of years Ivan the Great had vastly increased the standing and prestige of the Grand Principality and strongly asserted its claim to all-Russian sovereignty. Almost imperceptibly Muscovy had become the largest country in Europe. But when in 1468 the Holy Roman Emperor patronizingly offered Ivan the title of king, he declined it out of hand. By marrying fat Sophia Paleologue he had taken a first step towards declaring himself successor to the Emperors of Byzantium. If Byzantium, now fallen to the Turks, had been the second Rome, why should Moscow not become the third Rome? Increasingly the word Tsar, directly derived from Caesar, was employed to denote the Grand Prince of Muscovy. Ivan meanwhile was beginning to surround himself with all the outward and visible manifestations of imperial pomp. In the train of his bulky Byzantine bride he had imported a number of Greek and Italian craftsmen and architects, whom he now used to make Moscow a capital worthy of an Emperor, while to strengthen the autocracy, he created a new class of *pomeshchiki* or serving landowners, who, in return for a grant of land, rendered certain services, usually military, to the state.

Ivan the Great died in 1505. His son Vasili's first concern was to complete his father's work as Assembler of Russia. Like Ivan, Vasili III enjoyed power and wielded it absolutely. 'He holds', wrote Baron von Herberstein, twice ambassador of the Holy Roman Empire to Moscow, 'unlimited control over the lives and property of all his subjects.' 'It is a matter of doubt,' he added, 'whether the brutality of the people has made the Prince a tyrant or whether the people themselves have become thus brutal and cruel through the tyranny of their Prince' – a question observers of the Russian scene have been asking themselves almost ever since.

When necessary, Vasili also used his great power for private ends. Tiring of his wife Solomonia, who had hitherto borne him no children, he obliged the ecclesiastical authorities to let him divorce her on grounds of barrenness and marry instead the more attractive Polish princess, Helen Glinskaya, who in 1530 duly bore him a son, Ivan Vasilyevich, later famous as Ivan the Terrible. Solomonia, meanwhile, had been relegated to the Convent of the Intercession at Suzdal, where, however, on being urged to take the veil, she resisted sturdily and in the end had to be flogged into submission by a boyar with a horsewhip. Worse still, on entering the convent, Solomonia proved to be pregnant, presumably by the Tsar, and in due course gave birth to a baby son. As her husband's pretext for divorcing her had been that she was barren, her baby could not but be an embarrassment to a number of highly-placed people. Accordingly, to save its life, rumour had it, Sister Sophie, as she was now known, had her child smuggled out of the convent, at the same time announcing that he had died.

And there the matter seems to have rested until 1934, when, in the course of some excavations, a small sarcophagus was found close to Solomonia's own grave in Suzdal, containing not a body, but a tiny dummy, dressed in an embroidered silk shirt and looking for all the world like a baby. Which confirmed what until then had only been guessed at. The fate of the real baby will never now be known, though it is clearly quite possible that some of his descendants, with a far better claim to the imperial throne than any Romanovs, are today alive and well and living near Suzdal. As for Solomonia, she was later very properly canonized, continuing to perform miracles long after her death.

On his death in 1533, Vasili Ivanovich was succeeded by his three-year-old son by Helen Glinskaya, Ivan, fourth of his name, later to be known as *Grozni*, the Terrible or Formidable. The early years of little Ivan's reign were chaotic. With the autocracy temporarily in abeyance, the boyars plotted and bickered among themselves. To this, Ivan put an abrupt end. On attaining the age of fourteen, he addressed the chief boyars from the throne. Many of them, he said, were guilty. But he would only punish one. Prince Andrei Shuiski, the most powerful man in Muscovy, was then immediately taken out and executed. Three years later, having married Anastasia, the daughter of a minor boyar, Ivan had himself crowned Tsar of All Russia at the Uspenski Cathedral in the Kremlin. A notable reign had begun.

To start with, the young tsar introduced a number of much-needed reforms. He also raised a standing army, with which in 1552 he embarked on a war against the Tartars, quickly capturing the great Tartar stronghold of Kazan on the Upper Volga. It was to celebrate this victory that Ivan built on the Red Square in Moscow the astonishing Cathedral of St Basil with its cluster of multi-coloured onion domes. Four years later he took the Tartar port of Astrakhan at the mouth of the Volga, which he now effectively controlled as far as the Caspian.

By his victories over the Tartars Ivan opened up vast new areas to Russian colonization, notably Siberia. In 1558 he authorized Grigori Stroganov, a member of the famous family of merchant adventurers from Novgorod, to establish a first settlement and trading post on the Upper Kama River. A score of years later, in September 1581, the Cossack Hetman Yermak, with the encouragement of the Stroganovs, set out with a force of eight hundred and forty men to cross the Urals and conquer fresh territories in the region that lay beyond them.

Meanwhile, Ivan was also looking northwards to the Baltic and to the possibilities it offered for trade and other contacts with the West. In 1558 he attacked the Teutonic Knights, the weakest of Russia's western neighbours. But, while he won some victories against them, he made enemies of Sweden and Lithuania-Poland, with whom he now became involved in a prolonged and bitter struggle.

In the year 1560 Ivan's wife Anastasia died, of poison, he suspected. Immediately his character seemed to change. He had never liked the boyars, whom he suspected of seeking to thwart his designs; now he unleashed against them the full force of his pent-up hatred. Soon terror, suspicion, treachery and delation were rife. Then, in December 1564, the tsar all at once left Moscow, to reappear fifty miles away at Alexandrov, whence, in January 1565, he sent word that he had renounced the throne because of the treachery which surrounded him.

It was not long before a solemn-faced deputation arrived to beg him to reconsider his decision. This, in the end, he agreed to do. But on his own terms. First, he wanted the traitors punished. Secondly, he intended to set up his own *Oprichnina*, a powerful instrument of civil and military government, responsible only to himself. Quickly the Oprichnina, the forerunner of many similar organizations, became a state within a state, with its own corps of several thousand *Oprichniki*. Clothed in black, riding black horses and carrying a severed dog's head at their saddle-bows, the Oprichniki brought terror wherever they went. Perhaps their most spectacular exploit was the destruction in 1570 of Novgorod the Great, whose inhabitants, the Tsar suspected, possibly with reason, were plotting with the Poles. Accordingly their city was sacked and more than 60,000 of its people massacred, while its Archbishop Ivan was stitched in a bearskin and hunted to death by a pack of hounds.

For all their wanton savagery, Ivan's actions formed part of a carefully thought-out plan, designed to strengthen the autocracy, build up the *pomeshchiki* or serving gentry as a powerful counterbalance to the reactionary boyars and create a centralized service-state in which each and every class was bound to the autocracy by bonds of compulsory service. Further restrictions, meanwhile, were placed on the peasants' freedom of movement – a first significant step towards serfdom and total central control. In his own, rather unusual way, Ivan was a deeply religious man. After his mass executions, he would meticulously send the names of his victims to the monasteries so that the monks might pray for their souls. He even set up at his country retreat of Alexandrov a kind of private monastery at which weird ceremonies were performed with himself in the role of abbot.

It was during Ivan's reign that yet another characteristically Russian phenomenon first appeared. On the fringes of Russia's fast-expanding empire, thousands of freebooters began to group together in armed bands, plundering and marauding as the spirit moved them. From a Tartar word meaning 'horsemen' they came to be called 'Cossacks'. As we have seen, it was the Cossack leader, Yermak, who in 1581 set out with eight hundred and forty such men to conquer Siberia.

In the north, meanwhile, what was called the Livonian war still dragged on. By a peace signed in 1582, Ivan gave up all the Lithuanian territory he had captured and abandoned his claims to Livonia. A year later, in 1583, the Swedes, exploiting Moscow's temporary weakness, took back the strip of territory which the Russians had won from them on the Gulf of Finland and formally annexed Estonia. Ivan's far-sighted attempt at a breakthrough to the Baltic had failed.

Ivan died in 1584, a worried man. The good Sir Jerome Horsey of the English Muscovy Company has described his end and how, sitting in his rich treasure chamber, he would fondle certain of his precious stones in the lingering belief that they might have the power to heal him, though his soothsayers and the spiders they employed as a means of divination no longer held out any real hope.

Ivan's most important achievements had been the creation of a standing army and the use he made of it to break the power of the Tartars and open the way for the eventual conquest of Siberia. Though he failed to break through to the Baltic, his exploratory contacts with Western Europe and the encouragement he gave to western merchant-adventurers had helped prepare the way for more regular relations with the West.

It is not easy to form a balanced judgement of Ivan the Terrible, who was scarcely a balanced man. Russia has always been a difficult country to govern. The control he achieved and the reforms he introduced mark him out as one of the handful of great revolutionary leaders who over the centuries have changed the course of Russian history. Nor did his excesses alienate the Russian people, who, for their part, enjoyed the eccentric, dramatic side of his character, as when he had an elephant promptly cut to pieces for refusing to bow down to him. With time, however, he became the victim of his own suspicions, destroying not only the turbulent, treacherous boyars, but much that he himself had created: his army, his country's prosperity and ultimately his eldest son, Ivan Ivanovich, killed in a moment of irritation by a well-aimed blow from his father's steel-pointed staff.

It was thus that on Ivan's death Russia was left to be ruled over by his feeble-minded second son Fyodor, with, as next heir, Dmitri, the child of his seventh and more than dubious marriage to a certain Maria Nagaya. Whoever governed Russia, it would clearly not be Fyodor. In fact, power passed quickly to the new Tsar's brother-in-law, Boris Godunov, a minor boyar of Tartar origin. Able and quick-witted, Boris had somehow managed to win the confidence of the old Tsar, whose son had married his sister. He also had valuable family and other connections with the Oprichnina. Familiar with the methods by which Ivan had governed, Boris's approach was saner and more subtle. Having won the all-important support of the church, he formally assumed the regency, continuing his predecessor's policy of building up the gentry at the expense of the great nobles, while binding the peasants ever more closely to the soil. He also continued the colonization of Siberia, resumed the war against the Swedes, and maintained Russia's contacts with the West. The Oprichnina he replaced by a less spectacular, but no less efficient, internal security system. For a few years Russia enjoyed a measure of peace and prosperity. But it was not to last.

In May 1591 it was reported that an accident with a knife had ended the life of little Prince Dmitri, Ivan the Terrible's son by Maria Nagaya and, as such, the heir to the throne. Others said that the nine-year-old prince had been murdered by Boris Godunov. The truth was hard to come by and remains so to this day. Seven years later Tsar Fyodor died, leaving no heir. Russia was without a tsar. All things considered, it was scarcely surprising that at the ensuing election Boris emerged as the successful candidate. His principal rival, Fyodor Nikitich Romanov, was quickly despatched to a monastery and in September 1599 Boris himself was crowned Tsar.

Four years later, however, came a disquieting rumour. Little Prince Dmitri Ivanovich, it was said, had not after all been killed twelve years earlier, but was still alive, now aged twenty-one. Worse still, the King of neighbouring Poland was helping him to raise an army of Poles and Cossacks with which to evict the usurper Godunov and claim his just inheritance. Next came information that he was marching on Moscow and then, suddenly, the news that Boris Godunov himself had died.

The ensuing period of Russian history was to be known, with reason, as *Smutnoye Vremya* or the Time of Troubles. Glad to take their revenge, even posthumously, on Boris Godunov, the great boyars rallied to the Pretender. Encouraged by this, the mob stormed the Kremlin and murdered Boris's son and widow. A week later, the Pretender, whose identity has never been finally established, but who clearly believed himself to be Dmitri, entered the capital in triumph. The first person to affirm his authenticity was Dmitri's mother, Maria Nagaya, quite regardless of the fact that she had herself witnessed her own son's death fourteen years earlier.

The reign of the False Dmitri was short but eventful. From the first he showed considerable initiative and independence. The Poles had supported him on the understanding that he would spread Roman Catholicism and Polish influence in Russia. But, once installed, he made it clear that he was staunchly Orthodox and had no intention of serving as catspaw for the Catholic Poles. On the contrary, his first step on arrival was to appoint a new Orthodox Patriarch and then have himself crowned Tsar. He next recalled from exile the Nagois, Romanovs and other families banished by Boris and did what he could to revive the former council of boyars.

But in the long run the Polish connection was to count against him. In particular his marriage to Marina Mniszech, the beautiful daughter of an impoverished Polish nobleman, was resented by the people of Moscow, who also complained that his manners and way of life were not sufficiently regal. The troublemakers, as usual, were a group of disaffected boyars, led by Prince Vasili Shuiski. Early on the morning of 17 May 1606, barely a year after his accession, a mob burst into the Kremlin and murdered the Pretender, after which his remains were burned and the ashes fired from a cannon in the general direction of Poland. Two days later Prince Vasili Shuiski was proclaimed Tsar.

There followed a period of utter confusion. The new Tsar was immediately faced with a rising of dissident elements of all kinds under the leadership of a former galley-slave called Ivan Bolotnikov. Scarcely had this been quelled than a fresh Pretender emerged, to be known as the Second False Dmitri and claiming identity not only with little Dmitri who had died at Uglich, but also with the First False Dmitri, whose ashes had been publicly blown from a cannon barely a year before. He nevertheless found plentiful support. Having recruited an army consisting of Poles and whatever was left of the armies raised by Bolotnikov and the First False Dmitri, the Second False Dmitri marched on Moscow, besieged the new Tsar in the Kremlin and then set up court in the suburb of Tushino. There he was joined by the beautiful Maria Mniszech, who quickly recognized him as her dead husband.

In July 1610, the people of Moscow, tried beyond endurance, rose against Tsar Vasili Shuiski and dethroned him. In despair, the boyars and church authorities now decided to offer the throne to Wladislaw, son of King Sigismund of Poland, whose troops, besides besieging Smolensk, were by this time occupying most of Moscow, including the Kremlin. To this King Sigismund replied that he wanted the Russian throne, not for his son, but for himself – wanted, in other words, to make Russia a dependency of Poland. Meanwhile the Second False Dmitri had been murdered and a Third had made his appearance in far-away Pskov.

It was now that a number of Russian patriots, realizing the appalling danger that threatened their country, decided to make a stand against the Poles and their Russian collaborators. On Christmas Day 1610, a call went out from the Patriarch of Moscow to rise against the Polish forces of occupation. A first Russian attempt to storm the Kremlin was unsuccessful, but the resistance movement grew in strength and by the end of 1611 a kind of national militia had been raised by the joint efforts of Kuzma Minin, a cattle-dealer from Nizhni Novgorod, and Prince Dmitri Pozharski, a local boyar, who now assumed command of the Russian forces. Meanwhile the monks of the Troitsko-Sergyevski Monastery at Sergievo (now Zagorsk), successfully withstanding a prolonged siege, continued to act as a focus of national resistance. Finally, in July 1612, Prince Pozharski, having assembled his army at Yaroslavl on the Volga, marched on Moscow and after several days of savage fighting secured the surrender of the Polish garrison. Moscow was once again in Russian hands.

It now only remained to elect a tsar. This was done in February 1613 by a specially summoned *Zemski Sobor* or Territorial Assembly, who chose as tsar the sixteen-year-old Mikhail Romanov, son of the same Fyodor Nikitich Romanov, who had competed for the throne with Boris Godunov in 1598. A contemporary has left a lively account of Mikhail's election, not without topical overtones. Wishing to ensure that the Zemski Sobor picked the right man, a number of armed Cossacks called in an old friend, the Abbot of Sergievo, who, after celebrating Mass, addressed the assembled delegates as follows: 'You are not here to enjoy yourselves', he began sternly. 'You are here to elect a Russian Tsar ... A Tsar is the Father of the Nation. Moscow is the Mother of the Nation. You can neither select nor elect your father nor your mother. They are sent to you by God.' 'Amen!' replied the members of the Assembly devoutly, 'quite right. And now tell us who is sent by God to be Tsar.' 'Who but Mikhail Romanov?' said the Abbot promptly and then called for a vote. One hundred and fifty-six of the delegates could neither read nor write and asked the Abbot (who could) to fill in their voting papers for them, after which a vote was taken and Mikhail Romanov unanimously elected Tsar of All the Russias. After first being exiled to a monastery by Boris Godunov, the new Tsar's father, Fyodor Romanov, had later risen to be Metropolitan and, as such, had played a leading part in ecclesiastical and political affairs. For the time being a prisoner in Poland, he later returned to Russia where he was at once consecrated Patriarch and became in practice co-ruler with his son.

The country in which young Tsar Mikhail assumed power was in a dreadful state. The cities had been sacked and burned, the countryside devastated and the population reduced by massacre, starvation and disease, from 14 millions to 9. The treasury was empty; bands of armed marauders roamed everywhere; the boyars had destroyed themselves by their ceaseless quarrelling. Such hope as there was lay in the smaller landowners, who of recent years had emerged as the most stable element of the population and effectively dominated the Zemski Sobor, which for some years met regularly. In time, order of a kind was restored at home and peace patched up with the Poles and the Swedes.

On his death in 1645 Mikhail Romanov was succeeded by his sixteen-year-old son, Alexis the Gentle, an ineffectual ruler whose reign was marked by a variety of revolts and rebellions. Even the Orthodox Church was not immune. The consecration in 1652 of the Patriarch Nikon, a strong-minded cleric utterly set on reform, led to a schism which has lasted to this day, ultimately leading to the foundation of the Church of the Old Believers.

There was trouble, too, in the *Ukraina* or Borderland between Russia and Poland, roughly corresponding to the present Ukraine. Most of this area, including Kiev, had long been under Polish rule and the Russian Orthodox population were under strong pressure from the Poles to become Catholics. For the Ukraine's Polish rulers the Ukrainian Cossacks, who had found an effective leader in Hetman Bogdan Khelmnitzki, presented a serious problem. Taking the offensive with a force of Cossacks from the Dnieper, Khelmnitzki, whose striking equestrian statue still stands in front of St Sophia in Kiev, utterly routed three Polish armies. Now master of the Ukraine, he next appealed for help to Tsar Alexis, who, after formally proclaiming himself ruler of the disputed territories, duly declared war on Poland.

Bogdan Khelmnitzki died in 1657. Disgusted to find themselves less independent than they had hoped, the Ukrainian Cossacks now rose against the Russians, some of them even enlisting Polish support. The ensuing three-cornered conflict lasted for ten years, during which the entire area was devastated several times over. In 1667 Poles and Russians again made peace and dreams of an independent Ukraine faded, to be revived at intervals ever since, notably during the First and Second World Wars, when the Germans gave active encouragement to the idea. Meanwhile the balance of power between Russia and Poland had shifted decisively in Russia's favour.

But for Alexis the Gentle there was worse to come. In 1669 a band, this time of Don Cossacks, under a certain Stenka Razin, launched an insurrection against what they termed the oppressors of the Russian people. It spread like wildfire. Town after town fell to the rebels. From a Cossack revolt the movement became a national uprising. By 1670, Moscow itself was threatened. Only then did the government assemble an effective force of foreign-trained troops. These turned the tide. Betrayed by his fellow Cossacks, Stenka was taken to Moscow and there, in June 1671, quartered alive on the Red Square. Today a nearby street bears his name.

For more than six hundred years Moscow has stood at the centre of Russian history. Just as Moscow is the heart of Russia, so the Kremlin is the heart of Moscow. *Kreml* in Russian signifies fortress or stronghold. Here, at the beginning of the twelfth century, the boyar Kuchko built his palisade among some pine trees on a little hill a hundred and twenty feet high at the junction of the Moscow River and of a stream known as the Neglinnaya. And here in 1147 he was done to death by Prince Yuri Dolgoruki of Rostov and Suzdal, who, grasping the strategic and commercial advantages of such a site straddling the main waterways of Kievan Rus, killed Kuchko, carried off his beautiful daughter Ulita, whom he married to his son Andrei, and seized his stronghold for himself. From an isolated fortress, the Kremlin grew with the years to be a small fortified town.

Moscow benefited from the Mongol invasions. By the beginning of the fourteenth century its princes were well on the way to achieving supremacy over their neighbours. Their capital became the seat of the Metropolitan of All Russia and four fine stone cathedrals now made their appearance within the wooden walls of the Kremlin, symbolizing the essential 'holiness' of Russia and the close association of temporal and spiritual power. Of these, the first was the Metropolitan's own Cathedral of the Assumption (Uspenski Sobor), built in 1326. The second, built in 1329, was a belfry dedicated to St Ivan. The third, which followed in 1330, was the Spasski Sobor or Cathedral of the Redeemer. The fourth, dedicated in 1333 to the Archangel Michael, served as a burial-place for successive grand princes and tsars. Built on four sides of a square and richly adorned with icons and frescoes, they stood on the same site as the churches of the same name which stand there today and tellingly emphasized Moscow's spiritual and political supremacy.

The original rough stockade which ran round the Kremlin was in the fourteenth century first replaced by a solidly built wall of oak almost a mile long. On its eastern side a moat, separating it from what is now the Red Square, made it more easily defensible. Twenty-five years later, in the reign of Prince Dmitri Donskoi, its wooden fortifications were replaced by a longer wall of white stone, triangular in form, on an alignment corresponding to that of the present walls of the Kremlin and reinforced by nine stone watchtowers.

A century after this, under Ivan the Great, Muscovy's continuing military and political advance was marked by a wholesale refurbishing of the Kremlin and its cathedrals. By this time, the Tartar threat had receded. Rus was unified under Moscow. Ivan, as ruler of the largest country in Europe, clearly saw himself as successor to the Caesars. Encouraged by his heavyweight Byzantine wife, he imported a galaxy of fresh talent from abroad. Work began in 1475 with the building of a new Cathedral of the Assumption, Uspenski Sobor, the original church of 1329 having fallen down in an earthquake some years earlier. To build it, Ivan sent for Rodolfo Fioravanti from Bologna in Italy, first despatching him to Vladimir to study that city's ancient churches. The cathedral he built, with its five great domes and white limestone walls, can have changed very little in the last five centuries. Inside, all four walls and the great columns that support the vaulted roof are covered with a multitude of splendid icons, frescoes and paintings of saints, martyrs and angels, as is the great golden iconostasis. Here, through the centuries, successive tsars were crowned and successive Metropolitans laid to rest. The cathedral is lit by a number of gilded chandeliers hanging from the roof. 'We see Heaven!' cried Ivan, his courtiers and clergy, on first entering the newly completed building.

Fioravanti next addressed himself to the Kremlin walls and fortifications. Work on them was to continue for more than twenty-five years. The old white walls of a century earlier were demolished and the present battlements and watchtowers of red brick erected in their place. Simultaneously the moat on the east side was deepened and extended, so that the Kremlin had water on each of its three sides. Of the five great gate-towers each has its own name and is built in its own individual style: Spasskaya, the Gate of the Redeemer, Troitskaya, the Gate of the Trinity, Borovitskaya, the Gate of the Pine Wood, Nikolskaya, the elegantly neo-Gothic Gate of St Nicholas, and Tainitskaya, the Secret Gate.

Between 1480 and 1490, while work was going ahead on the fortifications, Russian architects from Pskov were celebrating the withdrawal of the Tartars by building the little church of Rizopolozheniye (the Laying-By of the Virgin's Vestments), modelling this too on the Cathedral of the Assumption at Vladimir. On the same side of the square the architects built the exquisite Cathedral of the Annunciation (Blagoveshchenski Sobor) with its nine golden cupolas, which served the grand princes and their imperial successors as a kind of chapel royal. Originally quite small, it was later enlarged by the addition of a covered gallery on three sides. Its floor is paved with agate and jasper, and it contains some remarkable early fifteenth-century frescoes.

Opposite the Cathedral of the Annunciation, on the south side of Cathedral Square, stands the five-domed Arkhangelski Sobor, the Cathedral of the Archangel Michael, built by Alevisio Novi from Milan between 1505 and 1509 on the site of the older cathedral of the same name. This served as the burial place of the grand princes and tsars. Next to the altar, in the holiest place of all, is the brass-bound coffin of Ivan the Terrible. Of the early tsars only Boris Godunov is buried elsewhere, in the Troitsko-Sergyevskaya Lavra at Zagorsk. To the north of the Cathedral of the Assumption stand the Palace of the Patriarch and the Church of the Twelve Apostles, both built in the middle of the seventeenth century.

High above all the other buildings of the Kremlin rises the bell-tower of St Ivan, popularly known as Ivan Veliki or Ivan the Great, with its shining golden dome. Built early in the sixteenth century by Bono Friazin, yet another Italian architect, on the site of an earlier fourteenth-century structure, it was raised a century later to its present height of two hundred and fifty feet by Boris Godunov. In times of trouble – and they were frequent – it was used as a watchtower and its great bell served as a tocsin to summon the inhabitants of the surrounding countryside to take refuge within the Kremlin walls.

The oldest surviving secular building in the Kremlin is the Granovitaya Palata or Palace of the Facets, built for Ivan III towards the end of the fifteenth century by two of the Italian architects who had helped Fioravanti design the fortifications, Marco Russo and Pietro Solario, and so called because of the faceted pattern of its walls. Its windows were added in the seventeenth century. The palace's lower floor was used for administrative purposes, while the upper floor contained a vaulted throne-room or audience-chamber.

Ivan III also built for himself the Teremnoi Palace, a name that comes from the Greek *teremnon*, meaning women's quarters. This was to serve as the official residence of the tsars. First built in about 1500, it was enlarged and reconstructed in the seventeenth century. Its five-storied façade, with its rows of ornate windows, elaborately decorated cornices and string-courses of brightly coloured tiles, offers a remarkable example of seventeenth-century plasterwork.

Within the precincts of the Teremnoi Palace are a number of small chapels or churches, of various periods and styles of construction, the eleven golden domes of which emerge above its roof. Adjoining is the Poteshni or Pleasure Palace, a tall, green-painted building dating from the mid-seventeenth century and the scene of the first theatrical performance ever given in Russia.

Part of the Kremlin's appeal lies in its diversity and the elegant, domed triangular building, devised in the eighteenth century to house a Duma or senate, fits well enough into its variegated surroundings. Over it today flies the Red Flag, floodlit at night – a suitably dramatic touch. In place of several older buildings, demolished to make way for it, the Great Kremlin Palace was built between 1839 and 1849 in a style ingeniously combining Byzantine with Classical and Ancient Russian elements. Painted a cheerful yellow, picked out in white, this massive building stretches boldly along the river frontage of the Kremlin. Adjoining the Great Kremlin Palace and later rebuilt in the same style is the Armoury; it contains an extraordinary collection of treasures, such as Yuri Dolgoruki's golden chalice, Vladimir Monomakh's jewel-studded, fur-fringed cap, Ivan the Terrible's throne of ivory, a jewel-studded throne presented to Boris Godunov by Shah Abbas of Persia, Peter the Great's immense top boots, made by himself for himself, and some of the most remarkable diamonds in the world.

In the years that followed the Great Fire of 1812, Moscow, as the map shows, was rebuilt in a series of concentric circles spreading outwards from the Kremlin and marked by broad, tree-lined boulevards, roughly corresponding to the line of the former for-tifications. The containing wall of the Kremlin, which thus forms, as it were, the core of the city, is triangular in shape. One side faces the Moscow River, another looks out on the Alexandrovski Gardens, marking the line of the former Neglinnaya River, now disappeared underground. The third, once protected by a moat, forms one side of the Red Square.

Immediately below the Kremlin wall is situated the low, dark red basalt mausoleum in which Lenin's embalmed body has lain for more than sixty years, sharing it for a time with that of his scarcely less famous successor, J. V. Stalin. Here, at the very heart of this vast country, stands the ultimate shrine of Marxism–Leninism, visited even in the most inclement weather by an endless line of devout pilgrims from every part of the Soviet Union, and symbolizing, as the Kremlin's churches once did, Moscow's combined spiritual and political supremacy and orthodoxy. Outside the door of the mausoleum two sentries with fixed bayonets stand guard night and day, the guards being changed at regular intervals with exemplary smartness and precision.

At the southern end of the Red Square is the altogether fantastic Cathedral of St Basil. Built in the reign of Ivan the Terrible, it was dedicated, appropriately enough, to Basil the Blessed, a mendicant miracle-worker or Holy Fool, to whom Ivan rightly or wrongly attributed his victory of 1552 over the Kazan Tartars. An extreme example of the exuberant native Russian style of the sixteenth century, it recalls the wooden-built churches of the countryside and marks, like them, a complete departure from the earlier Byzantine tradition. 'A masterpiece of caprice . . . This box of crystallized fruits', the visiting Marquis de Custine called it with true Gallic irony a hundred and fifty years ago. Originally white all over, it was later repainted in all the colours of the rainbow. In front of it stands a handsome early nineteenth-century monument to the two leaders of the national rising of 1611, Kuzma Minin, the butcher, and Dmitri Pozharski, the prince, both looking equally heroic in their severely classical way. A hundred yards or so away is a plain raised circular stone platform, possessing gruesome associations – Lobnoye Mesto, the Place of the Skull, where over the centuries convicted traitors and others who had incurred the tsar's disfavour were publicly done to death.

Across the Red Square from the Kremlin on a site previously occupied by a handsome classical building is GUM, the great state department store, through which people pass at the rate of several hundred thousand a day. Built a century or so ago in the ancient Russian manner as a multiple shopping arcade on three floors under a lofty glass roof with footbridges spanning the intervening chasm and fountains tinkling merrily at the inter-sections, it most certainly repays a visit.

Moscow possesses a number of ancient monasteries, now put to a variety of uses and in varying states of preservation. One of the most important is the Monastery of the Don (Donskoi Monastir), situated on the southern fringes of the city, in a loop of the Moscow River. Built on the site of an older fortress of which the massive outer wall and twelve fortified towers still survive, it was founded in 1591 to commemorate the final defeat of the Golden Horde and is dedicated to the Virgin of the Don, whose gem-studded icon was kept until the Revolution in the largest of its seven churches, a five-domed baroque cathedral, built towards the end of the seventeenth century. The gravestones and monu-ments which stand under the trees bear the names of many great Russian families. Latterly the monastery has become an architectural museum.

On the left bank of the Moscow River, a couple of miles south-west of the Kremlin and surrounded by a high white wall, stands the Novospasski Monastir or Convent of the New Redeemer, its towers and domes and ramparts reflected in a fish-pond. Founded by Ivan Kalita in the fourteenth century and said to be the oldest monastery in Moscow, it was moved to its present site in the reign of Ivan III. Individually, none of its five churches, repeatedly destroyed and rebuilt, is of very great interest, but, taken together, with the belfry which rises above the entrance gate, they are impressive enough. Two more fine old monasteries near the centre of the city are the Upper Petrovski and Spaso-Andronikov monasteries, the latter containing a fine collection of icons.

Away to the south-west, once beyond the city's limits, is perhaps the most interesting of Moscow's many convents or monasteries: Novodevichi, the Convent of the New Virgin. Founded in 1525 and strategically sited at a bend in the Moscow River, Novodevichi formed a vital link in the chain of Moscow's outer defences. In 1591 its cannon repulsed an attack by the Khan of the Crimea and in 1612 it played an important part in the defence of Moscow against the Poles. Its massive sixteenth-century walls still stand four-square with a battlemented tower at each of the four corners and lesser fortifications in between.

The convent's principal church is the great five-domed Smolensk Cathedral, built in 1525 to celebrate the recapture of Smolensk and possessing a particularly fine seventeenth-century iconostasis. Novodevichi was always a rich foundation, being generously endowed by the numerous great ladies who for one reason or another were admitted to it as nuns. Over each of the main entrances is a typical late seventeenth-century gate-church; a tall bell-tower adjoining the Church of the Assumption and the refectory belong to the same period. The adjoining graveyard is still a fashionable place to be buried and, in addition to those recalling famous figures from the past such as Gogol and Chekhov, contains a number of handsome monuments to once-significant Soviet personalities, including the late N. S. Khrushchov, V. M. Molotov and J. V. Stalin's tragic wife, Nadezhda Alliuyeva, who, no doubt with good reason, shot herself in 1932.

Among Moscow's other monasteries pride of place must now go to the ancient Danilovski Monastir, founded in the thirteenth century, turned after the revolution to secular uses, now reconsecrated and lavishly refurbished in preparation for the 1,000th anniversary of Russia's conversion to Christianity and destined to serve henceforth as the official seat of the Patriarchate, due to return to Moscow after an interval of more than two and half centuries. At the time of writing teams of workmen under due ecclesiastical supervision, and crossing themselves as they go, are working hard to complete their task within the allotted time.

A good deal further afield, some fifty miles north of Moscow, at Sergievo or Zagorsk, stands the great fortified monastery of the Trinity and Sergei founded by Sergei in the fourteenth century and still an important religious centre. On a fine day it is a magnificent sight with its glittering domes brilliantly reflected in the waters of the moat. St Sergei himself, who blessed the assembled Russian armies before their great victory over the Mongols at Kulikovo in 1338, built much of the original timber structure with his own hands and lies buried in the oldest of the monastery's churches. This is the white limestone Cathedral of the Trinity, with its single golden dome, built in 1422, the year when St Sergei was canonized and formally proclaimed Protector of the Land of Russia. The nearby Church of the Holy Ghost, with a peal of bells ingeniously inserted under the drum of its single dome, was built fifty years or so later, in 1476, by craftsmen from Pskov.

The splendid five-domed Church of the Assumption, now the monastery's main cathedral, was begun in 1559, in the reign of Ivan the Terrible. The severity of its lines is relieved by its beautiful proportions and by the generous curves of its star-spangled onion domes. The frescoes within date from the late seventeenth century. Near the north-western corner of the cathedral is the family burial vault of the Godunov family and just outside the main entrance is the tomb of Tsar Boris Godunov himself. At the other end of the cathedral's west front is the elaborately decorated and cheerfully coloured late seventeenth-century Nakladezhnaya or Chapel-over-the-Well. Inside it rises a spring of cold clear water, a gulp of which, you are assured, will wash away your sins. Round it cluster a succession of penitents armed with mugs, cups and bottles. The refectory, the hospital, with church attached, and the Chertogi Palace, in which the Tsar used to stay when visiting the monastery, are all good examples of late seventeenth-century architecture. The Palace of the Metropolitan, on the other hand, took almost three centuries to build, being completed in the eighteenth century. The little Church of St Micah, near the Refectory, dates from the eighteenth century, as does the elegant classical Church of the Virgin of Smolensk with its baroque five-tiered, blue and white campanile. First built in about 1550, the monastery's walls successfully withstood a sixteen-month siege by the Poles sixty years later. Today it has become a popular place for church marriages and wedding parties proliferate. The singing in the churches is as good as you will find.

Due south of Moscow, agreeably situated on a bend of the Moscow River, is the village of Kolomenskoye which dates back to the thirteenth century. Adjoining it is a former royal estate, originally laid out in the fourteenth century by Dmitri Donskoi and later a favourite resort of Ivan the Terrible. Of the various buildings at Kolomenskoye, the most remarkable is the Church of the Ascension, built in 1533 with its extraordinary sugar-loaf spire which, in a moment of enthusiasm, the composer Hector Berlioz compared to the cathedrals of Strasbourg and Milan. Nearby is a tall, brick-built tower known as the Falcon Tower, where Tsar Alexis kept his hawks and falcons, with, next to it, a sixteenth-century campanile dedicated to St George. Some distance away, on the other side of a handsome gateway, the seventeenth-century Church of Our Lady of Kazan, with its bright blue onion domes, is still in use.

Two fine eighteenth-century mansions on the outskirts of Moscow are Ostankino and Kuskovo, both built entirely of wood and both once the property of the Sheremetiev family. Another great house of the same period is Arkhangelskoye, built by the Golitsins and later sold by them to Prince Yusupov. At Arkhangelskoye a frequent visitor was Alexander Herzen, the famous nineteenth-century revolutionary writer and thinker. Like Arkhangelskoye, Ostankino has its private theatre, built by Count Sheremetiev for Parasha, the beautiful young actress he eventually married. Parasha was herself a serf and the builders and craftsmen who created Ostankino, now in part a Museum of Serfdom, were equally all serfs from Count Sheremetiev's estate.

But already these last rural outposts are falling one after another within the capital's all-enveloping urban sprawl. Fifty years ago, when I first knew it, Moscow was still in many ways an overgrown village. Until not very long before, eighty-five per cent of all Russians had been peasants and most of the urban population still had strong links with the land. Even in the heart of the city you still came on unexpected green patches, while on the outskirts, mingling with nineteenth-century mansions and more modern tenements, began the dachas or country cottages so close to every Russian's heart, each with its own patch of cultivation.

Now much, though not all, of this has been swept away to make way for the extraordinary new urban developments which in half a century have transformed Moscow from a comparatively small, old-fashioned town into a fitting capital for a superpower. In the city centre more and more majestic new buildings keep springing up. Right through the heart of old Moscow runs the Prospekt Kalinina, which, with its massed high-rise public buildings, department stores and apartment blocks, recalls the main street of a mid-western city in the United States. Meanwhile, on the outskirts, vast new suburbs are reaching out in every direction to accommodate a population which in the forty odd years since the end of World War II (when Stalin's intensive building drive began) has doubled to 8.7 million.

But, for all this, Moscow has somehow managed to retain much of its old character, of which no one is prouder than the Muscovites themselves. In contrast to Leningrad, it is still at heart an Eastern city, plumb in the middle of the Russian land-mass, half-way to

Asia, to non-Russian eyes infinitely exotic and strange. Of the faces you see on the streets, many have an Eastern, even a Far Eastern, look, while the features, not only of visitors from further afield, but of actual Muscovites, often suggest an admixture of Tartar blood. The architecture of Moscow is equally exotic. Despite the best efforts of Ivan the Great's imported Italian architects, the Kremlin's towers and spires and even the onion domes of the churches clearly claim kinship with the mosques and minarets of Turkestan.

A good deal more, too, of the old Moscow has survived the bulldozers than you would at first suppose. In the centre of the city, a hundred yards on either side of the Prospekt Kalinina and in the streets round the Arbat, once the old Tartar marketplace, you can still find any number of quiet, tree-lined streets of old plaster-fronted or even wooden town houses, one storey high or taller, often with an old golden-domed church to complete the village atmosphere. Today, what is more, should one or other of these streets or houses be threatened with demolition, the local residents now get together to resist such desecration of their corner of the city. As elsewhere, conservationism is catching on.

Some would say, a little late. Forgetting for the moment the numerous acts of wanton destruction which followed the Revolution, the Prospekt Kalinina, however impressive in its all-American way, cut a swathe right through the centre of old Moscow, while the construction of the mammoth Hotel Rossiya on thirty acres of land in full view of the Kremlin, though possibly good for tourism, involved the sacrifice of any number of churches and other old buildings, only a few of which were in the end preserved.

Twenty years on, the Rossiya, originally intended as Moscow's answer to the Hilton, is no longer quite the sensation it once was. With its three thousand rooms decorated in pastel shades and furnishings, each with bath and telephone, accommodating, it is said, some five thousand guests, and its two glittering restaurants, each feeding a thousand or more at a time, it has now been slightly put in the shade by the more remote, but in some ways even more sophisticated Cosmos and Mezhdunarodnaya. Not that most visitors to Moscow would not still think themselves lucky to get a room at the Rossiya and dine there with nine hundred and ninety-nine other guests to the deafening din of amplified Soviet *dzhazz*. If they can manage it, however (and it is not easy), the more discriminating still seem to prefer to any of these the faded splendours of the National and Metropole, built at the turn of the last century with the clear intention of showing that, when it came to grand hotels, Moscow could be as grand as any place. In both establishments, the food is by local standards good and the old spirit of service with a smile has survived, always providing you can make friends with the head waiter. Round the corner from the Metropole amid the steam and birch twigs of the famous pre-revolutionary Sandunovski Russian Bath-House, the enterprising traveller can seek to lose such weight as he has put on, while purging his sytem of any vodka he has managed to consume. At the Praga on the Arbat, another old-established restaurant unfortunately demolished by an enemy bomb during the war, but since completely restored to its former glory of marble and gilt, I have of late found both food and service exceptionally good. It is one of the few places where, at the moment, you can count on getting a tender, juicy steak.

Just around the corner from the Praga, in place of what used once to be Arbat Street, there is now a trendy new shopping precinct, closed to traffic, where art students and others offer to paint portraits of passers-by and art books and artists' materials are offered for sale. To add to the variety of the scene, it has recently become a popular spot for break-dancing, now, like heavy metal, all the rage among the younger generation.

Discovering where to go in Moscow and what to eat and drink and what to avoid is a painfully acquired but thoroughly worthwhile art. Meantime, for those in a hurry, the self-service restaurant at the vast, bleakly modern Hotel Intourist can only be described as a godsend, while for those who wish to savour the cooking of Central Asia or the Caucasus without the trouble of actually going there, there are quite a number of Georgian, Armenian, Azerbaijani, Uzbek and other ethnic restaurants. For those, on the other hand, who fancy real, 100 per cent Russian food in a spectacularly Russian setting, I would recommend a short walk across the Red Square and down a side-street to the Slavianski Bazar, an Olde Russian restaurant, once the haunt of such celebrities as Chekhov, Chaikovski and Stanislavski and later lavishly refurbished in the ancient Russian manner for the benefit of serious seekers after local colour. It is, at the time of writing, one of the relatively few places where the present shortage of genuine Olde Russian vodka is not immediately noticeable. And now, of course, new privately or semi-privately run cafés and *traktirs* are beginning to spring up all over the city, each with its own individual atmosphere, and vying with each other to attract rather than rebuff the potential customer.

A great Russian institution, now sadly, it seems, on its way out, is the *dezhurnaya*, literally officer of the day, the solid, capable, middle-aged female who used invariably to sit at a desk on each floor of any Soviet hotel, keeping a more or less friendly eye on the guests, as they came and went, and attending within reason to their needs, notably providing steaming glasses of tea from her samovar, extra towels, bedside lamps, bottles of mineral water and often sound advice in an emergency. She will, if the tendency to do away with her continues, be sadly missed, by no one more than the present author.

To write of Moscow or Russia without touching on the theatre or ballet would be to leave out a whole side of Russian life very close indeed to the heart of almost every Russian. Both theatre and ballet appeal strongly to something deep down in most Russians, to their love of language and music, of movement and colour, of drama and romance. Anyone who has ever visited the ballet schools of Moscow or Leningrad or witnessed the performances of the Bolshoi or Kirov companies or seen the plays of the Moscow Arts or Mali Theatres will without difficulty understand the total dedication required of their actors or dancers. He will also appreciate the amazing sophistication of the audience they play to. Both theatre and ballet are part of a deeply Russian tradition, though by Western standards historically not a very old one. In Soviet society, the stars of the theatre and ballet occupy the same position of honour as they did in the days of the tsars. Whenever they can, ordinary Russians will flock again and again to watch critically and with informed enthusiasm the plays of the great Russian nineteenth-century dramatists which, if you come to think of it, is only natural in a country which produced such outstanding dramatists and, in a wider sense, such giants of the theatre. As for the ballet, it is even more popular, providing amongst other things a ready escape from the somewhat drab reality of everyday life ('Just like your royal weddings', said a Russian friend recently.)

For the best part of a thousand years practically the only forms of pictorial art in Russia were formalized church art and iconography. Indeed it was not until the eighteenth century that Russians really began to paint ordinary pictures. Following this late start, native Russian painting has yet to reach supreme heights. (Socialist Realism, itself a form of religious art, has in its turn likewise held up Russia's artistic development.) But, besides magnificent icons, both the Tretyakov Gallery in Moscow and the Russian Museum in Leningrad contain a fascinating collection of nineteenth-century Russian portraits, landscapes and conversation pieces, as well as a number of enormous paintings celebrating different important episodes in Russian history, all, insofar as they portray aspects of life now gone for ever, of very real interest to the student of Russia and its people. Nor should the art enthusiast on any account miss the magnificent collections of Western European Art in the Pushkin Museum in Moscow and the Hermitage in Leningrad, both of which, thanks to the good taste of some rich Russian private collectors at the turn of the century, include some remarkable paintings by the French Impressionists. As for the future of Russian art, Socialist Realism now seems, not before time, to be making way for newer, more adventurous and less ideological schools of painting.

3

Window on the West

Here there shall be a town.
PETER THE GREAT
ON HARE ISLAND, 16 MAY 1703

On his death in 1676, Tsar Alexis the Gentle was succeeded by the son of his first marriage, Fyodor, a partly paralysed boy of fourteen. Next in the line of succession came Fyodor's short-sighted and half-witted brother, Ivan, and, after him, Peter, aged four, the handsome, lively intelligent child of their father's second marriage to the beautiful Natalya Narishkina. On Fyodor's death in 1682, the Narishkins, with the support of the boyars and the Patriarch, declared Ivan incapable of ruling and proclaimed Peter tsar and his mother regent. They had, however, reckoned without Ivan's hideous but extremely determined elder sister Sophia, who, calling out the *streltsi* or musketeers, gave them ten roubles each to march on the Kremlin and massacre any Narishkins they could lay hands on. Sophia was then proclaimed Regent on behalf of Ivan and Peter, who were declared co-tsars. After which Sophia installed herself with Ivan in the Kremlin, while Natalya withdrew to the village of Preobrazhenskoye outside Moscow, taking little Peter with her.

For the next seven years, while Sophia ruled Russia, Peter and his mother lived quietly at Preobrazhenskoye, not far from the Nemetskaya Sloboda or Foreign Settlement, where the foreign colony dwelt even then in seclusion from the rest of the community. Natalya did not share the prevailing distrust of foreigners and her son was accordingly able to acquire much useful knowledge from the craftsmen and experts of the foreign settlement. The boy's inclinations were military and the war games he played were so realistic that, while still a youth, he managed to form the nucleus of two famous regiments, the Preobrazhenski and Semyonovski Guards. At Preobrazhenskoye he also acquired, as he grew older, a taste for strong drink and a flaxen-haired German mistress named Anna Mons. When he reached the age of seventeen, a suitably noble consort, Evdokia Lopukhina, was found for him by his mother, but, like Vasili's unfortunate wife, St Solomonia, before her, soon packed off by him to the Convent of the Intercession at Suzdal with scarcely time to produce a first-born before she took the veil.

Sophia, meanwhile, not content with being regent, seems to have hatched a plot to get rid of Peter and declare herself autocrat, again with the help of the *streltsi*. But Peter's supporters were taking no chances. On an August night in 1689 the young co-tsar was roused from his bed and rushed to the nearby Monastery of the Trinity and St Sergei, now Zagorsk, where he was joined by some leading boyars and a considerable number of loyal troops. Soon more nobles and clergy joined him. He was by now in a position of some strength. Relegating his half-sister Sophia to the Convent of Novodevichi, he gave orders for the arrest and execution of a large number of her supporters. The question of who was tsar had finally been resolved.

For the next five years Peter left his mother to govern the country, while he himself built up its defences. In 1695 the outbreak of war with Turkey gave him an eagerly-seized opportunity to demonstrate his skill as a military commander. His first move was to lay siege to the Turkish port of Azov. But several months later the Turkish garrison, able to receive supplies by sea, were still holding out. Peter spent the winter of 1695 building up a fleet with which to blockade the port. By March 1696 it was ready and, sailing with it down the Don, he launched a fresh attack on Azov, which quickly fell to the Russians. More convinced than ever of the need for a strong Russian navy, Peter now built new shipyards, imported more foreign experts and trained ever larger numbers of Russians in shipbuilding. In 1697, with the idea of forming a Grand European Alliance, the young tsar himself led an Embassy Extraordinary to Germany, Austria, Holland, Poland and Great Britain, thereby considerably widening his experience and his knowledge of the world. For all that, he remained a true Russian. 'We shall need Europe for a few decades', he said to a friend, 'and then we can turn our backside to her.'

While in Vienna in the summer of 1698, Peter received the news that, in his absence, the *streltsi* had mutinied. Hurrying back to Moscow, he executed a couple of thousand of them in a matter of weeks, himself giving the executioners a helping hand. Further investigation left him in no doubt as to the guilt of his half-sister Sophia, even though she was still languishing in the Convent of Novodevichi. She was accordingly shorn as a nun and placed under still closer restraint with three dead *streltsi* dangling outside her window as a reminder. On his return, Peter also sought to instil in his courtiers some of the new Western ideas he had picked up on his travels, forcing them to shave their beards and discard their old-fashioned kaftans. Nor was this all. A larger-than-life character and an enthusiastic reformer in every field, he intervened vigorously in all branches of government, working his subjects harder than ever and strengthening his own autocratic control.

It was by now clearer than ever to Peter, as it had been to Ivan the Terrible before him, that Russia must have an outlet to the West. This could only be achieved by breaking through to the Baltic. Here his main obstacle was Sweden, where King Charles XII, a boy of eighteen, had recently come to the throne. In King Augustus of Poland and King Christian of Denmark Peter found ready allies for what he had in mind. In the summer of 1700, after first concluding peace with Turkey, he despatched a force of forty thousand men to the Gulf of Finland.

But Charles of Sweden was not so easily disposed of. Seizing the initiative, he first struck in strength at neighbouring Copenhagen. Then, turning on the Russians, he utterly defeated them at Narva on the Gulf of Finland. Peter, who left the field of battle well ahead of his troops, had underestimated his opponent. He was, however, not easily put off. Within weeks of his defeat at Narva, he had already started to assemble a bigger and better army.

It was Charles who now blundered. Instead of following up his advantage, he let himself become involved in a prolonged campaign against the Poles. Reorganizing his forces, Peter mounted a fresh attack. While one Russian army threatened the Swedes in Poland, another made for the Baltic and the Gulf of Finland, moving gradually nearer to the mouth of the River Neva. In the autumn of 1702, Peter joined his northern army, captured the important Swedish stronghold of Nøteborg on the Neva and, pressing on down the river in the spring of 1703, seized the fortress of Nyenschanz at the junction of the Neva and the Okhta. Here, on a little island known to the local fishermen as Hare Island, he laid in May 1703 the foundations of the future fortress of St Peter and St Paul and of the great city that was to bear his name – St Petersburg. By the autumn of 1703 ships were being built on nearby Lake Ladoga and a naval base had been established on the Island of Kronstadt. The following year the Russians captured Narva and two or three other strongpoints.

Overall, however, the outlook was far from reassuring. By drastic reforms and heavy taxation, Peter, himself a man of abounding physical energy, had put a heavy strain on his country, on his people, indeed on the whole machinery of government. Meanwhile, Russia's ally King Augustus of Poland had been defeated by Charles of Sweden who was now preparing to march on Moscow; there was unrest among the Cossacks in the Ukraine and on the Don and the Ukrainian Hetman, Ivan Mazepa, was intriguing with Russia's enemies, the Swedes.

Charles of Sweden launched his planned offensive early in 1708, advancing through Poland in the direction of Smolensk, while another Swedish force under General Loewenhaupt marched south to join him with additional supplies. Then, just as he seemed about to attack Smolensk, he suddenly turned south into the Ukraine. This gave the Russians their chance. Intercepting General Loewenhaupt before he could join Charles, Peter captured the entire Swedish baggage train. At the same time Prince Menshikov, commanding another Russian force, struck hard at Mazepa, nipping his intended insurrection in the bud.

It was thus that, with winter coming on, Charles found himself entirely surrounded by Peter's armies. Having failed to break out in the direction of Moscow, he decided in the spring of 1709 to lay siege to the Russian fortress of Poltava, two hundred miles southeast of Kiev. But in the event the Russian garrison held out just long enough to let Peter come to their help and on the morning of 8 July 1709 Swedes and Russians met in battle at Poltava. By midday the fight was over. Half Charles's army had been killed or captured. The remainder were in full retreat to the Dnieper, where Menshikov was lying in wait for them. Charles himself, badly wounded, was carried across the Dnieper into Turkish territory.

Peter's victory at Poltava placed Russia in the front rank as a military power and firmly established her supremacy in north-eastern Europe. By his decisive defeat of the Swedes, he had consolidated her foothold on the Baltic and given her 'a window on the West'. 'The final stone', he declared, 'has been added to the foundations of St Petersburg.'

Other wars followed – an unsuccessful campaign against Turkey and a prolongation of the war with Sweden, which dragged on until 1721. Upon Peter were bestowed in gratitude the styles of 'The Great', 'Pater Patriae', and 'Emperor of All Russia'.

For more than twenty-five years, Peter, unresting, had kept his country continuously at war. At the same time he had relentlessly driven through a series of radical reforms. Every Russian from the great nobles downwards had been forced into the service of the state. Ninety per cent of the population were now serfs. The nobility and gentry were liable to a lifetime of military or other government service. Meanwhile, untiringly and at enormous cost in treasure and in human lives, he pressed on with the project which in a sense symbolized his achievement, the creation on the marshy banks of the Neva of a fitting capital for the newest of the great European powers, Russia, as the old Muscovy was now formally renamed. In January 1725, Peter died at the age of fifty-two. For Russia his reign marked a watershed between the Middle Ages and modern times. It is perhaps not surprising that two hundred years later he should have been hailed by Stalin as the First Bolshevik.

Peter's only son Aleksei had died under torture in the Fortress of St Peter and St Paul, where he had been confined on his father's orders on suspicion of treachery. For the two years that followed Peter's death the throne was occupied by his much-loved widow Catherine, a former servant-girl from the Baltic who rode and swore and drank like a man and who now ascended it with the timely support of a former lover, Prince Menshikov, and of the Imperial Guards. On her death in 1727, she was succeeded by Peter's twelve-year-old grandson Peter Alekseyevich, but three years later little Peter caught smallpox and died. Again the Imperial Guards, destined henceforth to play an ever more important part in Russian affairs, intervened, replacing him by Peter's niece, Anna, widow of the Duke of Kurland on the Baltic. From Kurland Anna brought with her to St Petersburg a horde of Baltic German advisers, who quickly formed an all-pervading German mafia which governed Russia for the next ten years, while the empress gave herself up to the unrestrained pursuit of pleasure.

On Anna's death in 1740 her three-month-old great-nephew Ivan of Brunswick-Bevern was proclaimed Tsar Ivan VI. Again the Guards intervened, sweeping away Ivan, his mother and their German entourage, and putting on the throne Peter the Great's younger daughter Elizabeth Petrovna. The new empress was not much interested in politics, preferring parties and young men and building palaces. 'Not an ounce of nun's flesh about her,' aptly reported the British Minister. French influence now abruptly replaced German and, in the Seven Years' War, Russia intervened vigorously against Prussia, occupying Berlin in 1760. Fortunately for Frederick the Great, who by now was facing disaster, Elizabeth died on Christmas Day 1761 and her death was followed by yet another sudden change in Russian policy.

The reason for this lay in the person and character of her successor, her nephew, Karl

Peter-Ulrich, Duke of Holstein, a fanatical admirer of everything German, who at once made peace with Prussia. Brought to Russia from Germany in 1742 and married three years later to the sixteen-year-old Princess Sophia Augusta of Anhalt-Zerbst, re-baptized Catherine on her entry into the Orthodox Church, Karl Peter-Ulrich, who now ascended the throne as Peter III, was a decidedly poor specimen. His young bride, on the other hand, was highly intelligent, highly sexed and bursting with energy and charm. Though German through and through, she quickly transformed herself into an enthusiastic Russian.

The new Tsar had few friends and it was not long before a conspiracy was hatched by his wife's most recent lover, Grigori Orlov, and once again by the Imperial Guards, to put Catherine on the throne in his place. In the summer of 1762 Catherine, who was living outside St Petersburg at Peterhof, rode into the capital in uniform, escorted by two Guards regiments, and was proclaimed empress. The following day Peter abdicated. A few days later he was dead, murdered, it was thought, by Grigori Orlov's brother Aleksei.

Catherine, who at the age of thirty-six now assumed control of the Russian empire, was by any standards a remarkable woman. In addition to immense vitality and strength of character, she possessed considerable political acumen. Her greatest successes were achieved in the field of foreign affairs. Russia's neighbour and old enemy Poland had by this time been reduced by the bickering of her nobles and by repeated outside interference to a state of total confusion. In 1768 the Russians, despatching a military force to Warsaw, established what amounted to a protectorate over Poland. Urged on by France, the Turks, who in the south still had a common border with Poland, now declared war on Russia.

To Catherine, who had long entertained designs on Turkey's European possessions, the war was not unwelcome. It began with a series of Russian victories. By the autumn of 1769 one Russian army had reached the Balkans. In July 1770 the Russian fleet under Aleksei Orlov utterly destroyed the Turkish Fleet in the Bay of Chesme, while another Russian army conquered the Crimea. In 1774 the Peace of Kutchuk Kainardji gave Russia a firm hold on the northern shores of the Black Sea and formally recognized her interest in the Sultan's Christian subjects in the Balkans and elsewhere, by which time large areas of Poland had been duly distributed between Russia, Prussia and Austria.

At home the situation was less happy. In the summer of 1773 a rebellion had broken out under the leadership of Emelian Pugachov, a roving Don Cossack, who, suddenly appearing on the Ural River, announced that he was Catherine's murdered husband Peter III. Soon, from a variety of discontented elements, he had assembled a force of twenty-five thousand men and by the spring of 1774 was threatening Moscow. In the end a strong force under the famous General Suvorov managed to get the better of him; savage reprisals were inflicted on all who had sided with him; and he himself was finally hunted down, brought in a cage to Moscow and there publicly dismembered.

With the aid of her latest lover, Prince Grigori Potyomkin, Catherine now turned her attention to the need for a measure of domestic reform and a more effective internal security system. Not before time, the Cossacks were brought under the control of the regular army; Russia was divided into fifty Governments; and a Charter of the Nobility gave the nobles the status of an officially recognized ruling class.

Catherine did not allow her internal preoccupations to interfere with her ambitions abroad. By her peace with Turkey she had secured vast areas of the rich grain-producing Black Sea steppe, well known for the famous *chernozem* or black earth which today makes the Ukraine one of the most prosperous parts of the Soviet Union. To this she gave the name of New Russia and appointed Grigori Potyomkin to be its first viceroy. Simultaneously her thoughts turned to the creation, at Turkey's expense, of a new Byzantine Empire under Russian control with a Russian-held Constantinople as its capital.

Friendship with Austria had by now replaced Catherine's earlier alliance with Prussia. Early in 1787 she set out on a state visit to her new southern territories and to their Viceroy, Prince Potyomkin, accompanied by the Emperor Joseph II of Austria and by Stanislas Poniatowski, another of her former lovers, since 1763 King of Poland. Greatly to her satisfaction, the Turks took her tour as an act of deliberate provocation and in September declared war on both Russia and Austria. It had been Catherine's intention that her army should now sweep in triumph through the Balkans to Constantinople. To her surprise the Turks more than held their own. Eventually General Suvorov himself took over command and things went better, but by now Russia was exhausted, the Austrians had already made peace and the Turks, for their part, were only too glad to come to terms. By a treaty of peace signed in January 1792, Russia made do with Ochakov, the Black Sea littoral between the Bug and the Dniester, and formal recognition by Turkey of her right to the Crimea.

In 1789, General Suvorov had stormed the Turkish fortress of Hadji Bey on the Black Sea coast. A year or two later he was directed by Catherine the Great to build a Russian fortress on the same site. Soon a town sprang up there. To this was given the name of Odessa. By the beginning of the nineteenth century, Odessa was already a flourishing port and the chief town of New Russia. The well laid-out city of today dates from this period. Its principal architect, after Suvorov, was none other than the Duc de Richelieu, who, having left France at the time of the Revolution, somehow became Governor of Odessa and Viceroy of New Russia, before returning to France to serve as Prime Minister under Louis XVIII. It was Richelieu who gave the new city the character of a typical French provincial town of the period with spacious squares and broad, tree-lined avenues. The good work was continued by Prince Michael Vorontsov, a hero of the Napoleonic Wars, who held the post of Governor-General from 1823 to 1854 before going on to the Caucasus; he added many more fine buildings in a continuing classical tradition which later culminated in an exuberantly baroque opera house, to this day the pride and joy of every Ukrainian. Prince Vorontsov's statue now dominates the Square of the Soviet Army, while a handsome bust of the poet Pushkin, who for a time was both one of his aides and his wife's lover, adorns the public gardens in front of his former palace. As for the Duc de Richelieu, his statue stands majestically in toga and laurel wreath at the top of a flight of granite steps, since made famous by Eisenstein in his great film *The Battleship Potyomkin*.

Before the Revolution, Odessa, like other maritime cities, had a large foreign population of Greeks, Jews, Italians and others. To this day it possesses a more cosmopolitan flavour than most Soviet towns, together with a southern, a Mediterranean atmosphere. First and foremost a port, it handles an enormous amount of Soviet and foreign shipping and of recent years two vast man-made harbours have further expanded its capacity.

In the course of the eighteenth century and of their various conflicts with the Turks and Persians, the Russians had gradually gained first a foothold and then more than a foothold in the Caucasus and Transcaucasia. In December 1800, as the new century began, came Russia's formal annexation of the ancient Kingdom of Georgia, thereafter to serve as a springboard for further conquests.

For Russia Poland, too, still held the promise of further territorial gains. In 1793 came the Second Partition, reducing what remained of Poland to a Russian dependency, followed four years later by a Third and, for the time being, final Partition, under which Prussia took the Polish territories lying between the Niemen and the Vistula, including Warsaw; Austria was given Cracow and Lublin; while Russia received the largest share of all, namely Kurland and the remainder of Lithuania. As a country, though not as a nation, Poland had ceased to exist.

In 1762 Catherine the Great had usurped the throne which should have gone to her son Paul. Thirty-four years later she was again planning to exclude him from the successions by making his son Alexander her direct heir, when on 17 November 1796 death overtook her at the age of sixty-eight and Paul in his turn became Tsar of All the Russias. Catherine's reign had marked an important stage in Russia's rise to greatness, but Catherine, unlike Peter the Great, was no real revolutionary. The radical ideas she had once favoured had by the end of her reign become abhorrent to her. By refusing to face the looming problem of serfdom, she bequeathed an uneasy heritage to her successors, while by the westernization of the Court, a deeper chasm than ever was set between the ruling classes and the Russian people as a whole. The key to Catherine's greatness lay rather in her abounding energy. By sheer force of character she deeply influenced the life and style of her time, made St Petersburg one of the most magnificent capitals of Europe and brought Russia greater territorial gains than any sovereign since Ivan the Terrible.

Paul, who succeeded his mother at the age of forty-two, had had a sad upbringing. His father had been murdered. His mother, who disliked him, had seen as little of him as possible, excluding him from her life, seeking to exclude him from the throne. Odd-looking and mentally unstable, he had spent most of his time in the seclusion of Gatchina and Pavlovsk, his estates outside the capital. His eldest son, Alexander, he quite rightly distrusted.

Paul's first act on coming to the throne symbolized his hatred of his mother and his desire to reverse as many of her policies and actions as possible. On his orders, his murdered father's body was exhumed from its resting-place in the Monastery of Alexander Nevski and carried in procession through the streets in its coffin, to be laid in the end next to Catherine's in the Cathedral of St Peter and St Paul. Behind it was forced to walk Peter's reputed murderer, Count Aleksei Orlov, carrying the imperial crown. As for Catherine's one time lover, Prince Grigori Potyomkin, who had died four or five years earlier, his body was, on the new tsar's instructions, dug up and cast into the common pit.

Paul's original intention on coming to the throne had been to keep Russia out of foreign wars. But already Holland, Belgium, Switzerland, part of Germany and most of Italy had been overrun by the revolutionary armies of France and Napoleon Bonaparte was now threatening Egypt. For a time Paul held back. Then in 1799, with Britain and Austria, he joined the Second Coalition and despatched an army under General Suvorov to Northern Italy to support the Austrians. Suvorov was an outstanding general. Soon one Russian victory followed another. But Paul did not receive the support he had hoped for from his British and Austrian allies and in February 1801 he withdrew from the coalition and resumed relations with France. A few weeks later he was busy planning to invade British India.

By this time the nobles had had enough of Paul. With the connivance of his son the Tsarevich Alexander, and, not unnaturally, of the British ambassador, a plot was hatched to eliminate him. He was now living, surrounded by elaborate security precautions, in the fortress-like Michael Castle, which he had built to protect himself against just such an eventuality. Here the conspirators, who included the commander of the palace guard, whom he mistakenly believed he could trust, came upon him on the night of 23 March 1801 and, having half-strangled him with an officer's silk scarf, finished him off with a malachite paperweight.

The young man who at twenty-four now ascended the throne as Alexander I was to be known as the Enigmatic Tsar. From an early age he had had very sensibly learned to conceal his thoughts and trust no one. The Michael Castle had unpleasant associations for him. With his attractive young wife he moved into the more cheerful Winter Palace. Though credited with liberal inclinations, he soon found that there was a limit to what could be done in the way of liberalization without imperilling the autocracy, and of this there could naturally be no question. In the end he left things as they were.

In 1805, after a period of non-alignment, Alexander, alarmed by the scale of Napoleon's latest victories, joined the Third Coalition against France with Austria and Great Britain. Not long after, a Russian army was despatched to Central Europe, where it arrived in time to be defeated at Austerlitz. As further discouraging defeats followed, Alexander's enthusiasm for the Alliance began to wane. In the summer of 1807 he and Napoleon met at Tilsit. Dramatically alone on a raft in the middle of the River Niemen, the two Emperors discussed peace terms and ended by concluding an alliance mainly directed against Great Britain, under which, in broad terms, France would control Western and Russia Eastern Europe.

The Franco–Russian Alliance was never likely to last. In June 1812 Napoleon, assembling his forces, invaded Russia. After a bloody but indecisive battle at Borodino, he entered Moscow on 2 September to find it abandoned. He was now ready to make peace. A few days after this, the city was set on fire and largely destroyed. The Russians rejected Napoleon's overtures. Alexander was by this time determined not to make peace so long as a single enemy soldier remained on Russian soil. In this he had the support of the Russian people. From a quarrel between Emperors, the war had, it could be said, become in the modern phrase, 'a people's war'.

The autumn found Napoleon a thousand miles away from any secure base, in a deserted, burnt-out town, lacking both shelter and supplies with winter coming on. The population was hostile. The French had no hope of receiving reinforcements. Their morale had suffered from the long march, the slaughter of Borodino, and the hatred of the Russian people. The Russians, on their own territory, were gaining in strength every day. After wasting a month in Moscow, Napoleon decided to withdraw. The retreat began in the first half of October. Winter came early that year. As the French retreated, the Russians swooped down on them guerrilla-fashion. Wounded men and stragglers froze to death or were massacred by angry peasants. By the time he reached the Berezina, Napoleon had lost almost the whole of his army.

Having willy-nilly rejoined the Grand Alliance, the Tsar now saw himself as the saviour not only of Russia but of all Europe. In January 1813, the Russian armies crossed the Niemen and Alexander called on his allies to join him in a fresh coalition. In December 1813, he led the Allied advance into France, French resistance collapsed and on 31 March 1814, he and the King of Prussia entered Paris at the head of their troops. On 6 April, Napoleon abdicated, to reappear briefly, but spectacularly, the following year before being finally relegated to St Helena.

At the Congress of Vienna, the victorious allies met to decide the future of Europe. Here, again, Alexander played a leading part. He had by this time come to see himself as an instrument of the divine will. At his instance the allied sovereigns now formed a Holy Alliance under which their mutual relations were to be governed by 'the supreme truths dictated by the eternal law of God the Saviour'. These high-sounding principles were first applied to the problem of Poland, which was now once more partitioned between Russia, Prussia and Austria. Nor, in Russia itself, was any more heard of the liberal ideas which the Enigmatic Tsar had once seemed to favour.

Despite a story that in fact he lived on for another forty years as a hermit in Western Siberia, after stowing away in a yacht owned by his old friend Lord Cathcart, Alexander, enigmatic to the last, is generally believed to have died at Taganrog on the Sea of Azov in the winter of 1825. Though he in no way fulfilled the liberal hopes he had raised as a young man, his reign was nevertheless marked by the first stirrings of a new national feeling and of a rudimentary public opinion. The new ideas found expression in the writings of Alexander Pushkin and other Russian writers who flourished at this time. They were shared by many liberal-minded young officers and noblemen. Both the ideas and their proponents were deeply suspect to those in authority.

The heritage which Alexander left to his successor was not an easy one. Nor was there a smooth transition from one reign to another. In the normal way, Alexander's successor would have been his brother Constantine. Constantine had, however, secretly renounced the succession in favour of his younger brother, Nicholas, though neither Nicholas himself, nor the officials concerned, had been clearly informed of this. Accordingly, on Alexander's death, a confused situation arose which was only resolved when Nicholas, realizing the dangers of delay, decreed on 14 December that the army and civilian population should forthwith swear allegiance to him as tsar.

But by now the harm had been done. For some years groups of young officers and others had been meeting secretly to discuss the prospects of reform. Constantine was for some reason credited by them with liberal tendencies and aspirations. Nicholas, they knew, was a reactionary. The sudden substitution of Nicholas for Constantine made up the minds of the conspirators – of some of them, at any rate. On the day the decree was made, about three thousand soldiers, encouraged by their officers, assembled rather half-heartedly in the Senate Square near the statue of Peter the Great, refusing to take the oath of allegiance to Nicholas and vaguely cheering for the Grand Duke Constantine and for *Konstitutsia*, a Constitution, under the impression, it is said, that Konstitutsia was Constantine's wife.

For a time nothing happened. Then, with night coming on, the new tsar decided after some hesitation on drastic action. The mutineers were surrounded by loyal troops and first cavalry and then artillery employed against them. Soon the square was littered with corpses. Numerous arrests followed. Of those arrested, one hundred and twenty were brought to trial and five executed. They were to be known to history as the Decembrists. 'I think,' wrote the British Minister in St Petersburg, with remarkable foresight, 'the seeds are sown which one day will produce important consequences.'

By the beginning of Nicholas's reign, St Petersburg had for more than a century been Russia's capital and also, no less significantly, her window on the West, a channel for new fashions and new trends of thought.

Peter the Great's choice of a site for the city that for two centuries was to bear his name was highly personal. Landing on Hare Island on 16 May 1703, he cut himself two strips of turf with a bayonet and laid them one across the other. 'Here,' he said, 'there shall be a town', and there and then in his new-found enthusiasm for things Dutch, he named it: *Sankt Piterburkh*. Soon he decided to make the new town his capital. In 1710, after his victory at Poltava, the court moved from Moscow to St Petersburg, where all the great nobles were required to build themselves suitable palaces. For himself Peter built a small Summer Palace in a pleasant formal garden on the south bank of the Neva, designed by the Swiss–Italian architect Domenico Trezzini and closely resembling a medium-sized Dutch or English manor-house of the period.

From the first, Peter took a keen personal interest in the building of the city that was to bear his name, lavishing on it enormous sums of money and the lives of tens of thousands of wretched labourers who left their bones in the swamps amid which it was built. Even so it was some time before St Petersburg could be said to have been completed. In 1705 Peter himself was carried away and almost drowned by a sudden flood along the new Nevski Prospekt, while as late as 1714 two sentries were devoured by wolves while on duty outside the great palace Prince Menshikov had built for himself on Vasilyevski Island. But in time the ever-encroaching waters of the Neva were diverted into an almost Venetian network of canals which, reflecting the elegant palaces which lined them, lent the growing capital a character all of its own.

By 1712, when it was officially proclaimed capital of the empire, St Petersburg had begun to extend along both sides of the Neva as well as to Vasilyevski Island, the triangular wedge of land blocking the mouth of the river and dividing the Greater from the Lesser Neva. But the original Fortress of St Peter and St Paul on Hare Island remains the focal point of the city. Within its walls stands Trezzini's Cathedral of St Peter and St Paul, its slim golden spire thrusting upwards to the sky. A rather austere, classical building from without, its interior is exuberantly baroque. Here Peter and his successors lie buried, all save Alexander I, whose coffin mysteriously proved to be empty, and Nicholas II, the last of the Romanovs, who lies at the bottom of a disused mine-shaft in Siberia.

Across the river from the fortress, on the south bank, were the shipyards, soon to be known as the Admiralty. Between these and his own Summer Palace, Peter built a Winter Palace, a relatively modest dwelling. In an easterly direction from the Neva ran the famous Nevski Prospekt, at the far end of which was the Monastery of St Alexander Nevski, where, in the Cathedral of the Trinity, said to stand on the exact site of the Saint's great victory of 1241 over the Swedes and the Teutonic knights, Peter reinterred Alexander's remains, especially brought there by him from Vladimir.

Forty yards wide and three miles long, the Nevski Prospekt was with time to become one of the most celebrated streets in the world, rivalling on its own terms the rue de la Paix, Fifth Avenue, and Bond Street. Here, before the Revolution, fashionable ladies would take tea at Yeliseyev's the pastrycook's, shop for bejewelled Easter eggs round the corner at Fabergé's, for new-fangled sewing-machines at Singer's and for almost anything else at Gostiny Dvor the great eighteenth-century department store across the street, which to this day seeks, rather unsuccessfully, to compete with Moscow's GUM.

Just off the Nevski lies the old-established Hotel Europe, still worth a visit for its *art nouveau* dining-room, if not for its food. But in 1912 the Europe was to be outclassed by the Astoria, built, as its name indicates, in the best capitalist tradition, right across the square from St Isaac's cathedral, with a prancing equestrian statue of Tsar Nicholas I immediately outside its front door. Today the Astoria's mock Louis XV bedrooms still have a certain charm. Otherwise not much remains of its former glory, though it is still infinitely preferable to the Leningrad, its vast modern concrete rival further north.

On Vasilyevski Island across the river is the university with its twelve identical colleges, originally intended as ministries. Peter later decided that this should be the academic centre of the new city and the tradition was continued by his successors. On University Quay, in addition to Trezzini's twelve colleges and the university library, is the city's first museum, Peter's blue and white Kunst-Kamera, built for him by Zemtsov. To ensure its immediate success, the Emperor generously offered a free glass of vodka to every citizen who visited it.

Nearby are the Academy of Science and Academy of Arts, both built later in the eighteenth century and still used for the same purposes. One of the most impressive buildings on Vasilyevski Island, across the river from the Admiralty, is the splendid Palace of Peter's favourite, Prince Menshikov, built in 1710, but later extensively altered. Another building which recalls the city's beginnings is Kikina Palata, the elegant residence of A. V. Kikin at Smolni, built in 1714. Kikin was for a time one of Peter's closest associates, but came to grief and was executed for high treason in 1718, only four years after finishing his beautifully proportioned house, still painted the fashionable dark red of the period.

But St Petersburg's true splendour dates from the reigns of Elizabeth Petrovna, Catherine the Great and their successors. Much of the credit for this must go to the Italian Bartolomeo Francesco Rastrelli, appointed chief architect in 1736. His first major assignment was to build a larger and more magnificent Summer Palace, which has not survived. After various other assignments, he built for Elizabeth, at that time toying, however improbably, with the idea of becoming a nun, the splendidly baroque blue-and-white Convent and Cathedral of the Resurrection at Smolni. For some tastes an even finer example of Russian baroque is the slightly smaller Cathedral of St Nicholas (Nikolski Sobor) built by Rastrelli's talented pupil Cherakinski at the other end of the city and commonly known as the Sailors' Church. It is today one of the most popular 'working' churches in Leningrad.

Rastrelli is, perhaps, best known for his final version of the Winter Palace, work on which began in 1754. Green and white in colour and baroque in style, its magnificent façade looks northwards across the Neva to the Fortress of St Peter and St Paul. It possesses fifteen hundred rooms and a hundred or more staircases. Of Rastrelli's original interior, part was remodelled under Catherine the Great and more destroyed by fire in 1837, but his great Staircase of the Ambassadors leading down to the main entrance of the palace on the Neva has fortunately survived much as he designed it.

Not surprisingly, Catherine the Great made as powerful and immediate an impact on the architecture of the capital as on every other aspect of Russian life. For the baroque exuberance of twenty or thirty years before she substituted a plainer, more classical style. Typical of this is her austerely classical School for the Daughters of the Nobility, built at Smolni by another Italian, Giacomo Quarenghi, in complete contrast to Elizabeth's baroque convent nearby. An earlier project was the Little Hermitage, built for Catherine to the designs of Vallin de la Mothe as a private residence for herself adjoining the Winter Palace and housing her collection of pictures, which subsequently grew so rapidly that in ten years it became necessary to build yet another palace for them, now known as the Old Hermitage. To this a small private theatre was added by Quarenghi in 1784 and yet another palace, the New Hermitage, in the first half of the nineteenth century. Further along Palace Quay is the splendidly classical Marble Palace, designed for the Empress by Rinaldi and presented by her to her lover Grigori Orlov.

Towards the end of the nineteenth century, the purely Russian portion of Catherine's collection of pictures was transferred to the Mihailov Palace, built by Alexander I in about 1820 for his brother Michael to the designs of another great Italian architect, Carlo Rossi, and now known as the Russian Museum. The square of which it forms one side was also built to Rossi's designs and includes the famous Mali or Little Theatre. Alexander's Mihailov Palace is not to be confused with the nearby Mihailov Castle, built by the Emperor Paul in the vain hope that its massive walls would somehow save him from assassination. Another of Rossi's notable achievements was the splendid Alexandrinski (now Pushkin) Theatre, built to his designs in 1832 in a little garden off the Nevski. From immediately behind it, the former Theatre Street, now Rossi Street, with its matching pillared façades, leads into a fine classical crescent.

But by most Rossi's greatest achievement of all is held to be his completion of Palace Square immediately behind the Winter Palace by the addition on the north side, facing the

Winter Palace, of a vast crescent, housing the Ministries of War, Finance and Foreign Affairs, with, at its centre, a great double triumphal arch, surmounted by a chariot and Winged Victory leading through to the Nevski Prospekt. Right in the middle of the square stands a tall pink granite column to the memory of Alexander I, surmounted by the statue of a winged archangel holding a cross.

To the west of Palace Square, at one end of the Nevski Prospekt, is the Admiralty, built by Zakharov at the beginning of the nineteenth century on the site of the former shipyards. Its slender golden spire, matching the golden spire of St Peter and St Paul across the river, rises from a massive yellow and white entrance-gate. Opposite the two wings of the Admiralty, the old Senate, built in about 1830 by Rossi in the classical manner, is linked by a bridge across the street to the former Synod building. Not far away a splendid gate leads from the Moika River to the part of the shipyards known as New Holland.

High above the Admiralty looms the vast golden dome of St Isaac's Cathedral. Begun under Alexander I in 1818 and designed to hold a congregation of thirteen thousand, it took forty years to build. In front of it, facing the Neva on Senate Square, the Bronze Horseman, Falconet's famous equestrian statue of Peter the Great rears up from its massive granite plinth, symbolizing in its way the ruthless energy which first brought the city into being. A few hundred yards along the Nevski Prospekt, the Cathedral of Our Lady of Kazan, built fifteen or twenty years earlier than St Isaac's on a scarcely less imposing scale, is clearly modelled on St Peter's in Rome.

For my taste the finest of all the palaces that line the Nevski Prospekt is that built by Rastrelli in about 1760 for Prince Stroganov at the point where the Nevski meets the Moika. The handsome pillared front of the palace, originally painted orange and white, but now green and white, is mirrored in the canal. Further along, at the corner where the Nevski crosses the Fontanka, stands the Anichkov Palace, also facing the canal. This was the work of more than one architect, but Giacomo Quarenghi gave it its present strictly classical character and endowed it with the splendid colonnade reflected in the waters of the Fontanka. Adjoining the Anichkov Palace is the Vorontsov Palace by Rastrelli. Not far away, on the Moika, is the palace built for the Yusupovs by Quarenghi, where in December 1916 Prince Felix Yusupov and the Grand Duke Dmitri together murdered Grigori Rasputin. Two scarcely less imposing palaces on the Fontanka are those of the Sheremetyevs and Shuvalovs.

Situated at some distance from the centre of the town, on a bend in the river not far from Smolni, is the Tavricheski or Tauride Palace presented by Catherine the Great to her lover Grigori Potyomkin, whom she created Prince of Tauris in 1787 as a reward for his victories against the Turks in the Crimea. Built to the designs of I. E. Starov in the purest neo-classical style, it was completed in 1789. In the middle of its golden yellow façade stands a portico of six white Doric columns supporting a plain pediment and flattened green cupola. From a vestibule you pass into the Cupola Hall, a vast octagonal room rising to the full height of the dome and thence into the great colonnaded hall or ballroom, more than a hundred and twenty feet long, supported by a double row of Ionic columns.

Across the main stream of the Neva from the Admiralty, Vasilyevski Island is joined to the southern bank of the river by Palace Bridge, which leads to the eastern-most point of the Island, known as the Strelka or Arrow. Here are two more fine classical buildings, the early nineteenth-century Bourse and the rather later Tamozhnaya or Customs House. At this point the Neva is almost a mile wide and the Strelka commands a magnificent view of the river and both its banks, northwards to the Fortress of St Peter and St Paul and southwards to the Admiralty and Winter Palace.

Of the islands in the Neva delta two are certainly worth a visit: Kamenni Ostrov, the Isle of Stones (now Workers' Island), and Yelagin Island, now the Kirov Central Park of Culture and Rest. On Kamenni Island, Catherine the Great built in about 1780 a fine neo-classical palace for the heir to the throne. On Yelagin Island, Alexander I commissioned the young Carlo Rossi to build a splendid porticoed palace for this mother, the Dowager Empress Maria, and at the same time to landscape the whole island, converting it into a park in the English manner.

Beyond the river, to the north, is the Finland Station, where, in 1917, Lenin arrived from Switzerland in his sealed carriage and where the locomotive that pulled his train is still piously preserved, while, lying at anchor in the Neva nearby, is the cruiser *Aurora* from which was fired the salvo of blanks which in November heralded the storming of the Winter Palace, both reminders, if reminders were needed, that Leningrad, and not Moscow, is the City of the Revolution.

'Petersburg', Tsar Nicholas I would say, 'is Russian but it is not Russia.' Over the two-and-a-half centuries that have elapsed since Peter the Great first founded his city, it has in many ways remained the 'Window on the West' which he meant to make it. On the banks of the Neva, with its majestic monuments, its vistas of elegant classical palaces, its quays, its bridges and canals, it has, despite everything, remained in essence a Western city, possessing in contrast to land-bound Moscow an outward-looking, aquatic, maritime character of its own, all the more striking, if, arriving there by sea, you land right in the centre of the city and are at once surrounded by its incomparable beauty. To its other characteristics Leningrad's appalling ordeal in the Second World War, when, reverting to its original role of northern stronghold, it held out against the Germans for nine hundred days, losing during this period no less than 833,000 of its citizens by starvation or enemy action, has added a sadder, a more solemn quality, of which the visitor cannot but be aware, when he contemplates the city's striking memorials to its dead. Some pages from a diary kept by thirteen-year-old Tanya Savich, which have somehow survived, tell the story of one Leningrad family. 'Uncle Lyosha', runs an extract, 'died at 4 o'clock. Lena died at five in the morning 27 March 1942. Now all the Savich family are dead. Tanya is alone.' But Tanya herself died not long after.

Leningrad shares many of its characteristics with the great imperial country residences which lie within easy reach of it. Of these perhaps the most famous is Tsarkoye Selo or, as it is now called, Pushkin, situated some fifteen miles due south of Leningrad and originally built as a hunting-lodge for Peter the Great by his wife Catherine in 1718. On becoming Empress a score of years later, their daughter Elizabeth started to transform her father's modest stone house into a great palace. Building was one of her great enthusiasms. The palace Rastrelli built for her has a pillared blue-and-white baroque façade a thousand feet long with a splendid pavilion at one end and a great golden-domed church at the other. Eighty tall French windows with wrought-iron balconies are separated from each other by gigantic caryatids. On the far side, the palace gives on to a formal garden with trees and ornamental water and a baroque hermitage. Inside the building the Great Hall, with its two rows of windows looking out on to the park and its tall gilded mirrors, made a perfect setting for the balls and receptions in which Elizabeth took such pleasure.

As we know, Catherine the Great's taste differed from that of her predecessor. 'There is going to be a terrible upheaval at Tsarkoye Selo', she wrote with evident glee some years after her accession to the throne. For the baroque exuberance of Rastrelli she substituted restrained, neo-classical elegance. In Charles Cameron, an expatriate Scot, she found the perfect architect for what she had in mind. Having first completed the decoration of three suites in the palace, Cameron turned his attention to what Catherine described as a 'terrace garden with baths below and a gallery above', enabling her to walk straight out of her apartments on the first floor of the Great Palace into the Hanging Garden, which in turn led to Agate Pavilion or Bath House. Adjoining the Hanging Garden is the Colonnade or Cameron Gallery, jutting out at right angles to the Great Palace and lined with bronze busts. Only a few hundred yards from the Great Palace at Tsarskoye is the yellow-and-white Alexandrovski Palace, built by Catherine in the Palladian manner for her much-loved nineteen-year-old grandson the future Tsar Alexander I, to the designs of Giacomo Quarenghi.

In 1777, Catherine the Great presented her son Paul with a sizeable estate two or three miles south-east of Tsarskoye Selo. The Palladian palace which Charles Cameron built there for him was given the name of Pavlovsk. As work progressed, other architects were brought in, but Cameron's plan prevailed. The palace, painted a warm golden yellow, has a square central block of three storeys, the upper two spanned by tall white Corinthian columns supporting an ornamented architrave and pediment. From the roof rises a low green dome, supported by a colonnaded drum encircled with slender white columns. In front two curving wings form a courtyard.

From the entrance a fine state staircase takes you by way of the Egyptian vestibule on the ground floor to the state vestibule on the first floor. Thence you pass through Cameron's splendid Italian hall to the even more magnificent Grecian hall, supported by massive columns of fluted green marble with white marble bases and white Corinthian columns. Turning left or right from the Grecian hall, you come on the one side to the apartments of the Grand Duchess Maria Fyodorovna and on the other to those of her husband Paul, all in the grandest possible manner. At Pavlovsk, the park, too, has survived unspoilt, with its ornamental water, its trees and flowers and classical temples.

Half-way between Tsarskoye Selo and Leningrad in the middle of a dreary housing estate, the real enthusiast will find the altogether fantastic church and adjoining palace of Chesme, built by Catherine the Great in the 'Turkish' manner to celebrate Aleksei Orlov's naval victory over the Turks off Chesme on the coast of Anatolia in 1780.

But of all the palaces round Leningrad, perhaps the most spectacular is Peterhof. Its site, on the Gulf of Finland, a dozen miles due west of the new capital, was chosen by Peter the Great himself. While striding by one day with some of his nobles, the Emperor came upon an ideally situated spring of water and, without further ado, the palace of Peterhof was forthwith planned and built above a Grand Cascade, gushing from the hillside and flowing down a series of tall stone steps marked by a line of fountains interspersed with gilded statues. Looking up from below, you see a long, splendidly-proportioned, three-storeyed, yellow-and-white building, built by Leblond and later extended by Rastrelli. Against this majestic background, the terraces of the Grand Cascade, with their gushing fountains and rows of glittering golden statues, form a dazzling foreground. Many of Rastrelli's magnificent interiors were destroyed during the Second World War, but a number still survive or have been restored with such loving care as to be indistinguishable from the originals. At Peterhof the grounds are divided by the palace itself into a small Upper Park and a much larger Lower Park which lies between the palace and the Gulf of Finland.

Five miles along the coast from Peterhof stands Oranienbaum, the great palace built for himself before his downfall by Peter's favourite Prince Menshikov, its massive central block linked by semi-circular galleries to large domed pavilions. Presented much later by the Empress Elizabeth to her nephew, the future Tsar Peter III, it was re-decorated by the Italian architect, Antonio Rinaldi. In 1762, Catherine the Great, having disposed of Peter but kept his architect, commissioned Rinaldi to build her a small Chinese Palace in the park at Oranienbaum. Although the main palace was badly damaged and is at present undergoing restoration, the little Chinese Palace remained untouched during the War and is well worth a visit. A baroque single-storeyed pavilion of seventeen rooms, on a stone terrace overlooking a little lake, it is particularly charming, both inside and out. Only the mixed Rococo and *Chinoiserie* of three or four of the rooms (with Rococo predominating) justifies the name by which it is known. But that, if you consider the superior quality of its decoration and contents, is scarcely important. In addition to a number of magnificent state rooms, the Chinese Palace possessed a handsome suite of private apartments, but, while she sometimes used it for entertaining, Catherine never, as far as is known, spent a night there, though that, like so much else in Russian history, must clearly remain a matter for speculation.

Not far away from the Chinese Palace is Katalnaya Gorka or the Switchback Pavilion. The Russians have always enjoyed tobogganing (hence the phrase *montagnes russes*), on ice runs in winter and in roller-coasters during the rest of the year. Built in three tiers with columns, pilasters and balustrades at all levels, with a bell-shaped dome on top to round it off, painted sky blue and white, Katalnaya Gorka resembles nothing so much as an immense wedding cake. Launching themselves boldly from its upper terraces, members of the imperial court would hurtle merrily down specially prepared chutes and slides at breakneck speed to the delight of the onlookers, assembled on the balconies of the pavilion. Others, meanwhile, took refreshments inside in an exquisitely-decorated Circular Hall and a no less exquisite Porcelain Room, the walls of which are adorned with gilded Rococo brackets supporting specially designed pieces of the finest Meissen.

4

Baltic Seaboard

A revolution of expectations.
MIKHAIL SERGEYEVICH GORBACHOV

Russia's breakthrough to the Baltic was, as we have seen, completed in the course of the eighteenth century by her conquest of what are now Estonia, Latvia and Lithuania. After a brief period of independence between the First and Second World Wars, followed by four years, first of Russian and then of German occupation, these were in 1944 once more forcibly reincorporated in the Soviet Union by the advancing Red Army, a *fait accompli* as yet unrecognized by the governments of Great Britain and the United States. More recently, in the light of *glasnost* and *perestroika* and of their own phenomenal social and economic development, the Soviet Baltic republics have achieved a new prominence, becoming in the process something of a display-case for Mikhail Gorbachov's new ideas.

Setting out for the Baltic recently in late June, the season of White Nights and Midnight Sun, I was not at all certain what I should find there or whether I should like what I found. I had been to the Pribaltika or Baltic Seaboard twice before, on both occasions to the Latvian capital of Riga, once in the doom-laden spring of 1939, when the three Baltic Republics were still independent 'bourgeois' states, and once a dozen years or so ago, by when all three countries had spent some three years under German occupation, as part of Hitler's Ostland, and the next thirty years as Soviet Socialist Republics.

My pre-war visit had been largely spent in the company of attractive White Russian émigrés, who took me with them to what, after a couple of years in Stalin's Moscow, seemed to me a supremely glamorous Russian night-club, and also to Easter Mass in the vast nineteenth-century Russian Orthodox Cathedral. As a result, I left Riga captivated by Slav charm (I was in my twenties) and with the impression of a somehow miraculously preserved enclave of Tsarist Russia. Of the Latvians, I must admit, I was barely aware, beyond registering the fact that their nice little country seemed prosperous and well run.

Thirty-odd years later, I found Soviet Riga not so very different from any other Soviet city, though I noticed signs of greater sophistication and a somewhat higher standard of living. Perhaps not surprisingly, I failed to find the night-club which held such happy memories for me. Nor did I revisit the Russian Orthodox Cathedral. Instead, I concentrated on the Latvians themselves and on Riga's older buildings which recalled a remoter past. The yellow-walled Castle, built in 1330, had once been the headquarters of the Teutonic Knights who bulked so large in Latvian and early Russian history. The great Domkirk, with its mighty spire and Gothic cloisters, first built in 1211 as the Cathedral Church of the Archbishop of Riga, has since been rebuilt and reconstructed many times. Sold by the last Catholic Archbishop to the Lutherans for 18,000 marks at the time of the Reformation, it has now been turned by the Soviet authorities into a concert hall, boasting what was once the biggest organ in the world. The ancient churches of St John and St Peter likewise date from the Middle Ages and have also been rebuilt more than once, while Peter the Great's handsome mansion and coach-house recall Russia's first conquest of Latvia. In one museum I found a reminder of more recent times – a series of commemorative portraits of leading members of the pre-war Latvian Communist Party, most of whose lives, I noticed, ended with deadly regularity in 1937, the date of Stalin's drastic purge of theirs and many other Parties.

And now, after a considerable interval, I was going back to the Baltic. Punctual to the minute, the long sky-blue Estonian Express pulled smoothly out of Moscow's Leningrad Station, the attractive Estonian conductress brought me a welcome glass of tea in an ornate metal holder and, at the end of an exacting week in the capital, I settled down in my comfortable bunk to enjoy the leisurely fourteen-hour train ride to Tallinn. When I was not contemplating a restful prospect of woods and green fields sliding gently past the window or making my way along to the well-equipped restaurant car, it offered a perfect opportunity to catch up on reading and sleep.

Tallinn, the capital of Estonia, once known as Reval, which we reached at an eminently reasonable hour next morning, was in many ways different from what I had expected, different, too, from most other towns in the Soviet Union. In many ways the Viru, the vast new hotel at which I stayed, was indistinguishable from an equivalent hotel in, say, Helsinki or Stockholm, a feature it shared with much else in Estonia. More important, this high-class establishment was only a few minutes' walk from the old town, which was what I really wanted to see and which you enter by the ancient Viru Gate, from which the hotel takes its name.

The history of Estonia, like that of neighbouring Latvia and Lithuania, goes back a long way. Tallinn is one of the oldest cities in the Soviet Union. The earliest historical mention of it occurs, surprisingly enough, in the writings of Abu Abdullah Mohammed Idris, an early Arab traveller and geographer, who in the twelfth century referred to it as 'a small town resembling a large fortress', a description which, as far as the Upper Town is concerned, still holds good today. Of the inhabitants of Estonia, Idris wrote: 'they are tillers of the soil, their income is meagre, but they have many cattle'. This, too, is still largely true. Wherever you go in the Baltic Republics, you see large herds of contented-looking Friesian cattle and the fields are remarkably well tilled. As for the Estonians' per capita income, I should say at a guess that here collective agriculture is more efficient and the income from it higher than anywhere else in the Soviet Union.

Peasants, fishermen and beekeepers, akin by race and language to the neighbouring Finns, the Estonians, who, like the Finns, doubtless reached the Baltic from Mongolia or thereabouts a great many centuries ago, have over the ages played a relatively small part in the history of their own country. Nor has life ever been easy for them. As early as the middle of the ninth century, Rurik's Varangians or Vikings swept through Estonia on their way south, leaving, as was their wont, a trail of death and destruction in their wake. A century later St Vladimir of Kiev's able but ruthless son Yaroslav the Wise made a vigorous if unsuccessful attempt to convert the reluctant Estonians to Christianity. A century and a half after that, the Germans, approaching the task with characteristic thoroughness, proved more successful. In the year 1200 a certain Bishop Albrecht von Buxhoerden arrived off the estuary of the River Daugava with five hundred heavily armed German Crusaders in twenty-three ships. Two years later he was authorized by Pope Innocent II to found the crusading Order of the Knights of the Sword, killers to a man. Having established themselves on both banks of the Daugava, the Germans next embarked with Danish help on the conquest of Estonia.

By 1227, despite spasmodic Estonian resistance, they had achieved their objective, though the Danes, who had fortified Tallinn on their own account (its name is said to signify 'Danish castle'), retained a hold on much of the area for another hundred years or so. In 1237, the Knights of the Sword were merged with their fellow Crusaders, the kindred Order of Teutonic Knights, who in the meantime had been busy converting the Prussians, another pagan tribe akin to the neighbouring Lithuanians. Five years later both Orders marched together against Alexander Nevski's Russians, who, as we have seen, successfully repulsed them in a great battle fought on the frozen expanse of Lake Peipus.

Having made peace with the Russians and completed the conquest of Latvia, the Teutonic Knights were by 1290 masters of most of what they called Livland or Livonia, comprising most of present-day Latvia and Estonia. Like Novgorod, a member of the Hanseatic League since 1288, Tallinn became during the fourteenth century one of the largest and most prosperous of Baltic towns, being ideally situated at the northern end of the regular trade route between the Baltic and Byzantium. Converted by this time to Christianity, the Estonians, like their neighbours the Latvians, had long since lost all vestiges of independence and became mere serfs of the Teutonic Knights, who were to rule over their country for the best part of two centuries, endowing it with a heavily Teutonic heritage.

The original aim of the Teutonic Knights had been to unite Livonia with Prussia and so gain control of the whole of the Pribaltika. But Lithuania, which lay between the two, was in 1385 saved from them by a timely dynastic union with Poland. Twenty-five years later, in 1410, came the crushing defeat of the Teutonic Knights at Tannenberg at the hands of the Poles and Lithuanians who, on this occasion, enjoyed both Russian and Mongol support. This effectively destroyed the Order's military power; in 1525 the last Grand Master became a Lutheran and was subsequently created Grand Duke of East Prussia by the King of Poland, after which the Order was secularized and finally disbanded.

Bogolyubovo

The Kremlin, Pskov
OPPOSITE In the Cathedral, Pskov
PREVIOUS PAGE The Palace of Weddings, Kaunas

View from the Kremlin, Moscow

OPPOSITE The Kremlin, Moscow

Ivan the Great, the Kremlin, Moscow

OPPOSITE Zagorsk

Leningrad

For most of the sixteenth century, Livonia, in other words Estonia and Latvia, Lithuania being by now in effect part of Poland, was fought over by Poles, Lithuanians, Russians and Swedes. In 1502 Ivan the Great of Muscovy sought to conquer it but was repulsed by the Teutonic Knights near Pskov. In 1558 his successor Ivan the Terrible, reaching out in his turn for the Baltic, captured Narva. But three years later the Swedes seized Tallinn and with it most of Northern Estonia. In 1581 they drove the Russians from Narva and Estonia, together with parts of Latvia, was annexed by Sweden, while the rest of Livonia fell under Polish dominion. Though most of the land remained in the hands of German feudal lords, Estonia with much of Latvia was for the next century and a half a Swedish province. Under Sweden the native Estonians seem to have fared better than under the Teutonic Knights, but the 'good old Swedish days' came to a sudden end early in the eighteenth century, when Peter the Great, after defeating Charles XII of Sweden at Poltava, finally broke through to the Baltic. Under the Peace of Nystad in 1721 Sweden ceded all its Baltic provinces to Russia. These were now divided into the three Governments of Estonia, Livonia and Kurland. Lithuania, since 1385 part of Poland, did not fall into Russian hands until 1795, following the third Partition of Poland.

With Latvia and Lithuania, Estonia remained part of the Russian Empire until 1917. After the October Revolution all three Baltic countries took advantage of the prevailing confusion to declare their independence. They remained prosperous, independent 'bourgeois' republics until 1940, when, under the terms of the Soviet–German Pact of August 1939, they were reincorporated in Russia. But not for long. The German invasion of the Soviet Union in June 1941 quickly brought all three under German occupation and made them part of Hitler's Ostland – to the great satisfaction, be it said, of many of their surviving ethnic German inhabitants. It was not until the autumn of 1944 that, after much heavy fighting, the German forces of occupation were finally driven out by the victorious Red Army and all three countries reabsorbed in the Soviet Union. Though at the end of the War tens of thousands of their inhabitants were deported or fled, active resistance to the Soviet regime seems to have continued in all three republics until as late as 1951. Of the famous German Baltic Barons, successors and in many cases descendants of the original Teutonic Knights, who had for so long played such a prominent part in Baltic and latterly in Russian history, few, if any, survived the vicissitudes of that last fateful decade.

Despite its disturbed history, the old town of Tallinn has kept much of its mediaeval appearance, many of its ancient buildings having either somehow survived untouched or else been skilfully restored. The people of Tallinn are rightly proud of their beautiful city and large sums are spent on its maintenance. With many of its massive walls and battlements still intact, the Toumpea's ancient fortress still dominates the Upper Town. Under the Teutonic Knights this was the seat of the town's military and ecclesiastical rulers, while the Lower Town was the preserve of rich merchants whose Guilds and Council enjoyed a considerable measure of independence.

Until the seventeenth century a single steep lane, Pikk Jalg Street, led down from the Upper to the Lower Town. Of the fortress's tall towers, three still stand, the Landskrone, the Pilsticker and Pikk Hermann. As it did in the Middle Ages under the Teutonic Knights, the Toumpea today still serves as the local seat of government. From the tallest of the towers, Pikk Hermann, for seven centuries and more a look-out tower over land and sea, flies the flag of the Estonian Soviet Socialist Republic, while in a handsome pink baroque palace nearby, built in the time of Catherine the Great, the Council of Ministers of the Republic now hold their meetings. Nearby, on an agreeable, tree-shaded square, stands the seven-hundred-year-old Gothic Cathedral, the Domkirk or Toomkirik, still in use as a Lutheran Church. Its baroque spire was added in the eighteenth century. One of its many handsome tombs, designed by the great Giacomo Quarenghi himself, commemorates Admiral Samuel Greig, a Scottish sailor who, with his fellow-Scot Admiral Elphinstone, helped win the sea-battle of Chesme for Catherine the Great in 1780.

From the Upper City's battlements you look down on the gables, the red-tiled roofs, narrow winding streets and tall church spires of the Lower Town, equally old and likewise once surrounded by a strong ring of fortifications and towers, of which a number still survive, notably the curiously named Kiek in de Kok (signifying, one is told, Peep in the Kitchen) and the massive Dicke Margarete, adjoining the city's Great Coast Gate through which Pikk Street passes on its way to the coast. For centuries the Market or Town Hall Square was the centre of life in the Lower Town. The Gothic town hall, built in the latter part of the fourteenth century, with its elegant spire and vaulted arcades, has been admirably restored, as have most of the other old buildings surrounding the square. At the far end of the square is the Town Council's Old Apothecary or Chemist's Shop, for centuries owned and operated by successive generations of the same Hungarian family.

Of the churches in the Lower Town the Niguliste or Church of St Nicholas, dedicated, like its namesake in Leningrad, to St Nicholas of Bari, the patron saint of mariners, was built in the second half of the fourteenth century with funds contributed by rich local merchants. The even older Church of the Holy Ghost, with its stepped pediments, once served as a chapel for the Town Council. On Pikk Street the Church of St Olaus or St Olaf, said to have been so called after King Olaf III of Norway, killed at the Battle of the Trondheim Fjord in 1033, was built in the fifteenth century. Its four-hundred-foot Gothic spire serves as a convenient landmark on one's strolls around the Old Town. Some of the finest houses in Tallinn are on Pikk Street, which runs diagonally across the Lower Town from Pikk Jalg Street to the Great Sea Gate. Adjoining St Olaus is a particularly fine mediaeval dwelling house known, from its triple gable, as the Three Sisters and no doubt once the residence of some rich local merchant. Among a number of early guild houses is the sixteenth-century Schwarzhäupterhaus or House of the Black Heads, the meeting place of a Brotherhood of that name founded in 1349 by the merchants of Tallinn and other Baltic cities (notably Riga) as a local defence force. The Brotherhood survived until 1940 when, as can be imagined, its members were overtaken by events far beyond their control. They owed their name to their patron, St Maurice, who, coming – it is said – from Egypt, was heraldically represented as a blackamoor and appears as such in the coat-of-arms above their door.

If, as I strongly recommend, you take a sauna on the twenty-second floor of the newest of all Tallinn's hotels, the Olympia, you will be able to look out, as you sit gently perspiring in a big glass box or taking an occasional refreshing plunge in the adjoining pool, right across the spires and towers and red-tiled gables of the Old Town to the sparkling blue waters of the Bay of Tallinn beyond. This at once gave me the idea of going for a swim from the elegant and well-equipped *plage* and yacht club at Pirita. Another nearby amenity, for those who like pop, rock or folk concerts, is Pirita's gigantic concrete open-air stage and auditorium where 30,000 singers can entertain an audience of no less than 100,000 and, owing to the remarkable acoustics, not lose a note in the process.

On our way to Pirita next morning, we stopped to admire the handsome baroque seaside palace which Peter the Great had built for his wife Catherine by the architects Zemtsov and Michetti, then working in St Petersburg, in an agreeable park at Kadriorg or Katherinenthal, not far from the little cottage he himself occupied there. Nearby a bronze angel commemorates the crew of the *Rusalka* or Mermaid, an Imperial Russian battleship which sank with all hands in the Gulf of Finland in 1893, while a little further on is a monument to Yevgeni Nikonov, a Russian sailor, taken prisoner by the Germans in 1941, who, defiant to the last, was tied to a tree and burned alive, for which he was posthumously created a Hero of the Soviet Union. Along the coast at Rocca di Mare, on the other side of Tallinn, an outdoor ethnological museum contains a collection of old wooden peasant houses transported there from all over Estonia and even a made-to-order village green, where folk dances are performed with becoming gusto in Estonian national costume.

As I climbed into the aeroplane which was to carry me via Riga to Vilnius, the capital of Lithuania, I took away with me from Tallinn the impression of a nation of friendly, energetic, independent-minded people, proud of their national heritage, of what they have managed to achieve under sometimes difficult circumstances and not least of their own native efficiency, their open-mindedness and high standard of living. Proud also of the many other ways in which they more than hold their own with any other republic in the Union. By their exceptional efficiency and by their bold experiments in the field of financial and other incentives and of measures designed to encourage individual initiative in industry and agriculture, they and their neighbours in the Pribaltika are at a critical time leading the way in a very positive direction. Though they only account for one-and-a-half out of the Soviet Union's two hundred and seventy millions, they could long term set an example and exercise an influence out of all proportion to their numbers.

After Tallinn, I felt that Vilnius could only be a disappointment, but in no way was this so. Though the destinies of Lithuania and Estonia run parallel and sometimes overlap, we are talking about two distinct nations with separate histories and of this you become aware as soon as you leave one for the other. Unlike the Estonians, the ethnic Lithuanians, who account for some eighty per cent of the population of their republic (there are more Russians in the cities), speak a language closely akin to ancient Sanskrit and are thought to have reached their present habitat at least two thousand years ago, apparently via the upper reaches of the Dnieper. As early as the fifth century AD there are signs to be found of some kind of federation of Lithuanian tribes, while much later, at the height of its power, the Grand Duchy of Lithuania was to reach all the way from the Black Sea to the Baltic. Earlier, in the Middle Ages, it served as a last bastion against the advance of

Christianity, a fact noted with pride by present-day Soviet historians some of whom would, I suppose, be only too glad to see this happen again. Following the arrival of the crusading Teutonic Knights in neighbouring East Prussia in 1230, the Lithuanians banded together under their leader Prince Mindaugas to resist Christian and German encroachment. Though in due course baptized and recognized as Prince of Lithuania by Pope Innocent IV, Mindaugas later repudiated Christianity and reverted to Paganism, further emphasizing his point by defiantly sacrificing his Christian prisoners to the old gods. His successor, Prince Gedimnas, who reigned from 1316 to 1339, greatly extended his country's frontiers, actually reaching out and taking Kiev and founding the city of Vilnius. As part of a political deal with the Pope he, too, was in the end baptized, but for his part remained a professing Christian, many of the city's churches dating back to his reign. Ablest of the dynasty he founded was Algirdas or Olgird who reigned from 1345 to 1377 and who, while keeping the Teutonic Knights at bay, still further extended Lithuania's empire.

In 1385 there occurred an event of great importance for Lithuania and the Lithuanians. Olgird's son Jagiello married Jadwig or Hedwig, Queen of Poland, thus effecting a dynastic union between their two countries. Lithuania now enthusiastically embraced Roman Catholicism which has remained the predominant religion there ever since, while Jagiello was duly crowned King of Poland. For the next four centuries Lithuania and Poland were in effect one large and powerful country, Roman Catholic by religion and playing an ever-bigger part in European affairs. In 1410 at Tannenberg, to be the scene of another historic encounter with the Germans in 1914, Poles, Lithuanians, Russians and Tartars together decisively defeated the Teutonic Knights. With time, however, the Lithuanians came to occupy a subordinate position in the Union and Polish ascendancy was firmly established. Later still, Lithuania shared in Poland's decline and, with the third partition of that luckless country in 1795, almost the whole of Lithuania was absorbed by Russia. Of Russia it remained part until the Revolution, when, after various vicissitudes, it gained its independence, only to lose it once more, with the other Baltic states, in 1940. During the Second World War Lithuania, like her neighbours, endured three years of German occupation, in the course of which most of her large Jewish population were slaughtered.

Just as the Lithuanians are by race, religion and to a great extent history, distinct from the Estonians, so Vilnius, their capital, is a very different city from Tallinn. Pleasantly situated a couple of hundred miles inland amid wooded hills at the confluence of two rivers, the Vilnios and the Neris, of which the latter divides the town in two, it was between the wars part of Poland. More than six-and-a-half centuries after its foundation by Prince Gedimnas, who, according to legend, was very sensibly directed to built it on its present site by the persistent howling of a gigantic iron wolf, perceived in a dream, much of the mediaeval town still survives. From the summit of the wooded hill where Gedimnas dreamed his dream the massive Upper Castle which bears his name looks down on the narrow winding streets and ancient gabled houses below. Of the Lower Castle, built at the same time, nothing now remains, though parts of it are said to have been incorporated in the free-standing belfry of the former Roman Catholic Cathedral of St Stanislav. Now a picture gallery, the Cathedral stands on Gedimnas Square at the centre of the city on the site of an earlier pagan shrine dedicated to Perkunas, the God of Light, still energetically invoked by the Lithuanians in their oaths. Beneath the shrine once lay a vault full of holy snakes. Since it was first built by Jagiello in 1287 to celebrate his marriage to Queen Hedwig of Poland and consequent conversion, the Cathedral has endured numerous restorations and reconstructions, the latest of which, in the eighteenth century, turned it into a handsome classical temple.

Parallel with the River Neris, the main street of present-day Vilnius, once the Bolshaya, now Lenin Prospekt, slopes gently downhill towards Gedimnas Square and the great white pillared cathedral. Turning to your right at its foot you quickly come to a remarkable group of ancient churches. At the edge of a little park immediately below the Upper Castle stands the sixteenth-century brick-built Gothic Church of St Ann, still in use by a Catholic congregation, while immediately adjoining it are the fifteenth-century Church and Monastery of St Bernard and St Francis, likewise late Gothic in origin, but with later baroque additions. Across the street from these is the late sixteenth-century Renaissance-style Church of St Michael, now a Museum of Architecture. The principal throughfare of mediaeval Vilnius was Great Castle Street, now Gorki Street, which linked the Upper and Lower Castles with Ratuses, the Town Hall or Market Square situated at the centre of the Old Town. The former town hall, rebuilt at the end of the eighteenth century, is now an art museum.

Great Castle or Gorki Street is one of the city's oldest and best-preserved streets, most of its ancient houses and churches having either survived unscathed or else been carefully restored. Though my own more modern hotel on Lenin Prospekt was quite adequate, I could not help noting for future reference the little Hotel Astoria at No 59 Gorki Street, which attracted me both by its name and its engaging appearance. Across the street from it the early baroque Jesuit Church of St Kazimir is now a Museum of Atheism. Gorki Street abounds in beautiful buildings. Nearby are the Orthodox Church of the Holy Ghost, the Catholic Church of St Theresa and, at its upper end, the Ostrovorotnaya or Medinka Gate, once one of the city gates. Above this, in the Ostra Brama Chapel, is a miracle-working icon of the Virgin, revered by Catholics and Orthodox alike. At No 73, where Gorki Street ends, are the gates of the Monastery of St Basil, a particularly fine example of late baroque architecture, while not far from these is the beautiful seventeenth-century Catholic Church of St Peter and St Paul, built, it is said, by Italian architects on the site of an earlier shrine dedicated to Milda, the Pagan Goddess of Love. On the far side of the Old Town, on Garelio Street, stands the great Baroque Dominican Monastery and Church of the Holy Ghost, used under the tsars as a prison, but now, strangely enough, once again a place of worship. First founded in the fourteenth century, it was rebuilt in its present style in the seventeenth and eighteenth centuries.

To the right of Gorki Street rise the magnificent buildings of Vilnius University, which in 1979 celebrated its four hundredth anniversary. The university's main courtyard is enclosed on three sides by tall early seventeenth-century buildings built above open galleries or arcades, while the fourth is occupied by the imposing façade of the former university church of St John (now a Museum of Scientific Thought). First built in 1387 at the time of Lithuania's conversion to Christianity, the church was taken over and rebuilt two hundred years later by the Order of Jesus, who at the same time founded the University. After a fire in 1737 St John's, while retaining some of its earlier features, was rebuilt in the Late Baroque manner.

Following Russia's occupation of Lithuania in 1795, the university's career was a disturbed one. Recognized as a university by Tsar Alexander I, it was closed by his successor Nicholas I in 1832 after the Polish uprising of the year before. One famous alumnus towards the end of the century of the academy that eventually took its place was Felix Edmundovich Dzerzhinski from neighbouring Kaunas or Kovno, a close friend of Lenin and today greatly revered as founder of the latter's famous Cheka, predecessor of the OGPU, the NKVD, and the KGB.

A few hundred yards from the University, in Kutuzov Square, you come on the former residence of the Russian Governor-General. Previously the palace of the Catholic Archbishop of Vilnius, it was occupied by the Russians after their occupation of the city in 1795 and later rebuilt to the designs of their great Classical architect Stasov. After being used by Napoleon as his headquarters in 1812, it was taken over later in the campaign by General Kutuzov, for whom the Square is now named. Another Russian general who waged war in these parts and today has a square called after him is General of the Army Ivan Chernyakovski, twice Hero of the Soviet Union, killed in action at the age of thirty-nine in July 1944 during the battle for Vilnius, taken by his troops a few days later. These are only some of Vilnius's more important buildings. Anyone with time to spare and an interest in mediaeval architecture could happily spend weeks exploring the town and neighbouring countryside – the more so as the food in the city's restaurants, often situated in fine old buildings, is quite exceptionally good.

Eighteen miles to the west of Vilnius, in a land of lakes and forests, is the mediaeval stronghold and former capital of Trakai. Once the main centre of pagan Lithuanian resistance to the Christian German invaders, Trakai was first fortified in the fourteenth century, a hundred years or so after the Lithuanians had first come together in a more or less centralized national state. Subsequently destroyed in the wars that followed, it was over the years re-sited and re-built a number of times to meet the requirements of its defenders. The surviving castle, an imposing structure built in the fifteenth century of brick and stone on an island in Lake Galve has, with what remains of the old town, been carefully restored to something like its original state. Through the main gate of the castle, which is linked to the shore by a footbridge, you enter a forecourt surrounded by a high outer wall with round towers at its corners and adequate casemates for supplies and ammunition. This is separated from the main keep of the castle by a moat. Crossing what was once a drawbridge, you pass into the castle's galleried inner courtyard, with flights of steps connecting the galleries which lead in turn to the living rooms and banqueting halls. On one side of this inner courtyard a tall watch-tower commands a wide view of Lake Galve and the wooded hills beyond. After it had ceased to be a fortress, the castle became for a time a residence of the Princes of Lithuania, but by the seventeenth century had already been eclipsed by nearby Vilnius and fell into disuse. After clambering all over the castle on a hot June day, nothing could have been more agreeable than a swim in the limpid waters of Lake Galve which surround it and which, I was glad to find, provided every facility for those so minded.

Another fifty miles beyond Trakai you come to Kaunas, prettily situated on a tongue of land between the Vilya and the Niemen and now a city of some four hundred thousand inhabitants. Between the wars, when Vilnius was still part of Poland, Kaunas, or Kovno as it was then called, served as the capital of independent Lithuania. The ruins of its ancient castle which, like Trakai, played an important part in the wars against the Teutonic Knights, still survive, though in rather diminished form. Near it is the Town Hall Square, once the city's commercial, and administrative centre. The elegant Baroque town hall, which stands in the middle of it, now serves, appropriately enough, as a Palace of Weddings and provides a welcome contrast to Vilnius' squat, ultra-modern concrete Wedding Palace. It is said to process, if that is the word, no less than forty weddings a day. Across the square the vast red-brick Gothic Church of St Peter and St Paul, also known at the Church of Vytautas, is the largest Catholic church in Lithuania and was, I found, still open for services. Adjoining it is a Catholic seminary.

On a green hillside some way outside the town stands Fort IX, a grim Nazi death-camp in which between 1941 and 1944 tens of thousands of Lithuania's Jews and Resistance-fighters met their end and which is now preserved as a museum and a monument to those who died there. On a pleasant summer's day it serves as a sobering reminder of Lithuania's troubled and bloodstained past.

Strolling down the agreeable, tree-lined pedestrian precinct which traverses present-day Kaunas, window-shopping in its stores, well-stocked with high quality locally produced goods, looking at the well-dressed, attractive passers-by or lunching at one or another of its excellent restaurants, one is again forcibly reminded (as are visiting Russians) of the relatively high standard of living enjoyed by Lithuanians, Estonians and Latvians alike. Today all three countries are giving a clear lead to their neighbours, not merely economi-cally, but by their positive and human approach to life, while at the same time showing considerable ingenuity in adapting themselves to the exigencies and limitations of a rigid and often unresponsive system. Over the past couple of years a beginning has been made in the Pribaltika with self-financing cooperatives. These have by their success more than justified this limited experiment in private enterprise which is now being tried out in other parts of the Soviet Union including Moscow. In the Pribaltika industry, whether light, heavy or science-based, is more efficient and uses more up-to-date methods. The same applies to farms and fisheries. Quite clearly all these Baltic republics are making the most of their not inconsiderable natural resources – not least their outstanding human resources, already responding well to the worthwhile inducements now being offered them.

In Tallinn pie-shop proprietor Viktor Rodin's only complaint is that his premises are no longer big enough for the amount of business he now does. 'Under the old system', he says, 'twenty-three people used to work here and make 14,000 roubles a month. Now we are on our own, we only employ a staff of sixteen and make twenty-four or five thousand.'

Last year, of the eight hundred taxis in Tallinn one hundred and sixty were already private. 'The state salary was 168 roubles a month', said one private driver 'but, now I'm on my own, I'm earning 450.'

Toivo Mangels, the youngish Head of Labour Resources at Gosplan, the official State Planning Authority, himself a bureaucrat, was very frank about the way things were going. 'Bureaucrats', he explained, echoing the new Party line, 'obstruct not only economic reforms, but anything that's new all over the world, including Estonia. But as the new ideas take over, they will in end be shown up and forced to cooperate.'

Though undoubtedly there, the heavy hand of the system is less glaringly in evidence in the Pribaltika. There are fewer scarlet banners bearing political and ideological slogans, fewer exhortations to fulfill the resolutions of the latest Party Congress, fewer icon-like portraits of leaders past and present – fewer and less forceful reminders, in short, that these are no longer the degenerate 'bourgeois' republics they once were, but integral parts of the USSR.

On the outskirts of the three Baltic capitals, as on those of other Soviet cities, vast new suburbs of high-rise buildings are going up, here rather better built and better planned than most. But, as in a number of other Soviet republics, Georgia for example, the City Fathers, one soon finds, are at least as proud of their ambitious schemes for the conservation and restoration of their city's older buildings, on which, much to the benefit of local tourism, large sums are now being spent. In Tallinn, millions of roubles and a great deal of thought and skill are devoted annually to this purpose and periodic song and folk-lore festivals, displays of vintage cars and other such unexpected entertainments are regularly held to raise more money and so promote what is now regarded as a worthy cause. And the same is equally true of Vilnius and Riga. Needless to say, in the Pribaltika, as in Georgia and elsewhere, such occasions are inclined to have a somewhat nationalistic tinge. For, as recent demonstrations, now tolerated by the authorities, have shown, nationalism is far from dead in the Baltic Republics.

To claim, after a visit to the Baltic Republics, that, to adapt the words of the ineffable Lincoln Steffens, you have seen the future for the Soviet Union and it works, would as yet be going a good deal too far. What can, I think, be said without undue optimism is that here is an example of one way in which the existing system can, with adjustment, be made to work considerably better than elsewhere and that what is happening in one area might well in time be found to have a wider application. It was therefore perhaps natural that in February 1987 Mikhail Gorbachov should have chosen to make a much publicized tour of the Baltic Republics and there declare his utter determination to press ahead with his revolutionary plans for change, at the same time emphasizing that what is now known as 'the Estonian model' was henceforth to be promoted throughout the Soviet Union. Nor, from this author's own observation, was it surprising that he should have found in the Baltic Republics what he called 'a revolution of expectations' and a general demand for 'a speedy social and material return'. Thereafter the need to satisfy the mood of expectancy which he himself had generated there and elsewhere was to become a prime consideration of his policy. Whatever else he did, he could not afford to stand still. And, like other Russian reformers before him, he still had a long way to go.

5

Winds of Change

The spirit of the people could very easily
pass from one integrated faith to another integrated faith,
from one orthodoxy to another orthodoxy
which embraced the whole of life.

NIKOLAI BERDYAYEV

The December Conspiracy of 1825 had convinced Nicholas I that his mission in life was to save Russia from Revolution. Security measures were intensified. 'A state of siege', wrote one observer, 'has become the normal state of society.' 'The Tsar's leaden eyes', according to Alexander Herzen, the revolutionary thinker, 'looked out at a boy from everywhere', much as Stalin's eyes were to look out at a later generation. But the intellectual and creative ferment continued nonetheless. 'We have in secret freedom', wrote the poet Pushkin, words quoted many years later, but no less aptly, by our own contemporary Yevgeni Yevtushenko.

In Russia the nineteenth century was marked by an extraordinary flowering of the creative arts. This was the age of Pushkin and Lermontov, of Tolstoi, Gogol, Dostoyevski and Chekhov, who, directly or indirectly, each in his way contributed to the prevailing ferment. Only when literature ceased to be written, remarked Nicholas's Minister of Education, Count Uvarov, would he be able to sleep soundly in his bed.

Abroad, a forward policy, further stimulated by the intensely nationalistic Slavophile and Pan-Slav movements, was a far from stabilizing influence. Like his predecessors, Nicholas had his eye on the Balkans and Constantinople. Over the past half-century Russia had made considerable territorial gains at Turkey's expense and under a treaty concluded in 1833 Nicholas became the self-appointed guardian of what he was pleased to call 'the Sick Man of Europe'. But his evident determination to make the Black Sea a Russian lake was disturbing to both France and Great Britain. When in 1853 Russia invaded Turkey's Danubian Provinces, the French and British fleets appeared in the Bosphorus and in March

1854 both countries entered the ensuing war on Turkey's side. Its main theatre was the Crimea, where the Allies landed an expeditionary force in September 1854, laying siege to Sebastopol, then, as now, a major Russian naval base. The Allied conduct of the campaign was almost as inept as that of the Russians and the siege and the war dragged on inconclusively for month after month. For Nicholas personally the Crimean War was deeply disillusioning, revealing as it did the inefficiency not only of his military machine but of the system as a whole. He died early in 1855, a saddened and disappointed man.

His son Alexander II, who was a realist, came to the throne with the conviction that, if future disaster were to be averted, drastic reforms were essential. Sebastopol finally fell to the British and French in the autumn of 1855 and in March 1856 peace was signed in Paris. The war over, the new tsar turned his attention to domestic problems, first and foremost to that of the serfs. For years it had been clear that a main cause of Russia's backwardness was serfdom. Alexander's predecessors had talked of freeing the serfs. He freed them. 'The existing system of owning souls,' he said in the spring of 1856, 'cannot remain unchanged. It is better to abolish serfdom from above than to wait for it to abolish itself from below.' But it was not enough to free the serfs. Once freed, they needed land of their own. Early in 1861 an Imperial Edict was issued, abolishing serfdom and allowing some forty million freed peasants to buy individual holdings with the help of long-term loans from the state.

Though the Peace of Paris had temporarily checked Russia's ambitions in south-eastern Europe, there was nothing to prevent her expansion in Central Asia and the Far East. Reaching out across Siberia, the Tsar's armies took from China between 1858 and 1860 what are now the Soviet Far Eastern provinces and, establishing the port of Vladivostok on the Pacific seaboard, made their country a Far Eastern power. Nearer home, after finally crushing the rebellious tribesmen of the Caucasus, they vastly extended their dominions in Central Asia, absorbing in a few years an area the size of all Western Europe. Nor had the Russians forgotten their role as protectors of the Christians in the Balkans. When in 1875 and 1876 rebellion broke out against Turkish rule in Bosnia-Herzegovina and Bulgaria, thousands of Russian volunteers flocked to fight for their fellow-Slavs and in April 1877 Russia declared war on Turkey, attacking simultaneously through the Balkans and the Caucasus. By February 1878, after much fierce fighting, a Russian Army stood before Constantinople, but, following a confrontation with the British Mediterranean Fleet in the Sea of Marmara, the Russians in the end withdrew and a peaceful settlement was eventually arrived at. Which only went to show how right Lord Palmerston had been when he said: 'The policy and practice of the Russian government has always been to push forward its encroachments as far and as fast as the apathy or want of firmness of other governments would allow it to go, but always to stop and retire when it met with decided resistance.'

In Russia, meanwhile, despite vigorous repression, the revolutionary movement was still very much alive, and in March 1881, after several unsuccessful attempts, a terrorist group known as The People's Will finally managed to assassinate Tsar Alexander, who had that very morning agreed to sign a proclamation marking a first step in the direction of constitutional government. The immediate reaction of his burly son Alexander III on ascending the throne was to tear this up and a fresh period of repression now ensued. Alexander III died on 1 November 1894. He had kept his country out of war and himself avoided assassination. His son Nicholas II was to be less fortunate.

By the end of the century, the population of the Russian Empire had reached 128 millions, three-and-a-half times what it had been a hundred years earlier. Though the peasants still accounted for much the greater proportion of the population, Russia was no longer as exclusively rural as a hundred years before. By 1900 some three million workers were employed in industry as against barely twenty thousand a century earlier. Thirteen per cent of the total population now lived in towns, compared with four per cent in 1800. Iron works and coal mines were being developed in southern Russia, textiles in St Petersburg and Moscow, oil in the Caucasus. The railroad system was growing fast, work on the Trans-Siberian line having begun in 1891. To Russia's other problems was now added that of a rootless and restless industrial proletariat. Large sums were raised at home and abroad to finance industrialization and a new class of industrialists and entrepreneurs had begun to emerge. From patriarchal or feudal, Russia was to a limited extent becoming industrialized and capitalist.

Simultaneously, in February 1898, the first Marxist party was founded in Russia: the Russian Social Democratic Labour Party. In 1902 it split into two factions, Mensheviks and Bolsheviks, the latter, led by Vladimir Ilich Ulyanov, otherwise known as Lenin, being rather more radical. More obviously dangerous to the regime were the openly terrorist Social Revolutionaries. Confronted with this new upsurge of revolutionary activity, Plehve, the Minister of the Interior, gave it as his view that 'a successful little war' was needed to distract attention.

When it began early in 1904, the Russo–Japanese War must have seemed an answer to his prayer. But from the first it went badly for the Russians, several earlier defeats being followed by the total annihilation of the Russian Fleet at Tsushima in May 1905. A humiliating treaty of peace was signed three months later. Meanwhile, Plehve himself had, ironically enough, been assassinated by the Social Revolutionaries. In the event, the war only aggravated popular discontent. On Sunday 22 January 1905 a great crowd of workers, carrying holy icons and singing hymns, converged on the Winter Palace to petition the Tsar. In the confusion that followed, the troops on duty were ordered to fire on the crowd, several hundred people were killed and by nightfall the government were facing a genuinely revolutionary situation.

Strikes, riots and demonstrations persisted throughout 1905. All over the country there were peasant risings and mutinies in the armed forces. In October came a general strike and the formation in St Petersburg of a Workers' Council or Soviet, led by a lively young revolutionary called Bronstein or Trotski. On 30 December the Tsar reluctantly agreed to the election of a National Assembly or Duma. Russia, it could be said, now enjoyed something approaching constitutional government.

But already the storm clouds were gathering over Europe. 'A war,' said Lenin in 1913, 'would be a very helpful thing for the Revolution.' Twelve months later his wish was granted. The Russians entered the war of 1914 with an army that was badly equipped, badly led and badly supplied. In three years they lost a couple of million dead. At the front, the Russian soldier fought, as always, with great courage and endurance, but he was let down by confusion, incompetence and corruption at the rear. Revolutionary propaganda fell on fertile ground.

Few individuals contributed more to the decay and eventual overthrow of the old regime than the infamous Grigori Rasputin, a self-proclaimed holy man and faith healer from Siberia, who, gaining the confidence of the Tsar and Tsaritsa, used his position at court for his own ends, making and breaking ministers and generals at will and enjoying, it is said, the favours of numerous highly-placed ladies. Bearded, gigantic and unkempt, he was a peculiarly Russian phenomenon. 'His pupils,' wrote the French ambassador, 'seem to radiate magnetism. He carries with him a strong animal smell, like a goat.' In the end, Rasputin was murdered, not without difficulty, by Prince Felix Yusupov and the Grand Duke Dmitri, who, having first invited him to the former's palace and plied him with wine and chocolate-cakes, liberally laced with cyanide, then in panic shot him again and again, and in the end dumped his bullet-riddled body, still apparently alive, through a hole in the ice of the nearest canal. There it was later found, frozen stiff, clinging to the supports of the nearest bridge. But their gesture had come too late.

War, in Trotski's pungent phrase, was once again to prove itself the Locomotive of History. Early in March 1917, the shortage of bread led to rioting in St Petersburg or Petrograd as it had now been renamed, to give it a more Russian ring. Organized demonstrations followed. Tens of thousands of workers came out on strike and thronged the streets, stoning the police when they tried to disperse them. The Cossacks, called out in support of the police, did nothing. Events now succeeded each other with frightening rapidity. On 10 March the Tsar dissolved the Duma and a Soviet of Workers and Soldiers and Soldiers' Deputies quickly took over one wing of the Tauride Palace. On 12 March, two regiments of the Imperial Guard mutinied and distributed their weapons to the crowd. Already 200,000 workers were on strike. On 14 March a provisional government was formed. On 15 March, under pressure from the members of his own high command, the Tsar, in his railway carriage at Pskov, signed his abdication. By the end of the week the Revolution of March 1917 was an accomplished fact. But there was more to come.

On 16 April, Lenin, having with German connivance travelled by train from exile in Switzerland, arrived at the Finland Station in Petrograd. What he stood for, he declared, on arrival, was no bourgeois revolution, but an immediate socialist proletarian revolution in Russia and everywhere else. As a first step, he demanded power for the Workers' Soviets and peace, bread and freedom for the people. This won him widespread popular support. Food and an end to the war was what most people wanted. By promising the redistribution of agricultural land and workers' control in the factories, he made a strong appeal to both peasants and industrial workers. During the weeks that followed Bolshevik influence grew rapidly. At the front, discipline began to break down. In the countryside, the peasants took possession of the landlords' estates. In the industrial areas more and more factories were taken over by the workers. Power, meanwhile, was passing to the Soviets, now springing up all over the country. In the newly formed All-Russian Congress of Soviets, the Bolsheviks were still heavily outnumbered, but Lenin's leadership and singleness of purpose more than made up for any lack of numbers. In July an attempt at armed insurrection (in which the Bolsheviks joined) was put down by force by the Provisional Government, but by this time Lenin had escaped across the border to Finland, thence to make his dispositions for the eventual seizure of power.

The leadership of the Provisional Government was now in the hands of Alexander Kerenski, a Socialist lawyer with considerable powers as an orator but little administrative ability or overall grasp of the situation. Within the Petrograd Soviet, the Bolshevik faction had quickly achieved almost complete ascendancy and Lenin, returning clandestinely to Petrograd at the beginning of October, decided on armed insurrection. On 7 November detachments of mutinous troops and armed factory guards under Bolshevik control occupied the principal buildings in Petrograd. To the accompaniment of a salvo of blanks from the six-inch guns of the cruiser *Aurora*, lying at anchor in the Neva, the Winter Palace was seized by Red Guards and most of the members of the Provisional Government placed under arrest. In the capital the Bolsheviks had won a quick and easy victory. In Moscow there was stronger resistance and it took them several days to establish their authority. In the rest of Russia, confusion and uncertainty prevailed, to be resolved in due course by a bloody Civil War.

On the evening of 8 November 1917 a new government was formed in Petrograd, the Soviet Narodnikh Kommissarov or Council of People's Commissars, with Lenin as its Chairman. It at once issued two decrees. The first called for an early peace. The second announced the abolition of the private ownership of land. On 18 January 1918 a Constituent Assembly met in the Tauride Palace, but was dispersed next day by the Bolshevik guards on duty. In Lenin's scheme of things there was, as he put it, no place for 'parliamentary illusions'. In July 1918 it was formally announced that sovereign power would henceforth be vested in the Congress of Soviets, which now ratified the carefully drawn-up constitution of a Russian Socialist Federative Soviet Republic. Of the Bolshevik or Communist Party no mention was made in the new constitution, but in practice it was the cement that held the whole structure together.

The most urgent problem confronting Russia's new rulers was how to end the war with Germany and Austria. Peace negotiations with the Central Powers were already in progress. The Soviet Government had of their own accord granted the right of self-determination to the subject peoples of Poland, the Ukraine, the Baltic States, Finland, Central Asia and Transcaucasia. But the German peace terms were so unfavourable to Russia that even the Bolsheviks, who were committed to peace at almost any price, hesitated to accept them. In the event, Lenin's influence proved decisive. Fearing for the future of the Revolution if hostilities were resumed, he threw all his weight on the side of peace. Harsh though they were, the German terms were accepted and on 3 March 1918 a Treaty of Peace was signed at Brest-Litovsk.

The Bolshevik government's wide-scale requisitioning of grain and their expropriation of the more prosperous peasants had made them unpopular in the countryside. The Whites, as the forces of counter-revolution were called, gained strength. A small volunteer army, raised in Southern Russia to resist the Bolshevik take-over, had originally found its chief support in the Cossack country of the Kuban and Don. Now, under General Denikin, the movement spread further afield. In the spring of 1918 the Allies, worried by Russia's withdrawal from the war, despatched small expeditionary forces to Murmansk, Archangel and Vladivostok, to be followed later by others sent to Transcaucasia, Central Asia and the Crimea in the pious hope that these would somehow get rid of the Bolsheviks and, with the help of the Whites, bring Russia back into the war on the side of the Allies. The Bolsheviks for their part now took a step which greatly increased the horror with which they were regarded in the West. In July 1918, Tsar Nicholas and his family were taken down into the cellar of the house where they were being kept at Ekaterinburg in Siberia and shot.

Relatively little blood had been shed during the November Revolution. The Civil War which followed it was a thoroughly bloody business. At first things went well for the Whites. By October 1919 General Denikin, advancing from the south, had reached Orel, barely two hundred miles from Moscow – Moscow, whither the Bolsheviks had by this time transferred the seat of government, thereby making a symbolic return to Muscovy, the Russian heartland, and rejecting the Western values and influences symbolized by St Petersburg.

For a time the capital and ultimate victory seemed within Denikin's grasp. But by now the Red Army had grown to be a formidable fighting force and in November 1919 the Red Cavalry broke decisively through the enemy lines. Divided among themselves, the Whites lost their initial advantage. Early in 1920 Denikin fell back on the Crimea, whence he later took ship to Constantinople. By December 1920 the Civil War was to all intents and purposes over, only a few foreign troops remained on Russian soil, and by and large the Bolsheviks were in control of the country.

Six years of war, revolution and civil war had brought Russia to the verge of collapse. Lenin needed a respite. His New Economic Policy involved a limited return to capitalism and the re-emergence of a notorious entrepreneurial class popularly known as NEP-men who made instant hay while the sun shone. But this retreat, it was made clear, was to be purely tactical. Once Lenin had taken advantage of the respite thus gained, he would devote all his energies to building a Socialist and ultimately a Communist state. Already the Bolsheviks were extending their authority to every corner of Russian territory. By 1924 the stage was set for the formation of the Union of Soviet Socialist Republics, consisting of the original Russian Socialist Federative Soviet Republic (which now included Siberia), the Ukraine, White Russia and, following a brief period of independence, Transcaucasia and Central Asia. Soon most of the great powers had recognized the new State.

It was at this moment that Soviet Russia suffered a grave loss. In January 1924, at the age of fifty-three, Lenin died. To most people Trotski, successively Commissar for Foreign Affairs and Commissar for War, must have seemed the obvious successor. In fact he had a formidable rival. In May 1922 Josip Vissarionovich Stalin, the Georgian, who since 1917 had served as People's Commissar for Nationalities, had been appointed Secretary-General of the Central Committee of the Party, potentially, as all concerned were soon to discover, a position of enormous power. In the political in-fighting that now followed he made the fullest use of it, displaying quite exceptional ruthlessness, resilience and skill.

As a realist, primarily concerned with the here-and-now, the doctrine which Stalin favoured was that of Socialism in One Country. This brought him into immediate conflict with Trotski, who still clung to the wider concept of World Revolution. Stalin dealt with his rival stage by stage. In 1926 Trotski was removed from the Political Bureau of the Party. A year later he was expelled from the Party itself, in January 1928 exiled to Alma Ata in Central Asia, and in 1929 expelled from the Soviet Union. His assassination in Mexico by a man with an ice-axe followed a dozen years later. Stalin's other potential opponents came quickly to heel. For the next quarter of a century power was to be concentrated in his hands, far greater power than that exercised by Lenin or by any of his imperial predecessors, power unquestioned and absolute. 'Imagine Jenghiz Khan with a telephone', Tolstoi had once said with frightening foresight.

Having secured his own position, Stalin turned his attention to the task of building Socialism in One Country. To this he brought the same energy and ruthlessness he had displayed in other contexts. There was no longer room for more than one point of view – Stalin's. Stalin's portraits were everywhere. The Party Line, which he dictated, was absolute and all-embracing. His own personal censorship of speech, of the press, of the creative arts was total. 'Who, whom?' Lenin had asked. There could no longer be any doubt at all as to the answer to that question.

Stalin's aim was to transform a backward agricultural country into a modern industrial state, self-sufficient and capable of holding its own against a hostile world, and to do this in the shortest possible time. His programme took the form of a series of Five Year Plans, launched in October 1928 and rushed through, against all probability, well ahead of the appointed time. To the attainment of this end everything else was sacrificed. Hand in hand with the Five Year Plans for industrialization went a programme for the collectivization of agriculture, at the same time designed to cure the peasant of the bourgeois concept of private property (Lenin's NEP-men had long since bitten the dust), to increase agricultural output by widespread mechanization and finally to release surplus peasant labour for work in industry.

The implementation of this policy involved a fierce struggle with the peasants, several millions of whom died in the process. But in the end Stalin won. 'It was', he told Winston Churchill ten years later, 'all very bad and difficult. But necessary.' By 1933 collectivization was a fact, the first Five Year Plan successfully completed and the second already begun. Stalin was well on the way to doing what he had set out to do. Meanwhile, though still contenting himself with the title of Party Secretary, he had in ten years become the *Vozhd*, the supreme Leader of the Soviet Union.

But the year 1933 brought something else: Adolf Hitler's accession to power in Germany. Though no one could at this juncture have wanted war less, Stalin felt obliged to prepare for one. In his latest Five Year Plan, greater emphasis than ever was placed on defence. Meanwhile to the current purge of Trotskyists and other native deviationists was added a no less intensive hunt for foreign spies and saboteurs.

The result was a reign of terror unparalleled in the whole of Russia's bloodstained history. No one was safe. No one could trust anyone else. Like a poisonous mist, fear and suspicion seeped in everywhere. Children denounced their parents and parents their children. On the flimsiest charges, millions were executed or sent to Siberia. All dreaded the fatal knock on the door at two in the morning. The people at the top were in the greatest danger of all. At a series of nightmarish treason trials the flower of the Party, of the army, navy and airforce, of every branch of the government service, ritually confessed to every conceivable crime before being taken away and shot. Stalin's power and the power of his ubiquitous and notorious Secret Police, the NKVD, as it was now called, were paramount.

Coming when it did, the conclusion of the Soviet–German Pact on 23 August 1939 made war a certainty. It broke out a week or two later. By his deal with Hitler, Stalin hoped to gain or regain for Russia half of Poland, Finland, the Baltic States and part of Roumania. While occupying his share of Poland, he had, or so he thought, managed to keep out of a war which with any luck would weaken both sides, greatly to Moscow's advantage. In the event, Finnish resistance to an attempted Soviet take-over and Hitler's successful *Blitzkrieg*, followed by the rapid collapse of France, threw out his calculations, though, by occupying the Baltic States and part of Roumania in July 1940, he reinsured his position as best he could. The German occupation of the Balkans came as another unpleasant surprise. Even so, despite warnings from a number of quarters, he seems to have remained convinced that the Germans would not attack him.

On 22 June 1941 Hitler invaded Russia with 175 divisions. Town after town fell to the Germans. By September they had reached the outskirts of Leningrad. By October the battle for Moscow had begun. For a couple of months the outcome hung in the balance. Then Soviet reinforcements were brought up from further east and in the course of the winter – the worst in living memory – the German advance was held.

With Russia's involvement, the War, from being the Second Imperialist War, became for the Russians a Patriotic War, a People's War, a War of National Liberation; all the resources of the nation, including the Orthodox Church, were now harnessed behind the war effort. In addition to Party Secretary, Stalin was made Chairman of the Council of People's Commissars, Commissar for Defence, Marshal, and Generalissimo.

Leningrad, meanwhile, remained beleaguered and further south the Red Army continued to withdraw until, in the late summer of 1942, a stand was made at Stalingrad on the Volga. There, by super-human efforts, the Germans were halted, the threat to the Caucasus and its oil fields averted and, after a siege lasting six months, a German army of one hundred thousand men under Field-Marshal von Paulus was successfully encircled and forced to surrender. It was a turning-point in the war. Allied victories followed on other fronts and by the early summer of 1944 the Germans had started to withdraw from Russia. In June came the opening of the Second Front in the West and the simultaneous advance of the Red Army through Eastern Europe. In the spring of 1945 the armies of the Soviet Union and the Western Allies met on the Elbe. Their meeting was quickly followed by the unconditional surrender of Germany and victory in Europe. In the Far East a well-timed Soviet declaration of war on Japan came six days before the Japanese surrender, in time to bring the Russians considerable advantages.

In the four years of war the Soviet Union had suffered appalling losses – more than twenty million dead and millions more wounded – and appalling destruction. But the Russian people were, as always, courageous, disciplined and infinitely long-suffering. As soon as the war was over, they turned once more, under Stalin's guidance, to the strenuous task of building Socialism in their devastated fatherland.

The hard-won victories of the Red Army and the heroic conduct of the Russian people had won the admiration of Western opinion. But no sooner was the war with Germany at an end than a Cold War began between her former enemies. In Eastern Europe, the Russians, apart from their own considerable territorial gains, sought to protect themselves against any real or imagined threat of encroachment by creating a cordon of Communist satellite states, stretching from the Baltic to the Balkans and constituting an extended Russian Empire which greatly exceeded the wildest dreams of the Romanovs. In Winston Churchill's words, an 'Iron Curtain' descended across the Continent.

Stalin died in March 1953. His death left an immense vacuum. The man who eventually succeeded him possessed an entirely different character. Where Stalin had been pre-ternaturally cautious and pathologically suspicious, Nikita Sergeyevich Khrushchov was by nature an extrovert and a gambler, a man who in the ultimate analysis was prepared to take a chance. The chance Khrushchov now took was considerable. To dismantle or even partially to relax a totalitarian dictatorship is a difficult and dangerous operation. Yet this in effect was what he set out to do, in the realization that you cannot run a modern technological society with a lot of brain-washed helots, that the carrot is sometimes as necessary as the stick. 'Under Stalin,' he said to a friend of mine, 'the whole machine was fast seizing up.' In certain fields people had to be taught to think for themselves. At the same time Khrushchov shifted the balance of the Soviet economy slightly more in the direction of the consumer. Soon people were better fed, better dressed and better housed than they had ever been before. Again Khrushchov was taking a risk. If people were taught to think for themselves on technological subjects, they would soon start thinking for themselves on other subjects too. Given a slightly better standard of living and rather more freedom of speech, they would soon be demanding a much better standard of living and much more freedom of speech.

In matters of foreign policy Khrushchov likewise showed himself more flexible. In 1955 he even arrived at a *modus vivendi* with President Tito of Yugoslavia, who seven years earlier had dared to defy Stalin and survived. But, when this was followed by signs of unrest on the part of the satellite countries, the Soviet Union's new leader did not hesitate to crush it, notably in Hungary in 1956. In his relations with the West he was more forthcoming, meeting the President of the United States, visiting the United Kingdom and making a spectacular appearance at the United Nations. Peaceful co-existence, it was announced, had taken the place of Cold War.

But none of this endeared Khrushchov to his own people or indeed to his own colleagues.

71

His handling of Soviet relations with China and his Cuban adventure in 1962 when, after seeking to establish a Soviet missile base under the noses of the Americans in Cuba, he was in the end, forced to remove it, further diminished him in their eyes. A first confrontation with the Party hierarchy in 1957 had brought victory to Khrushchov. A second, in October 1964, ended differently. A majority came out against him, he was removed from office and his place at the head of affairs was taken by one of those who had engineered his overthrow, Leonid Ilich Brezhnev, a man, once again, of rather a different stamp.

Leonid Brezhnev's eighteen years as Secretary of the Party and subsequently State President were marked first and foremost by a substantial increase in the military power of the Soviet Union. In particular the phenomenal growth of the Soviet Navy under Admiral Gorshkov gave Soviet armed strength a new dimension world-wide. In nuclear arms the Soviet Union quickly achieved approximate parity with the West, while far outstripping NATO in conventional forces. No one could now question the Soviet Union's claim to full Superpower status – something to which its leaders understandably attached considerable importance.

Some four years after assuming power, Brezhnev gave his name to the Brezhnev Doctrine, under which the Soviet Union claimed the right to intervene, by armed force if necessary, in the affairs of any Soviet satellite that showed signs of deviating from orthodox Soviet-style Communism. This was first invoked to justify Soviet armed intervention in Czechoslovakia in 1968 for the purpose of putting an end to the wretched Alexander Dubcek's ill-fated efforts to endow Communism with a human face, though anyone recalling what had happened in Hungary twelve years earlier might have felt that the doctrine was not in fact an entirely new one.

Eleven years later, in December 1979, just as memories of Czechoslovakia were beginning to fade, the Russians again had recourse to military action, this time in neighbouring Afghanistan and apparently planned as a brief incursion, with a view to establishing there what they regarded as a more trustworthy government. Their intervention, which encountered vigorous and prolonged resistance on the part of the local population, evoked world-wide criticism, but once again no effective counter-action. As the casualties multiplied and continued and no positive conclusion seemed in sight, it was to invite increasingly apt comparison with the ill-fated American campaign in Vietnam.

In 1980 the emergence in Poland of a nationwide and genuinely proletarian movement for independent trade unions, actively supported by the Catholic Church, posed a deeply disturbing problem in yet another border state. In the end this was contained by the Polish government themselves without recourse to Soviet armed help. The resulting strain on East-West relations was nevertheless considerable.

During the 1970s, Dr Fidel Castro, having, for his part, managed to survive the Cuban Missile Crisis of 1962, continued, in return for a subsidy of over four billion dollars a year, to give active support to Soviet policies worldwide, notably in Africa and Central America, often using his troops as Soviet surrogates, with varying degrees of success. In Central America the indirect threat which these and kindred Soviet-sponsored activities presented to United States interests was profoundly upsetting to American susceptibilities, provoking not always very carefully thought-out counter action.

During Brezhnev's tenure of office, arms limitation talks continued spasmodically between East and West, without, however, arriving at any very definite conclusion, while on both sides defence budgets continued to escalate. In 1972 President Nixon visited Brezhnev in Moscow and in 1973 Brezhnev returned his visit. Negotiations on strategic arms limitation made some progress and there was again some talk of *détente*. After Nixon's sudden downfall in 1974 this continued under Presidents Ford and Carter, but was abruptly cut short in 1979 by the Soviet invasion of Afghanistan. Any early and never very substantial Soviet hopes that President Reagan might somehow prove easier to deal with than his predecessors were quickly dispelled. With China, despite the obvious desirability of countering American attempts to play the China card, Soviet relations continued strained.

In the domestic field, though the unsatisfactory working of the economy continued to cause concern, no very far-reaching measures were taken to put matters right. From the first, one of Brezhnev's chief aims was to reverse the liberalizing trends introduced by his predecessor and considered in Party circles to have been carried a great deal too far. Here he was not unsuccessful. With time a large number of leading dissidents were successfully removed from circulation and a variety of trends obnoxious to the Party and Government firmly discouraged.

For all this, a complete return to Stalinist methods was no longer possible and, despite an all-round tightening up, the largely spontaneous evolutionary process initiated by Khrushchov continued, though at a considerably slower pace. Moreover, despite the less than satisfactory functioning of the economy overall, the public were kept relatively happy by a continuing consumer boom. To pick a now almost universal criterion, in 1964 less than one Soviet family in four owned a television set; by 1982 nine out of ten had sets. Meantime the numbers of motorbicycles and radios had doubled and those of washing-machines trebled, while refrigerators jumped from one for every ten families in 1964 to nine for every ten in 1984. By when a wider choice of food stuffs was available to store in them. What is more, with the increasing availability of goods in the shops the real value of money increased in proportion.

In his efforts to establish a greater measure of control Brezhnev had been ably abetted by Yuri Vladimirovich Andropov, who, from 1967 until early 1982, was head of the KGB. Accordingly, when, after a long illness, Brezhnev died towards the end of 1982, no one was greatly surprised to see Andropov succeed him as Party secretary and soon after as Head of State. Clearly his prolonged connection with such a formidable and ubiquitous organization furnished an invaluable power base.

Having assumed office, Andropov, by now in his sixty-ninth year, at once set about rooting out a number of the abuses and irregularities of one kind or another which had crept in during Brezhnev's declining years. He was not, however, vouchsafed time to carry his reforming policies to fruition. After barely fifteen months in power, during the last six of which he was too ill to appear in public, he in his turn succumbed, being succeeded almost as a matter of course, both as Party Secretary and President, by Konstantin Ustinovich Chernenko, a slightly older contemporary who, like him, had for many years been closely associated with Brezhnev. In poor health from the first, Konstantin Ustinovich finally died in March 1985, his death after barely a year in power seeming still further to underline the geriatric character of the regime.

In fact, however, it was to mark the end of one era and the beginning of another, the news of his demise being followed within hours by an announcement from the Central Committee that his place as Party Secretary had been taken by Mikhail Sergeyevich Gorbachov, a vigorous, decisive, self-confident man of fifty-four who with luck and good management could look forward to another twenty years of active political life.

Born of peasant stock in Stavropol in 1931, Mikhail Sergeyevich had been only fourteen when the Second World War ended. He had thus largely escaped its traumas and those of the Stalinist era, which came to an end while he was still a student. Exceptionally bright and ambitious, he first took a law degree at Moscow's prestigious Lomonosov University, followed by a degree in agriculture on his return to his native Stavropol, where he was soon put in charge of several collective farms. Meanwhile he had been vigorously pursuing what was to prove a meteoric political career, first in the Komsomol or Young Communist Movement and then in the Party itself, becoming in 1970, before he was forty, First Secretary of the Stavropol Party. Having by his energetic conduct of affairs in Stavropol attracted favourable attention in the Kremlin, notably that of the influential Mikhail Suslov, he was in 1978 called to Moscow and appointed the Central Committee's Secretary for Agriculture. Under the personal sponsorship of Yuri Andropov, whose attention he had also caught, his rise now became even more meteoric. In 1979 he was made a Candidate-Member of the Politburo and a year after that, while still in his forties, a full Member. By the mid-1980s he was clearly a likely candidate for the highest office of all.

Lacking much first-hand experience of the outside world or of international affairs, Gorbachov, as Chairman of the Foreign Affairs Commission of the Supreme Soviet, was in 1984 picked (or picked himself) as leader of a Soviet Parliamentary Delegation to the United Kingdom. There he impressed all he met (including the present author) by his obvious self-confidence, his positive and energetic demeanour, his toughness, his affability and his sharp sense of humour. This, said the British Prime Minister immediately, was someone she liked and felt she could do business with. His elegant, attractive, and obviously highly intelligent wife, Raisa, whom he first met when they were both students at Moscow University, made an equally favourable impression, while at the same time giving the delighted media a field-day – something no Soviet politician's wife had ever done before. To his new job Mikhail Sergeyevich brought a new approach and an entirely new style, taking frequent opportunities to talk to ordinary people in the street and, with Raisa, to listen to what they had to say and give them his views in return – a startling innovation by Soviet standards and one that went down remarkably well.

Though Gorbachov's appointment as Secretary of the Party came as no great surprise to Kremlin-watchers world wide, it clearly heralded a complete departure from what had gone before. 'We must', said the new Party Secretary, speaking in Leningrad in May 1985, 'all change our attitude' – a remark which was rightly taken by most people as a direct reference to his old rival Grigori Romanov, the high-living, hard-drinking Leningrad Party boss. Soon Mikhail Sergeyevich made it abundantly clear by deeds as well as words that it was his firm intention to introduce a wide range of badly-needed reforms, the necessity for which he had already hinted at in a widely reported speech made shortly before taking office in which he declared that what the Soviet Union wanted was 'a bold, creative quest, fresh thinking and a vigorously-presented struggle against everything hypocritical and out of date'. Something that soon became out of date was drunkenness, always a serious problem in Russia. Previous attempts to fight it had been half-hearted. Gorbachov left no one in any doubt as to the seriousness of is intentions. Vodka disappeared from official receptions and under a series of measures promulgated in May 1985 heavy penalties were imposed on drunkenness and on the operators of illicit stills, while sales of alcohol were severely restricted. Within a matter of months its production had fallen by well over thirty per cent.

Though at all times careful to emphasize that the reforms he had in mind were to be sought 'not outside Socialism, but within the framework of our system', his overriding mission, Gorbachov repeatedly announced, was to reform and rejuvenate the creaking Soviet economy and drag it, if need be, kicking and screaming, into the era of high technology. And indeed, despite his oft-declared loyalty to Socialist principles, he had within two years of taking office caused a law to be presented to the Supreme Soviet, officially authorizing on a small scale numerous forms of private enterprise and giving greater autonomy to individual enterprises. Had not Lenin himself after all, back in the days of his New Economic Policy and the wicked NEP-men, declared that 'Communists must learn to trade'?

Though limited in scope, hedged about with restrictions and in fact doing, for the time being, little more than legalize the unofficial status quo, this measure clearly represented a major departure from standard Marxist–Leninist orthodoxy. Moreover, to those who understood the workings of Russian (and, more especially, Transcaucasian) human nature, it seemed to open up endless new possibilities. Others, revealingly, took it all as a matter of course. 'I can see nothing wrong with going to a private dressmaker', said one great lady dismissively to an enquiring foreign journalist. 'It never really crossed my mind to do otherwise, just as I used to send my son to a private kindergarten. It cost more money, but he was looked after much better.'

By March 1987 a first cooperative restaurant had opened on borrowed money in elegant premises at 36 Kropotkinskaya, once the Moscow home of Prince Trubetskoi, with eighteen partners working from 7 am to 11 pm, serving an appetizing à la carte menu including roast sucking-pig to fifty appreciative Muscovites, while hundreds more queued in the snow outside. 'If they make a loss', commented the *Moskovskaya Pravda*, 'no one will bail them out. They will go bankrupt.' But this, on the face of it, seemed highly improbable. 'We are used to cafés where the food is uneatable and they treat you like dirt', said one contented customer. 'This is something extraordinary.' 'Better than Paris!' cried another.

On my very next visit to Moscow, I made a point of investigating this remarkable establishment in person. From outside the National Hotel the Metro carries you comfortably in five minutes flat to the Kropotinskaya, a pleasant avenue of elegant, early nineteenth-century town houses called, appropriately enough, after that noble anarchist of the period, Prince Peter Kropotkin. Making our way along it, we came in another five or ten minutes to the Kropotinski Pereulok, a leafy side-street on the corner of which a discreet doorway with a couple of glossy private cars outside it indicated the entrance to what we had by then learnt to call the Cooperative Café.

Our first surprise came as, crossing the threshold, we entered a smartly furnished foyer, where we were at once made welcome by a friendly youth in immaculate white shirt and dark trousers, who, on learning that we had a reservation, immediately led us across the thickest of thick carpets to our table in one of the most agreeably and imaginatively furnished restaurants I have ever sat down in.

Surprise now succeeded surprise. Half a dozen tables were laid on two sides of the room between white classical columns, in windows draped with full-length curtains of dark velvet. Shaded table lamps shed a discreet light on elegant chinaware and cutlery, bright against a cloth of mulberry-coloured patterned linen damask. Glasses glistened. Tall jugs of freshly-made iced blackcurrant juice awaited us. (A licence to sell wine has been applied for.) Across the room a youthful orchestra dispensed pleasantly dated palm-court music and classical jazz. From an elegantly pillared pavilion at the far end of the room an extremely pretty girl in white blouse and dark skirt presided over the proceedings, while two or three other, equally pretty girls, similarly attired, took orders and waited at table, providing service unheard of in any other Russian restaurant.

The menu, reasonably priced and neatly written out in white chalk on a blackboard, was limited to a dozen cleverly chosen dishes, depending on whatever first class raw materials had been available at the peasants' free market early that morning to the partner in charge of marketing, particular pride being taken by all concerned in a regular supply of fresh fruit and vegetables – unobtainable at the ordinary state foodstores. The meat, too, was no less carefully chosen, one particularly delicious speciality of the house being slices of the finest smoked and marinated fillet of beef, and another, shashlik of veal, worthy of a good restaurant anywhere. We finished our dinner with fresh fruit salad, an unheard-of delicacy in most Moscow restaurants.

But what struck me most was the intimate atmosphere of the place, its elegance and the youthful desire to please which pervaded it, the warm welcome we were given and the personal attention lavished on the individual. The foreign customers, I noticed, included that night a party of middle-aged middle-class Frenchmen, than whom no one is more demanding or more critical of other nations' cooking, but who in this instance were loud in their praises of both fare and service. Probing further after dinner I came on an inner room with four or five more tables, rather reminiscent in décor and atmosphere of a good London club and full of knowing-looking parties of native Russians, clearly enjoying every moment of it.

That this bold experiment has been a resounding success, there can be no doubt at all. Started by three professional chefs, who were already friends ('much older than us – almost forty', said the prettiest of the waitresses) and then recruited another fifteen boys and girls to bring the cooperative up to the authorized maximum of eighteen, the team (and they now are a team in every sense of the word) are after only four months already preparing to open a further *traktir* on the floor below in what was once Prince Trubetskoi's cellar and frankly I can't wait to try it out when the time comes.

Strolling home after dinner past the fine classical façades of the Kropotinskaya, I could not but reflect on the importance of what I had just witnessed. This, without any doubt, was a big breakthrough if only in one small field. Here, with the full approval of the powers that be, human nature had taken hold, all kinds of latent, half-forgotten talents and impulses had emerged, achieving immediate and demonstrable success. An entirely new spirit was abroad. These young people, you could see, were happy in their work, actively enjoying themselves, having fun dispensing good cheer with good grace in congenial surroundings – something that deep down has always appealed to the innate Russian instinct and gift for hospitality so long stifled and frustrated by bureaucracy and all-encompassing red tape. 'Will there soon be more places like this?', we asked our friend the waitress as we left. 'Of course there will', was her cheerful reply. 'Lots more!'

On coming to power, Gorbachov lost no time in getting rid of as much dead wood as he could in the Party and government, replacing tired, complacent and often stubborn old-stagers with active men of his own generation and way of thinking. One of the first to go, to no one's surprise, was his own principal rival, the Leningrad Party boss, Grigori Romanov, notoriously a heavy drinker, who on 1 July 1985, retired 'for reasons of health'. He was followed before the end of the year by another old rival, Viktor Grishin, the Moscow Party boss. In the spring of 1986 the 27th Party Congress, over which he presided barely a year after taking office, replaced nearly half of the Central Committee's 307 members and further strengthened his majority in the 12-man Politburo. In his first two years of office two thirds of the government ministers were likewise replaced.

Someone whose services Gorbachov had from the first been quite ready to dispense with was old Marshal Sergei Sokolov, whom Chernenko had made Minister of Defence not many weeks before his death. As things turned out, an unexpected occasion for the aged Marshal's dismissal was conveniently provided in May 1987 when, to everyone's amazement, an enterprising West German teenager, Matthias Rust, landed his light aircraft on Red Square in broad daylight, having managed to fly it all the way from the frontier on Frontier Guards' Day without any attempt being made to prevent him. Not surprisingly, the air defence chief Marshal Alexander Koldunov, and a number of other senior officers, followed their minister into disgrace. Quite clearly the ensuing appointment as successor to Sokolov of Dmitri Yazov, a relatively junior general, whom Gorbachov had met in the Far East, was a personal appointment by the Party Secretary, who in this way neatly and effectively re-inforced his control over the armed forces, a wise move in a country whose rulers have always kept a sharp look out for real or imagined Bonapartism. Ready confirmation of this move's political implications came almost immediately in a hard-hitting speech from Boris Nikolayevich Yeltsin, the new Moscow Party boss and one of Gorbachov's staunchest supporters in the Politburo. Following Herr Rust's landing, people, said Yeltsin, were demanding that the officers of the Soviet Army should 'look them in the eye and explain just how something like this could happen'. And in the same tone he went on to accuse the army of inertia, nepotism, cliquishness, capriciousness and, worst of all, of resisting *perestroika* (restructuring).

Perestroika clearly was sweeping all before it. Then, in the autumn of 1987, just as all concerned were preparing to celebrate with due solemnity the seventieth anniversary of the Bolshevik Revolution, came a sudden, somewhat disturbing interlude. On 21 October a meeting of the Central Committee of the Party (duly reported in *Pravda*) was marked by a characteristically vigorous outburst from Boris Nikolayevich Yeltsin, complaining that *perestroika* was proceeding at far too slow a pace and that his own efforts in that direction were meeting with obstruction. This provoked in turn an angry reaction from a more conservative (or should one say less revolutionary) faction led by Yegor Ligachov, the next senior member of the Politburo to Gorbachov himself. Once it had become clear to him that the conservatives now commanded the support of a substantial majority, Gorbachov found it advisable, in the all important interests of Party unity, to make a sharp personal attack on his own leading supporter, who, it was now explained, had badly overstepped the mark in more ways than one, and had, as it happened, also had a heart attack. Following an abject admission of his guilt, for some unpleasantly reminiscent of the nineteen-thirties, the unfortunate Yeltsin was accordingly removed from his post at the head of the Moscow Party.

But, to everyone's surprise, there was more to come. Hard on this somewhat unnerving exercise in practical democracy came the embarrassing discovery that Yeltsin and his policies possessed a fair number of all too vocal supporters, who now protested publicly at his dismissal, expressing 'bitterness and bewilderment' and providing in the process yet another vivid illustration of the awkward problems to which *glasnost* and 'democratization' could in practice give rise. Fortunately, in Moscow, as elsewhere, with a strong hand on the helm, such little local difficulties rarely prove insurmountable. In the event, Yeltsin was given another, rather less desirable job. His alleged heart attack was found to be less serious than had been supposed. His place at the head of the Moscow Party was taken by Lev Zovikov, a senior member of the Politburo and another staunch Gorbachov supporter, and, after this slight buffeting, the ship of state proceeded once more serenely on her way.

For Mikhail Gorbachov, meanwhile, it had become clearer than ever that it was possible to push *perestroika* too hard and that for him the key question still remained just how far and how fast he dared go. As for the seventieth anniversary of the Revolution, he had celebrated it relatively quietly a couple of weeks earlier with a carefully balanced speech, dwelling at some length on past achievements and past errors (including, in both instances, those of Generalissimo Stalin), restating his aims at home and abroad and emphasizing yet again the need to press on with *perestroika* at a suitable pace. 'What happened with Yeltsin?' he said nonchalantly afterwards, when interviewed on American television 'Well, look – in fact it's just a normal process for any democracy'.

Unlike his predecessors, Mikhail Sergeyevich had not himself at once assumed the state presidency, preferring instead to bestow it on the veteran Andrei Andreyevich Gromyko,

Foreign Minister for over thirty years. As Gromyko wittily remarked, the new Secretary-General had a nice smile, but teeth of iron, a judgement quickly borne out by his actions and utterances both at home and abroad. Gromyko himself was now quickly replaced as Foreign Minister by Edvard Shevardnadze, newly promoted to full membership of the Politburo, a personable, quick-witted Georgian with the reputation of having as Party Secretary handled any little local difficulties in his own republic with energy and, where necessary, ruthlessness. (He had quite recently sent the Georgian Minister of Finance to do thirteen years in a labour camp.) It seemed unlikely, however, that in the long run Gorbachov would entrust the ultimate control of Soviet foreign policy to anyone but himself.

Yet another early casualty in Gorbachov's clearance of Brezhnevite dead wood was old Dinmukhamed Kunayev, Party Secretary of Kazakhstan, for the past fifteen years a member of the Politburo and a close and allegedly corrupt crony of Brezhnev himself. Curiously enough, Dinmukhamed's removal from his long-held office and his replacement by an ethnic Russian from the Volga provoked a strong and probably unexpected reaction in his native Kazakhstan, where crowds of what were described as 'nationalists and hooligans' were quickly out on the streets rioting and protesting at what they clearly regarded as an affront to Kazakh national pride. The fact that the rioting (which was promptly and firmly dealt with) was freely reported in the official press was in itself a tribute to Gorbachov's new policy of *glasnost*, or openness. Another non-Russian Brezhnevite survivor to be eliminated was Geidar Aliyev, a former KGB Chief from Azerbaijan, who in October 1987 found it necessary to resign from the Politburo for reasons of health.

Meanwhile, there had also been a marked change in the Soviet attitude towards dissidents. In mid-December, after a number of other prominent dissidents had in the course of 1986 been released from custody and allowed to leave the Soviet Union, Mikhail Gorbachov made a sensational personal long-distance telephone call to Dr Andrei Sakharov in Gorki, where the great nuclear scientist and Nobel prize-winner, long the subject of fierce controversy, had for the past six years been living in exile, and personally informed him that he was now free to return to Moscow and resume his scientific work there.

This dramatic and well publicized move was clearly intended to herald a definite change in policy in the much-debated matter of human rights and thus generally improve the image presented by the Soviet Union to the world. The fact that it coincided with a leading article in *Pravda* blaming Brezhnev personally for the mistakes and shortcomings of recent years was yet another clear signal that a new era had begun, a message driven home even more forcibly a month or two later by the arrest of Brezhnev's own son in law, Yuri Churbanov, a former Deputy Minister of the Interior, on charges of bribery and corruption.

Though fully occupied at home, it was only natural that Gorbachov should also wish to make an early mark in the international field. While the usual sharp exchanges between the Superpowers continued for the time being unabated, the idea of a 'summit' was before long once again being floated. No doubt sharing Gorbachov's curiosity and mindful of his own reputation as a great communicator, President Reagan responded positively and in November 1985 a meeting took place between the two in Geneva, the first such encounter since those of more than ten years before, between Presidents Nixon and Brezhnev. In the event, the two world leaders were duly photographed chatting amicably together by the fireside and appropriate communiqués were eventually issued, reporting frank exchanges of views. If it achieved nothing else, this bold initiative had at least demonstrated for all to see that such meetings were possible, did no apparent harm, and might, with luck, be repeated. It therefore came as no great surprise when in October 1986, less than a year after their first meeting, the leaders of the two Superpowers again met at Reykjavik in Iceland. Though again nothing very definite seemed to have been achieved and there was even a certain amount of mutual recrimination, the two protagonists were at one in proclaiming that their meeting had despite everything been useful and that they must continue their efforts to bridge the gap still separating them, thereby holding out to their respective electorates and to the world at large hopes of better things to come.

Secretary Gorbachov subsequently continued his exchanges with political leaders from all parts of the world. In particular he wisely showed every sign of seeking a genuine reconciliation with Communist China, thereby suggesting that he shared President Reagan's constantly repeated view that the future of the world lies in the Pacific and further underlining his determination, vigorously expressed in an important speech made at Vladivostok in July 1986, that the Soviet Union should in future play its full part as a Pacific power. Meanwhile being the continuing presence of some 120,000 Soviet troops in Afghanistan remained a major blot on the Soviet Union's clean new image as well as a continuing drain on its resources and an obstacle to better relations with a number of neighbouring countries, including China. That Gorbachov, who had himself described Afghanistan as 'a bleeding wound', would welcome an opportunity to withdraw his forces, seemed certain, always provided that this could be achieved without too great loss of face and without the prospect of a permanently hostile neighbour on his sensitive southern border.

After less than a year in power Gorbachov had placed on the table for all to see his grandiose plan for a nuclear-free world by the year 2000. This he followed up in February 1987 with the proposal, already discussed at Reykjavik and elsewhere, that both super-powers should remove all their medium-range nuclear weapons from Europe, this time, however, without making it an absolute condition that President Reagan should abandon or defer the development of his controversial Strategic Defence Initiative. In this manner he opened the way for a resumption of top-level talks between the Superpowers after their breakdown at Reykjavik and at the same time threw a timely life-line to the one-time detractor of his Evil Empire, who, as it happened, was then going through a difficult period in his Presidency and would clearly welcome relief from any quarter. Once again Gorbachov's timing, tactically, was hard to fault.

It was at this juncture, towards the end of March 1987, that, on Mikhail Gorbachov's invitation, the British Prime Minister, for so long 'the Iron Lady' of Soviet demonologists, paid a brief, but in the event extremely significant, visit to Moscow. While it had always been clear that any comprehensive agreement on nuclear disarmament would need to be between the Superpowers, there can be no doubt that Mrs Thatcher's ten or twelve hours of talks with Secretary Gorbachov served most effectively to clear the way for such an agreement. Indeed on her return to London she was able to announce to the House of Commons that there was now every prospect of an agreement on intermediate-range missiles by the end of the year.

Even more significant was the personal and working relationship, clearly based on mutual respect, which Margaret Thatcher and Mikhail Gorbachov were able to establish with each other and which in itself marked a massive breakthrough, not only in Soviet-British, but in East-West understanding. In the course of their prolonged and hard-hitting discussions on a wide range of controversial subjects, including the respective merits and demerits of Communism and capitalism, social conditions and the exercise of human rights under both systems, their own respective political aims and objectives, the necessity or otherwise for a nuclear deterrent and, last but not least, the continuing Soviet military presence in Afghanistan, neither protagonist pulled any punches whatever, whether in public or in private. At the same time it was obvious throughout that each retained a friendly regard for the other and found the other's company highly stimulating. 'There was', Mrs Thatcher said afterwards, 'an ability to argue with passion and not without temper, but with a certain amount of banter too.' Their talks she said had been 'lively, without jargon'. 'It has', she added, 'been the most fascinating visit I have ever made abroad as Prime Minister.' Secretary Gorbachov, she went on to say, was not only a man she could do business with, but a man who, once he gives his word could be expected to keep it. As for Gorbachov, he hailed their talks with equal enthusiasm, publicly describing them as 'of great significance'. That the two got on well together was clear to everyone. 'They look more like a newly-married couple than two leaders who are supposed to have disagreed on almost everything', exclaimed one astonished Muscovite, surveying a picture of them cheerfully sharing an elegant Empire settee on the front page of *Pravda*.

Certainly Secretary Gorbachov went out of his way to give Mrs Thatcher the warmest of welcomes and to make her visit as big a success as possible; no doubt sensing that here was a kindred spirit, someone of his own generation, as bright, as capable, as tough and as much of a radical as himself, whom he liked and with whom he, too, could do business. Sensing also that in effect Mrs Thatcher spoke for the Western Alliance and that at such a crucial time domestically and internationally there was for his country and for himself every advantage in cultivating such a relationship.

Mikhail Sergeyevich also made Mrs Thatcher's visit the occasion for an unprecedented display of *glasnost* and, it may be added, of self-confidence. Not only was the Iron Lady encouraged to mingle with the crowds on the streets of Moscow and Tbilisi and shake hands with as many excited Soviet citizens as she could; not only did she make, with Mikhail Sergeyevich and Raisa, a spectacular appearance in the Imperial Box at the Bolshoi to loud cheers and the strains of God Save the Queen; but the wider-ranging and by Soviet standards highly controversial speech she delivered at a great Kremlin banquet was promptly published in full in *Pravda*, while her long and extremely hard-hitting television interview with three Soviet correspondents was put out nationwide at peak viewing time to an estimated 120 million astonished Soviet citizens. In a witty article afterwards one of the three, to whom she had given a particularly rough time, denied rumours that he had since been banished to the Kurile Islands, his colleague from *Pravda* demoted to cloakroom attendant and the third, a well-known television personality, banned from ever again appearing on TV. What they had felt very keenly, he admitted, was that they were treading a path hitherto completely unknown to Soviet journalists and one that in currently changing circumstances required urgent exploration.

Nor was this all. In Moscow Mrs Thatcher was able to meet and talk at length with Dr Andrei Sakharov and the newly-released Jewish dissident Dr Josif Begun, while on the Sunday after her arrival she attended divine service at Zagorsk, where she publicly lit a candle as a gesture of solidarity with the country's thirty million Christians. No less significantly, as a tribute to the twenty million Soviet dead of World War II, she laid a wreath on the grave of the Unknown Soldier under the Kremlin Wall.

All in all, her visit marked a whole series of remarkable departures from precedent, the breaking down of any number of barriers and the establishment at long last of something approaching normal, human communication and even a measure of understanding between East and West. Never, as the London *Times* most perceptively observed, had there been a clearer case of the right person in the right place at the right time. It was thus in no way surprising that in December 1987 Mr Gorbachov should have stopped off in London on his way to attend a summit meeting with President Reagan in Washington, announced not long before, at which, amid public acclaim and mutual demonstrations of good will, the leaders of the two superpowers duly concluded an agreement for the joint elimination of their intermediate-range nuclear forces and at the same time agreed to open negotiations for further cuts in their nuclear arsenals.

PART TWO

OUT OF ASIA

We shall go Always a little further;
it may be Beyond that last blue mountain barred with snow,
Across that angry or that glimmering sea.
JAMES ELROY FLECKER

1

Faster than Fate

We are they who ride faster than fate.

JAMES ELROY FLECKER

The history of European Russia is only a part of the history of the Soviet Union. Scarcely less important to our understanding of that enormous country is the history of Central Asia, the vast area out of which over the centuries successive hordes of nomad invaders swept into what is now Russia, making an impact and leaving an imprint which endures to this day, an area which later itself fell under Russian domination, so that today the Soviet Union is as much an Asian as a European power.

Geographically, what we call Central Asia is bounded by the Caspian Sea on the west and by Lake Baikal on the east. To the north is Siberia. To the south rises the most formidable mountain barrier in the world: the Pamirs and the Himalayas, flanked on the west by the Elbruz and the Hindu Kush and on the east by the Tien Shan and Altai. Beyond these lie Iran, Afghanistan, parts of China and, still further south, the Indian Subcontinent. Between these natural limits is a vast expanse of desert, the Kara Kum or Black Sands to the west and the Kizil Kum or Red Sands to the east. Two mighty rivers traverse it, rising in the great mountain ranges to the south and flowing northwards into the Sea of Aral: the Oxus or Amu Darya, and the Jaxartes or Syr Darya. Along their fertile valleys and those of their tributaries civilization gradually took root and flourished. Here the caravans from China, from the Near and Middle East and from Europe had their staging posts. Cities were built and soon, side by side with the wandering pastoral existence of the nomads, a more sedentary, urban way of life began.

From the earliest times conquering armies and marauding nomad hordes swept across the length and breadth of the Asian landmass, dealing death and destruction as they passed and leaving behind them little trace of what had gone before. Samarkand, we know, was already a great city when Alexander of Macedon sacked it in 329 BC. For some centuries it had been a part of the Persian Empire. After defeating the Persians and making the territories he had taken from them between the Oxus and the Jaxartes a province of his own far-flung empire, Alexander pressed on southwards across the Hindu Kush in search of further conquests. It was a hundred years or more before the province he left behind him was overrun by a fresh wave of invaders and long after that memories of the Greeks and their civilization lingered on in Central Asia. To this day Alexander, or Iskander, is still remembered by the story-tellers in the bazaars of Bokhara and Samarkand.

For the next eight or nine hundred years Central Asia presents a confused picture, with fresh waves of marauders sweeping across it and vast areas changing hands at frequent intervals. In 250 BC the Emperor of China, determined to defend his Celestial Kingdom against all comers, wisely began to build the Great Wall, thus deflecting the invading hordes westwards into what remained of Alexander's Central Asian dominions. By the dawn of our own era two hundred and fifty years later, power in Central Asia had passed to the Tushans, a Tartar tribe whose vast empire straddled the Hindu Kush, stretching into Central Asia to the north and India to the south. After holding sway there for four centuries, the Tushans were in their turn overthrown around 430 by the White Huns, like them of Tartar or Turko-Mongol stock. Meanwhile in Persia a new dynasty known as the Sasanids had established themselves, remaining in power for the next four hundred years. Further north the Turks emerged as a major power; while the Eastern Turks held sway over an area stretching from the Urals to Mongolia, their western khanate controlled everything between the Altai Mountains and the Jaxartes. For a time, Turks and Persians joined forces against their common enemies, the White Huns. Bactria now became a Persian province, while the Turks established themselves in Transoxiana, the territories beyond the Oxus. But soon the former allies were again at odds.

Such was the situation in Central Asia when in 632 the Prophet Mohammed launched from his native Arabia the wave of conquests which in a surprisingly short time were to bring a great part of the then known world under Mohammedan dominion. Within twenty years the Arabs had conquered the whole of Persia, followed in due course by Bactria and Transoxiana. By the end of the eighth century the Caliph Harun al Rashid ruled from his palace in Baghdad over dominions which extended from the frontiers of China to the Atlantic coast of Spain.

Within this vast empire the Persian provinces, having duly embraced Islam, enjoyed virtual independence under their own rulers, the Samanids, whose dominions included the whole of Transoxiana or, as the Arabs called it, Mawara-al-Nahr, the Land Beyond the River. In the year 999, however, the Samanids were overthrown by the Turkish Karakhanids, who in their turn ruled over Transoxiana until the middle of the twelfth century, when their place was taken by the Karakitais, nomads of Chinese culture and in all probability Mongol origin. From Merv in what is today Turkmenistan a new power, the Seljuk Turks, now ruled over most of Moslem Asia including not only Persia and Afghanistan, but Anatolia, Mesopotamia, Syria and Palestine. For a time their dominions included Khorezm or Khiva, as it is now called, but in due course there arose in Khorezm yet another Turkish dynasty, the Khorezmshahs, who, establishing themselves in Samarkand and Bokhara, had by the beginning of the thirteenth century become the paramount power in Moslem Central Asia.

It was at this point in history that the startling phenomenon of the Mongol invasions burst on an astonished world. Until then the Mongols had been just one of a number of nomad tribes who ranged over the rolling country to the north of the Gobi Desert and to the south and east of Lake Baikal. It was here that in about the year 1154 Jenghiz Khan was born, the son of an obscure local chieftain. After spending the first fifty years of his life consolidating his position in his own country, Jenghiz had by 1206 united under his leadership all the tribes of Mongolia and had turned their combined armies into a formidable striking force of a quarter of a million men. With this he now invaded China. By 1214 his armies stood before the gates of Peking.

Having captured Peking and all its treasures, the Mongols turned westwards, over-running the territories of the Karakitais in what is now Kazakhstan. This brought them into conflict with the Shah of Khorezm who, in addition to Khorezm and Transoxiana, was by this time master of most of Afghanistan and Persia as well as northern India. Jenghiz's attack on the dominions of the Khorezmshah was as carefully planned as his invasion of China. In 1219 he struck with his main force at Otrar, following this up a year later by seizing Bokhara and Samarkand, while other Mongol armies occupied other Khorezmian territories and the Khorezmshah himself fled to an island in the Caspian. After wintering on the Oxus, Jenghiz next attacked Balkh, the capital of Bactria, while one of his sons raided Khorasan in Persia. Crossing the Hindu Kush in the spring of 1221, he defeated what remained of the Khorezmian forces on the Indus and then, having spent the summer in the northern foothills of the Hindu Kush, made his way back to Mongolia.

After overrunning northern Persia, yet another Mongol force of some twenty thousand men had by this time reached the southern foothills of the Caucasus and penetrated deep into Georgia. In 1222, they returned in strength, utterly defeating the Georgians and then taking possession of the Ukraine and the Crimea, where they spent the winter. The following summer, after routing a Russian force sent out to meet them, they once more withdrew eastwards.

In 1226 Jenghiz set out from his capital at Karakorum to crush an insurrection in China. It was to be his last campaign. In August 1227, at the age of seventy-two, he died and his body was brought back to Mongolia for burial. But Jenghiz's death scarcely checked the Mongol advance. Using the formidable military machine they had inherited from him, his sons and grandsons sustained his initial impetus for another half-century. 'They made up their mind,' wrote the Venetian traveller, Marco Polo, 'to conquer the whole world.'

To his grandson Batu, Jenghiz had allocated a vast expanse of territory, comprising much of what is now Siberia and Kazakhstan as far as the borders of European Russia and known as the Golden Horde. His second son, Chagatai, inherited most of Turkestan, while his third son, Ogetai, succeeded him as Ka-Khan or Chief Khan, at the same time taking possession of Eastern Jungaria, Mongolia and the parts of China under Mongol rule. To his fourth son, Tolui, went his household and treasury, the ancestral territories and pastures and, most important of all, the seasoned core of shock troops who constituted the main striking force of the Mongol armies.

For the Mongols the next thirty years were to be a period both of consolidation and of further expansion. Their hold on Persia and Khorezm was strengthened, Azerbaijan, Armenia and Georgia were added to their dominions, Korea invaded and China north of the Yangtse annexed. But the most spectacular conquests of all were those of Batu and his Golden Horde. Between 1237 and 1242 they struck deep into Russia, Poland and Hungary. In Russia town after town fell to the invaders. While one Mongol force threatened Breslau, another overran Lithuania and East Prussia. Early in 1241 they reached Pesth; soon all Hungary was in Mongol hands. It seemed as though nothing could stop them.

Then in 1242, just as Batu was preparing to continue his advance into Austria and Bohemia, came news from Mongolia that his uncle Ogetai, the Ka-Khan, had died. Abandoning his proposed campaign, he set out for Karakorum to help elect a new Great Khan. By the time he returned to Europe, he had abandoned the idea of fresh conquests. Instead, establishing his headquarters at Sarai on the Volga, he settled down to consolidate what he had already conquered on the west of that river.

Ogetai was succeeded as Great Khan by his son Güyük. But two years later Güyük died mysteriously and by 1251 all Ogetai's other male descendants had also died. The title of Ka-Khan now went to Möngke, the son of Jenghiz's fourth son, Tolui. Möngke's reign, from 1251 to 1259, marked the zenith of the Mongol Empire. Power by now had passed to a fresh generation of Jenghizkhanids, as determined as their predecessors to maintain, indeed to extend the conquests they had inherited. While Batu was advancing into Hungary and Poland, another Mongol force had swept across Anatolia to defeat the Seljuk Turks at Kayseri and Erzerum. In 1253 Möngke's brother Hulagu invaded northern Persia and Mesopotamia. By 1257 he had seized all the main strongpoints in the Elbruz Mountains. In 1258 he captured Baghdad. From his capital in northern Persia he now ruled over a kingdom which reached from Kashmir to the Lebanon.

In China, meanwhile, Möngke's brother, Kublai, had done so well that in 1257 Möngke, growing uneasy, took command there himself. But two years later Möngke died and Kublai, having duly disposed of another brother, himself assumed the title of Ka-Khan, ruling for the next thirty-five years over an empire which in time came to include the whole of China. With the years, Kublai, as Ka-Khan, spent more and more of his time in China, falling into Chinese habits and losing touch with the Western khanates.

During the ensuing hundred years or so, the central control of the Mongol Empire was further weakened, while, with the opening of oceanic trade routes, the importance of the transcontinental caravan trade diminished and the process of disintegration continued. In the end the Yuans, as the Mongol dynasty now called themselves, were replaced in China by the native Mings and Mongolia itself became no more than a remote Chinese province. And then a remarkable thing happened. Over the next six centuries the once warlike Mongols underwent a complete transformation. Lamaist Buddhism, first introduced from Tibet, grew to be a dominant influence. The Bogda Gegen or Living Buddha of Urga became ruler of the country and soon almost half the male inhabitants were celibate, unproductive lamas who kept Mongolia in a state of mediaeval stagnation, while the population dwindled to only a few hundred thousands.

The nineteenth century brought one important change. From a province of China,

Mongolia became a Russian protectorate. This, save for four tumultuous years between 1917 and 1921, it has remained ever since. Today the People's Republic of Mongolia is bound to the Soviet Union by strong military, economic and political ties, while across the border Inner Mongolia has become an integral part of China.

The People's Republic of Mongolia is roughly the size of Western Europe. In so large a country, a population of a million or so is thinly spread. The green rolling steppe stretches endlessly away to a distant horizon of hills. Having provided yourself with a Soviet jeep, you can drive for hours without meeting more than an occasional shepherd, a herd or two of horses or cattle, or some nomads on the march, with their belongings loaded on to a string of camels. Every now and then you come on clusters of the traditional round tents in which the bulk of the population still live and which they carry with them on their camels when they move. In these, if you stop to ask the way, you will be entertained to nourishing meals of tea and cheese and great bowls of fermented mare's milk.

There are few roads in Mongolia – just a series of rough tracks from which to take your choice. Further south, the steppe merges gradually into a desert or *gobi*, made a wilderness, it is said, by the trampling of Jenghiz Khan's myriad cavalry. The Mongols are still a nation of horsemen. Racing, after wrestling, is their most popular pastime. Their national emblem is a horseman and on the main square of Ulan Bator stands a prancing equestrian statue of Sukhe Bator, the revolutionary hero who in 1921 founded modern Mongolia. Jenghiz Khan's capital of Karakorum was sacked six or seven centuries ago. All that is left of it today is a solitary stone tortoise, the stones of the original city having been used long since to build the neighbouring Lamaist monastery of Erdeni Tsu, now in its turn falling into decay.

Within the frontiers of the Soviet Union is another former stamping-ground of the Mongol hordes and of their various nomad predecessors: the Soviet Socialist Republic of Kazakhstan. Sprawling across the north of Central Asia from the frontiers of European Russia in the west to the borders of China in the east, Kazakhstan comprises much of what was once the territory of Batu's Golden Horde. With its fifteen million inhabitants spread over almost three million square kilometres, it is, like Mongolia, still thinly populated, consisting very largely of desert, the Red Sands or Kizil Kum, but also of steppe, prairie and rolling grassland, providing pasture of a kind for sheep and cattle.

If you travel by rail from the north, as I first did fifty years ago, the change from Siberia to Central Asia comes soon after you enter Kazakhstan. For a couple of days the track runs across desert, as flat, but more desolate than Siberia. At the halts along the line the peasants who ride in with food to sell are no longer European Russians, but native Kazakhs and Kirghiz with strongly Mongoloid features; the women in strange high mediaeval-looking head-dresses; the men in long padded coats and skull-caps or helmet-shaped hats of thick white felt with sharply upturned brims. Here and there are groups of their circular skin or felt tents or yurts.

Then, after a day or two spent crossing the sandy waste, you suddenly catch sight, far away to the south, of a mighty range of mountains, their lower slopes veiled in cloud and vapours, their snow-clad peaks glittering in the sunlight. These are the Tien Shan, the

Mountains of Heaven, part of the great mountain barrier which divides Russian from Chinese Turkestan and beyond that from Tibet and India. As you approach Alma Ata, the capital of Kazakhstan, which lies at their foot, you suddenly find yourself amid exuberantly green cultivation: apple orchards, fields of corn, plantations of melons, rows of tall poplars. In Kazakh 'Alma Ata' means 'Father of Apples' and the apples grown in its orchards are as fine and juicy as any in the world.

Alma Ata, formerly Vierny, founded by the Russians in the mid-nineteenth century as a garrison town, is laid out in wide avenues of elms and poplars running at right-angles to each other. Today it is a typical Soviet city with the usual blocks of flats, department stores, opera, university and imposing new government buildings. But the green avenues of tall poplars and the old, brightly-painted wooden and stucco bungalows of the early settlers still give the town a pleasantly bucolic character.

Under the tsars, the Kazakhs, like the Mongols, were wandering nomad herdsmen, pitching their tents where they could find pasture and possessing no permanent abode. Alma Ata has retained its European character and the greater part of Kazakhstan's inhabitants are now European Russians or Ukrainians with only a minority of native Kazakhs. Its good climate and the fertility of the soil have always made it suitable for colonization by Europeans. The imperial government actively encouraged European Russians to settle there and their Soviet successors have, after their own fashion, followed their example. Even so the replacement in December 1986 of the aged Dinmukhamed Kunayev, the local Party boss, by an ethnic Russian was enough to bring large numbers of native Kazakhs out on the streets in protest at this jolt to their national susceptibilities.

Economically Alma Ata's significance sprang from the opening in 1931 of the Turkish Railway which linked it up with the main Trans-Siberian line. Quickly it became a boom town with a population that increased from fifty thousand in 1931 to two hundred and thirty thousand in 1938 and has gone on increasing ever since until it has now almost reached a million. Soon Kazakhstan produced more copper, lead and zinc than any other republic in the Union and was third in production of coal and oil. It is also the biggest producer of sheep and cattle, while grain production from the arable areas is more than 16 million tons a year.

The Kazakhs vary considerably in type. Most of them have dark, reddish-brown complexions and flat, round moon-like faces with high Mongoloid cheek-bones; some have oval faces and more aquiline features. Their language, like most of the native tongues of Soviet Central Asia, is akin to Turkish. Many of the peasants still wear national dress, but in the towns European clothes have long been more usual.

From Alma Ata you can make your way by bus and on foot into the foothills of the Tien Shan or Ala Tau. At first the countryside is green and fertile and the hamlets are set among orchards and well-cultivated fields. Next you come to pinewoods and alpine pastures and then, leaving the tree-line behind you, to the rocky snow-capped peaks of Kirghizia or Kirghiztan, the mountainous little Soviet Socialist Republic which forms a natural barrier between Soviet and Chinese Central Asia.

Formerly part of the Government of Turkestan, Kirghizia consists for the most part of a massive mountain range rising to some 24,000 feet, which since 1860 has marked the border between Russia and China and which, here too, bears the name of Tien Shan or Ala Tau. Further west it merges into the even higher Pamirs of Soviet Tajikstan, which likewise possesses a common frontier with China. High among the mountains of Kirghizia, forty or fifty miles due south across the border from Alma Ata, lies Lake Issik Kul, an immense freshwater lake a hundred miles long and thirty miles wide. On its shores, great Tamerlane had a favourite castle and beneath its waters a whole city is said to lie buried.

Like their neighbours and cousins the Kazakhs, with whom they have much in common, the Kirghiz, coming originally from further east and north, took refuge in the Tien Shan at the time of the Mongol invasions. Under the tsars they remained for the most part nomads and horsemen, living in movable round felt or skin yurts and migrating with their flocks and herds from the winter to the summer pastures and back again, while, as in Kazakhstan, large numbers of Russian colonists settled in the fertile low-lying areas. Dark-skinned and black-haired, with slanting eyes and high cheekbones, the Kirghiz, like the Kazakhs, speak a language akin to Turkish. With the ruthlessly enforced and disastrous collectivization of agricultural land which followed the Revolution and which they strongly resisted, their way of life changed drastically and large numbers of them were obliged to exchange a pastoral for an urban existence. Now no more than a few herdsmen and their families lead a semi-nomad existence up in the high hills within the framework of state or collective farms, while the rest follow more settled pursuits.

Frunze, the capital of Kirghizia, which lies at the foot of the great mountains, is an agreeable enough town. Over the last seventy years it has grown from the little township of Pishpek, with a population of fifty thousand, consisting partly of Kirghiz and partly of Russian settlers, to a fine modern city of nearly three-quarters of a million inhabitants, lavishly provided with imposing public buildings and scarcely less imposing apartment blocks. From Moscow it can be reached by air in three-and-a-half hours or in little over an hour from Tashkent. Should you on the other hand choose to travel by train, you will emerge from a handsome station building to find yourself facing a large equestrian statue of the city's most famous son, who gave it its present name, Mikhail Vasilyevich Frunze, a Russian settler who served as People's Commissar for War in the early days of the Bolshevik regime and played an important part in establishing Soviet power in Central Asia.

Mikhail Vasilyevich's statue stands at the top of a broad, tree-lined boulevard dedicated to the memory of his no less famous contemporary, Felix Edmundovich Dzerzhinski, founder and inspirer of Lenin's security police, the Cheka, forerunner of the OGPU, NKVD and KGB. Just across the street from the station is the Hotel Ala Too, which, like the station itself and most of Frunze's older public buildings, dates from the Stalin era and, if a trifle old-fashioned and, for some tastes, rather ornate, is a good deal better built, more commodious and a great deal more comfortable than its modern no-nonsense concrete rivals. Here, on a recent visit I found myself occupying for no very good reason a luxury suite, including not only a pleasant bedroom and a bathroom dispensing plentiful hot water, but a large private sitting-room with a dining-room seating eight, a massive sideboard, a desk and a couple of comfortable chairs, leaving plenty of room for a grand piano, had I needed one.

Dzerzhinski Boulevard, with its fine double row of trees, runs right through the best residential part of the town, where the whitewashed bungalows of the early Russian settlers alternate with larger buildings of the Stalin era and big modern apartment blocks. From the railroad station it leads to the inevitable statue of Lenin and to a kind of piazza with the city's principal public buildings arranged around it – Party Headquarters, various ministries, the Supreme Soviet, the Opera, theatres, Lenin Museum, Philharmonic and so on, including a most impressive new building, at present still under construction, boasting a massive dome and converging colonnades. But what strikes one most about Frunze is its greenness. It is in the truest sense a garden city. Every street, square or public park is planted with tall, well-grown poplars, sycamores or silver birches, recalling in its way the residential areas of some American cities. On the outskirts, as in almost every Soviet town, more big new apartment blocks are being built on a lavish scale. Like the centre of the town, these, too, will have their share of greenery. In Kirghizia land is abundant and the new developments are well laid out with plenty of space for future planting.

Although of recent years there has been much industrialization and on the edge of the city you find an increasing number of new factories pouring their fumes into the clear Central Asian air, cattle and sheep remain the basis of Kirghizia's economy. By tradition, every Kirghiz, like every Mongol, is from childhood at heart a horseman or horsewoman. Frunze itself possesses a much-frequented race-course and equestrian prowess is still greatly applauded. As in other Central Asian countries, one of the most popular sports is *buzkashi*, a game half-way between polo and American football, played by a dozen or more horsemen. First, a goat is beheaded. A violent scramble then ensues for the carcass. Having once succeeded in seizing hold of this, a player gallops off with it as hard as he can go with the others in hot pursuit, trying to grab it back from him. No holds are barred and it is surprising how few of the players or horses are seriously injured. At the end of the game, the goat, having been thoroughly tenderized, is roasted and devoured with great gusto by all concerned.

Another favourite pastime is wrestling on horseback, the players pairing off and endeavouring, usually without much success, to pull each other off their horses. No less popular than the pursuit of a goat is the pursuit of a girl, when a man on a horse chases a girl on a horse with the object of catching hold of her and kissing her. In this he is usually successful, though, should she not welcome his advances, she is free, amid loud applause, to hit him as hard as she can across the face with her whip, making on the whole for a more exciting finish.

In Kirghizia, as in Mongolia, a popular drink is *kumiss* or fermented mare's milk, an effervescent and mildly intoxicating beverage, mid-way between yoghurt and champagne, said to be a sovereign cure for rheumatism, tuberculosis, and numerous other ailments. As a race, the Kirghiz are compulsively hospitable. Horseflesh in various forms is a greatly-prized delicacy, liable to be lavished on you if you are lucky enough to be entertained at a yurt in the mountains. At such feasts, when sheep or goat rather than horse is on the menu, the partly dismembered carcass is placed in the middle of the festive board, with its head facing the oldest person in the yurt (by now almost invariably the present author) who is then invited to cut it up and distribute eyes, ears and brain to his fellow guests, a not entirely simple task, unless you happen to be a butcher by trade and carry with you an unusually sharp knife.

No one is prouder than the Kirghiz to possess as their favourite son one of the Soviet Union's most successful and most controversial novelists in the robust person of Jinghiz Aitmatov, whose books sell hundreds of thousands of copies at home and abroad. Though, as a Lenin Prize winner, a member of the Supreme Soviet, and a Hero of Socialist Labour, Jinghiz is undoubtedly a leading light of the Soviet establishment, he clearly welcomes (what author would not?) the lively controversy aroused by his latest novel, *The Chopping Block*, which deals with such daring themes as drug addiction among the young and what he calls his own search for God. ('It is beginning to look as though they were afraid I might find Him!' he says, clearly delighted at the attacks made on him in various influential organs of the Soviet press.) Active in politics and now a leading force in the Writers' Union, he is personally one hundred and fifty per cent in favour of Gorbachov's campaign for *perestroika* and, more particularly, for *glasnost* – greater freedom of expression. He is also the first leading Soviet personality I have met to give the late N. S. Khrushchov the credit he deserves for his early efforts to dismantle or at any rate relax Stalin's dictatorship. That so prominent and popular a public figure as Jinghiz should be at the centre of such controversy and actually enjoy it seems in itself to point to increasing freedom of discussion and an increasing measure of the *glasnost* at which Gorbachov is aiming – in itself an encouraging sign.

I left Kirghizia with the impression of a people by now not unhappy with the existence which some seven decades of Soviet rule have brought them. In the mountains they lead in modified form the pastoral life of their forebears. In the towns they enjoy some of the advantages of modern life and, as far as one can see, not too many of its disadvantages. Whatever its attraction may have been, the existence led by a nomad in the high Pamir must have possessed a number of drawbacks, while in contrast to other parts of Central Asia, there was little for them to lose in the way of long-established cultural or religious traditions. Though the crumbling ruins of a few ancient Mohammedan shrines survive in the parts of the country bordering on Uzbekistan, Islam does not seem to have made much impact on the Kirghiz who, insofar as they had a religion, inclined rather to vague forms of Shamanism and spirit worship. In the old Kirghiz burial-grounds you see by the roadside, the monuments are as often as not shaped like big bird-cages with a crescent on top, no doubt symbolizing the yurts the deceased once occupied. Whether or not the crescent possessed some religious significance, no one seemed to know, although I feel it almost certainly did. Of Kirghiz national dress all that survives is the strange helmet-shaped felt hat with its sharply-upturned brim, still worn by most Kirghiz men along with their standard Soviet suits. Their national musical instrument, a twanging contraption made of wire, struck me as identical with a Jew's Harp. By nature the Kirghiz are a cheerful, friendly people, proud of their country, of its achievements and of their rapidly growing and increasingly impressive capital city. Owing to the active encouragement given by the central government to white settlers over the last hundred years, European Russians and Ukrainians now come close to outnumbering the native Kirghiz, especially in the towns, but, as a result of a higher Kirghiz birthrate, will not necessarily do so in the future. Relations between natives and incomers seem friendly enough, though, as elsewhere in Central Asia, there seems to be a tendency on the part of both races to keep themselves to themselves and there is less intermarriage than might be expected.

2

Golden Road

For lust of knowing what should not be known,
We take the Golden Road to Samarkand.

JAMES ELROY FLECKER

Just as Kublai and his heirs became with time increasingly Chinese in their outlook and habits, so the rulers of the Western khanates of the Mongol empire gradually shed many of their Mongol characteristics, at the same time loosening the links which bound them to Karakorum and the ruling Ka-Khan. When Batu, the first Khan of the Golden Horde, died in 1255, he was succeeded by his brother Berke, who, embracing Islam, made it the predominant religion of the Horde, while Turco-Tartar replaced Mongol as its *lingua franca*. Already relations between the Western khanates were far from friendly. While the khans of the Golden Horde quarrelled with the Il-Khans of Persia over territories in Transcaucasia that were claimed by both, the Il-Khans for their part were perpetually at odds with their northern neighbours, the unruly Chaghatai khans of Turkestan.

This confused state of affairs was brought to an abrupt end by the emergence in the second half of the fourteenth century of yet another great conqueror, Timur-i-Lenk, Timur the Lame or Tamerlane, who regarded himself, perhaps not surprisingly, as a reincarnation of Jenghiz Khan. Born in 1336 at Shakhr-i-Sabz, just south of Samarkand, Timur, the son of a local Tartar chieftain, had by 1370 achieved a dominant position among the tribes of Mawarannahr and placed himself at the head of a formidable military force. Making Samarkand his capital, he spent the next ten years strengthening his position at home and subduing his immediate neighbours in Kashgaria and Khorezm. Then in 1380 he invaded the Persian province of Khorasan. The Il-Khans were no match for him. Soon he was master of most of Persia and had begun to encroach on Azerbaijan and Georgia. For a time he allied himself with Toktamish, Khan of the Golden Horde, but soon they fell out, raiding each other's territory and competing for possession of Transcaucasia and the Caucasus. Having defeated Toktamish in battle near Samara, east of the Volga, Timur resumed his Persian campaign, pressing on through Persia into Mesopotamia and Anatolia. But the power of the Golden Horde had not yet been broken and in 1395 Timur, massing his forces, again struck hard at Toktamish, this time defeating him decisively near the lovely minaret of Tatartub on the River Terek in the northern Caucasus. Sweeping on across the Kuban Steppe, he then utterly destroyed the capital of the Golden Horde at Sarai on the Volga, at no great distance from the scene, some five hundred and fifty years later, of the equally decisive battle of Stalingrad.

Just three years after his victory over Toktamish, Timur, 'marching so fast that he overtook the birds', invaded northern India, crossed the Hindu Kush, and sacked Delhi and Meerut. In 1399 he returned to his favourite hunting grounds around Karabag in the Southern Caucasus. Setting out thence two years later, he stormed Baghdad and Damascus and broke the power of the Mamelukes in Syria. Next he turned against the Ottoman Turks, already a power to be reckoned with. Advancing westwards through Anatolia, in 1402 he defeated the Ottoman Sultan Bayazid at Ankara and, taking him prisoner, carried him off in a cage.

Master by this time of all Western Asia from the Aegean to Turkestan, Timur now returned to Samarkand, which he had made one of the most magnificent cities in the world. Arriving there in September 1404, Don Ruy Gonzalez de Clavijo, Ambassador of King Henry of Castile, found Timur seated on a raised dais under the portal of a most beautiful palace. 'A fountain', he tells us, 'threw up a column of water into the air backwards and in the basin of the fountain were floating little red apples.' 'His Highness', he continues, 'was dressed in a cloak of plain silk without any embroidery and wore on his head a tall white hat on the crown of which was displayed a balas ruby, the same being further ornamented with pearls and precious stones.'

While Clavijo was in Samarkand, Timur was building a mausoleum for a favourite grandson, killed fighting the Ottoman Turks. Dissatisfied with the original building, he had given orders for it to be rebuilt in ten days. Its fluted turquoise dome rose from an octagonal base. On either side of the entrance stood twin minarets. The interior was lined with alabaster and green marble. Entitled the Gur Emir, it was to serve in due course as Timur's own burial-place and remains to this day one of the most beautiful buildings in the world.

Of the many other fine buildings in Samarkand Clavijo and his companions were struck in particular by the Bibi Khanum, the great Mosque which Timur had built to the memory of one of his favourite mothers-in-law. But Timur, for his part, found the entrance gate too low and, giving orders for this, too, to be pulled down and rebuilt, had himself carried each morning to the building-site in a litter to urge on the workmen, throwing down cooked meat and coins to them, 'as one might cast bones to dogs in a pit'. To accommodate the rich merchandise brought into the city from Cathay, India, Tartary and many quarters besides, a great new bazaar was also being built, 'a street', Timur had decreed, 'passing right through Samarkand with shops on either side of it in which goods of all kinds shall be sold'.

Timur was now sixty-eight, 'infirm', says Clavijo, 'and old'. After spending the month of December 1404 assembling his armies, in January 1405 he set out, already a sick man, to invade China, whose Emperor's attitude he resented. Early in February he crossed the frozen Jaxartes. By this time his health was failing fast. At Otrar he fell seriously ill and on 17 February he died and was buried 'with great magnificence' in the Gur Emir. 'And be it known', writes Johann Schiltberger, a young German who served him for six years, 'that after he was buried the priests that belonged to the temple heard him howl every night during a whole year . . .'

Tamerlane's sarcophagus bore, it is said, the following inscription: 'He who opens this tomb will bring upon his country an invader more terrible than me.' Just over 536 years later, in the long hot summer of 1941, the tomb was in fact opened and Tamerlane's remains taken out and carefully exhumed, showing him to have been a tall, powerfully built man with a straggling reddish moustache, and lame, as his name indicates, in one leg. And then, just as the distinguished Soviet archaeologist who had opened the tomb stood looking down at all that was left of Tamerlane, one of his assistants burst in with the staggering news that a few hours earlier Hitler's armies had crossed the Soviet frontier.

Tamerlane was succeeded by his younger son, Shakh Rukh, a devout Moslem and a man of peace, who in the course of his long reign of forty years did much to consolidate the empire which his father had left behind him. With time this became an ordinary Moslem khanate, with its centre in Khorasan. Mawarannahr was governed as part of it by Shakh Rukh's son, Ulug Beg, a man of wide learning and a famous astronomer, who endowed both Samarkand and Bokhara with some of their finest buildings. On Shakh Rukh's death in 1447, Ulug Beg succeeded him, but only to be murdered two years later by his own son, Abd el-Latif.

Towards the end of the fifteenth century power in the lands between the Oxus and the Jaxartes passed to the Uzbeks under their leader Mohammed Shaibani. By 1500 he had taken Bokhara and Samarkand and conquered all of Mawarannahr, or, as it is now called, Uzbekistan, which was to be ruled over for the next hundred years by his descendants, the Shaibanids.

Bokhara had by this time come to be considered one of the holiest cities of the Moslem world. Elsewhere, it was said, light came down from heaven; from Bokhara it went up. Both Bokhara and Samarkand were renowned for the fanaticism of their inhabitants. Few infidels found their way there and those who did were unlikely to come back alive. With time, the opening up of fresh sea routes and the consequent decline of the caravan trade further increased their isolation and over the centuries few travellers from the West managed to reach Central Asia, remote behind its barrier of mountains and deserts. One who made the journey and, surprisingly, lived to tell the tale was the famous English merchant-adventurer, Anthony Jenkinson, who, setting out for Bokhara from Moscow in April 1558 with a cargo of English cloth and a letter of introduction from Ivan the Terrible of Muscovy, left a lively account of his adventures.

Over the next three hundred years Bokhara, under different dynasties, became even more isolated. In the neighbouring khanates of Khiva, as Khorezm was now called, and Kokand, other independent monarchs held sway, while east of the Caspian, tribes of fierce

Turkmen nomads ranged over the desert at will, raiding caravans and selling the prisoners they took as slaves. Far away to the north and west, what remained of the Golden Horde had by this time long since begun to disintegrate. By the middle of the fifteenth century it had broken up into a number of independent khanates, at Kazan, at Astrakhan on the Volga, in the Crimea, north of the Caspian and in Siberia, all at odds with one another and all by this time under growing pressure from the Russians, now beginning to encroach on them from the north.

With the disintegration of the Golden Horde in the fifteenth century, it had become increasingly easy for the Russians, already a considerable power in their own right, to play off their former conquerors against each other. Soon the roles were reversed and the Tartars were well on the way to becoming Russian vassals. By the beginning of the eighteenth century the tsars, in addition to their conquests further north, had established a loose suzerainty over the various nomad khans who ruled over the Kazakh and Kirghiz tribes of Southern Siberia. This they followed up during the first half of the nineteenth century by annexation and colonization, establishing a first garrison at Vierny, the present Alma Ata, in 1854.

Further west, the Russians, still in search of fresh territories to conquer, were poised for the conquest of Turkestan. Earlier expeditions had failed. Their next campaign was better prepared. Turkestan was at this time divided between three weak independent states: Khiva (the ancient Khorezm), Bokhara and Kokand. In 1855 the Russians seized from the Khan of Kokand the fort of Ak Mechet (later Perovsk) on the Syr Darya and dug themselves in along the river. Further east, Vierny served as a base. In the spring of 1864, operations were resumed in Central Asia and in May of that year, one Russian column started from Vierny, while another set out from Perovsk. In June the former seized Auli Ata, while the latter took the town of Yasi. The two columns then joined forces and in September stormed the citadel of Chimkent, easily routing the native garrison. A few weeks after this their commander, without bothering even to ask for instructions, added to his other conquests the Kokandi city of Tashkent.

Two years later the Russians resumed their advance, invading Bokharan territory in the spring of 1866 and then decisively defeating the Khan of Kokand, who readily sued for peace. On 11 July 1867 an imperial decree established a Government-General of Turkestan with Tashkent as its capital and appointed General K. P. von Kaufmann as its first Governor-General.

General von Kaufmann, a most capable commander, lost no time in making his presence felt. In the spring of 1868 he invaded the Emirate of Bokhara in strength. On 2 May he took Samarkand and, pushing southwards into the foothills, occupied Urgut and Katta-Kurgan. A month later he routed the Bokharan army on the nearby heights of Zerabulak. Under the ensuing treaty of peace the Emir ceded Samarkand to the Russians and agreed that what was left of his country should become a Russian protectorate. In Central Asia only the Khan of Khiva, safe, as he hoped, behind his barrier of deserts, precariously retained his independence, while further south, on the borders of Persia, the marauding Turkmen tribes of the desert continued to prey with impunity on passing caravans.

'For lust of knowing what should not be known,' sang Flecker's pilgrims, 'we take the Golden Road to Samarkand.' Today, when anyone with the price of a package tour can make the Golden Journey, it is hard to imagine the aura of mystery and glamour and above all remoteness that surrounded Samarkand and Bokhara when I first managed to make my way there just on fifty years ago or the feeling of triumph I experienced when I finally alighted at Samarkand station from the hardest of railway carriages and hitched a lift to the famous Registan in the back of a passing truck. Twelve months later came Bokhara, remoter and even more mysterious, within its ring of crumbling fortifications. To reach it at all seemed an enormous achievement, for in those days the whole of Soviet Central Asia was a forbidden zone. Now that one can fly there from Moscow in three or four hours and stay there in reasonable comfort, Central Asia has lost some of its mystery and remoteness. There is a hideous new concrete hotel in Samarkand and the ancient walls of Bokhara have largely been torn down. But the splendid turquoise domes, the mosques and minarets, the bazaars and *chaikhanas*, are still there and, though few Uzbek women now wear the veil, it is still possible to drink green tea in company with any number of turbaned worthies resplendent in their striped *khalats*.

From the airport you approach Samarkand across a wide dusty plain, scattered with ancient tombs and crumbling ruins. This is Afro Siab, the site of Maracanda which Alexander the Great once stormed and sacked. Continuing on your way, you suddenly catch sight of the city's glittering domes and minarets spread out before you against a green background of gardens and trees. Though in Marco Polo's day it was already 'a very large and splendid city', Samarkand is first and foremost the city of Tamerlane, who made it his capital and lies buried under the magnificent turquoise dome of the Gur Emir. His burial chamber is lined with jasper and alabaster, while his tombstone is made from a single slab of dark green jade from China. In a corner of the courtyard lies Kok Tash, the Blue Stone, a long low block of bluish-grey marble on which he and his successors were crowned. If you examine this closely, you will find that its surface has at some stage in its history been neatly marked out for the game of Nine Men's Morris which, it appears, originated in these parts.

At the centre of the old city, the paved expanse of the Registan, now sadly overlooked by a cinema and a modern apartment block, is enclosed on three sides by ancient Mohammedan religious colleges or *medressehs* with their fluted domes, their minarets, their great arches and their spacious courtyards. On the northern side stands the Tillah Kari or Golden Mosque Medresseh, built in the middle of the seventeenth century and called after the great mosque which forms part of it. On the western side, to your left as you face the square, is the smaller but older and more beautiful Medresseh of Tamerlane's grandson, Ulug Beg, the scholar and astronomer, who built it in 1417. (He also constructed a remarkable observatory, the remains of which can still be seen on the outskirts of the city with its vast stone quadrant and other instruments still in position.) To your right, on the eastern side of the Registan, opposite the Medresseh of Ulug Beg and built to balance it, is Shir Dar, the Lion Bearer, dating, like the Tillah Kari, from the seventeenth century. Across the top of its great central arch sprawl the splendid yellow lions or more probably tigers that give it its name. On either side of the façade are beautifully-proportioned twin domes of dazzling blue. Behind the façades of the three medressehs lie enclosed and arcaded courtyards, into which open what were once the cells of the religious teachers and their pupils.

Not far from the Registan stands the great Cathedral Mosque of Bibi Khanum, built, like the Gur Emir, in the last frenzied year of Tamerlane's life. Bibi, one version of the story runs, was a beautiful Chinese princess who became Timur's wife and the mosque, it is said, was built by a Persian architect who, while Tamerlane was away on one of his campaigns, fell in love with the lonely Bibi and kissed her so passionately that the mark of his kiss remained for all to see. Noticing this on his return from the wars, Tamerlane sent his men to kill the Persian, but he, fleeing before them to the top of the highest minaret, sprouted wings and flew safely back to Persia. Such is the legend. In fact, however, it seems more likely that this is the mosque which Tamerlane built in memory of a favourite mother-in-law and which Clavijo called 'the noblest of all we had seen in the city of Samarkand'. A crumbling ruin when I first saw it, it has now been so thoroughly restored and even extended that it might have been built yesterday.

Today the Bibi Khanum and the great mosques and medressehs of the Registan are no longer places of worship. But a mile or two away in the suburbs of the old town is the mosque of Hodja Akhror, built in the seventeenth century by an uncle of the reigning Emir and called after the saint of that name who lies buried there. Under the ancient plane trees which surround the central pool, devout Moslems still come to pray and you may see robed and turbaned figures deep in prayer or silently prostrating themselves in the direction of Mecca. Outside the main precinct lies the tomb of the saint, with lesser monuments clustered about it.

To the north of the city cluster the cupolas of a superb avenue of ancient tombs built up the side of a hill on both sides of a narrow passageway, Hazreti Shakh-i-Zindeh, the Shrine of the Living King. Kasim Ibn Abbas, the martyred monarch who gave the shrine its name, was, it is said, a cousin of the prophet Mohammed, who, having converted Sogdiana to Islam in the seventh century, was later hunted down and beheaded by zealous local Christians. Begun in 1326, the building of the Shakh-i-Zindeh was continued under Tamerlane and Ulug Beg, but for pious Moslems it was a place of pilgrimage long before that and still remains one today.

From the great gate at the foot of the hill, built by Ulug Beg, you climb a steep flight of steps. At their head stands a white arch and beyond this a paved alleyway leads between the tiled façades of two lines of exquisite shrines to yet another arched gateway. Through another arch at the end of the alleyway you enter a beautiful courtyard. From this a dark passage leads to the magnificently-decorated mosque and octagonal mausoleum of the Living King, built in 1334–5, where Kasim's mortal remains lie buried under a fine blue-tiled tomb-stone. But those who know better will tell you that in fact he is still alive and lurks nearby in a disused cistern, waiting, with his severed head under his arm, to emerge and claim his kingdom.

In old Samarkand life still centres round the bazaar which lies across the way from the

Registan near the single dome which is all that remains of the original covered bazaar. In the shade of some ancient trees nearby is the main *chai-khana* or tea house of the city, where everyone meets to sit cross-legged and talk and drink green tea.

From Samarkand a short drive takes you up into the foothills of the Zeravshan Range where, not far from the village of Urgut, you can picnic by a pool in the shade of a giant sycamore, said to be seven or eight hundred years old. For Moslems this, too, is a place of pilgrimage and passing wayfarers pause to pray beside the clear waters of the pool. Continuing in the same direction and crossing the craggy Zeravshan Range at five thousand feet by the Takhtakaracha Pass, you reach at a distance of some fifty miles south from Samarkand the ancient town of Shakhrisabz, famous as Tamerlane's birthplace and also known as Tsishi or Kesh. In spring or early summer the drive is an agreeable one, the wooded valleys of the Zeravshan being bright with almond and white acacia blossom and wild tulips.

Shakhrisabz means 'green city'. Situated at two thousand feet above sea-level, it has a relatively temperate climate and the town itself, which lies in a fertile valley amid vineyards, orchards, mulberry plantations and cotton fields, is generously planted with trees and flowering shrubs. The first thing you see as you enter it is the gigantic ruined portal of Ak Sarai, the vast White Palace, built for himself near the graves of his ancestors during the closing years of the fourteenth century by Tamerlane, before he finally decided to make Samarkand his capital. The great gateway with its splendid mosaics is all that now remains of the palace, destroyed, so they say, a hundred years or so later by Uzbek invaders led by the great Shaibani Khan himself. At the head of his troops, Shaibani, according to one version of the story, caught sight of Ak Sarai from a great distance and, misled by its enormous size and believing it to be nearer than it really was, put spurs to his horse in his haste to reach it ahead of his army. But in reality the palace was further away than he thought and after he had galloped across country at high speed for a great many miles, his horse expired, leaving him with a dead horse and still a long way from his destination. This so infuriated him that, when he did in the end arrive before its gates, he gave orders for its immediate demolition. According to another, less dramatic account, it simply fell down due to faulty construction and has remained a ruin ever since, though now there are signs that some indefatigable Uzbek antiquaries are about to undertake its restoration.

Tamerlane, it is said, himself originally planned to be buried in Shakhrisabz and you are still shown a modest hole in the ground which supposedly marks the site of his proposed sepulchre, but scarcely bears comparison with the Gur Emir. Near the centre of the town are a number of fine old buildings dating back to the days of Tamerlane and the Timurids, notably the Mazar of Shamseddin Kulyal, the working Cathedral Mosque of Kok Gumbaz and the mausoleum of Gumbazi Selidan, built in 1435. The single dome of the fifteenth-century charsu, now bright with neon lights, indicates the site of the ancient covered bazaar. Nearby a contemporary *hammam* is still in use. The domed Khanaka of Malik Azhdar and the Mosque of Kazy Guzar, its fine *aivan* or pillared recess supported by tall, finely carved wooden columns, belong to a later period. In the south-eastern part of the town is the massive fourteenth-century Mausoleum of Dzekhangir and the adjoining

Mosque of Khazret–Imam. Shakhrisabz was a stopping-place on the Silk Road to China and in August 1404 was visited, on his way to Samarkand, by Don Ruy Gonzalez de Clavijo, who observed with interest the building of the Ak Sarai.

A hundred and fifty miles westwards from Samarkand along the fertile valley of the Zeravshan River, lies the ancient city of Bokhara. With its three hundred and fifty splendid mosques and one hundred religious colleges, it was known as Bokhara es Sherif, Bokhara the Noble. Writing in the thirteenth century, Marco Polo speaks of it as *'une cité moult noble et grant'*, and three hundred years later the English traveller Anthony Jenkinson wrote of its 'high wall of earth and its many houses, temples and monuments of stone, sumptuously builded and gilt'. When I first saw Bokhara in 1938, making my way there by night, on foot, in company with a caravan of heavily laden Bactrian dromedaries, its 'high wall of earth' was still intact, with, within it, a fairy-tale city of ancient houses of sun-baked clay each looking inward on its own courtyard. Now its ancient city walls have for the most part been demolished and a big boulevard driven through it, 'to let in the air'. But, for all that, the city still retains many reminders of its prodigious past. Above the dusty expanse of the Registan looms the thousand-year-old Ark or Citadel, containing within its fortifications a tangle of tumbledown palaces, mosques, harems and offices. Part of it was destroyed when the last Emir set fire to it as, in response to a warning telephone call, he fled before the oncoming Red Cavalry in the troubled summer of 1920, dropping favourite dancing boy after favourite dancing boy along his route in the hope of thus delaying their advance. The great entrance gate is flanked by twin turrets, between which once hung the clock made for the Emir in about 1840 by an Italian, Giovanni Orlandi of Parma, who was eventually bludgeoned to death for refusing to become a Mohammedan or, it is sometimes said, for allowing the Emir's watch to stop.

You enter the Ark by a steep, dark, winding passage-way, flanked on either side by sinister-looking guard-rooms and torture chambers and cells for prisoners, and leading to the courtyard where the Emir's throne still stands. This was the way taken on his arrival in Bokhara on 27 April 1844 by the Reverend Dr Joseph Wolff, curate of the parish of High Hoyland in Yorkshire, who had set out from London six months earlier to try to discover what had happened to two British officers, Colonel Stoddart and Captain Conolly, sent by Her Majesty's government on an ill-defined mission to the court of the Emir Nasrullah, the bloodthirsty ruffian at that time ruling over Bokhara. Dr Wolff learned the answer soon enough. After months of imprisonment the two envoys had been consigned to a well, full of vermin and reptiles. When, two months later, 'after masses of their flesh had been gnawed off their bones', they still refused to embrace Islam, they had been taken out and beheaded. Dr Wolff himself was luckier and after many adventures escaped from Bokhara alive, to the amazement, be it said, of the population.

Behind the Ark stands the Zindan, the prison where you may still see the vermin-pit in which Nasrullah kept his victims. Not far from the Ark is Kok Gumbaz, the turquoise-blue dome of the great Kalyan Mosque, rebuilt in the fifteenth century by the Shaibanid Khans on the site of an earlier cathedral mosque. Here the Emir worshipped in person.

High above it and above all Bokhara looms menacingly the elaborately decorated twelfth-century Kalyan Minaret or Tower of Death, from which condemned criminals were once cast down to their destruction. 'Like large parcels' wrote Monsieur Moser, a nineteenth-century French traveller, who 'by way of distraction' observed their descent, twisting and turning as they fell.

Of the hundreds of other mosques and medressehs which formerly adorned Bokhara, a fair number still survive. Opposite the main entrance of the Kalyan Mosque stands the smaller Medresseh of Mir-i-Arab, built in 1535 with funds derived from the sale into slavery of several thousand Persians and still in use as a religious college. To the south-east of the Registan are the Kosh-Medresseh or twinned Medressehs of Abdullah Khan, built in 1588, and of Madar-i-Khan, built in memory of Abdullah's mother a score of years earlier. Like those of Samarkand, the mosques and medressehs of Bokhara are constructed from sun-baked bricks. The design of the façade consists of a central arch, or *pishtak*, with, on either side, a double row of smaller arches. The central arch serves as the entrance to a courtyard surrounded by cloisters and the cells of the seminarists.

Many of the buildings in Bokhara have by now lost the coloured tiles which once adorned them; but one pair of medressehs, those of Ulug Beg and Abdul-Aziz, which stand facing each other across a narrow lane not far from the Tower of Death, have retained much of their former splendour, their façades being still decorated with their original intricate arabesques. The Ulug Beg Medresseh, like the medresseh of the same name in Samarkand, was built by Ulug Beg in the early fifteenth century, the Medresseh of Abdul-Aziz more than two centuries later.

A few of the lesser mosques are still in use, but for the most part they stand abandoned or have been turned to other uses. Of the buildings which stand round the Liabi Khaus, the tree-shaded pool in the centre of the town, the seventeenth-century Nadir Divan Begi Khaniga or guest-house is – or until recently was – a billiards club and the adjoining Nadir Divan Medresseh an hotel, while the local public record office is housed in the one hundred and sixty cells of the sixteenth-century Kukeldash Medresseh. By the side of the pool a rather rough-and-ready restaurant does a brisk trade in local delicacies: pilaff or *plov*, meat balls, chicken stew, jam pancakes and green tea, which you collect yourself in a couple of bowls and carry off to consume sitting cross-legged on a carpet-covered platform under the trees nearby. To this day water is carried through all Bokhara by a series of open channels, linked with the Liabi Khaus and other pools and ultimately, by way of the Shakh Rud or Royal Canal, with the Zerafshan.

Near the Tower of Death are the baths and the covered bazaars, once the richest in Central Asia. Now little is left of them and where priceless merchandise once changed hands a desultory trade is carried on in sweets and ice-cream and synthetic lemonade, for the Uzbeks still have a sweet tooth. Yet another survival from the Middle Ages are the caravanserais, where the caravans arriving in Bokhara from the outside world once came to rest. Today they are apt to be inhabited by teeming families of Bokharans. On top of almost every building in Bokhara a stork has built its nest and each summer the air resounds with the clicking of their beaks. Some distance away from the centre of the town is the Char Minar, an unusual architectural fantasy built in 1807 by a rich Bokharan merchant as gatehouse to a medresseh which has long since disappeared. Its four bulbous minarets, each with its stork's nest, dwarf a low central dome.

When I first visited Bokhara, its walls and battlements and eleven gates and watch towers still stood in all their crumbling magnificence. Now they have for the most part been demolished, though here and there enough remains to give you some idea of what they once were like. Outside the city a little way beyond the main covered bazaar are two buildings of great antiquity: Chasma Ayub, or Job's Spring, said to have been built by Tamerlane on the site of a miraculous spring which gushed forth there at the behest of the Prophet Job, and the Mausoleum of Ismail Samani, a strange structure decorated with elaborate floral designs in fired brick that was built as a burial place for himself by the founder of the Samanid Dynasty in the ninth century of our own era.

In Bokhara, more even than in Samarkand, many of the inhabitants have kept their national dress and way of life. In the bazaar, in the *chai-khanas* and on Fridays in the mosques you may still see the men wearing their turbans and brightly striped robes. For most Uzbek women, on the other hand, the veil is a thing of the past, though even now you occasionally get a glimpse of a completely veiled figure.

Whenever I return to Bokhara, which I seem to do surprisingly often, there is nothing I like better than to take a stroll through the winding, dusty alleyways of the old town, far more of which survives than one might at first sight suppose. Passing between the high uneven walls of sunbaked clay, I quickly recapture the mood and atmosphere of fifty years ago and rediscover the old sights and sounds and smells – the bright-eyed little Uzbek children in their miniature *khalats*, scuffling in the dust or peeping through windows and half-closed doors; the old men and women sitting outside their houses talking and drinking tea or preparing the food for the family's next meal; the scent of wood smoke and the very eastern aroma of Bokharan cooking; the sour smell of the all-pervading dust; here and there a sheep or goat tethered to a post; every now and then the sudden, persistent braying of a donkey; and sometimes, glimpsed through half-closed doors, an assembly of turbaned elders, in conference or at their devotions.

For me the ancient carved doors of Central Asia, set in the high clay walls of the houses, with their heavy bronze or iron bolts and hinges, have always held a particular fascination. From the street, the blank walls, the barred windows and padlocked doors give nothing away; behind them all is mystery – the stuff, one feels, of *The Thousand and One Nights*. But, like all Uzbeks, the Bokharans are in fact easy-going hospitable people, always ready to befriend a stranger, welcome him to their homes and ply him with green tea and other exotic delicacies, while exchanging views about life in general. Following a preliminary exchange of greetings you are quickly across the threshold and in an often astonishingly spacious inner courtyard with an apricot tree or two, a tall pillared and carpeted veranda and a number of conveniently sited wooden day-beds on which you sit cross-legged while consuming large quantities of strange sweetmeats and bowl after bowl of steaming green tea.

In Bokhara, as elsewhere in Central Asia, there is often more than meets the eye. Behind the high walls and closed doors, in the privacy of their own houses, some many hundreds of years old, some newly built in the same traditional style, many Bokharans, whether professing Moslems or not, still lead the traditional Moslem way of life, which has changed remarkably little over the centuries and which sixty-odd years of Soviet rule have, once you get below the surface, left relatively undisturbed. In its essence the culture of Central Asia is a religious, an Islamic culture. Seventy years after the Revolution, despite much discouragement, religious practices continue everywhere. Such mosques as remain open are packed and religious festivals are meticulously observed. Family influence is strong; young couples are married in the mosque; there is not much intermarriage between Uzbeks and Russians; for professing Moslems traditional Moslem funerals are a matter of course. Of late many young Uzbeks have, it appears, found a fresh interest in the Islamic traditions and culture of their own people. Side by side with the official activities of the Grand Mufti in Tashkent, who, like his father before him, is very much a part of the Soviet establishment, another, unofficial, one might almost say underground, Islamic cult exists. There are unofficial mosques, unregistered *mullahs* and *imams* and, even, if you know where to look, *sufis*. All of which, in its way, helps fill the spiritual vacuum left here as elsewhere by modern life.

I have been going to Samarkand and Bokhara on and off for many years. Their beauties remain undiminished. But from inaccessible eastern cities, steeped in mysterious lore, they have, superficially at any rate, become highly-developed tourist centres. For me this has robbed them of some of their charm and on recent journeys, I have looked elsewhere for a fresh insight into the customs and life of present-day Central Asia.

From Tashkent, the capital of Uzbekistan, you can in forty minutes fly to the town of Ferghana, formerly New Margilan. Surrounded on three-and-a-half sides by the foothills of the Pamirs, with access through a narrow gap in the mountains, the Ferghana Valley, in which Ferghana lies, was until its annexation by the Russians in 1875 part of the old Emirate of Kokand. Since the Middle Ages it has been famous for its fertility, for the speed and endurance of its horses and for its inhabitants' explosive nature and fanatical devotion to the Moslem faith.

More even than most journeys in Central Asia, the forty-minute flight from Tashkent brings home to you dramatically the difference between cultivation and desert, between the lush greenness of the oases and the bleak nothingness that lies all round them. From the air you can follow the course of the rivers, the Jaxartes or Syr Darya in particular, down from the great mountain ranges, where they rise, into the plain below, and also make out the intricate network of irrigation canals which of recent years have brought vast new areas under cultivation.

Certainly the Ferghana Valley more than lives up to its reputation for fruitfulness. I have tried only a few of the eighty different kinds of melon grown there, but the bazaars are full of them and those I have tasted were, like the peaches, grapes, nectarines and pistachio nuts enough to convince me I need look no further. Built as a Russian garrison town just over a hundred years ago, Ferghana is laid out in broad, tree-lined avenues running at right-angles to each other. Here and there modern blocks of flats have replaced the stucco villas built for the Tsar's officers and administrators, but in the main the town has kept its original character.

The day after we reached Ferghana was not only a Saturday, but some kind of public holiday and therefore, we reckoned, a good day for a trip into the mountains. The place we chose was Hamzabad, originally known as Shakh-i-Mardan after Ali Mardan, a famous Arab conqueror and holy man, who built a mosque there in the eighth century. In Central Asia, resistance to Soviet rule persisted for some years after the Revolution and in 1920 forty-eight hard-pressed Red Army soldiers found it necessary to fall back on Ali Mardan's mosque and make a stand there, whereupon the Basmatchi, as their opponents were called, burned it down with the unfortunate soldiers inside. In the years that followed it fell to Hamza, a local poet and keen supporter of the new ideas, to re-indoctrinate the unrepentant inhabitants of Shakh-i-Mardan. But this evidently proved an uphill task, for in 1929 Comrade Hamza was in his turn stoned to death by counter-revolutionaries, a fate he shared with a progressive school-mistress, who advocated the abolition of the veil for women, and a local actress, who persisted in appearing on stage unveiled. After those responsible had been duly punished, a handsome shrine in traditional Uzbek style was erected to the martyred Hamza on the site of the former mosque and the name of Shakh-i-Mardan changed to Hamzabad.

To make our journey to Hamzabad an even more memorable occasion, an Uzbek acquaintance had offered to accompany us and cook us some real Uzbek *plov* for our midday meal. *Plov*, in other words, *pilaff*, made of mutton and rice, and a great many others things as well, is an Uzbek speciality which I greatly appreciate and we accepted his invitation with enthusiasm. Before setting out from Ferghana we went shopping for the ingredients. Most of these, currants, onions, rice, carrots, spices and pistachio nuts, we bought in the bazaar. Meat was harder to come by, but after shopping around we found a piece of fat lamb in a village along the road. There had once been a mosque in the village, known as the Mazar or Shrine of the Pigeons. This had by now disappeared but from its dovecote, which still survived, a cloud of pigeons flew out and fluttered around. At a *chai-khana* under some ancient trees the village elders sat cross-legged, sipping green tea. Next to it was a baker's shop with ovens going full blast, producing large quantities of *nan*, the flat local unleavened bread. Fruit was no problem and thus provisioned we set out for Hamzabad.

Our map showed that on the way to Hamzabad we should for a few miles be passing through a valley which belonged to the neighbouring Republic of Kirghizia and, sure enough, the villagers we met by the roadside during the Kirghizian part of the journey had the flatter, more Mongoloid faces one associates with the Kirghiz and, instead of turbans or skull-caps, were wearing the strange mediaeval-looking white felt helmets which are their national headgear. But when we came to the next village a few miles along the road, there could be no doubt that we were back in Uzbekistan. Under the shade of an enormous sycamore, said to be eight hundred years old, several typical Uzbek family parties were drinking green tea at a *chai-khana*, the men in their traditional skull-caps and *khalats*, the women in beautifully-patterned dresses of fine Uzbek silk.

At Hamzabad, a holiday mood prevailed. A band was playing. There were booths in the streets at which you could buy ice-cream or hot pies or lollipops or get your photograph taken against an elaborately-painted backdrop, and the swings and roundabouts of a fairground were working full-time. Following the crowd, we climbed a steep paved stairway to a kind of plateau overlooking the town. This was where the Mosque of Ali Mardan had once stood. Now some monumental statuary commemorated the sad end of the forty-eight Red Army soldiers, while not far away was poor Hamza's miniature mausoleum.

But on this particular day, people's minds were not on the past. Nearby a drum was beating and a great crowd of excited Uzbeks was gathering round a troupe of native acrobats and weight-lifters, led by a man with bulging muscles, a stentorian fairground voice and an unrivalled gift for patter. At regular intervals a collection was taken up to which the crowd contributed enthusiastically, tossing whole handfuls of rouble notes into the ring. Looking round me, I noticed that acrobats and spectators, men, women and children, were all Uzbeks. There was not a Russian among them. Indeed the only incomer I met that day was a friendly old Tartar from the Crimea who had presumably been deported to Central Asia with the rest of the Crimean Tartars during the war on grounds of unreliability. By now he seemed quite contented with his lot and hospitably insisted on buying us a packet of biscuits.

Meanwhile, in a secluded valley four or five miles further up into the valley, our friend was busy cooking the *plov*, a process requiring several hours. The site he had chosen was a charming one. Over a rushing mountain torrent, several open pavilions had been built, on bridges spanning the stream. Nearby the *plov* was simmering on a primitive cooking stove, while the caretaker of this idyllic spot looked on with his wife and two pretty daughters. By now the *plov* was passing through its final stages. Rice, vegetables and mutton were solemnly mixed together over the glowing charcoal and carried in triumph to one of the pavilions where, sitting cross-legged on a carpet, we scooped it up with greasy fingers and stuffed it into no less greasy mouths. With it we drank fragrant green tea from elegant porcelain bowls, finishing off our feast with magnificent grapes and melons from the bazaar, while nearby a herd of yaks picked a scanty living from the stony hillside, lending an exotic air to the landscape.

One of my purposes in going to Ferghana was to visit the neighbouring city of Kokand, the capital of the former Emirate of that name. This, rather to my surprise, turned out to be practicable and the following morning we set out by car in a north-westerly direction without being very sure what we should find when we got there. The country we passed through was typical of Central Asia; white, dusty roads under the August sun, rows of poplars along the irrigation ditches, emerald green patches of cultivation, heavily laden vines and fruit trees, and a line of blue mountains on the skyline. Here and there along the road we passed villages and individual farm houses, mostly built of mud-bricks. At one point we crossed the famous Ferghana Canal which fills the irrigation ditches and brings fertility to the whole area.

Further on, we stopped at the little town of Rishtan, where, even more than in Ferghana, the bazaar is the centre of local life, its stalls, under a trellis of vines, piled high with produce and its alleyways teeming with a jostling, brightly-dressed crowd of Uzbek men, women and children, buying and selling for all they are worth. At the entrance a heavily-bearded bootmaker was plying his trade. Just inside I was delighted to find a turbaned snuff-merchant selling the pungent green Uzbek snuff, to which I have long been addicted, at fifty kopeks a bottle. Not far away a woman had a stall full of the traditional black and white skull caps, originally turban-bases, which are worn throughout Turkestan while once or twice we actually caught sight of a completely veiled woman, hidden from head to foot in a *paranja*, a horse-hair contraption like a meat-safe. Here, far more than in Ferghana, one felt oneself totally immersed in the life and traditions of Central Asia.

For centuries a stopping-place on the Silk Road from China, Kokand has kept much of its original character. It was here that the first silk-worms were brought from China, concealed in a hollow stick, and to this day the area is still the centre of a flourishing silk industry, which even produces pure silk portraits of Lenin. Scattered through the town are the ancient caravanserais where the merchants from China made halt on their long journeys westwards. Of recent years nothing has come from China save abuse and the caravanserais for the most part serve other purposes.

The immense Jami or Friday Mosque built by Omar Khan in 1811 with its spacious courtyard and forest of carved columns is no longer in use, but at least one mosque is still working. This, with the medresseh or religious college attached to it, I found to be a most agreeable place, patronized by a number of friendly elderly gentlemen, who, when not at their devotions, seemed to use it as a club as much as anything. In the forecourt, vines grew on trellises and one of the greybeards, nimbly climbing a ladder, hospitably handed us down a bunch or two of grapes.

Noticing a Moslem funeral makings its noisy way through the streets, I followed it to the adjacent graveyard. This centres round two rather handsome early nineteenth-century royal mausoleums, the Dakma-i-Shakhan and the Madar-i-Khan. It also contains a number of recent monuments to local Mohammedan notabilities including a fine new marble monument to Nadir, the wife of one early nineteenth-century Emir, who seems to have won the retrospective approval of the Soviet authorities by her allegedly forward-looking attitude towards women's rights.

In a pavilion nearby some Uzbek girls and women were busily stitching away, elegant in their silk *khalats*. 'What are they making?' I asked. 'Shrouds,' came the answer. Meanwhile all through the graveyard a dozen small boys, lively as only little Uzbeks can be, were playing hide-and-seek among the turbaned tombstones, while several dozen more were bathing with merry shrieks in the fountains of the nearby public garden, climbing up the statuary and taking headers into the pools below, their brown bodies glistening in the midday sun.

One is reminded that Kokand came under Russian rule not much more than a hundred years ago by the semi-fortified former palace of the Emirs, finished in 1873. In the event, the last Emir did not enjoy its somewhat tawdry splendour for long; nor did its fortifications stand him in very good stead. 'Every spring ends in autumn. Nothing is for ever', runs an apt inscription above the entrance gate. Its truth was to be proved all too soon. Having made his peace with the Russians and duly accepted the suzerainty of the Tsar in 1865, he was swept from his throne in 1875 by a national insurrection of such violence that the Russians were also obliged to withdraw only to return in strength a few months later, this time without the Emir. Today his palace is a museum, its state apartments containing some rather moth-eaten stuffed animals and a number of historical exhibits vividly depicting the horrors of life under the Emir and clearly designed to convince the public that they are probably better off now than they would have been under any previous regime.

With the architectural splendours of Samarkand and Bokhara, Kokand has little to compare. The city's interest lies rather in its people and their way of life, best observed in the bazaar and the *chai-khanas*, in one of which – brand-new, but built in the traditional style – we refreshed ourselves with a pot or two of green tea before returning to Ferghana.

Racially almost all the peoples of Soviet Central Asia have a strong Turanian strain and the languages they speak are akin to Turkish. But the Tajiks, who live high up in the valleys and foothills of the Pamirs, where the frontiers of the Soviet Union converge with those of China, Afghanistan, Pakistan and India, are by race, language and civilization more akin to Persians and within living memory still managed to smuggle small sums of money across the frontier as tribute to their religious leader, the Aga Khan. Ninety-three per cent of the Republic of Tajikstan is mountainous; indeed it can boast some of the highest mountains in the world and, not unnaturally, hydro-electric power has played an important part in Tajikstan's industrial development. Dushambe, the capital, once Stalinabad, is a completely modern town of a quarter of a million inhabitants and the centre of a thriving cotton industry. It has a Park of Rest and Culture with an ornamental lake for bathing and boating and a modern speedway leading up into the mountains. The local mullah told me that it now has four mosques, as against one before the Revolution, though then, of course, it was no more than a village. Certainly the mosque I visited was thronged by a numerous and devout congregation and afterwards there was a great gathering of bearded and turbaned elders in the streets outside, while as recently as the winter of 1986/87 religious rioting in and around the Tajik town of Kurgantepe, following the arrest of a popular local *mullah*, showed that Islam was still a considerable force there.

From the ruins of the ancient town of Pendjikent, also in Tajikstan, on the Uzbek border, a few hours' drive south-east from Samarkand, you look across to the foothills of the Pamirs where, far away to the south, China meets Afghanistan. A Sogdian settlement, dating back to the fifth or sixth century of our era, Pendjikent was deserted by its inhabitants after the Arab invasion of Central Asia in the eighth century, when they took to the nearby hills for a final stand against the Arabs. The remains of the town, which cover an area of nearly fifty acres, have now been thoroughly excavated and to the trained eye of the archaeologist, though not to mine, reveal an intricate network of intersecting streets, a market square, various places of worship and large numbers of dwelling houses. Indeed, from their discoveries there, the experts have managed to piece together a remarkably complete picture of life in pre-Moslem Central Asia.

Seventy years after the Revolution, the Mohammedan religion is still very much alive in Turkestan. On Fridays and Holy Days the remaining mosques are crowded and, as the cry of the muezzin sounds from the minaret, you may see a great concourse of worshippers bowing down and standing up and intoning the responses and prayers, while afterwards alms and gifts of food are distributed to those in need. Even those shrines which have officially been deconsecrated and turned into museums still receive a steady stream of visitors whose interest is clearly religious rather than cultural and in Samarkand, in the Shakh-i-Zindeh, as you climb from one blue-domed mausoleum to another, you are apt to break in on the meditations of devout worshippers. But the powers that be are no longer seriously concerned as they were immediately after the revolution. Fifty or sixty years ago, the Soviet authorities were still having trouble with the mullahs. Now there are few signs of conflict and from his headquarters in Tashkent, the Grand Mufti of Central Asia, whose late father I met when he held the same office thirty years ago, maintains the most amicable relations with the regime, indeed has become in many ways a pillar of the Soviet establishment. There were, he told me recently, now probably as many as thirty or forty million Moslems in the Soviet Union. Meanwhile everywhere the old order is making way for the new. Ancient customs and traditions are disappearing and new ones are taking their place. New buildings are going up and a new, more efficient, more hygienic, though less picturesque way of life is taking shape.

The former Kokandi town of Tashkent, once the seat of the Tsar's Governor-General of Turkestan, is today capital of the Soviet Republic of Uzbekistan and, with a population of close on two million, has kept its position as the chief city of Central Asia and the focus of a flourishing cotton industry. Just on fifty years ago, when I first went there, it was still neatly divided into a European and an Uzbek city, with the cantonments of the conquering race arranged in well laid-out avenues and the native quarter clustering round the bazaar. With the help of an earthquake, the old native town has by now almost completely disappeared and been replaced by magnificent new parks and avenues and blocks of flats and hotels and well-stocked department stores and an immense stadium. But at heart it remains a Central Asian city and of late I have eaten many a delicious al fresco meal of *plov* and green tea and strange Oriental sweetmeats in one or other of its open-air restaurants and *chai-khanas*. While here, as elsewhere, in private Uzbek homes, individual Uzbeks continue to lead their private Uzbek lives.

3

The Black Sands

Rejoicing through the hush'd Chorasmian waste.

MATTHEW ARNOLD

In 1873 the Russians, having conquered the greater part of Turkestan, turned their attention to the still independent Khanate of Khiva, long the centre of a flourishing slave trade. Here an able-bodied Russian, male or female, could be bought in the bazaar for less than a pound sterling – in itself something of a provocation. Previous expeditions had been defeated by the waterless desert surrounding the oasis – the Kara Kum, or Black Sands. By now well established as Governor-General of Turkestan, General von Kaufmann left nothing to chance. His force was divided into four columns. In May 1873 the main column, under Kaufmann himself, started from Tashkent. Another set out from Orenburg, on the borders of European Russia, and two more from the Caspian ports of Krasnovodsk and Fort Alexandrovski. The column from Krasnovodsk suffered so much from heat and lack of water that they were obliged to turn back, but by the end of May, after a notable approach march across the desert, the other three columns had reached their objectives and on 10 June Khiva fell almost without a fight. Kaufmann now entered the city in triumph, and a couple of months later he and the Khan sat down to sign a treaty, under which the latter ceded a large part of his territory to the Russians and placed the remainder under Russian protection.

Today, though some of its inhabitants, after a few years' absence, have been allowed to return, Khiva remains in essence a museum town. The real life of the district centres round the neighbouring town of New Urgench and the thriving cotton plantations and sheep farms of the oasis, which with improved systems of irrigation is rapidly growing in size and fertility. Even so, Ichan Kala, the walled and fortified Inner City of Khiva, still presents a remarkably complete picture of a Central Asian city precinct, with its fortress, its walls and gates, its caravanserais and covered bazaar, its mosques and palaces and baths and ordinary dwelling houses, all standing exactly as they were in the days of the last Khan.

Built of clay and sunbaked bricks, the walls, ramparts, bastions and gates of the Inner City, are still intact. Ichan Kala lies roughly north and south. Entering it by the West Gate, you come immediately upon Kunya Ark, the Old Citadel, which until the early nineteenth century also served as the Khan's residence and seat of government. A fortress within a fortress, its walls enclose a man-made mound, crowned with crumbling ruins. From this you look out across the gardens, mulberry trees, orchards and vineyards of Dishan Kala, the Outer City, to the irrigated fields of the oasis and beyond them to the howling wilderness of the Kara Kum.

The Old Citadel dates from the seventeenth century. Of the complex of courtyards and buildings where the Khans once held court, took counsel and dispensed justice, much has disappeared, but from the ruins of the castle you still look down on the *aivans* or pillared recesses of the mosque built by Allah Kuli Khan (1825–42) and of the older Kurinishkana. Curiously enough, most of the buildings in Khiva, though very similar in style to those of Samarkand or Bokhara, are by contrast of quite recent origin, dating in the main from the first half of the nineteenth century. To the south of the Old Citadel are the mosque, medresseh and minaret of Madamin or Mohammed Amin Khan, built in 1851–2 and recently converted into a hotel. Madamin's intention was that they should outshine every other building in Khiva and that their minaret should be the finest and tallest in all Central Asia. But, before the minaret could be finished, he was killed by marauding Turkomans and the great minaret, magnificent as far as it went, remained unfinished, a truncated stump, known as Kalta Minar, the Short Minaret.

One of the most beautiful buildings in Khiva is the Mausoleum of Pahlavan Mahmud with its fine octagonal blue and white dome. Built between 1810 and 1835, it stands in the southern quarter of the Inner City and served as a burial place for the reigning dynasty. The interior of the cupola is decorated with magnificent majolica tiles. Pahlavan Mahmud, the holy man whose name it bears and who lies buried in it under a handsome green-tiled tomb, lived in the fourteenth century. He was also a poet, a more than adequate wrestler and a first-class furrier. High above his mausoleum and above the rest of Khiva towers the minaret of Islam Khoja, built, together with the nearby mosque, by a Grand Vizir of that name in the reign of the last Khan of Khiva, who held sway from 1910 until, like his neighbour in Bokhara, he was driven out by the Red Army in 1920.

On the far side of the Inner City, three or four hundred yards from the Ark, a group of diverse buildings cluster round Palvan Darvaza, the East Gate of the city and its turreted gate-house. Here, just outside the walls, are the caravanserai and covered bazaar, the Mosque of Allah Kuli Khan, the older Ak-Mechet or Blue Mosque, the Mosque of Kutlug Murad and the Baths built in 1657 by Abulgazi Khan to celebrate a victory over the Bokharans.

Here too is the Tash Hauli, the new royal palace which Allah Kuli Khan built for himself in the 1830s. Within its solid outside wall, the Tash Hauli consists of three main courtyards. The first of these was used as a harem, the second for banquets, audiences and other state occasions and the third as a court of justice. Giving on to the courtyards are a number of two-storeyed buildings, the rooms on the upper floor opening on to a gallery supported by finely-carved wooden columns. All the buildings are lavishly decorated with fine majolica tiles. As in the smaller Khivan houses, the *aivans* face north, being carefully designed to catch any cool breezes in the hot weather and channel them into the rooms within. In winter low brick platforms in the courtyards provided a base for the yurts or circular felt tents, heated by braziers, in which the Khan and his entourage, reverting to the habits of their nomad forebears, sought refuge from the cold.

By bringing Khiva under their protection the Russians virtually completed their conquest of Turkestan. Between the frontiers of Russia and those of Persia and Afghanistan only the desolate region known in tsarist days as Transcaspia and today as Turkmenistan remained to be subdued. This was inhabited by the unruly Tekke-Turkmens, the most notorious marauders in Central Asia. Since 1869 the Russians had held the port of Krasnovodsk on the Caspian, which for administrative purposes was included in the governorship-general of the Caucasus. From this base, a strong Russian force set out across the desert in September 1879 to attack the Turkmen stronghold of Geok Tepe, but were driven off by the Turkmens with heavy losses. A second expedition was accordingly mounted under the command of the dashing and flamboyant General Skobelyev, popularly known as the White General, who in January 1881 with a force of over 7,000 men took Geok Tepe by storm and massacred every one of its defenders. 'The harder you hit them,' he would observe, 'the longer they will stay quiet afterwards.' Soon after this, Transcaspia was annexed to Russia, leaving the remote oasis of Merv to be mopped up three years later.

By 1885 Russia's conquest of Central Asia was complete. Her territories marched with those of China to the east and Afghanistan and Persia to the south. At one point they were barely separated by a narrow strip of Afghan territory from the borders of British India. Of the independent khanates and emirates with which Central Asia had once abounded, only Bokhara and Khiva survived, both as Russian protectorates.

With the outbreak of the Russian Revolution in 1917 and the ensuing civil war and Allied intervention, Central Asia was again thrown into turmoil. Briefly, Bokhara and Khiva recovered their independence, while for a time a British force occupied parts of Transcaspia. But in the end the whole area was reabsorbed by Soviet Russia and five Soviet Socialist Republics created in Central Asia – Kazakhstan, Kirghizia, Uzbekistan, Tajikstan and Turkmenistan.

Today the flight westwards by Tupolev jet from Tashkent to Ashkhabad, capital of the Soviet Socialist Republic of Turkmenistan, takes a couple of hours, for the most part over the Kara Kum or Black Sands, a howling wilderness which makes most other deserts I have visited look like garden suburbs. As we approached our destination, a line of blue mountains appeared to the south, the Kopet Dagh, which marks the Soviet border with Iran. At Ashkhabad airport the thermometer stood at 120 degrees and the midday sun blazed down mercilessly on the tarmac. On this, my first visit, we found the portentous-looking new concrete Hotel Ashkhabad closed for repairs and were relegated to an older, smaller and altogether more agreeable hotel where we were given a large airy first-floor bedroom and sitting-room opening on to a wide veranda with, beyond that, a green tree-shaded garden. A fountain tinkled. Two Turkmen girls in long dark-red dresses and kerchiefs with their hair in plaits brushed up the leaves and from the ceiling of our room the massive blades of an ancient electric fan kept the air gently moving. It was all rather like pre-war British India.

Our hotel had no restaurant and for dinner we were directed to the Brigantine. The Soviet Union is full of surprises and the Brigantine certainly came as one to me. A single-storeyed, kidney-shaped, air-conditioned, surrealist night-club, built from ferro-concrete and glass round a central courtyard filled with brightly-lit exotic plants and culminating in an intensely expressive wrought-iron ornament is somehow not what you expect in deepest Turkmenistan. Like all good restaurants in the Soviet Union, it was packed. Fortunately there was one table left, which we seized. Rather a good band, silhouetted against a red glow, was playing the Charleston and a large number of the more sophisticated citizens of Ashkhabad were dancing it with enthusiasm and skill.

One couple stood out from the rest: a tall, sallow cadaverous Turkmen in a pale tangerine-coloured shirt, with aquiline features and a long drooping moustache faced an equally tall, fair, elegant Russian girl with high cheekbones, a body like indiarubber and a fantastic sense of rhythm, who danced like one possessed, swinging and jerking a long string of beads further to accentuate the beat. 'Bye, bye, blackbird. Blackbird, bye, bye,' went the band, putting everything they had got into it, as the dancing became faster and more furious. Meanwhile in a corner of the room, two gigantic Georgians with black curly hair and moustaches were busy dancing their own national Georgian dances, circling and prancing to the beat of some quite different rhythm which only they could hear.

Ashkhabad, which started life as a remote Russian garrison town, a far-flung outpost of empire amid a potentially hostile population, has nothing much to offer the sightseer in the way of antiquities except for the remains of the Gorka, an ancient Turkmen mud fortress of indeterminate age and shape, and the Russian governor's charming late nineteenth-century palace. Until barely a century ago, the Turkmens, like the Kazakhs and Kirghiz, were largely nomads, moving with their flocks and herds from one scanty patch of pasture to another and supplementing their slender earnings by carpet-weaving, brigandage and the slave trade, the slaves and the carpets being marketed in Bokhara and Khiva. Indeed what are usually known in the West as Bokhara carpets are in fact Turkmen in origin and an expert can tell at a glance by which Turkmen tribe they were made. Today you can still see them being woven on hand looms by rows of Turkmen girls in their national dress.

With a rather fierce air that distinguishes them from their more stolid Uzbek neighbours, the Turkmens, beneath their enormous shaggy sheepskin busbies, are a fine-looking race. The women, dressed for the most part in national dress, are often extremely pretty and make me wonder whether, after robbing a Russian or Persian caravan, their forebears had not kept back some of the better-looking captives as mates for themselves.

There are, so far as I know, no working mosques left in Ashkhabad, but a few miles outside the town we found the fifteenth-century Mosque or Mausoleum of Khan Abdul Kasim Babur. Though both the mosque and the much older Sassanid fortress inside which it was built had been badly damaged by an earthquake, it was still possible to identify two white dragons on a blue ground above the sixty-foot arch. Despite seismic and ideological vicissitudes, it has remained a holy place and pious Moslems are still taken there to be buried.

Since my first visit the main bazaar of Ashkhabad has long since been roofed in and another massive concrete structure built to meet the growing demands of the private sector of agriculture. Most of the more prosperous peasants now bring their produce to market in their own cars, which, with those of their more well-to-do customers, are parked in rows outside. Many of the peasants still wear the traditional sheepskin busbies and I know of no finer sight than two of them, thus accoutred, racing neck-and-neck down the main road on the bright red Czechoslovak motor-bikes which have replaced their once famous Turkmen horses. Camels, on the other hand, are still plentiful in Turkmenistan and out in the country you see any number of them, grazing by the roadside or moving in stately procession across the desert.

On my latest visit I found to my dismay that the old hotel where I used to stay no longer admitted foreigners and that, whether we liked it or not, we had been accommodated in the new, bigger, more solid, but far less commodious Hotel Ashkhabad, a massively-built concrete structure in the sub-Mexican-prehistoric style now favoured by the government of Turkmenistan, which to my mind compares most unfavourably with the grander, more oriental manner encouraged by Generalissimo Stalin in his heyday. I was equally disappointed to discover that since my last visit the Brigantine, so recently the rendezvous of the *beau monde* of Ashkhabad, had been half demolished and left to moulder, while the bold bit of symbolic metalwork which once served as its sign now projected disconsolately and incongruously from a hole in the ground just across the road from the local Institute of Marxism–Leninism. The night-life of Ashkhabad, however, had found a fresh venue in the restaurant of the Hotel Ashkhabad, where both Turkmens and Russians still rock happily to the latest and noisiest American jazz.

Meanwhile present-day Ashkhabad is expanding rapidly in every direction as ever higher high-rise buildings accommodate an ever-growing urban population and the old Turkmen way of life recedes ever further into the past. Watching a film one night on Turkmen television about a blonde Russian village maiden who goes to Moscow, is caught up in big-city show business, love and romance, appears briefly in a variety show in top hat, white tie and tails, but finally gives it all up and goes home to tend her dying mother and marry the companion of her youth, I could not help reflecting, not without a touch of melancholy, on the growing sum of similarities between the two Superpowers. On the other hand, I comforted myself with the thought that, however trashy, the film I had been watching at least held the attention and, as far as I could see, conveyed no political or ideological message whatever beyond the vague and universally acceptable assumption that East, West, Home's Best (though not always quite such fun).

If you are lucky (and extremely persistent), Ashkhabad can serve as a jumping-off place for a trip to one of the most fascinating places in the Soviet Union: the ancient ruined city of Marghiana or Merv, once Queen of the World. Accordingly, on a recent visit, having applied to the local branch of the Department of State Security, in other words the KGB, for the special visas required to visit Merv, a hundred and fifty miles away across the desert, and knowing from past experience that I would not get a decision immediately, I spent the next couple of days exploring the country round Ashkhabad itself.

Twenty or thirty miles away, at the foot of the Kopet Dagh range, the crumbling walls and watchtowers of Nisa, capital of the Parthian kings from the second century BC to the third century AD enclose a vast area of ground. After scrambling over them for two or three hours in the blazing sun, I was gladder than I would normally have been to drink a large tumbler of sour camel's milk at a wayside tavern, followed by several welcome glasses of vodka with three jolly Soviet infantry subalterns, two Russians and a Turkmen, out for the day from the nearest barracks.

Next day a rather less rewarding expedition took us some fifty miles to Bakharden, where, with a number of other seekers after health, we swam claustrophobically in the dark in a hot underground sulphur lake, hundreds of feet beneath the Kopet Dagh and at no great distance from the Iranian frontier. On the way there we stopped briefly at Geok Tepe where, behind the railway station, I managed to find the remains of the great Turkmen fortress stormed by General Skobelyev in 1881, together with a rather battered monument celebrating the event. A few miles away to the south, on the border with Iran, we could see the spur of the Kopet Dagh from which Edmund O'Donovan, Special Correspondent of the *London Daily News*, watched each phase of the battle and ensuing massacre, before making his way to Merv. Asked how she felt about things, an immensely old Turkmen woman, who had actually been a child of six at the time of the massacre, put it all in a nutshell. 'Too many Tsars!' she said wearily. 'Alexander, Nicholas, Lenin, Stalin, Khrushchov, Brezhnev – too many Tsars!'

Next day I was informed to my surprise and delight that our visas for Merv had been granted and the day after that we took off for our slightly improbable-sounding destination in a tightly-packed local plane, full of howling babies and squawking hens, rather like a local bus in the Highlands of Scotland. After successive dynasties and civilizations had flourished there in turn over the centuries and made of it one of the most famous cities in the world, the end came quite suddenly for Merv in the late eighteenth century, when the neighbouring Bokharans, in the course of a periodic bout of bickering, hit on the ingenious idea of simply changing the course of the neighbouring Murgab River, thus depriving the population of their water-supply and transforming the once flourishing oasis into the arid wilderness it is today.

For all this, Merv is still by any standards an extraordinary place, littered with the ruins of its remarkable past. Here, scattered over fifty square miles of desert, are the remains of four or five walled cities. Of these the northernmost and also the oldest is Iskander-Kala, the Fortress of Alexander, so called after its founder, Alexander the Great of Macedon. To the east is Giaour-Kala, the Fortress of the Infidels, dating in part from the second century BC. This was a Sasanid city which later possessed a large population

The Mountains of Heaven from Alma Ata

Horsemen, Kirghisia

Gur Emir, Samarkand

OPPOSITE The Short Minaret, Khiva

The Bazaar, Samarkand

The Bazaar, Samarkand

OPPOSITE Shakh-i-zindeh, Samarkand

Shirdar, Samarkand

OPPOSITE Shirdar, Samarkand

Mother and Child, Bokhara

OPPOSITE The Registan, Samarkand

Outside the Mosque, Bokhara

'Green Tea', Bokhara

OPPOSITE At Prayer, Bokhara

Bokhara

OPPOSITE The Tower of Death, Bokhara

A Kirghiz Shepherd and Son

Mother and Son, Hamzabad

OPPOSITE An Uzbek

'Green Snuff', Rishtan

of Nestorian Christians. It also contains, if you know where to look, the remains of some Buddhist shrines. To the west is Sultan-Kala, the Fortress of the Seljuk Sultans, once destroyed by the Mongols but later rebuilt. At its centre stands the great domed *mazar* or mausoleum of the famous Seljuk Sultan Sanjar who made the whole area fertile by damming the Murgab and whose work was undone six hundred years later by the Emir of Bokhara when he destroyed the dam.

Some of the ruins, including the eleventh-century Mosque of Sultan Sanjar, are being restored by highly qualified experts, one of whom told me that they had found fresh evidence to show that it was much older than had previously been believed. (He went on to expound some theories about early UFOs, which, I must say, rather shook my faith in him.) Several other Moslem shrines and holy places, such as the mosques of Mohammed Ibn Seid and Talkhatan Baba, which date back to the eleventh and twelfth centuries respectively, have been kept in repair by local Moslem worshippers. In one we found an immensely old woman, rather like Rider Haggard's Gagool, who seemed to be living there permanently and readily brewed us a most welcome cup of tea. Though there were no signs of a *mullah* or anyone else, little bits of coloured rag tied to the trees and bushes and numerous banners and flags testified to fairly frequent visits by the faithful. Other buildings go back to pre-Moslem times, before the Arab invasion, notably a number of strangely corrugated fortresses that rise gauntly from the surrounding desert.

Merv, ruins and all, finally fell to the Russians in the year 1884, three years after the fall of Geok Tepe, causing what the then Duke of Argyll wittily called a moment of 'Mervousness' to the British government of the day, already seriously disquieted by the speed of the Russian advance in Central Asia. During its last few months of independence, the oasis was briefly ruled over by that enterprising Irish reporter, Edmund O'Donovan of the *Daily News*, who, having made his way there from the stricken field of Geok Tepe, was on his arrival promptly elected Khan by the inhabitants in the, as it turned out, vain hope that the election of a British Khan might encourage Queen Victoria's ministers to rescue them from the advancing Russians.

After a prolonged inspection of the ruins in the sweltering heat and a copious meal of *plov* and iced beer in a wayside *chai-khana*, presided over by a massive Turkmen manageress, I caught the plane back to Ashkhabad, happy in the knowledge that Soviet Central Asia now held no more mysteries for me.

From Ashkhabad, if that is how you choose to go, a direct flight carries you swiftly to Baku and within an hour or so of take-off we were soaring high above the green metallic waters of the Caspian en route for the scenic and other marvels of the Caucasus and Transcaucasia.

PART THREE

MOUNTAIN OF LANGUAGES

We Romans conducted our affairs there
with the aid of one hundred and thirty interpreters.

PLINY

1

Military Highway

By thinking on the frosty Caucasus.

WILLIAM SHAKESPEARE

If ever there was a frontier, it is the Caucasus, the great mountain barrier stretching from the Black Sea to the Caspian, dividing Europe from Asia, West from East, Christendom from Islam. With its foothills the main range stretches from east to west for about six hundred and fifty miles. Of this the highest mountains, at the centre, account for some four hundred miles, the foothills falling away gradually for another hundred miles or so to the Black Sea on the west and to the Caspian on the east.

To the ancients the Caucasus was the End of the World. Here Jason and his Argonauts came in search of the Golden Fleece. Here, in the magic land of Colchis, Medea cast her spells. Here Prometheus was chained by the gods to Mount Kazbek and an eagle sent to tear at his liver. Here, today, the frontiers of three countries meet – Turkey, Iran and the USSR. And here, in this great tangle of mountains and valleys, you will find a mixture of races, languages, religions and civilizations such as exists nowhere else in the world. 'The Mountain of Languages', the Arabs called it and Pliny tells us that the Romans conducted their affairs there with the aid of no less than one hundred and thirty interpreters.

Transcaucasia, the land beyond the Caucasus, is now divided into three Soviet Socialist Republics: Georgia, Armenia and Azerbaijan. Azerbaijan, before becoming part of Russia, was a Tartar khanate, not very different from its neighbours across the Caspian. The history of the two Christian countries reaches back into the remotest antiquity. Noah's Ark, we know, came to rest on Mount Ararat. While the Armenians trace their descent from Noah's great-great-grandson, Haik, and call their country Hayastan, or Land of Haik, the Georgians claim that they go back to Haik's brother Karthlos and call themselves Kartvelhi or Karthlians, and their country Sakartvelo or Karthli.

Although there are numerous other ways of doing so, I would from choice approach the Caucasus and Transcaucasia from the north, so as to savour more fully the sudden transition from the rolling steppes of southern Russia to the entirely different world you enter as soon as you reach the northern foothills of the Caucasus. As a jumping-off place I would choose the little town of Pyatigorsk in the northern Caucasus and, following the foothills of the main range, make my way thence by car to Ordzhonikidze at the northern end of the Georgian Military Highway, the great strategic road which the Russians began building two centuries ago and which takes you right across the Caucasus to Tbilisi, the capital of Georgia, a distance in all of about one hundred and twenty miles.

Pyatigorsk, made famous by the poet Lermontov, who lived there for a time, while serving as a soldier in the Caucasus, is easily reached by air or, more agreeably, by train from Moscow. In Russian Pyatigorsk means Five Hills. The hills in question rise abruptly from the plain to the west of the town, while a sixth, Mount Mashuk, dominates it from the north-east. Far away to the south, on the horizon you can, on a clear day, see the whole of the Caucasus spread out before you with the snowy peak of Mount Elbruz towering high above the rest.

Pyatigorsk is first and foremost a watering-place. Most of its hot springs and mineral baths are pleasantly situated in some well-tended public gardens above the town. In any one of a number of handsome early nineteenth-century buildings you can, if you feel so inclined or your doctor tells you to do so, drink their warm sulphurous waters or soak yourself in them to your heart's content. On a hill overlooking the gardens are the Elizabeth Gallery and Elizabeth Spring and, another seven or eight hundred feet above that, stands a kind of belvedere from which proceeds, as it did in Lermontov's day, the agreeable humming of an aeolian harp. For Lermontov, you will find, is still the presiding genius of Pyatigorsk, Lermontov, who spent the last months of his short life there and met his end in an unnecessary but somehow predestined duel at the foot of Mount Mashuk. Not far away is the thatched whitewashed cottage which he rented and which now contains an ingeniously assembled collection of his sketches and manuscripts. In the centre of the town the former Assemby Rooms with their fine classical portico recall the famous ball described by him in *A Hero of Our Time*.

From Pyatigorsk it is an easy day's drive eastwards to Ordzhonikidze, skirting along the northern foothills of the Caucasus. Some forty miles before reaching Ordzhonikidze you come to the River Terek and the lonely Minaret of Tatartub, marking the famous ford across the Terek, where in 1395 Tamerlane defeated Toktamish and finally broke the power of the Golden Horde. Formerly known as Vladikavkaz, the Ruler of the Caucasus, Ordzhonikidze was originally a garrison town which in due course developed into a fashionable resort. Today it is the principal city of Northern Ossetia. A double row of lime trees planted down the middle of the main street make it a pleasant enough place for a stroll between the cheerfully painted, stucco-fronted shops and houses. Nearby, on the banks of the fast-flowing Terek, are public gardens with swings and roundabouts, a boating-lake and stucco statues of generously built sports-girls. In the green garden-restaurant of the early nineteenth-century hotel, a regular coaching inn, you can dine well and discreetly in your own vine arbour or, if you are lucky, join in the liveliest of local reels to a blast of primitive but nonetheless invigorating pipe music, for here already you are in tribal country.

Before leaving Ordzhonikidze, it is worth spending a day or two exploring some of the northern valleys of the Caucasus. Setting out in a westerly direction by a road which skirts the northern foothills, you reach after an hour or so a gap in the hills marking the entrance to the valley of a tributary of the Terek, the Fiagdon or Crazy River. Turning southwards along it you pass through the Kurtatinski or Kurdish Gorge, so named after some mediaeval Kurdish invader who, tired of campaigning, married a local girl and made his home there. Then, as the valley broadens out, you come to a succession of ancient fortified Ossetian villages dating back to the days of the Mongol invasions.

There have been few changes since the time of the Mongols. Here towers take the place of houses: high look-out towers, from which to watch for the approach of an enemy; fighting towers for warriors, with arrow-slits and loopholes from which to meet an attack; dwelling-towers into which animals, women, children and old people could be herded in case of danger; and finally towers for the dead, each with a narrow hole through which the family's corpses were pushed until there was room for no more. In the last six or seven hundred years some of the towers have fallen down and been rebuilt and some have been extended and adapted. But the people who live here still lead a simple pastoral existence with which they seem well content and which, they proudly tell you, produces a record number of centenarians. In one village I met an old lady of at least eighty, carrying a roast chicken and a bottle of wine who, as she strode off up the hill-side, proudly announced that she was on her way to visit her granny, who was not feeling too fit.

Further along the valley is the village of Tsimitar, poised four or five hundred feet above the river and commanding the valley in both directions. Here too are watch-towers, fighting-towers, dwelling-towers and death-towers. In the valley below stands a bronze horse with empty saddle, commemorating the local Ossetian villagers, mostly cavalrymen, who died fighting Hitler's Germans.

These glens and valleys have a bloodstained past. Not far from the Fiagdon is the valley of the Gizeldon or Red River, so called because it ran red with blood at the time of the Mongol invasions. Nearby another memorial recalls that at this same point seven centuries later, in 1942, the invading Germans were at long last thrown back after yet another bloody battle. A little way from the main memorial another more personal monument represents a flight of seven cranes, commemorating seven Ossetian brothers born in the nearby village and all seven killed in the last war. The brothers, whose memory is still proudly cherished locally, are the subject of some famous lines by the poet Rasul Gamzatov from neighbouring Daghestan:

I sometimes think that warriors brave
Who met their death in bloody fight
Were never buried in a grave
But rose as cranes with plumage white

Since then until this very day
They pass high overhead and cry.

Is that not why we often gaze
In silence as the cranes go by?

Twenty miles west of the Fiagdon, near the town of Alagir, the valley of the Ardon, also a tributary of the Terek, marks the starting-point of another famous strategic road, the Ossetian Military Highway, leading across the mountains to Kutaisi in Western Georgia and likewise built to help the Russians control the turbulent tribes of the Western Caucasus.

Crossing the main range of the Caucasus by the Georgian Military Highway is never dull. Even the Alps seem tame by comparison. Starting from Ordzhonikidze, you begin by following the course of the River Terek to where it emerges from the mountains. At first the river valley, strewn with enormous boulders, is relatively wide. But gradually it closes in. Wooded hills rise steeply on either side of the road. Beyond them, above the tree-line, rise higher rocky peaks and, in the side valleys, strategically sited in case of sudden attack, are more Ossetian villages with their watch-towers and their clusters of stone huts.

Soon you come to a massive old Russian fort once no doubt an outpost of the famous Cossack Line. At this point the valley narrows dramatically. The Terek is by now a rushing mountain torrent and on both sides of the road vertical precipices of granite five or six thousand feet high tower immediately above you. This is the famous Darial Gorge, Dar-i-Alan, the Gate of the Alans, as the forefathers of Ossetians were called, and here the Iberian Gates marked the limit of the Roman advance under Pompey. Perched on a rocky crag high above the river are the ruins of an ancient fortress, claimed to be the castle of the famous Georgian Queen Tamara, who is said by some to have had her discarded lovers thrown down from its battlements into the raging torrent below.

Another ten miles further on the road dips down to the level of the river and, rounding a great shoulder of rock, you suddenly find yourself looking, if the weather is clear, at the towering snow-capped mass of Mount Kazbek, sixteen and a half thousand feet above sea-level and eleven thousand feet above Kazbek village, which lies immediately ahead of you. It was to this mighty mountain that Prometheus was chained by the gods.

After Kazbek village, the road starts to climb in earnest, zigzagging up several thousand feet to the Krestovi Pass or Pass of the Cross, so called after an enormous cross erected there by Queen Tamara many centuries ago. The last village before you reach the watershed is Kobi, an Ossetian settlement where within living memory pagan sacrifices were still offered at an altar adorned with goats' horns. From the rocks in which it rises, the Terek here comes leaping down in a rushing torrent. On one craggy pinnacle high above the road, I recently noticed painted in letters six feet high the words 'Long Live Stalin', on another 'Christ the Saviour of the World' – neither inscription, it might be said, without its message for the student of Soviet affairs. Beside the road the remains of brown-streaked glaciers scarred the hillside.

Twenty miles beyond Kazbek, at eight thousand feet above sea-level, you reach the top of the Krestovi Pass. Here the landscape changes and for a few miles the road traverses pleasant green pastures, with, in summer, sheep and cattle grazing and peasants gathering the hay. Looking down into the valleys from on high you catch sudden glimpses of tiny villages thousands of feet below. From the Alpine meadows at the top of the pass the road descends in a series of eighteen terrifying zigzags to the little village of Mleti. As you begin the descent, a tremendous panorama of snow-capped peaks opens up: Mount Gud, Krestovaya Gora, the Mountain of the Cross and finally the Seven Brothers and the Red Mountains, two massive ranges of red volcanic rock. From Mleti, the road follows the valley of the White Aragvi. Once more the landscape changes; the slopes on either side of the road are wooded; in summer the fields are green with rye and barley and in the villages the fruit trees are in blossom.

At Pasanauri, a dozen miles beyond Mleti, the White Aragvi joins the Black to become one river and for a hundred yards or more after the confluence you can see the two streams flowing side-by-side without mingling, the light and the dark. You are now on the Georgian side of the watershed. Wooded hills, the haunt of brown bears, slope steeply down all round and in the morning the peasants from the neighbouring valleys bring their beasts and farm produce to market.

For me stopping at Pasanauri is one of the chief pleasures of crossing the Caucasus. Here, at an old-established open-air restaurant, which got an enthusiastic mention from Baedeker as far back as 1914, you can, with luck, lunch al fresco in a green bower off freshly-caught trout and *shashlik*. On a recent visit, the fact that we were now in Georgia was immediately brought home to us by the appearance of a party of young Georgians who had come out for the day from Tbilisi and, having lunched well rather than wisely, were now dancing Georgian dances with true Georgian abandon. 'Where are you from?' they asked and, on learning that we came from the Highlands of Scotland, immediately launched into a panegyric of mountain races, braver, sturdier, handsomer and of course much, much heavier drinkers than anyone else in the world. It was several hours before we continued on our way, having made a number of life-long friends and consumed large quantities of exotic food and drink – a foretaste, as we well knew, of what lay ahead.

From Pasanauri we were soon spinning merrily down the wooded valley past the great fortress of Anauri, its towers and battlements golden against the setting sun. For centuries the stronghold of the Eristav or hereditary viceroy of the Aragvi, Anauri stands splendidly above the valley. Within its battlements rise a massive square watch-tower and two churches. From a secret hiding-place beneath the ramparts reserve bodies of men-at-arms once sprang out to surprise the enemy and in the church wall just behind the altar there is a spy-hole from which, during the service, a look-out watched for the approach of a foe.

Here, after passing a new man-made lake, you emerge from the great mountains into the mellow Georgian countryside and another thirty miles or so bring you to Mtzkhet, the ancient capital of Georgia and one of the oldest inhabited towns in the world. Nearby are the crumbling ruins of Beblistikhe, in pre-Christian times the fortress of the Georgian kings, while not far away lies a burial-ground dating back to the Iron Age. Now no more than a village, Mtzkhet stands at the confluence of the Aragvi and Kura rivers, dominated by the great cathedral church of Sveti Tzkhoveli, where for centuries the old kings of Georgia were crowned and buried.

Like many Georgian churches, Sveti Tzkhoveli is strongly fortified, being ringed round by a high battlemented wall, with look-out towers at intervals. To Georgians it is a place of special sanctity and on feast days the cathedral is thronged with worshippers. Nearby are the Church and Convent of Samtavro, where Mirian, the first Christian king of Georgia, lies buried. High on a hilltop above Mtzkhet stands Dzhvari, the Church of the Cross, built fourteen centuries ago on the spot where, two centuries before that, Nino or Nouni, the holy slave-woman from Cappadocia who converted the Georgians to Christianity, first set up a cross.

Arriving in Mtzkhet one fine day in early September, I found myself caught up by chance in the biggest religious festival of the year. Being autocephalous and therefore independent of the Russian Orthodox Church, the Georgian Church has a strongly national character and this was as much a national as a religious festival. An immense and devout congregation thronged the cathedral and many hundreds of Georgians, young and old, men and women, followed the Patriarch, as, preceded by banners and icons and magnificent in golden vestments, he and his attendant clergy issued from its great door and walked in procession round the cathedral precincts. In celebration the bells rang out merrily from the watch-towers, while all through the town clowns, wrestlers and mummers in mediaeval dress entertained the delighted crowds, while the wine, as always in Georgia, flowed freely.

From Mtzkhet I recently drove up a precipitous side-valley to the ancient Monastery of Shio Mgvime, built at the head of the valley against a backdrop of limestone cliffs. Founded in the sixth century and extended, restored and rebuilt many times since, but now unoccupied, it is on a site which clearly illustrates the necessity to pick a place which a handful of determined men could hold against the assaults of a multitude of Turks, Persians, Mongols, or Huns. One of the oldest of the monastery buildings is a pleasing little conical tower dedicated to St John the Baptist.

The importance in those days of picking a good strategic site is no less clearly shown by a tiny single basilica all by itself on a nearby mountain top. But the climb which most severely tested the powers of our sturdy jeep-type Niva and eventually of our own legs took us to the neighbouring fortress of Zedazeni, built round an ancient church. The sun was setting as we reached the summit and, looking northwards, we could see the whole mighty snow-capped range of the Caucasus culminating in Kazbek, dramatically outlined against the evening sky.

Once in Georgia, you soon realize that its history goes back a long way. Mtzkhet itself has existed as a town for two or three thousand years. In Homer's day, Colchis, roughly corresponding to Western Georgia, was well known to the Greeks. Both Medea the sorceress and her father Aeëtes, King of Colchis, were, it seems, historical characters and Jason and his Argonauts are now known to have come to Colchis from Greece in search of trade. Many centuries later, in 400 BC, Xenophon traversed Georgia on his way to the sea, and seventy or eighty years after that it became a dominion of Alexander the Great of Macedon. Thereafter Georgia was ruled over by successive dynasties of semi-independent native kings, living in uneasy proximity to their Persian and Armenian neighbours. For a time Colchis was part of the dominions of Mithridates Eupator, King of Pontus. But in 66 BC, following Pompey's invasion of Georgia or, as the Romans confusingly called it, Iberia, both Eastern and Western Georgia fell under Roman hegemony. It was not long however before the Georgians showed an excessive measure of independence and in AD 114 Georgia was again invaded, this time by the Emperor Trajan. For a century or so, Roman and Persian influence existed side by side. Then, with the rise of the Sassanid dynasty in Persia, Persian influence came to predominate.

It was under the Persian-born King Mirian that, in about the year 330, Georgia was converted to Christianity by St Nino, who first won the confidence of Mirian's Queen, Nana, by miraculously curing her of a mysterious complaint. Next, the king himself, while out hunting, suddenly found himself enveloped in total darkness, which as suddenly dissolved when he invoked Nana's new God. This made a Christian of him and he gave orders for a Christian church to be built forthwith at Mtzkhet. Work on the church was, it appears, at first held up owing to the difficulty of hoisting the central pillar into position, but one morning the pillar was found hovering miraculously in mid-air, after which it lowered itself neatly onto its base. The first church at Mtzkhet was made of wood and only later replaced by a stone building. In recognition of its miraculous construction, it was given the name of Sveti Tzkhoveli, the Church of the Life-Giving Pillar, and is said to have been built on the spot where Christ's coat without a Seam was first found after the Crucifixion, having been brought there from Golgotha by a wandering Jew named Elioz.

The Georgians' conversion to Christianity, coinciding as it did with that of the Emperor Constantine, was of more than purely religious significance. Their country now became an important outpost of Christianity in the Middle East. Henceforward, the Church played a central part in the life of the Georgian nation and their Christian faith helped the Georgians, as it did the neighbouring Armenians, to preserve their national identity through the centuries that followed.

The dynasty founded by King Mirian ruled in Georgia for two centuries, his most famous descendant being King Vakhtang Gorgaslan, the Wolf-Lion, who reigned from about 446 to 510 and in the course of his long reign moved his capital from Mtzkhet a dozen miles along the Kura valley to Tbilisi. After Vakhtang's death, the Georgian monarchy was so weakened by internal strife that in the middle of the sixth century the kings of Persia assumed direct control of Georgian affairs. For the next two or three hundred years local Georgian chieftains simply ruled over as much territory as they could control under Persian or Byzantine or, after the Arab invasion of the seventh century, Arab suzerainty.

But towards the end of the eighth century a new dynastic force emerged in Georgia: the Bagrationi, princes of Speri or Ispir, who in 866 formally assumed the title of King. It was to remain in their family for the best part of a thousand years. Claiming descent from David and Bathsheba, the Bagrations boldly displayed on their coat-of-arms the Lion of Judah, David's sling, the Psalmist's harp, Solomon's scales, and Christ's Coat without a Seam. In our own times, members of the family are known to have gone into mourning for the festival of the Assumption of the Virgin Mary on the grounds that it marked a family bereavement.

Under the new dynasty the unification of Georgia continued and in 1008 King Bagrat III became king of both Eastern and Western Georgia. His reign coincided with a period of high achievement in church architecture. To this period belong the great cathedral churches at Kutaisi in Imeretia, at Alaverdi in Kakhetia, and finally at Mtzkhet, where a magnificent stone cathedral was built on the site of St Nino's little wooden church. Tbilisi meanwhile remained in Moslem hands.

During the second half of the eleventh century, the Seljuk Turks swept into Asia Minor from across the Caspian; Georgia was overrun and it was not until the end of the century, when the feeble King George II abdicated in favour of his sixteen-year-old son David IV, that the outlook improved. David IV, who has gone down in history as Agmashenebeli, the Builder, was not only a patron of the arts, but a considerable statesman and military leader. Between 1100 and 1121 he won a whole series of victories against the Turks, drove the Moslems from Tbilisi and annexed large parts of Armenia. Soon Georgian influence reached from the Black Sea to the Caspian. It was during David's reign and under his personal supervision that the splendid monastery was built at Gelati in Western Georgia where he himself lies buried and where, at the academy he endowed, Joane Petritsi founded his famous School of Philosophy.

David the Builder died in 1125. The task he had begun was ably resumed half a century later by his great-grand-daughter Tamara, a remarkable woman, who reigned from 1178 to 1213. Under her auspices Georgia's power and prestige reached their zenith. Like her great-grandfather, Queen Tamara was an outstanding military leader and fought several successful campaigns against the Persians. Having quickly discarded her first husband, the Russian Prince George Bogolyubski, a vicious, drunken adventurer, she took as her consort David Soslan from neighbouring Ossetia, to whom she bore a son and a daughter. Tradition has it that the great Georgian epic poet, Shota Rustaveli, author of *The Knight in the Panther Skin*, lived during her reign, became her Chancellor of the Exchequer, and fell madly in love with her, ending his days broken-hearted in a monastery in Jerusalem.

In 1221, Jenghiz Khan's Mongols, having overrun Persia, quickly routed the Armenian and Georgian armies that were sent against them; Tbilisi was taken and Tamara's daughter, Queen Rusudan, forced to take refuge in the mountains of Imeretia. The Mongol invasions put an end to Georgia's Golden Age and, for the time being, to her independence, her kings now becoming vassals of the Mongol Il-Khans. In the fourteenth century came signs of a national revival, but soon Transcaucasia was to become a battleground for Tamerlane, who more than once overran and devastated it in the course of his campaigns against the Persians, the Turks and the Golden Horde.

Alexander I, last king of a united Georgia, reigned from 1412 to 1443. Under his sons the country was split up into three smaller kingdoms, each ruled over by a different branch of the Bagration family and each at variance with the others. Henceforward the senior branch reigned over the kingdom of Karthli, namely Tbilisi and Central Georgia. From Kutaisi a second branch governed Western Georgia or Imeretia. A third ruled over Eastern Georgia or Kakhetia, while several lesser princely families set up as minor monarchs on their own in various outlying areas.

With the fall of Constantinople to the Ottoman Turks, Georgia was completely cut off from Western Christendom and the Georgians fell an easy prey to their southern neighbours. In 1510 the Turks invaded Imeretia and sacked Kutaisi. Soon after this the Shah of Persia attacked Karthli. Towards the end of the sixteenth century the Turks, taking advantage of the disturbed state of Persia, seized the whole of Transcaucasia. But under the great Shah Abbas the situation was quickly reversed and the Turks driven right out of Eastern Georgia, which now became a Persian province. Over Imeretia, meanwhile, and the lesser principalities of Western Georgia the Turks retained a loose suzerainty.

In the centuries that followed, Georgia remained, in practice, partitioned between Persia and Turkey. There were moments when the Georgian kings enjoyed a greater measure of independence, but for most of the time they were mere satraps of the Shah, hovering judiciously between the Christian and Moslem faiths and dividing their time no less judiciously between Tbilisi and Isfahan. In the eighteenth century, during the long reign of the olive-skinned and highly astute King Hercules II, there came a partial revival of their power. But by this time the Georgians had begun to come under pressure from the north as well as from the south.

Sustained relations between the Russians and the tribes of the Caucasus date from the second half of the sixteenth century. The Cossack bands of marauding horsemen who first made their appearance during the troubled times which followed the Mongol invasions had gradually come to occupy most of the disputed frontier areas to the south and east of Russia, until in the end what became known as the Great Cossack Line stretched right across the northern Caucasus.

Henceforth the plight of Christian Georgia provided the Russians with a permanent pretext for crossing the Caucasus and confronting the encroaching Turks and Persians. Under King Hercules II the relationship between Georgia and Russia grew closer. In the past the Russians had been content to stand on the Cossack Line. Now, with the accession to the throne of Catherine the Great and her successive campaigns against the Turks, Russian interest in the Caucasus became keener and in 1763 a first Russian fortress was built at Mozdok on the Terek. Besides upsetting the local tribesmen, this also offended their protector, the Sultan of Turkey, who in 1768 declared war on Russia. The ensuing conflict lasted for five years and was fought on several fronts. One of the most spectacular successes of the campaign was achieved by General von Todtleben, who, crossing the main range with four hundred men and four guns, took Tbilisi. The following year he invaded Western Georgia, took Kutaisi, the capital, and, routing a Turkish force of twelve hundred men, fought his way down to the Black Sea coast. Three years later, however, Catherine suddenly decided to withdraw her forces to the Cossack Line and in July 1774 Russians and Turks made peace at Kutchuk Kainardji.

Once more the Russians now concentrated on strengthening and reinforcing the Cossack Line, thus preparing the way for an eventual advance across the Caucasus. The chief threat to Georgia came at this time from Persia and, when in 1783 the new Shah sought to reimpose his suzerainty, King Hercules immediately appealed to Russia for help. Count Paul Potyomkin, the Russian Commander-in-Chief, quickly responded to his appeal. The fortress of Vladikavkaz was built, the rough bridle path linking it to Tbilisi was made into a road and in November 1783 a small Russian force was sent across it to Tbilisi. Not long after the Empress formally took Georgia under her protection.

But even now the Russians did not remain in Georgia for long and in 1795 the Persians, returning in strength, sacked Tbilisi and massacred the inhabitants, at the same time hamstringing any virgins they could find. Again Russia intervened and the Persians were driven out. When three years later they once more massed on the frontier, the Georgians again appealed to St Petersburg, asking this time for full union with Russia, with the result that, early in 1801, Georgia became an integral part of the Russian Empire. Having established themselves in Tbilisi the Russians next brought the adjoining areas under their control. By the end of 1804 all the former territories of the old Georgian monarchy, divided up four hundred years earlier, had been reunited, this time under Russian rule, and the Tsar's dominions stretched the whole way from the Black Sea to the Caspian.

2

Marching through Georgia

Le peuple Géorgien aime à donner.
ALEXANDRE DUMAS PÈRE

Even after being ruled from St Petersburg or Moscow for close on two centuries, the Georgians are still very different from the Russians. They are of a different race and speak a different language; their historical and cultural background is different; and they possess a completely different temperament and national character – all of which becomes obvious the moment you enter Georgia and even more so when you reach Tbilisi, which lies no more than a dozen miles beyond Mtzkhet.

Tbilisi, capital of Georgia since the sixth century, is a most agreeable city. In Georgian, *tbili* means 'hot' and Tbilisi owes its name to its hot sulphur springs, first discovered by the great King Vakhtang Gorgaslan while out hunting over fifteen hundred years ago. A wounded deer fell into the bubbling hot water and re-emerged as vigorous as before it had been hit. This so impressed the monarch that he at once built a town there and made it his capital. To this day the hot, health-giving, sulphurous water still bubbles up in the marble baths of a magnificently equipped *hammam*, to be found not far from a fine new equestrian statue of King Vakhtang, erected to his memory by the present Georgian government.

Tbilisi is built, like Rome, on several hills and likewise stands on the banks of a rushing river, the Kura. A long narrow town with a population of around a million, eighty per cent of whom are Georgian and a high proportion of the remainder Armenian or Tartar, it stretches for several miles along both sides of the river. The oldest part of the city lies to the south-east, where the hills come suddenly together in two rocky promontories. High on the northernmost of these stand the Avlabar, the old Georgian citadel and, within it, the ancient church of the Metekhi Virgin, built originally in the fifth century, destroyed by the Mongols, and rebuilt in its present form in the thirteenth century. All along the high rocky cliffs which here form the river bank, the houses of the old Georgian quarter, with their deep verandas, overhang the swirling waters of the Kura, the original bridge across which is said to have been built by Alexander the Great. Facing the Metekhi across

133

the river the ancient Persian fortress of Narykala dominates the confused tangle of little streets and terraces and alleyways of the old Persian, Tartar and Armenian and Jewish quarters. First built in the fourth century, it was put back into working order by the Turks in the sixteenth century. Below the ridge on which it stands, among tumbledown shacks and balconied houses, are a mosque, an Armenian church, a Jewish synagogue, all still in use, and finally the blue-tiled *hammam* with its constant hot, bubbling sulphurous water.

Not more than a couple of hundred yards from the *hammam*, where a wallow in a fine marble bath and a brisk massage had given me a healthy appetite, I was delighted on my last visit to come on a vaulted beer-cellar where they were serving the best hot toasted cheese or *khatchapuri* I have ever tasted, liberally washed down by several litres of excellent local draught beer, which served as a welcome chaser to several generous tots of vodka sent across to our table by a friendly fellow-customer from Azerbaijan. Whether he was a practising Moslem or not I did not enquire. Nor did I seek his views on the latest restrictions on the sale of hard liquor, then only newly introduced. Just round the corner from the beer-cellar is an underground *khashnaya* where, if you are bold enough, you can dine off *khash* or *khush*, a fearsome Armenian dish of pigs' trotters and garlic, or less adventurously off excellent mutton *shashlik*.

Further along the embankment, where another bridge crosses the Kura, you come to a number of imaginatively restored and gaily painted old Georgian houses, in one of which I have more than once been lavishly entertained by a distinguished Georgian friend who was recently lucky enough to obtain possession of it. In addition to dwelling-houses, these attractive buildings also include an excellent restaurant and a stone-flagged vault which dispenses first-class Turkish coffee.

Below the Narykala were once the bazaars. Now their place has been taken by the modern department stores of the new town, built in the last century when Tbilisi was capital of the Russian vice-royalty of the Caucasus. On your way from the old town to the new, you pass the Sioni Cathedral dating back to the seventh century or even earlier, and, like the town itself, destroyed and rebuilt many times since. Here in a splendid silver shrine is the miraculous cross which in the fourth century St Nino plaited from vine stems and bound with her own hair. The singing in the cathedral is magnificent and the services well attended. It is also a fashionable church in which to be married. In a comfortable house next door resides the Patriarch.

A little further on, just off Lenin Square, the main square of the city, you come to the Museum of Art, a handsome classical building. A marble plaque at the entrance proclaims that this was once the theological seminary where Josif Vissarionovich Stalin was brought up to be a priest before embarking on his career as a revolutionary. The museum possesses a splendid collection of mediaeval Georgian icons and artefacts, including the famous Kakhuli Triptych, a masterpiece of Georgian mediaeval craftsmanship.

It would be surprising if the Georgians, whose art reached such heights in the Middle Ages, had not at some later stage in their history produced a school of painters worthy of our attention. In addition to its remarkable collection of mediaeval icons, the Museum of Art contains a number of more recent paintings by Georgian artists which are well worth looking at. The oldest of these, dating from the end of the eighteenth and first half of the nineteenty century, are portraits of members of the Georgian royal family and of connected princely houses, painted in a stiff, formal, oriental manner, matching the stiff formal garb of their subjects and recalling Persian portraits of the same period. The next product of Georgia's native genius are the naïve or primitive paintings of Nico Pirosmani or Piromanishvili, a peasant from Mirzaani in Kakhetia, who died a drunkard in 1918. His paintings for the most part portray prosperous Georgian peasants at table in rustic surroundings, solemnly eating and drinking their way through gargantuan feasts, and were no doubt commissioned by the peasants themselves as a means of perpetuating the memory of these happy and characteristically Georgian occasions, while at the same time providing Pirosmani with his much-needed supplies of wine. Only occasionally do they represent something more dramatic, for example a rich peasant preparing to cut his wife's conveniently bared throat.

Hardly had Pirosmani drunk himself to death, than a lively new school of young Georgian painters sprang into being in Paris in the 1920s. The work of three of these is represented in the Museum of Art: Shalva Kikodze, David Kakabadze and Lado Gudiashvili. Of the three, Lado Gudiashvili survived to be the Grand Old Man of Georgian Art, People's Artist of the USSR and Hero of Soviet Labour, dying quite recently at the age of over ninety. Immensely aristocratic in manner and appearance, he resided in what was once the town house of Princess Orbeliani, on the walls of whose vast and agreeably ornate ballroom hung large numbers of his paintings, varying from enormous classical battle-scenes featuring splendidly naked Amazons falling full-frontally from their chargers to clever little portraits rather in the manner of his close friend Modigliani. On my last visit to him, finding him hard at work on a prancing scarlet nude, I asked him about Socialist Realism. 'To paint tired, dirty workers is silly', he replied dismissively and carried on painting.

Shalva Kikodze, who died young, left a kind of frenzied rake's progress of *déjeuners sur l'herbe* and similar scenes, faintly allegorical in flavour and tinged with cynical despair, as though to suggest that wine and women, though essential to life, might somehow not be its sole aim. A striking self-portrait leaves one regretting his early death, accelerated no doubt by a ceaseless search for ever stronger sensations.

David Kakabadze, who died thirty years ago, was probably the most considerable painter of the three, displaying remarkable virtuosity in a wide variety of manners and styles. His pre-1914 experiments in abstract painting and collage show that in this field he was, like some of his Russian contemporaries, ahead of his time, while from his experiments in Cubism (wisely acquired by an American university) he would clearly hold his own with the leading exponents of that genre. In Paris he was evidently much influenced by the Impressionists and Post-Impressionists and here again his work bears comparison with that of more famous painters. All his life, his widow told me, he was obsessed by the view of a certain hillside in Georgia which he painted again and again in his Impressionist manner. Several versions hang in his studio; there is also one in the Museum of Art, painted in 1942, with as foreground a procession bearing red banners. It was apparently his single excursion into ideological art.

Northwards from Lenin Square runs the main street of Tbilisi, known in tsarist days as the Golovinski Prospekt, but since renamed Prospekt Rustaveli in honour of the great mediaeval Georgian poet, Shota Rustaveli, whose statue stands at the far end of it. With its well-grown plane trees, happily mingled architectural fantasies, and cheerful chattering crowds of pedestrians, this bustling boulevard has a Parisian quality, duly noted in his day by Alexandre Dumas, a discriminating and enthusiastic visitor to Georgia. Here you will find the best shops, hotels, restaurants and cafés, theatres and cinemas. Here, opposite the site once occupied by the old Hotel Orient, is the imposing modern building which houses the Government of the Soviet Socialist Republic of Georgia. Here is the former palace of the viceroy, now a children's club. And here the young people of Tbilisi gather each evening towards sunset to walk up and down and take the air and admire each other in their form-fitting blue jeans and T-shirts. Meanwhile, side by side with old Tbilisi, of which the inhabitants are justly proud, a fine new town is springing up in which clever use has been made of the lie of the land and where contemporary Georgian architecture successfully blends the modern with the traditional.

In Tbilisi, in the summer, life is largely lived out of doors in the streets and public parks and in the courtyards of the old houses. Wherever you go, something is always happening and there is always a crowd looking on. People are buying and selling things, playing games or musical instruments, looking in the shop windows or at each other. There is never a dull moment. Before the Revolution, it was calculated that one in seven of the male population of Georgia was a prince. Certainly the Georgians still have a style and an elegance all of their own: the men with their marvellous bearing and fierce hawk-like good looks; the women darkly beautiful with their flashing eyes, white skins and aquiline features. They are also a proud race and enjoy showing off. But they are not arrogant. Indeed they are among the friendliest, most convivial and most hospitable people I know.

On meeting a stranger, the first thought that enters the head of any Georgian, whether he be a man of consequence or the poorest peasant in the remotest mountain village, is to entertain him as hospitably as he can. And, should there be no strangers to entertain, the Georgians entertain each other constantly and lavishly. At every restaurant or eating-place, in every town or village, you will find at any hour of the day parties of four or more Georgians, almost invariably men, sitting round a table laden with bottles of wine, skewerfuls of *shashlik*, and dishes of strange herbs, engaged in the liveliest conversation. Any stranger appearing on the scene will, in my experience, at once be drawn into one of these feasts, any attempt he may make to pay his own bill being indignantly rejected. As Alexandre Dumas remarked, no doubt on the basis of similar experience, '*le peuple Géorgien aime à donner*'. In Tbilisi, one has only to look inside a courtyard or get into conversation with a stranger in the street to be immediately asked in and lavishly entertained, often to a full-scale meal. One old lady was hard at work with her rolling-pin making dumplings under the tree in her backyard. 'Come back in half an hour and they'll be ready', she said, and sure enough thirty minutes later we were sitting down to a dish of delicious meat-filled dumplings and being treated to a detailed account of our hosts' family history.

Nor is this lavish and universal hospitality purely a matter of eating and drinking. Along with the food and wine goes, especially among intellectuals, a vigorous exchange of ideas on every conceivable subject. Even the toasts that are an important feature of such gatherings tend to turn into little speeches and are used to develop a theme which then becomes a subject for general conversation. They also provide the Georgians, who are by nature expansive and big-hearted, with a welcome opportunity to display the goodwill and affection they feel for their companions and, as the evening progresses, for humanity at large.

Only some of these convivial occasions take place in restaurants. Whenever possible, Georgians prefer to entertain their guests in their own houses and are always on the lookout for a pretext to ask in friends, relations, colleagues, work-mates or indeed the passing stranger. Then the usual enormous array of bottles are opened, the female members of the family scour the markets for provisions and get to work in the kitchen, the maximum number of people are crammed round the largest available table, and the party begins. A word of warning to the novice: never assume that the display of smoked fish, caviar, cheese and cold sucking-pig, which you find on the table when you sit down, is all that you are going to get. After anything up to an hour some soup is likely to make its appearance, followed by course after course of roast and grilled meats, fruit, pastries and other confections, accompanied by quite surprising quantities of wine. Just how many hours the ensuing symposium lasts, how much food and drink is consumed, how many toasts are drunk and to whom, and how much singing and dancing takes place, depends purely on the mood of the company present.

Many of the Georgians' national characteristics – elegance, gaiety and dash – emerge in their dancing. Georgians old and young will dance at the drop of a hat wherever they find themselves, in the street, by the roadside, in a restaurant, anywhere where there is room to manoeuvre and where they can find someone to play the drums and accordion. Among all the many national dance groups performing today in the Soviet Union, the Georgian State Dance Company has achieved a unique position, not only domestically but in the world at large. That this is so is due first and foremost to the inspired and dedicated work over the years of a tremendously talented couple, Nino Ramishvili and her late husband Iliko Sukhisvili. Both brilliant dancers, Nino and Iliko were married some fifty years ago while still in their teens. Their work for the Georgian Dance Company began just after the war. During its early years the company, in Nino's words, were 'short of everything except enthusiasm'. Later, following their early successes, came increasing official re-cognition and – no less important – official support. Now their company is the State Dance Company and Nino bears the much-coveted title of People's Artist. Until ten years or so ago, both she and Iliko danced themselves. Now instruction, choreography, administration and organization take up most of Nino's time although she is always ready to demonstrate any step or movement for the benefit of the pupils. Watching her at work or at leisure, one realizes at once how close is the relationship between her and the members of her company and its importance in what she is seeking to achieve. Of the total devotion she inspires there can be no doubt. And the same can be said of her son Tenghiz and daughter-in-law Inge who, themselves both first-class dancers, are carrying on the family tradition with equal dedication.

There can be no doubt that they are fortunate in their human material. Not only are the Georgians as a race remarkably good-looking, with instinctive style and elegance and an innate gift for display; they are also natural dancers. Equally rich are the sources of inspiration on which they can draw for their themes. In every part of Georgia, there are age-old local traditions of national dancing. Every village and every valley has its own local reel, round-dance or sword-dance, performed to the acompaniment of some exotic musical instrument, the drums and bagpipe included, and usually based on some dramatic incident in Georgia's long and turbulent history. For thirty years or more, Nino and her husband travelled to the remotest parts of the country in order to research these traditions on the spot and, having discovered a new dance, to adapt it to their requirements, often transforming it in the process, while retaining its essential characteristics. The result is a repertory of immense diversity and interest which in its own way bears comparison with that of any of the great ballet companies. Ballet, it has been said, is the language of movement. The dancing of the Georgian State Dance Company expresses better than anything the pride, the style and the beauty of Georgia.

No less remarkable are the performances of the Rustaveli Theatre Company. For sheer brilliance and originality they rival those of any theatre in the world. In the company's lead actor, Ramaz Chikvadze, its enormously gifted director Robert Sturua has found a talent which matches and as it were complements his own, while the other members of the company are in their various ways of comparable excellence. To the plays they put on they bring a new freshness and force. One of the company's great triumphs is Shakespeare's *Richard III*. This they present in a way which makes you feel that never before have you fully grasped that story's fearful import, endowing it with unbelievably sinister overtones of treachery and doom, while also enhancing and intensifying our understanding of the original play. Brecht's *Caucasian Chalk Circle*, on the other hand, they completely transform, lending it a lightness and wit which Brecht himself sometimes lacks, while, if anything, strengthening its satirical content.

Neither of these very different plays is without its political message. Each is in its own way a fable for our times and in each this is brought home with elegance and force. This is in itself not only a tribute, if tribute were needed, to native Georgian inventiveness and talent; it also reveals an encouraging political awareness. Such, moreover, is the force of the acting that it is only after leaving the theatre that you realize that the play which has enthralled you was given in a language of which you do not understand a single word.

Of recent years, the Georgians have also been producing a number of unusual and remarkable films, an outstanding example being Eldar Shengalaya's savage satire *The Blue Mountains* which despite or, one hopes, because of its devastating attacks on Soviet bureaucracy, recently won a greatly coveted official prize. More significant still was Tenghiz Abuladze's *Repentance* with its telling denunciation of Stalin, Stalinism and, for the matter of that, neo-Stalinism.

Both by tradition and inclination, the Georgians are wine-drinkers, leaving beer and vodka to the Russians. Wine production is a major industry and wine as important in Georgia as in France. Georgians will tell you that wine was first produced in Georgia and that *ghvino*, the Georgian word for it, was its original name. The sunny foothills of the Caucasus certainly produce excellent vintages and both Kakhetia and Imeretia are rightly famous for their wines. 'We may assert', wrote that great Anglo–French seventeenth/eighteenth-century travel-writer, the Chevalier Chardin, 'that there is no country where they drink more or better wine . . . in truth, had I drunk as much as my neighbours, I had dy'd upon the spot.' It is a tradition which, in spite of everything, still persists. Fortunately for us all the rumour that Georgia's famous vineyards were to be uprooted as part of the recent campaign against alcohol has proved to be without foundation, though even in Georgia wine no longer flows quite as freely as it once did.

In Tbilisi, foreign tourists are now usually relegated to the Hotel Iveria, an ageing concrete skyscraper at the far end of the Prospekt Rustaveli. Whether for this reason or not, its restaurant has become a favourite haunt of local Georgians, large groups of whom sit out on its terrace in the summer eating and drinking and generally enjoying themselves. For four or five roubles you can get an adequate meal and plenty to drink with it. Anyone who prefers better cooking in more pleasing surroundings will do well to patronize the Hotel Tbilisi (formerly Palace) built in the grand manner of 1912. Here in a magnificent pillared dining-room amid a discriminating Georgian clientèle, you may savour at your leisure (and eating out in Tbilisi is invariably a leisurely proceeding) a selection of strange regional delicacies to the strains of traditional jazz skilfully dispensed by six grey-haired musicians led by a saxophonist worthy of the Savoy Orpheans of fifty years ago. A livelier evening's entertainment is provided at a new night-club in a nearby cellar, offering a jazzed-up Georgian floorshow and a 'gourmet dinner' with *flambé* dishes at thirty or forty roubles a head, a price which must put it beyond the range of all except the very rich or those who, for one reason or another, do not need to pick up the check. For more genuine local colour, one can always try a *shashlichnaya* where, in a cellar below pavement-level at a table with a plastic cloth you can, for two or three roubles, get a good enough Georgian *shashlik* with a litre of wine to go with it. Only occasionally do you encounter a family party. More usually the customers are knowing-looking men, obviously regular patrons of the establishment and on intimate terms with each other, the cooks and the waiters.

But in Tbilisi, as in most places, the best food and drink is to be found in private houses. 'I think you will like this little wine. It comes from my own vineyard', said a distinguished literary friend of mine recently, as we enjoyed his wife's delicious cooking and admired his private collection of works of art. In Georgia, as elsewhere, most housewives who can afford it patronize the flourishing free markets where peasants from state or collective farms sell the produce of their private plots and where the supplies are of quite a different quality, variety and freshness from those to be found in the state shops.

The advent of the private automobile has further enhanced life in Georgia. 'What kind of car do you have?' asked one young man I met whose family clearly had access to foreign currency. 'I'm getting a Jaguar for my birthday', he added, before I had time to mention my own snub-nosed Morris Minor. Another of the guests, a distinguished young academic, had a scarlet Italian sports car. One car in which we were fortunate enough to travel was equipped with television set 'to amuse the chauffeur', we were told by its owner, a leading man of letters, also active in politics. Now that so many of them are motorized, there is nothing most Georgians like better than to drive out into the country with their friends for an al fresco meal.

From Tbilisi it is an easy morning's drive to Telavi, the principal town of Kakhetia or Eastern Georgia. To reach it, you at first follow the wide dusty valley of the Kura, crossing a range of thickly-wooded hills to emerge into the parallel valley of the Alazani. As you enter Kakhetia, the landscape changes, the country becomes more fertile and, through a screen of green poplars, you find yourself looking across fields of vines and Indian corn to a distant line of blue mountains: the main range of the Caucasus. Telavi itself which, during the seventeenth and eighteenth centuries, often served as a refuge for the Georgian kings when Tbilisi was in the hands of the Persians or Turks, is dominated by the Batonistikhe, a massive fortress containing a number of palaces and churches, where Hercules II spent much of his long reign.

Telavi is at no great distance from Tsinandali. This was the home of the Chavchavadzes, an ancient Georgian family one of whom, Prince Alexander, an early nineteenth-century patriot and poet, is regarded with sufficient favour by the Soviet authorities for his house to be preserved as a museum. It was from this medium-sized country mansion with its wide verandas and big airy rooms that the young Princess Anna, wife of Prince David Chavchavadze, her sister, their children, and teenage niece were snatched in the summer of 1854 by a band of wild Moslem tribesmen and carried off into the mountains of nearby Daghestan as hostages of the Iman Shamyl, the great guerrilla leader, who held out against the Russians in the mountains for the best part of thirty years. Built of pink sandstone, the house stands in a well-planted park facing due north across the broad fertile valley of the Alazani to the mountains of Daghestan, where the princesses and their party were to spend several deeply unnerving months before being finally ransomed. At the far end of the park are the buildings where the wines for which Tsinandali had long been famous are still made and the cellars where they are laid up to mature. Here, sitting round a great polished table and nibbling at local cheese and fruit, you can savour at your ease some fine recent vintages and admire row upon row of ancient bottles going back to 1814 and used, I was told, rather to my disappointment, for purposes of scientific research.

Also within easy reach of Telavi are several of the most remarkable churches and monasteries of mediaeval Georgia. To the north-east, across the Alazani, is Gremi, which in the sixteenth century was capital of Kakhetia. Of the ancient city only a few crumbling ruins remain, but perched on a fortified hilltop above them stand two churches of the same period which – thanks perhaps to their strategic position and massive walls – survived the ravages of time and the disasters which overtook their neighbours below.

Not many miles north-west from Telavi are the ancient monastery and academy of Ikalto and the famous cathedral church of Alaverdi, built at the beginning of the eleventh century by King Bagrat III in the shape of a gigantic cross. Ringed with crumbling walls and watch-towers, the great cathedral rises splendidly above the green of the surrounding plain, while far away to the north, beyond cornfields and vineyards, the setting sun catches the distant peaks of the Caucasus. Carved in relief on one of the flagstones of the floor, the image of a single human hand recalls the heroic end of a local prince who, captured by the Turks and facing death, cut off his hand and sent it home, so that at least some part of him might be buried in consecrated ground. Alaverdi is also regarded as a holy place by the Moslem tribesmen who live in the surrounding hills and have a Moslem shrine of their own adjoining the Christian cathedral. On feast days the whole population turns out to celebrate with much drinking and eating and dancing within the cathedral precincts.

From Alaverdi it is a short drive to Ikalto, which, as far back as the sixth century, was the seat of a Christian monastery and of an academy famous throughout Georgia. Of the monastery and academy only a few crumbling walls still stand, but the adjoining three churches, of which two date back to the seventh and eighth centuries respectively, have remained in good repair.

West of Telavi and due south from Ikalto is the monastery of Old Shuamtha, the Place Between the Mountains. This stands in a clearing on a hillside from which it commands a wide prospect of distant blue hills. Its fine basilica dating back to the fifth century and its two domed churches, one large and one small, were built in the seventh century to much the same design as the slightly older Church of the Cross at Dzhvari, above Mtzkhet. Near Old Shuamtha is the monastery of New Shuamtha consisting of a large, rather clumsy-looking sixteenth-century church with a belfry and what were once dwelling-quarters for the monks.

Eastern Kakhetia is wine-growing country *par excellence*. Every village you pass through bears a famous name. Mukuzani produces the best red wine, while Tsinandali and Gurjani are well known for their white. At Gurjani, some miles east of Telavi, you are close to Kvelatsminda, the Monastery of All Saints, situated on a green wooded hillside beside a stream a mile or two off the main road. Kvelatsminda consists of an eighth- or ninth-century basilica with, most unusually, separate twin domes, and another smaller church. On the altar of the main basilica, still apparently in use, stood – when I last visited it – a roughly-carved and clearly immensely old representation of a ram, shining with candle-grease and evidently a traditional object of veneration. What could it be? Possibly the Lamb of God. But no less possibly some ancient pagan deity, still furtively worshipped in this remote spot. There was no means of telling and no priest to explain.

On a recent visit to Gurjani I was taken by my companions to lunch off excellent *shashliks* and toasted cheese on the veranda of a charming nearby country house, now a restaurant, but once the home of my friend film director Eldar Shengalaya's film-star mother, Nato Vachnadze, sadly killed in an aircrash while still quite young. Here the chilled white Gurjani we drank with our luncheon tasted far better directly under the hillside where its grapes had ripened under the warm Georgian sun than it could ever have done in some city restaurant.

Although it is a long way off the regular tourist route, permission is sometimes granted to visit the famous cave-monastery of Vardzia, far away to the south on the Turkish border. To reach it from Tbilisi, you first follow the Kura Valley north-westwards in the direction of Gori, passing the fine eleventh-century Church of Samthavissi, with its great cross standing out in sharp relief on the eastern façade. Only a few miles before Gori you come to the cave-city of Uplistsikhe, carved out of the rock in the Bronze Age and finally destroyed by the Mongols in the thirteenth century. Gori's chief claim to fame is that Stalin was born there in 1879. A neatly laid-out public park now surrounds the little flat-roofed house in which the Generalissimo first saw the light of day. This consists of two sparsely furnished whitewashed rooms, each about ten feet square, and a veranda. One room, it appears, was occupied by the landlord and the other by Stalin's father and mother. The whole structure is now enclosed within a magnificent pillared marble pavilion with a glass roof. All day long a stream of visitors go in, look around and come out again. In the main square of the little town a massive statue of its most famous son stands guard in front of the fine municipal buildings with which he endowed it, while from a hill on its fringes the battered mass of a ruined fortress, the Goristsikhe, broods over everything, as it has done for the past two thousand years and more.

Not many miles south of Gori, at the head of a narrow valley, high above a rushing mountain stream, is the little church of Ateni Sion, built in the first part of the seventh century and containing a famous fresco dating from the eleventh century. Like other early Georgian churches, the Church of the Cross at Dzhvari in particular, its dome rests on a faceted drum above a cruciform ground plan, the arms of the cross ending in four half-circles. Splendidly situated among the hills, Ateni Sion gives a feeling of enormous antiquity, serenity and strength.

From Gori you continue westwards along the valley of the Kura to Kashuri, where the valley turns southwards, climbing steeply between thickly-wooded hillsides to Borzhomi, a famous spa, where Grand Dukes once took the waters and where Chekhov and Chai-kovski and later the giants of the Revolution came to enjoy the mountain air. Through the town, the Borzhomka, a rushing poplar-lined tributary of the Kura, flows between rows of pretty nineteenth-century stucco villas, including what Baedeker, writing in the year 1914, called 'the Moorish-looking château of the Grand Duke Mikhail Nikolayevich'. At a mineral spring in the nearby park you can, if you so wish, drink your fill of warm, effervescent sulphurous water, a valuable antidote, I found, to Georgian hospitality.

From Borzhomi, a morning's drive along the valley of the Kura brings you to Vardzia. At Atskuri, where you enter the frontier zone and display your special passes to a detachment of smart green-capped frontier troops, an ancient fortress, high on a rock above the road, recalls the enduring strategic importance of this road. For invading armies, coming in either direction, this has always been a vital line of approach to Georgia or alternatively to Anatolia. From this point onwards the ruins of some ancient castle or fortification look down from every point of vantage.

Akhaltsikhe, or New Castle, a key Turkish strong-point and the scene of a hard-fought battle between Turks and Russians in 1828, stands at four thousand feet above sea-level. 'You may sooner snatch the moon from the heavens', ran an old Turkish saying, 'than the crescent from the Mosque of Akhaltsikhe.' Here the valley opens out and the town itself, with the citadel rising above it, lies in a bowl ringed round by mountains. Beyond it the valley narrows again, the craggy, rock-strewn hills on either side become higher and more precipitous. On a rocky cliff high above the river stands the great mediaeval castle of Khertvissi. Further on, the mighty ruins of yet another ancient fortress, destroyed by Persian invaders in the sixteenth century, are almost indistinguishable from the rocks on which they stand.

At Vardzia the Kura, as you near its source, narrows to a rushing torrent. On both sides of the valley the mighty volcanic cliffs are honeycombed with cave-dwellings and everywhere you can see traces of early terraced cultivation. But Vardzia itself is on an altogether different scale. Half-way up the cliff a whole city has been hollowed and tunnelled out of the rock with room for several thousand inhabitants as well as for churches, palaces, forts, monasteries, banqueting-halls, barracks, stables and wine-cellars, all interconnected by an endless labyrinth of caves and tunnels and passages and stairways, the pattern of which has been clearly revealed by an earthquake which at some period sliced away a part of the rockface. Here you may see the stalls in which the king's horses were stabled, the frescoed chapel in which he worshipped, the wine-presses from which his wine gushed forth, the great jars in which it was stored, the banqueting-hall in which he and his friends drank it and, in the rock above, a slit just wide enough for a lance to be driven through it into the neck of some unwelcome or expendable guest. Completed in the twelfth century, Vardzia was after four hundred years finally sacked by the Persians in 1552 and its inhabitants massacred to a man.

From Kashuri, where you branch off to Borzhomi, a splendid new mountain road now leads you amid lush tropical vegetation and through wild mountain gorges westwards to Kutaisi. No less than Kakhetia, Imeretia or Western Georgia has a character all of its own. This is Colchis, the kingdom of Medea's father Aeëtes, where Jason and his Argonauts sought their fortunes and to this day Kutaisi, its capital, bears the Golden Fleece as its municipal crest. A city of immense antiquity, Kutaisi is pleasantly situated on the Rioni River which rises further north in the main range of the Caucasus. With its elegant, stone-built, vine-wreathed town houses of different periods and styles, many standing in their own gardens, it is in some ways remoter and more exotic than Tbilisi and yet in others more Western or perhaps one should say, more Mediterranean, for, as Colchis, it was for centuries constantly open to Greek and Roman influence. Before the Revolution there was, strangely enough, an Italian Capuchin monastery there, of which the handsome classical church still survives, now used as a concert hall.

High above the river stands the great cathedral church built by King Bagrat III of Georgia in about the year 1000, when Tbilisi was still in the hands of the Arabs and Kutaisi had for the time being become the capital of the Georgian kings. Blown up by the Turks just seven centuries later, in 1699, it has been a ruin ever since. Behind it are the remains of a massive fortress tower from which on a clear day you get a fine view of the great mountains away to the north.

While admiring the cathedral, we fell in with some young Georgian art students who made an attractive foreground to the surrounding ruins. 'Do take my photograph!' they said. 'And mine! And mine!' clustering round me. With them, we scrambled down the hillside to the Botanical Gardens, where we were entertained to tumblers of local wine and large helpings of stew by the resident caretaker, an old soldier who remembered the wartime Big Three with enthusiasm and, coupling Stalin's name with those of Churchill and Roosevelt, invited us to drink their health, sitting side by side on his bed.

Better regarded in death than in life, especially in Transcaucasia, Stalin, we found, serves as a convenient focus for Georgian nationalism and for elderly grumblers who, in their cups at any rate, affect a not entirely convincing nostalgia for the smack of firm government. By the roadside further north I came on a mammoth-size painting of him on a rock and in the bazaar in Kutaisi, I found that privately-produced hand-coloured folk-art portraits of the Generalissimo were selling like hot cakes for three roubles each. Interestingly enough his companions in a set of three popular pin-ups were a bosomy, pistol-packing American blonde in tight jeans and a cowboy hat, and a rather Italianate representation of the Holy Family, a strangely-assorted triptych, with each of its three panels clearly representing an important socio-political trend in the Soviet Union of today.

Through the middle of Kutaisi flows the Rioni, here a rushing mountain torrent. Just below the main bridge is a beer-house with a balcony, an excellent vantage-point from which to watch the local boys boldly shooting the rapids clutching the inflated inner tubes of motor tyres.

Imeretia abounds in tea plantations and vineyards and produces wines that rival those of Kakhetia, including a better-than-average rosé, while Georgian green tea at three roubles a pound sells all over Central Asia and the Caucasus. The local bazaar, as one would expect, is a sight for sore eyes, with its piles of grapes, peaches and melons, fresh eggs, extremely expensive jars of honey and great bowls of sour cream.

A dozen miles to the north-west of Kutaisi, perched high on a hillside above the river in full view of the main chain of the Caucasus, is the splendid monastery of Gelati, endowed at the beginning of the twelfth century by King David the Builder. In King David's day Gelati became one of the most important religious and also cultural centres in mediaeval Georgia. Within its precincts are three churches, a bell-tower and the ruins of the academy founded with King David's support by the famous philosopher Petritsi.

Of the three churches, the largest is the great sandstone Cathedral of the Virgin Mary, containing some remarkable twelfth-century mosaics and frescoes. The two lesser churches are dedicated to St George and St Nicholas respectively, the latter being built on two storeys. From under its little free-standing belfry rises a spring of fresh clear water. King David himself lies buried under the archway of one of the gates of the monastery. It is said that, as a token of humility, he wished his grave to be walked on by as many people as possible. Nearby are the ruins of Petritsi's Academy, with its windows looking across the valley to the mountains beyond.

In the district of Racha, forty or fifty miles beyond Gelati, high up in the foothills of the Caucasus, stands the church of Nikortsminda, yet another magnificent example of Georgian mediaeval architecture. You approach it through an exuberantly fertile valley with, on either side of the road, tea plantations and vineyards, producing light, rather flowery wines that hold their own with the heavier vintages of Gurjani and Tsinandali. The little church stands on a low green mound on the outskirts of a village. Over the wall is the playground of the village school. Beyond it, green orchards and vineyards slope steeply down to a little mountain stream. Built of mellow, golden-coloured stone, the church is hexagonal, its conical cupola rising from a splendid drum, pierced by tall narrow windows with beautifully carved architraves. High on the north wall above three perfectly proportioned blind arches is a splendid figure of Christ. Beyond Nikortsminda the valley of the Rioni narrows, and the road – the Ossetian Military Highway – climbs up to the town of Oni and beyond it to the Mamison Pass, whence it descends, as we have seen, to Alagir on the far side of the Caucasus, not many miles from Ordzhonikidze.

One of the few surviving secular buildings of feudal times is the great ruined palace of the Georgian kings at Geguti, four or five miles to the south of Kutaisi, where the Rioni Valley opens out into a spreading plain. 'In the autumn of 1125,' we are told, 'King David the Builder came to Geguti, where he hunted and rested and, having settled all local affairs, in March departed for Karthli.' From the size of the great broken arch of its banqueting-hall which towers above a tumbled mass of bricks and masonry, it is clear that his onetime palace was on a grandiose scale.

From Kutaisi some years back I drove westwards through the mountains to the Black Sea, passing *en route* the ruins of several splendid castles and churches. Once or twice we strayed from the main road a few miles northwards into the foothills of Mingrelia and Svanetia. Might there be a chance of pushing on into the high mountains of Svanetia and reaching Mestia, its capital? It was hard to say. But by this time it had come on to rain in torrents; the dark-green hills were veiled in cloud and mist, and in the end we abandoned any further attempts at exploration and simply pushed on along the bumpy, then half-finished road, arriving at dusk at Sukhumi, capital of the Autonomous Republic of Abkhasia, a city said to have been founded by the Romans in the second century AD.

I am not sure what I had expected Sukhumi to be like, probably dazzling white concrete hotels and sanatoria and nothing much else. It was in fact quite different: a charming late nineteenth-century watering-place, set against a background of lush subtropical vegetation, with stucco villas, a promenade, a pier, a bathing-beach and boat-trips round the bay where Jason and the Argonauts first landed. Best of all there were peepshows – miniature pagodas, standing some five feet high and elaborately inlaid with ivory and mother-of-pearl. Through one of several sets of eyepieces, you gazed at stereoscopic views of the Folies Bergère, the Taj Mahal, King Edward VII on his way to open Parliament, Sarah Bernhardt as L'Aiglon, Lily Elsie as the Merry Widow, and Kaiser Wilhelm reviewing his troops in preparation for World War I. All were in constant use by a succession of fascinated Soviet citizens of all ages happily goggling at the slightly faded splendours of the past. Nearby the thud and ping of equally eager holiday-makers proving that great strength rings the bell and wins a prize reverberated merrily from under the palm trees.

Further along the front we discovered an intriguing-looking tavern named The Dioscuri after Castor and Pollux, the two sons of Zeus who accompanied the Argonauts on their journey. Built on a rocky promontory above the blue waters of the bay near the site of the old Turkish slave-market, it gives the feeling that you are dining in some airy marine cavern. Here relays of merry Abkhasians (who, though they might not like to be told so, are very like Georgians only more so) eat long, leisurely meals, washed down as usual by litres of the local wine. A little further along the promenade stands a monument to a number of Red Army soldiers killed while seeking to suppress the now long-forgotten nationalist insurrection of 1924. After lunch we spent two agreeable hours in Sukhumi's famous Botanical Gardens, founded in 1840 and containing a marvellous collection of subtropical and tropical plants. Three or four miles outside the town is a splendid eleventh or twelfth-century bridge over the River Besleti, said to have been built by the Venetians and proving, if this is so, just how far the influence of Venice extended in the Middle Ages.

After our preliminary probing of the foothills, the idea of somehow reaching Svanetia stayed with me for several years. A hundred years before, it had been a happy hunting-ground for the famous mountaineers of the nineteenth century, but since the Revolution, no more than a handful of foreigners had ever reached it. My Georgian friends, for their part, spoke of getting there as the easiest thing in the world. 'You just take a light plane from Tbilisi,' they said, 'or drive.' But, when it came to the point, the flights had a way of being cancelled. The weather had closed in. The snow had come earlier that year. Or the road, such as it was, had been blocked by an avalanche. And each time in the end the project had to be dropped. It was not until several years later that it once more seriously took shape and the necessary visas were granted for a journey by car.

The road from Kutaisi to the little town of Zugdidi, once the capital of Mingrelia and residence of its Dadiani princes, where you turn off northwards into the mountains, ran between plantations of tea and Indian corn and rich-looking patches of pasture across a flat fertile, alluvial plain – the valley of the river Rioni. Along the road, agreeably lined with poplars and plane trees, cows, calves and pigs of all sizes drifted haphazard, totally ignoring such oncoming traffic as there was. We were in Abkhasia and in front of their houses Abkhasian peasant women, in black from head to foot, their pale features peering from the folds of their black mediaeval-looking cowls, gossiped with each other or kept an eye on goats or pigs or children.

Turning north at Zugdidi, we started to climb. Then, all of a sudden, round a corner, a great panorama of mountains opened out before us. Soon we were climbing more and more steeply, as we followed the valley of the Inguri River, a rushing mountain torrent, now dammed at one point to form a great artificial lake. For the next three or four hours after this the road, still climbing steeply, ran upwards through a thickly wooded gorge with towering cliffs on either side and the grey waters of the Inguri a thousand feet below us. Then, all at once, at four or five thousand feet, the valley opened out and we found ourselves in a region of high Alpine pastures with cattle and sheep grazing and villagers getting in the hay, alternating, as in most mountain regions, with a pattern of small, intensely cultivated plots. As we followed the road with its backdrop of tall mountain peaks, we came first to one and then to another mountain village, each with its cluster of tall mediaeval towers, resembling in their way the roughly contemporary towers of San

Gimignano in Tuscany. Of the villages we passed, few could rival the little hamlet of Soli, with its dozen or so towers sharply outlined against a tremendous background of snow-capped mountains.

Finally, somewhat to our relief, for it had been a long hard drive over a bad road (seventy miles in six hours) and we had in the process climbed some four or five thousand feet, we reached our destination, Mestia, the principal town or rather village of Svanetia and found, again to our relief – indeed surprise – more than adequate accommodation.

At the local inn we were gratified to discover that we had as our fellow-guest no less a personage than His Holiness the Patriarch of All Georgia, in whose honour a somewhat rudimentary hot-water system was now switched on (to be no less promptly switched off on his departure next morning.) Before leaving, he partook, I noticed rather enviously, of a caviar breakfast, carried to his apartment with due deference by a lavishly-bearded acolyte. In these parts the Church is still held in high regard.

By now the sun was shining brightly, the snowy peaks had emerged from their encompassing mists and vapours, and following, we discovered, in His Holiness's footsteps, we set out in our sturdy Latvian-made minibus to climb another couple of thousand feet to Ushguli or Heart Without Fear, a complex of strongly-fortified towers and scarcely less strongly-fortified churches, which at six thousand feet above sea-level is said to be the highest village in Georgia, if not in Europe, spending six months of the year under thick snow. On our way there we again followed the valley of the Inguri, its swirling grey waters appearing at frequent intervals several hundred feet below us, while high above us towered two of Svanetia's highest mountains, Tednuli and the massive cleft peak of Ushba, both over fifteen thousand feet high. As we negotiated the road's frequent hairpin bends, I was interested to notice by the roadside a number of little tin letter boxes each fashioned to resemble a church with a tiny cross on top. They must, I reflected, have been a source of satisfaction to the Patriarch, as he passed that way.

At Ushguli we were warmly welcomed by the women of the village with a plentiful assortment of local delicacies, delicious freshly-baked *khatchapuri* (hot cheese pasties) *mehadi* (cornbread), white goat cheese and, as an accompaniment, handfuls of strange aromatic herbs. It was in Ushguli, we were proudly told, that Medea, the fair witch-maiden, the priestess of the grove, gathered her magic herbs with which to bewitch Jason and his Argonauts.

Perched high among Ushguli's ramparts we found no less than seven little Christian churches, all more or less in use. It was these, we discovered, that the Patriarch had travelled all the way from Tbilisi to visit. In one tiny tenth-century chapel where Easter is celebrated each year (the other Feasts being celebrated in the other churches), we came on some remarkable frescoes, crosses, and icons of the same period, proudly shown to us by the self-appointed curator, a serious-minded young man with a tawny beard and a tartan shirt who, after taking a degree in Tbilisi, felt irresistibly drawn back to his native Svanetia where he now led a happy existence working on a farm, painting in a variety of different manners and looking after this and Ushguli's other churches. The chapel's little outer porch, he told us, was where the congregation gathered on feast days before Mass and where, as part of the service, they still sacrificed farm animals brought with them for that purpose.

That his was a not unusual pattern for young Svanetians or Svans as they are called, to follow was likewise demonstrated by Rosika, an engaging and no less dedicated young woman, whom we found caring for the treasures of early Svanetian church art now assembled in the eleventh-century church of St George in Mestia itself. She too, it seemed, had felt the pull of her native mountains and abandoned a promising academic career in Tbilisi to return to her own country and her own people.

With Rosika's readily given help, I managed in a comparatively short time to fill in the many gaps in my knowledge of Svanetia and the Svans. Unlike their neighbours, the mainly Mohammedan Ossetians, the Svans are essentially of the same race as Georgians and speak a language which is in effect an archaic form of Georgian, though in addition to this they have a secret hunting language, designed to mystify both the beasts of the chase and any evil spirits that could be around. In their remote mountain fastnesses, the Christian Svans managed not unnaturally to retain throughout the Middle Ages a greater purity of race and language than their town-based compatriots in the plain, overrun as these constantly were by hordes of invaders. They likewise clung steadfastly to the ancient religious and other traditions of their race and to the very essence of Georgian nationhood. In times of trouble this is where many of Georgia's most sacred national treasures were carried for safe-keeping by the Svans, who thus became in a sense the custodians of Georgia's national heritage. During the repeated Persian and Turkish invasions of the seventeenth and eighteenth centuries, Svanetia was in practice cut off from the rest of Georgia and the Svans left largely to their own devices. But this periodic isolation in no way inhibited their cultural or artistic development and I saw many striking examples of the work of self-taught native Svanetian artists and craftsmen.

In appearance, the Svans are a good-looking race, possessing the clearcut features, proud bearing and independent spirit of the highlander. The Turks and Persians were not, it seems, alone in experiencing the full force of Svanetian resistance. Tales are still told of a revolt against the Russians as recently as the 1870s when the Tsar's tax collectors and excisemen were obliged to use cannon and even dynamite to dislodge the embattled villagers, still stubbornly holding out in their fortified towers.

On our return journey we broke our journey in the tiny hamlet of Luha, where we quenched our very considerable thirst with cups of refreshing home-made raspberry juice given us by a true matriarch, the widow Dadeshkiliani. Still very much the head of a family of seventeen, the old lady, whose husband had died some years back, was that morning holding the fort with one of her daughters-in-law and three little grandsons, while her two sons, her unmarried daughters and the rest of the family gathered in the harvest and herded the sheep and cattle in the high hills. Her house, a capacious one with a wide gaily-painted veranda hung with variegated strings of dried fruit, was typical of the Svan way of life, based on an extended family, all living together. Hanging on the wall of the roomy kitchen was the portrait of a heroic-looking character with flowing moustaches who turned out to be the family's forebear, the early nineteenth-century Svanetian poet Dadeshkiliani, whom his descendants and the Svans in general still hold in great honour. It was only later that I discovered that, before the Russian conquest, the Dadeshkilianis had also been the ruling princes of Svanetia and that I had therefore been entertained unawares by royalty.

Always interested in the private sector of Soviet farming, which contributes so much to the country's agricultural production, I learned that, with the orchards round the house, several rows of promising-looking hives producing the most delicious honey, a patch of land 'across the road', and the uplands where the two sons were busy with the harvest, the family were altogether farming some five hectares which clearly supported a more than adequate standard of living. As a sideline, meanwhile, the old mother was turning out a great number of the plain grey or white round felt hats worn by every male Svan, which afford protection against sun and rain alike. As we watched, she carefully moistened the grey and white wool and moulded it into shape.

Bumping and jolting back down the road to Zugdidi (which, even downhill, took six hours to reach) we drove on between the high wooded cliffs and past the great artificial lake till we again reached the valley of the Inguri and the fertile alluvial plain which reaches from Kutaisi to the sea, heading this time for Sukhumi. The open parkland through which we were now passing, dotted with clumps of well-grown park trees and with more trees lining the road, had a look of the English Home Counties. It was only when you saw that the fields on either side of the road were vineyards or tea, tobacco or orange plantations, that you realized where you were, namely approaching the Black Sea Riviera.

Soon we were driving past rows of smartly-painted holiday homes, each with its own well-tended garden containing at least one palm tree and no doubt worth a considerable sum were it ever to come on the market, though just how such transactions are conducted in a Communist society would not, I suspect, be an easy thing to discover.

Gutted by fire, the Hotel Abkhasia where I had stayed on my last visit to Sukhumi was now no more than an empty shell. But at the equivalent of fifty pounds a night for bed without breakfast (Sukhumi is not cheap), we were able to find accommodation at the Ritza, so called not, as might be supposed, after the illustrious Monsieur Ritz, but after a neighbouring lake of that name. Sukhumi, I soon discovered, had hardly changed at all. It still had the same slightly shabby charm which I had enjoyed on my previous visit and at the Ritza (built in 1914) my large airy room with its tall windows looking out on the palm trees of the esplanade was all that anyone could have wanted. In the adjoining rather dreary dining-room everything had a way of being 'off, Comrade', but a short distance along the front we found a large and cheerful open-air restaurant serving tough but tasty Abkhasian smoked meat, the inevitable *katchapuri* and a filling kind of corn porridge called *mamalinga*, washed down with badly-needed draughts of a raw Abkhasian red wine. Though they resemble them in many of their habits, the Abkhasians, I learned over dinner, are of a different race from the Georgians and among themselves speak an entirely different language.

From Sukhumi all the way to Sochi a kind of Black Sea Corniche carries you swiftly and smoothly along the coast from one fashionable resort to another, each with its palm trees and pier, its dazzling white hotels, its bathing beaches, boat-trips, public parks and white stucco colonnades, with on one side the blue waters of the Black Sea and on the other the dark hills of Circassia. On our way we stopped for an al fresco luncheon with a local group of professional centenarians who, magnificently decked out in national dress, were welcoming a recent recruit to their ranks and, despite the current drive against drinking, made it quite clear that it was not thanks to teetotalism that they had reached their advanced age.

Sochi, sixty miles further north, is, in complete contrast to Sukhumi, an entirely modern up-to-the-minute seaside resort in a splendid setting. From it we drove up into the mountains which here rise sharply from the sea. The valley we chose to explore, that of the River Mzymta, leads up through spectacular scenery into what was once Circassia. Egged on by an enterprising Scot called David Urquhart, the native Circassians fought the Russians fiercely for fifty years or more before being finally subdued in 1864, when many of them took refuge in Turkey, where their women were already in great demand for the better-class harems of the Ottoman Empire. Today few Circassians remain in the valley which, soon after their departure, was converted by the Tsar into an imperial game reserve and is now farmed by a variety of incomers from all over the country.

Together with Yalta in the Crimea which, like Sukhumi, possesses agreeably nineteenth-century overtones. Sochi and Sukhumi are the most sought-after of all Soviet holiday resorts. This is where the really big shots (or, as the Russians say, 'big birds') from the Kremlin have their villas and where the next level of high officials spend their holidays in only slightly less luxurious rest-homes. Here, too, many government departments and industries have their own 'sanatoria', where each year their workers are accommodated for two or three weeks, each in accordance with his rank and importance, for an all-in charge of two or three roubles a day.

At such establishments due emphasis is placed on health, regular meals, regular exercise, early nights and communal gymnastics, leaving not too much 'free time' for other activities. Nor are they to everyone's taste. 'My department has a simply marvellous rest-home,' one official boasted to me, 'with swimming-pools, tennis courts and running tracks – the lot. You never saw such a place.' 'You must enjoy that', I replied. 'Well,' he said, 'in practice I don't seem to go there much. I find it more of a rest to share part of a dacha with some friends on our own.' And immediately I had visions of smoke-filled rooms and endless tea and talk and an occasional bottle of vodka. Less healthy perhaps, but, to some tastes, better relaxation. For the younger generation, on the other hand, for school children, Pioneers (Communist Scouts and Guides), students and Young Communists, all kinds of holiday camps and healthful outdoor activities are admirably organized by those responsible and in the Caucasus you constantly come on sun-tanned groups of them hiking enthusiastically through the forests and mountains.

Alaverdi

Ananuri

PREVIOUS PAGE Mountain of the Cross, Georgian Military Highway   OPPOSITE Inside Ananuri

Mausoleum of the Shirvan Shahs, Shemakha

The Patriarch, Mtzkhet

OPPOSITE A Georgian Dancer

The Georgian Military Highway

Al fresco

OPPOSITE Mtzkhet

Mount Kasbek

Lermontov's House, Tbilisi

OPPOSITE Tbilisi

A Village War Memorial, Northern Caucasus

OPPOSITE The Towers of the Dead

LEFT St Gayane, Etchmiadzin

RIGHT Kachkar, Etchmiadzin

OPPOSITE Northern Caucasus

ABOVE The Katholikos of all the Armenians

Outside the Railway Station, Erivan

OPPOSITE Gelati

OVERLEAF Svanetia

3

Noah's Vineyard

The Armenians' martyrs are as characteristic
as their merchants.

From Tbilisi it is half-an-hour's flight or an easy day's drive southwards through the mountains to Erivan, capital of the Soviet Socialist Republic of Armenia. Situated some three or four thousand feet above sea-level in the valley of the Araxes, Erivan, a city proud to be ninety per cent Armenian and only three per cent Russian, was, they say, founded by Noah in person. A few miles to the south, just beyond the Turkish frontier, looms the vast mass of Mount Ararat, where the Ark came to rest after the Flood. 'Erivan!' cried the Patriarch, looking out of the porthole. 'It has shown itself!' and so gave the city its name. Noah's next move, as we know from the ninth chapter of Genesis, was to plant some vines, make some wine and drink it, thereby starting a happy tradition which has continued in Armenia to the present day, the wine produced there being more than adequate and the brandy even better. A hundred miles or so from Erivan, on the Persian frontier, glimpsed fifty years ago on a dimly-remembered railway journey, is the dusty little town of Nakhichevan or Noahville, where Noah himself, it is said, lies buried in a disused churchyard.

This takes us back to the Flood. Few people or countries have a longer history than the Armenians. Mention of their forerunners and probable forefathers, the Urartians, is made in an Assyrian inscription of the thirteenth century BC. By the ninth century Urartu, as Armenia was then known, was already one of the most powerful states in the Middle East. The transition from Urartu to Armenia seems to have taken place during the sixth century and in 521 BC we hear of Armenia as a satrapy of Darius the Great of Persia.

For almost two hundred years the Armenians remained under Persian rule. After Alexander the Great's victory over the Persians at Arbela in 331 BC, they next passed abruptly under the control of Macedonia, thereafter enjoying a measure of autonomy under Greek suzerainty. For forty years or so, from 95 to 50 BC, a native Armenian, King

Dikran or Tigranes the great, ruled over an independent Armenian Empire extending from the Caspian to the Mediterranean and from Mesopotamia to the Pontic Alps. Once again Armenia had become a major power in the Middle East, only to fall in the end under the dominion of Rome. Subsequent Armenian rulers sought, with varying degrees of success, to play the Persians off against the Romans and vice versa. With the defeat and capture of the Roman Emperor Valerian by the Great King Shapur I in AD 260, Armenia again became part of Persia. But in 286, under Diocletian, Rome recovered her former losses and it was under Roman auspices that King Trdat or Tiridates III was restored to the throne of his ancestors.

Following the conversion of Tiridates in the year 301 by his cousin, St Gregory the Illuminator (whom he had previously kept confined in a well full of reptiles), Armenia became a bulwark of Christianity in Asia. Henceforward the Armenian Church was to serve as a rallying-point for the Armenian nation. But the Persians kept up their pressure, the Armenians were divided among themselves, and towards the middle of the fifth century Armenia was reconquered by Persia. For a time the Armenians endured savage persecution at the hands of the Persians. Then, in the seventh century, came conquest by the Arabs and no less savage persecution at their hands.

During the centuries that followed, what had once been Armenia was bandied about between the Persians, the Byzantine emperors and the Mohammedan khalifs of Baghdad. It was not until the ninth century that she regained a measure of independence and some of her former glory. For a century and a half, a small Armenian kingdom with its capital at Ani flourished under the Bagratids, the princely Armenian family who also held sway in the neighbouring kingdom of Georgia. This was the high point of mediaeval Armenian civilization and prosperity. At Ani and elsewhere Armenian architecture and other national arts blossomed and flourished. But in 1064 both Armenia and Georgia were again overrun, this time by the Seljuk Sultan Alp Arslan. Ani, with its magnificent churches and palaces, was sacked and burnt and, under Turkish rule, has remained a ghost-town ever since.

Armenia's existence, even as a semi-independent state, was at an end. During the centuries that followed, her former territories were fought over by Mongols, Turks and Persians, and their inhabitants scattered far and wide over the world. Yet with stubborn tenacity the Armenians somehow retained their identity as a nation. In this the Armenian Church, independent of both Rome and Byzantium, played a vital part. Wherever they were, the Armenians clung to their religion with a zeal made all the more desperate by the knowledge that it was all that remained of their nationhood and through the centuries the Katholikos of Holy Etchmiadzin, to this day Head of the Armenian Church throughout the world, acted as a national as well as a religious leader.

After the Russian annexation of Georgia in 1801 the Armenians were no longer so completely cut off from outside help. In the Tsar they now had a powerful neighbour and friend, whose declared policy it was to bring the rest of Transcaucasia under his direct rule, in particular the areas populated by Christians. In 1804 a first attempt by Russia to seize the Persian-protected Khanate of Erivan was unsuccessful. In the summer of 1827, however, the Russians under General Paskevich again invaded Erivan, at the same time occupying Holy Etchmiadzin, to which the Persians immediately laid siege. A savage struggle for the monastery ensued, during the whole of which the embattled Patriarch Narses V bravely held aloft the monastery's most precious relic, the Holy Spear which pierced the side of Jesus, while at the same time praying hard to the God of Victories. In the end the Russians won the day. For a time the Persians continued to fight back fiercely, but in October Erivan itself finally fell to the Russians and Armenia, with Georgia, became part of the Russian viceroyalty of the Caucasus.

Just as Armenia's stony, rugged mountains contrast sharply with the smiling land of Georgia, so the Armenians and the Georgians, though near neighbours, possess very different national characters. The Georgians are chivalrous romantic extroverts, the Armenians hard workers, hard fighters and hard bargainers, who proudly claim that, while it takes three Greeks to get the better of a Jew, it takes at least three Jews to get the better of an Armenian. As a French observer once remarked, they have, in the course of their history, had *'juste le temps de s'enrichir entre deux massacres'*. Or, as someone else put it, 'their martyrs are as characteristic as their merchants'.

Anyone who spends even a few days in Armenia cannot fail to be impressed by the strength of the Armenians' national feeling. It is this that through the centuries has enabled them to survive. Over three million Armenians live in the Soviet Union, a couple of million of them in Soviet Armenia. Another million and a half are scattered over the world. Strong links persist between them all. Today, Erivan's hotels are full of expatriate Armenians visiting the old folk back home. Over the years many thousands of ethnic Armenians from all over the world have returned to settle in their homeland and there are now said to be direct flights between Los Angeles and Erivan.

Something that strikes one immediately about the Armenians is their penetrating intelligence. Nothing escapes them. They have read one's thoughts before these have had time to take shape. It is, incidentally, to a mythical Radio Armenia that other Soviet citizens usually attribute the more amusing *bons mots* about the regime. As for the business sense of the Armenians, this has been famous world wide for many thousands of years. Under Communism, the opportunities may be limited, but signs of business acumen are everywhere. How revealing, for example, that in Armenia there are more private cars per head of the population than in any other Soviet republic.

On a recent visit to Erivan II was privileged to witness the impact on an audience of seven or eight thousand young Armenians of the famous Russian pop star, Alla Pugachova, so called presumably after the eighteenth-century Cossack freebooter of that name. As the diminutive middle-aged blonde with her powerful personal magnetism and massive psychedelic and electronic back-up skipped or rocked about the stage, alternately crooning cosily into a microphone or belting out one of her favourite numbers in a voice that shook the concrete rafters of Erivan's vast new Sports Centre, it was fascinating to observe the strangely archaic features and big, liquid brown eyes of the solemn Armenian youths and maidens all around me take on an expression of even greater intensity than usual, as they paid their enthusiastic tribute to this triumphant manifestation of a culture as alien to Armenia as it is to Marxism–Leninism. In the local shops her latest discs and cassettes were selling like hot cakes, as were those of the Beatles and Bing Crosby, not to mention Amanda Lear, gazing from the sleeve with a wealth of epicene sex-appeal.

But while the Armenians welcome foreign talent in this field, the true heroes of the jazz scene in Erivan are the local Valagian Group, who not only appear regularly on local television and whose concerts are invariably a sell-out, but also tour the Soviet Union and appear in jazz concerts world wide. What they play, moreover, is not rock or pop, but pure classical jazz interpreted in their own essentially Armenian manner. None of which, be it observed, could come about without a measure of government and Party approval, indeed support – already a far cry from the grudging tolerance of former years.

Over the fifty years I have known it, Erivan itself has undergone a complete transformation. Hardly anything remains of the old town of roughly-built little flat-roofed houses I visited in the nineteen-thirties. Their place has been taken by an entirely new city of avenues and piazzas laid out in the grandest possible manner to house a population of more than half a million people. At the same time, Armenia as a whole has been heavily industrialized.

Like the Georgians, the Armenians have most successfully applied their country's traditional style of architecture to modern uses and in the buildings of present day Erivan it is possible to recognize the same designs and motifs, executed in the same reddish-yellow tufa, that are found in Armenian churches and monasteries of the early Middle Ages. One particularly striking modern building is the great covered market near the site of the former bazaar, where one need only watch, however briefly, the transactions between producer and consumer to realize that the Armenian is still nothing if not businesslike.

No one is more conscious than the Armenians of their tremendous past. 'The crest of the old Kings of Armenia', I was told as I passed some recently erected monument, and in the National Library, the Matenadaran, is an unrivalled collection of ancient Armenian books and manuscripts including no less than three codices and revealing in striking fashion the high standard of scholarship which prevailed in Armenia from the earliest times. Not far away from the bazaar, the Kok Jami, a handsome blue-and-yellow-tiled mosque and religious college built in the eighteenth century by Nadir Shah, recalls that not much more than a century-and-a-half ago Erivan was still a Persian city. But this is practically the only remaining trace of the Persian occupation.

To return to Noah, it seems likely that what he really said as he peered from the porthole of the Ark was not 'Erivan!' but 'Erebuni!' This is the name of an ancient walled stronghold standing on a hill in the northern suburbs of Erivan, which is all that is left of the original capital of Urartu. Erebuni was founded in the year 782 BC and in 1968 the people of Erivan proudly celebrated the 2750th anniversary of the foundation of their city.

The Armenian genius for architecture found its fullest expression in the magnificent early Christian churches and monasteries in which their country abounds. From the classical temples of the Hellenistic period was first developed a plain, domeless, vaulted basilica, similar to those found elsewhere in the Near East. By the sixth or seventh centuries, the Armenians, like the Georgians, had turned their attention to the problem of setting a central dome on a vaulted roof. Soon the cruciform church with a centrally placed dome had become the archetypal form of both Armenian and Georgian church architecture. For strategic reasons the churches and monasteries of Armenia were, like those of Georgia, often sited high up in the mountains or at the head of valleys in readily defensible positions. This and their solid construction has meant that large numbers of them survive in a good state of preservation; also that they frequently happen to be situated in magnificent natural surroundings.

A dozen miles due west from Erivan along the fertile Ararat valley, enclosed within a massive wall, is the oldest and most famous monastery of all: Holy Etchmiadzin. Here the Katholikos of Armenia has his See in a Cathedral originally built in 309 by St Gregory the Illuminator when Rome was still a pagan city. Thence he keeps in daily touch with Armenians the world over. In a crypt beneath his cathedral, you are shown on enquiring the remains of the Temple of Venus on top of which first a Christian altar and then the original Christian basilica was built. And after that the well into which the Katholikos's remote predecessor St Gregory, having first converted his cousin King Trdat III to Christianity, rudely pushed the local pagan gods, sealing them neatly off with a marble slab.

Nearby, the ancient Churches of St Hripsime and St Gayane are both still in use. The former was built in the seventh century to commemorate the martyrdom of Hripsime, a beautiful Christian maiden, who with her nurse Gayane had fled from Rome to escape persecution at the hands of the Emperor Diocletian. Struck by her exceptional good looks, King Trdat, at this stage still a pagan, sent his palace guard to fetch her. Having repelled his advances, Hripsime managed to escape, but was brought back and tortured to death. For this and other misdemeanours Trdat was turned by the Almighty into a pig and not suffered to resume human shape until he had agreed to release his cousin Gregory from the snake-pit and himself embrace Christianity.

The Church of St Hripsime, built in 681 on the site of an earlier *martyrion*, or martyr's shrine, and never since rebuilt or restored, is one of the most perfect examples of early Armenian Christian architecture. Cruciform, with its lofty central dome resting solidly on four apses and four supporting corner niches, its appearance from the outside is simple to the point of austerity, while within it is surprisingly light and harmonious. It was to serve as a prototype for numerous churches of this period, each in its way different from the others, offering endless variations on a single theme.

A few hundred yards from the Church of St Hripsime and similar to it in style is that of her nurse St Gayane, who shared her martyrdom. This was built some ten or twelve years later. An arched portico, added in the seventeenth century and containing the tombs of some high Armenian ecclesiastics, though perhaps detracting from its purity of style, adds greatly to its charm. Immediately in front of the church is a rough-hewn oblong block of stone. On feast days during the service, a lamb is led seven times round the stone, its throat cut, a fire lit and the roasted flesh distributed to the congregation.

A mile or two outside Etchmiadzin, looking across a vista of green vineyards to the snow-capped peaks of Ararat, are the ruins of Svartnots. These are all that is left of a gigantic three-storeyed Christian cathedral, a hundred and fifty feet high, built in about 643, at the time of the first Arab invasions and destroyed some three hundred years later by an earthquake or, according to other accounts, a Saracen raid. Circular in form, it rose in three stages to a single central dome. Broken columns, shattered walls, piers and buttresses, the remains of the high altar and crypt are all contained within a great circular rim of faced stone which once formed the perimeter of the cathedral and at the same time the three steps you climbed to enter it. Standing proudly out amongst the debris, carved on the capitol of a broken column, is the great heraldic Spread Eagle of the old Armenian kings. Svartnots probably represented the peak of Armenian architectural achievement. When it was completed, the Byzantine Emperor Constantine III who happened to attend its consecration, was so impressed by what he saw that he at once carried the architect off with him to build him a cathedral like it back in Constantinople. But the architect died on the journey and the Byzantines were left to make do with St Sophia.

Twenty miles due east of Erivan, dramatically sited on a triangular promontory high above a valley, with walls of sheer rock falling abruptly away on every side in a splendidly impregnable position, are the massive ruins of the ancient Urartian fortress of Garni. Built on the site of an even older Neolithic stronghold, its ruins date back to the eighth century BC, while stones inscribed in Greek, Aramaic and Armenian bear witness to its continued occupation by successive conquerors throughout the centuries. In Hellenistic times, Garni, which stands more than five thousand feet above sea-level and produces an excellent vin rosé, was the summer residence of the Armenian kings. Passing through the crumbling gates of the fortress, you come on a fine classical temple, built in the first century of our era, partly destroyed by an earthquake in 1679 but now carefully restored. Outside the walls of the fortress are numerous other ruins and remains.

In a secluded side valley not far from Garni you come on the dramatically-sited Monastery of the Holy Lance at Geghard standing in a commanding position near the head of the valley with precipitous cliffs of rock rising on all sides and a rushing mountain torrent sweeping past it. According to ancient tradition, Geghard has been a place of Christian worship since the fourth century and above the monastery itself are several little cells for hermits cut in the face of the rock and dedicated to St Gregory the Illuminator. Beside them are some fine early stone crosses or *khatchkars*. For devout Armenians, this is a place of particular holiness and the rockface all around in blackened by the smoke of innumerable candles lit over the centuries to the greater glory of St Gregory. Like St Gregory's shrine, the main church of the monastery, the much larger thirteenth-century Church of the Virgin, with its cruciform dome and connecting chapels, is cut largely out of the living rock. Here too, in accordance with ancient practice, farm animals are still brought by the congregation to be blessed and then sacrificed.

A visit to Garni and Geghard, another thousand feet above sea-level, and a clamber round the precincts leaves you with a healthy appetite for lunch at a handy *shashlichnaya* perched above a precipice only a few hundred yards below the monastery and commanding a splendid view of the valley beneath. There, if you make friends with the cook, you can feast in summer or winter alike off freshly grilled *kebabs* and *shashliks* along with great loaves of newly baked Armenian bread.

Travelling northwards by car from Erivan to Tbilisi you come on numerous other fine examples of Armenian mediaeval church architecture, notably the eleventh-century monastery of Kecharis, some twenty miles from Erivan. From Kecharis another twenty miles' drive in a north-westerly direction brings you to Lake Sevan, lying, like so much of Armenia, at more than six thousand feet above sea-level and larger, one is told, than all the lakes in Switzerland put together. 'There is', writes Marco Polo, who passed that way, 'a great lake at the foot of a mountain. And in this lake are found no fish either great or small through the year until Lent comes. But on the first day of Lent they find in it the finest fish in the word, and great store thereof; and these continue to be found until Easter-Eve. And after that they are found no more till Lent comes round again. And so it is every year.' Today, under a Soviet government, the fish in Lake Sevan ignore the Feasts of the Church and, passing that way at Whitsuntide, I have eaten more than one fine salmon-trout from its waters.

On a promontory reaching out into the lake stand two ancient churches dedicated respectively to St Karapet and to the Holy Apostles, and both dating back to the ninth century. They were founded, it appears, by a princess who fell in love with a fisherman. When her father forbade her to see her lover and banished her to a nunnery, she solved her problem with true Armenian ingenuity by building one for herself by the lakeside, where he could (and did) visit her nightly.

From Sevan the road carries you through wooded gorges and over a seven or eight thousand-foot pass to Dilijan, a pleasantly-situated health resort, once frequented by the famous Armenian composer Khatchaturian. Up a secluded valley, a dozen miles from Dilijan, the monastery of Haghartsin, stands among splendidly wooded hills. Looking out over the valley to a distant prospect of blue mountains, its three churches, refectory and outbuildings are harmoniously grouped at the head of a green glen above a rushing mountain stream, while all round the wind stirs the leaves of a mixed forest of beech, oak, elm, hornbeam and lime. Nearby, on green banks and under the trees, half-hidden in the grass, are a number of ancient shrines and finely-carved crosses, all testifying to the essential sanctity of the place. Of the three churches, the largest is that of St Gregory, built in the tenth century of rough white limestone. Near it is the thirteenth-century Church of the Virgin as well as another smaller church of the same period dedicated to St Stephen. There was no priest in sight when I last went to Haghartsin, but on the altar of the largest church some lighted candles were burning, proof enough that people still worshipped there.

To reach the nearby monastery of Sanahin (and it certainly repays a visit), you drive up a steep rocky track to a high plateau some three thousand feet above sea-level, commanding a panoramic view of the surrounding country. Across a precipitous gorge stand a line of dark copper-bearing cliffs. The oldest of the monastery buildings is an early tenth-century church of the Virgin. High up under the gable on its eastern wall, a charming contemporary carving depicts its founders, King Smbat and King Gurgen Bagrationi. The much larger Cathedral of St Saviour, built in the second half of the tenth century, is also cruciform. Near the Church of the Virgin is a tiny chapel dedicated to St Gregory the Illuminator, built at the end of the tenth century and later rebuilt. Adjoining this is an eleventh-century library possessing a fine pillared gallery. Its stone shelves and niches are now empty of books, their contents having been pillaged by the Mongols or some subsequent invader. Wedged between the Church of St Saviour and that of the Virgin, and thus protecting both from snow-drifts, is the long vaulted and pillared Academy of Gregory the Magister, a leading local scholar and divine who in the Middle Ages made Sanahin a famous centre of learning and culture. Nearby are the mausoleum of some local princes and a beautiful thirteenth-century belfry.

Five or ten miles away on another high plateau stands the Monastery of Akhpat, looking out to Sanahin across the intervening gorge. Of its three churches the oldest and finest is the Cathedral of the Cross, built between 977 and 991. On the eastern wall under the gable is carved another representation of King Smbat and King Gurgen, the founders it shares with Sanahin, both heavily bearded and turbaned and holding between them a model of the cathedral itself. Adjacent to St Cross are two similar domed churches, that of St Gregory, built in 1005, and that of the Virgin, built some two hundred years later, as well as a remarkable three-storeyed thirteenth-century belfry. From Dilijan it is no more than a hundred miles to Tbilisi, an agreeable drive through hilly country.

One carries away from Soviet Armenia the impression of a highly individual country different in any number of ways from other Soviet republics. More than a century-and-a-half of government from St Petersburg or Moscow has naturally left its mark, but it would in any case have been surprising if the Armenians, after clinging to their nationhood with such amazing tenacity, through a thousand years of Mongol, Turkish and Persian occupation, had not managed to retain their full share of national characteristics.

There can be no more fascinating experience, after attending High Mass in the sixteen centuries-old Cathedral of Holy Etchmiadzin, than to be received in audience by that most impressive ecclesiastic and statesman, His Holiness Vasgen I, Katholikos of All Armenians who, when I last saw him, was keenly looking forward to a visit from his Brother-in-God, the Archbishop of Canterbury, only one example of the world-wide contacts which serve to set Soviet Armenia apart from the other republics of the Union. Talking to him, you are at once conscious of the immense significance in Armenian eyes of the Church over which he so ably presides and over whose ancient traditions he stands guard so effectively.

Of this I was vividly reminded, while walking round the cathedral precincts, by the sight of a number of what were clearly early nineteenth-century cast-iron cannon-balls or rather shell-cases, each with a hole for the fuse, now used to edge the flower beds. These, I was told by the Rector of the theological seminary, had been left over from the siege of June 1827, when Narses, the Katholikos of the day, supported by two sturdy acolytes, had held aloft the Sacred Spear throughout the battle until General Paskevich's liberating army had finally thrown back the invading Persians.

As you admire the astounding treasures of Armenian ecclesiastical art assembled in the museum, donated to the Cathedral by Mr and Mrs Alex Manoogian of the USA, you are conscious, too, of the manner in which Holy Etchmiadzin still serves as a focus of loyalty for Armenians world-wide, something which is borne out by the surprisingly large numbers of Armenians who come each year from all over the world to settle in the Land of their Fathers and make their homes there. In few countries in the world is one so constantly aware of a number of recurrent themes, religious, patriotic and creative which, whatever the obstacles, have somehow persisted through the centuries. The same feeling of an intense and persistent national consciousness is inspired by the striking monument to the victims of the Turkish massacres of 1895 and 1915, which stands on a hillside outside Erivan. Until recently, when visiting it, one as often as not found oneself in the company of elderly Armenians who, as children, had either narrowly escaped death themselves or else had lost close relatives in the massacres. But with the passage of time, these are becoming fewer.

4

Eastern Enclave

We may be slaves, but enslaved by Russia,
the Ruler of the Universe.

M. Y. LERMONTOV

The Soviet Socialist Republic of Azerbaijan, occupying the south-eastern corner of Trans-caucasia, has rather a different history and background from the other two Transcaucasian Republics. Consisting originally of Baku and several other Tartar Khanates, linked his-torically with Persian Azerbaijan, it was for centuries a more or less integral part of Persia. Its capital, Baku, once the principal port of the Persian province of Shirvan, later a semi-independent khanate and now the fifth city of the Soviet Union, was, after various vicissitudes, finally taken by the Russians in 1806. Today not much remains to remind one of Baku's Tartar and Persian past. It is now largely a Western city in which the ornate buildings of the nineteenth century contend as best they can with the products of modern Soviet architecture. Only the Palace of the Shirvanshahs and a few fine old fourteenth- and fifteenth-century mosques and caravanserais recall its former Tartar and Persian rulers, while from the massively built Maiden's Tower on the sea front the beautiful daughter of some early khan is said to have cast herself down to avoid her lustful father's incestuous advances.

For more than a hundred years now, Baku, once the haunt of Persian fire-worshippers, who adored the sacred flames that sprang mysteriously from the soil and even from the sea, has been above all an oil-town. The smell of oil hangs heavily in the air and gaunt derricks marking the oil-wells stretch far out into the Caspian and advance in serried ranks across the barren hinterland. Its population consists of a mixture of Azerbaijanis, Russians, Armenians and other nationalities. By now European Russians are the most numerous, though in the rest of Azerbaijan the native Turko-Tartars still predominate.

Of the three Soviet republics which lie beyond the Caucasus, Georgia, Armenia and Azerbaijan, I have visited Azerbaijan less frequently than the other two, my experience of it having until recently been limited to Baku, the capital, and Lenkoran, a harbour in the far south, to which I paid an eventful visit just fifty years ago, when, having wandered inadvertently into the frontier zone with Persia, I was very nearly shot.

Usually I have reached Baku by train or aeroplane. On recent visits, however, after an agreeable few days in Georgia, I have tried a new approach, namely by car from Telavi, the ancient capital of Kakhetia or Western Georgia, my purpose being to see something of an area with a Tartar population and Moslem traditions going back well beyond the time of Tamerlane, whose favourite hunting-ground, the Karabag, lay in this region.

The sun was hot on my last visit and, feeling the need for protection against it, I decided to buy myself one of the traditional soft black felt pillboxes with a button on top which they still wear in Kakhetia. The leading hatter in Telavi had eight different portraits of Generalissimo Stalin in his tiny shop in the high street, but no hat that would fit me. 'But', he said, 'I will make you one in ten minutes.' This seemed improbable but, sure enough, ten minutes later he had two hats ready, one black and one white. Handing him four roubles and placing the black one firmly on the back of my head, I set out for Azerbaijan, with a backward glance at a fine new statue of King Hercules II of Georgia, magnificent on his charger, guarding, sword in hand, what remains of his former palace.

Not many miles from Telavi we came to Gremi with its two ancient fortified churches high on their hilltop. The road we were following ran along the fertile Alazani valley between vineyards bearing the names of such famous local wines as Tsinandali and Mukuzani. In the ditches beside the road, water buffaloes wallowed contentedly.

Soon after leaving Gremi we reached the frontier with Azerbaijan. To the north rose the highlands of Daghestan, a formidable barrier broken here and there by an occasional river valley, but nowhere, even today, by a road. These were the mountains in which, in the nineteenth century, the Moslem tribesmen of the great Imam Shamyl held out against the Tsar's armies for more than thirty years. Climbing a few hundred yards up the bed of the stream that marks the border, we stopped half-way between frontier posts to lunch off Soviet sausage and flat Georgian bread, helped down by a bottle of Tsinandali, cooled in the icy water.

Twenty miles inside Azerbaijan at Zakatali, you come to the ruins of one of Shamyl's strongholds and not far away is the grave of the Imam's ally, rival and ultimately bitter enemy, Hadji Murad. Here Tolstoi served as a young officer and here he must have heard the story of Hadji Murad of whom he later wrote so movingly. It was at Zakatali too that, in 1905, after their ill-starred mutiny, the sailors of the cruiser *Potyomkin* were imprisoned at a safe distance from any possible sympathizers.

Seventy miles beyond Zakatali, in the shadow of three massive mountain peaks, we reached the little hill town of Sheki, where I was to spend the night at a hostelry describing itself, with engaging frankness, as 'Hotel Shaky'. At Sheki the local tribesmen managed to throw back Pompey's legions in 66 BC, but were in due course overrun and subjugated in turn by Arabs, Seljuks, Mongols, Turks, and Persians. In the first half of the eighteenth century, Sheki became the capital of an independent or semi-independent khanate under Persian suzerainty. This it remained until taken over by Russia a century later. Within the walls of its fortress stands the Khan's former palace, built in 1796, an agreeable two-storeyed building with a pleasant, tree-shaded garden in front of it. The greater part of each floor is taken up by one long room lighted by windows of brightly-coloured glass and lavishly decorated with wall paintings. Round the upper room runs a long frieze recalling the Khan's victories over his enemies, neat piles of whose severed heads appear as a recurrent motif.

For centuries, Sheki was an important trading post on the Silk Road to China and it still boasts two fine old caravanserais, the upper and the lower. Here the itinerant merchants lived in comfort in spacious rooms giving on to the open galleries of the first floor. Their trading was done in the great central courtyard and their goods stored in the cellars below. Soon, I was told, the upper caravanserai was to revert to its original role and again provide accommodation for foreign travellers as a welcome alternative to the Hotel Shaky. But on a subsequent visit to Azerbaijan, I was disappointed to find that this ambitious project had still not materialized.

Some miles outside Sheki, perched precipitously on a hilltop commanding the river valley which alone gives access to the interior of Daghestan, are the crumbling ruins of the Gelersen Gyoresen or Come-and-See Fortress, so named to recall the challenge broadcast by the Khan of the day to his enemies, of whom only the more imprudent accepted it and did not usually live to tell the tale. Having scrambled up to the top of the hill through impenetrable scrub at sunset, I can bear witness to the hazards any would-be invader must have faced trying to reach the top, let alone storm the fortress when he got there.

Somewhat surprisingly, Sheki boasts a first-class restaurant, cleverly sited on a hillside overlooking the valley and rejoicing in the name of Happiness, where I recently dined most satisfactorily off grilled sturgeon from the Caspian and chicken *shashlik*, accompanied by a bottle of more-than-adequate local wine. Though historically a Moslem country, Azerbaijan produces large quantities of quite good wine, which the Azerbaijanis boldly claim equals that of Georgia. The Kura-Araksin Valley and the Plain of Shirvan in which Sheki is situated together form one of the most fertile regions of Azerbaijan with an almost subtropical climate which, in addition to wine, produces tea, rice and tobacco. Sixty or so miles beyond Sheki you come to the Aksu Pass, commanding a wide view of the surrounding region. Thence you descend abruptly into country bearing a strong resemblance to Persia, of which for many years it was part: tawny hills in the foreground, and to your north a continuing line of amethyst mountains, the south-eastern extremity of the main range of the Caucasus.

The town of Shemakha, reached an hour or so later, was founded in the sixth century by the Sasanids and for seven or eight hundred years was the capital of the Khanate of Shirvan, a region famous for its carpets, which are, in fact, still produced there. Like Sheki, it lay on the caravan route to China and in the sixteenth century, in the days of the great merchant adventurers, even possessed an English trading post. Loosely attached to Persia, Shirvan was taken by the Russians in 1820. In 1849 an earthquake wiped out most of Shemakha and today only a few old buildings survive: a tenth-century mosque, almost completely rebuilt in the last century, and the domed mausoleums of the khans of

Shirvan, standing above the town on a hillside bristling with Moslem tombstones. Outside Shemakha are the ruins of the twelfth-century fortress of Gulistan.

Today, wine production is Shemakha's principal industry. Arriving there some years back, hungry and thirsty after an early start and a long drive, I demanded lunch – with no success whatever. Forcing my way into a kind of canteen adjoining the impressive new Party headquarters, I found to my dismay that, even here, there was nothing to eat at all. The grape harvest was at its height and every man, woman and child in the place was out in the vineyards picking the grapes. Shemakha was like a city of the dead. The streets were empty. Every shop was shut. Fortunately, when all seemed lost, someone remembered a friend who was a baker and came back a few minutes later with an armful of flat round loaves straight from the oven and a hunk of hard white cheese to go with them. Gnawing these gratefully, I pressed on across the arid plain to Baku, where I was thankful to find awaiting me an invitation to dinner at a restaurant in the old part of the town called the Caravanserai.

The Caravanserai, a relative innovation, is nothing less than a stroke of genius. With surprisingly few structural changes, a fine fourteenth-century caravanserai, once the halting-place of merchants from beyond the Caspian, had been transformed into the sort of restaurant one dreams of in one's wilder moments of fantasy. Eight or ten vaulted alcoves, their walls hung with fine old Shirvan carpets, gave on to a paved central courtyard open to the sky. In each alcove, a low table, heaped with exotic delicacies, had room round it for a party of a dozen or more. In a neighbouring alcove, several native Azerbaijani musicians were playing with vigour, the drum predominating, while such guests as felt so inclined danced a variety of steps to its pulsating rhythm. The food was plentiful and delicious, the wine flowed freely and I was soon thankful that my luncheon menu had been relatively austere.

Next morning I set out to visit once more the ancient Palace of the Shirvanshahs, their mausoleum, their mosque, and their Court of Justice, the last thoughtfully provided with a hole in the middle of the floor through which the heads of those condemned to death could promptly be propelled into the Caspian.

Dating mainly from the fifteenth century, the former Palace of the Shahs of Shirvan stands on an eminence dominating the old Persian town, once completely enclosed by massive crenellated walls, of which a good part still survive. At different levels within the palace precincts stand the Shah's residence, the Divan Khaneh, where he received his subjects in audience and dispensed justice, his family mausoleum, his court mosque and minaret, his hammam, and finally a strange conical structure marking the tomb of one Yah-Yah, a famous fifteenth-century dervish. Within the precincts of the palace, poplars, tall cypresses, Persian lilacs, acacias, wisteria, myrtles, and irises set off the austere elegance of the stone buildings.

Beneath the palace walls stand the older eleventh-century mosque and minaret of Mohammed. In the nearby streets a number of fine old Persian houses have of recent years been skilfully restored. One of several former hammams has been transformed into a medical museum and working chemist's shop cleverly adorned with clusters of coloured glass flagons which at once provided me with a most effective prescription for the treatment of arthritis. Nearby a late nineteenth- or early twentieth-century mosque houses a magnificent collection of the Shirvan carpets for which the region is famous, while others are displayed in the spacious saloons of a club frequented before the Revolution by the rich merchants of Baku. Today the local upper crust seems instead to frequent the Caravanserai or the Hotel Azerbaijan on the sea-front, which for service and accommodation can hold its own with most Soviet hotels.

This time I had it in mind to look at oil-wells which I did in style the following day, driving far out into the Caspian along an immensely long jetty, which led to the first of a great line of derricks reaching for miles out to sea. As so often in Baku, a gale was blowing, recalling the city's Persian name, Badkube or Nasty Wind.

On our way back into the town we stopped in the village of Surakhani on the Apsheron Peninsula to inspect earlier evidence of the region's oil-bearing capacity, the temple of a sect of fire-worshippers who seem to have come there from India some three hundred years ago to prostrate themselves before the flames which sprang so surprisingly from the earth. There are known to have been fire-worshippers in the region of Baku from very early times, but the advent of militant Islam seems to have put an end to their cult and it was not until the latter years of the seventeenth century that it was revived by these Indian pilgrims who founded the present Temple of Ateshgah. 'Near the well,' wrote the French traveller Villot in 1689, 'a volcano appeared, spouting fire, and has been spouting for eight or ten months. They call this place Ateshgah, meaning Home of fires, and to this day it is honoured by Hindus and Hebrews. They come here from different places to worship and throw in silver and gold coins and even keep two dervishes to guard this sacred fire.' There have, it appears, been no practising fire-worshippers in Baku for many years, but the flames still burn brightly in their one-time temple and I was shown round it by an Azerbaijani maiden who clearly enjoyed her role as high priestess of an extinct cult.

To the south, Baku's immediate surroundings are bleak and uninteresting to anyone save an oil man. Dusty red hills merge into the dreary expanse of the Mugan Steppe. For a real contrast you need to take the steamer two hundred miles further south to the little port of Lenkoran only a few miles from the Iranian border. The climate of the Southern Caspian littoral is classed as subtropical. Though I have never encountered one, the fauna is said to include tigers and the flora is scarcely less exotic. Luxuriant green orchards and steaming tea-plantations reach almost down to the water's edge and further inland a line of distant blue mountains marks the frontier with Iran. When I first went there in 1937, Lenkoran was no more than a village, clustered round a bazaar with the red roofs and white-washed walls of the houses standing out against the vivid green of the trees. Of the old Persian fort, built for the Shah by the British and finally stormed by the Russians, I could find no trace, though I believe it is still standing. It was here, strangely enough, that in 1812 Captain Christie, the auctioneer's son, met his death in battle, fighting unofficially for the Persians.

Three hundred miles to the north of Baku, on a rocky headland overlooking the Caspian not far from the port of Makhach Kala, stand the remains of an old Russian fort, Fort Burnaya, meaning Stormy. Built in 1821, fifteen years after the capture of Baku, Burnaya was the easternmost of a line of forts stretching from Vladikavkaz to the coast and intended to control the warlike mountain tribes of Chechnia and Daghestan, whose territory lay in the Eastern Caucasus between the Georgian Military Highway and the Caspian. By the end of 1829, the Russians had defeated both Turks and Persians and were the undisputed masters of Transcaucasia. Once their southern frontier had thus been adjusted to their liking, it only remained for them to impose their will on the turbulent tribes of the Caucasus itself, over whom they had long claimed sovereignty. This, in the event, was to prove the most arduous task of all. From the tribes occupying the central massif of the Caucasus, the Russians were to have relatively little trouble. Trouble was to come, rather, from the Cherkess or Circassians in the West, encouraged by David Urquhart and, more particularly, from the warlike tribes of the eastern foothills, the Chechens in their dense beech forests and the various tribes who ranged over the barren mountain plateau and tablelands of neighbouring Daghestan.

For a war of resistance to succeed, two things are necessary: a strong, all-pervading idea and a leader. In the eastern Caucasus both were at hand. The Imam Shamyl, born in the mountain village of Ghimri in north-eastern Daghestan towards the end of the eighteenth century, was known from early youth for his amazing physical strength and total dedication to the Moslem faith. He was also, as it happened, an inspired leader of men. In Daghestan the arrival of the Russians had coincided with a religious revival known as Muridism after the Murids or Mohammedan holy men who inspired it. Soon the war of resistance against the foreign invader had become a holy war against the Infidel.

In May 1831 the Murids boldly attacked Vnezapnaya, Fort Surprise, and then ambushed and heavily defeated the Russian force sent to its relief. The insurgents were quick to exploit their initial success, and other Russian setbacks followed. The Russians now made a determined attempt to bring the situation under control and in the end the Murids fell back on Shamyl's native village of Ghimri. The Russian attack on Ghimri was launched on 17 October 1821, five hundred Murids being surrounded by ten thousand Russians. After much bitter fighting, no more than sixty Murids were left. Of these only two escaped alive. One was Shamyl, who, leaping clean over the heads of a line of Russian soldiers about to open fire on him, cut down three of them before a fourth ran him through with his bayonet. Plucking the bayonet from his chest, he promptly used it to dispatch its owner and thus made his escape into the woods.

It was a couple of years before Shamyl, who assumed the title of Imam in 1834, again brought resistance to its former pitch, but by the end of 1836 the insurrection was once more widespread. By now the Russians had realized the nature and extent of the Murid threat. In May 1837, an expeditionary force of some five thousand men and eighteen guns was sent gainst Shamyl's headquarters at Ashilta in Averia. The campaign lasted for most of the summer, but failed in its main purpose, which was to stamp out resistance in Daghestan and Chechnia and bring Shamyl to bay. Shamyl now spent some time strengthening his military position and building up his authority over the tribes. Then, returning to the mountains of Daghestan, he established his headquarters on the rock of Akhulgo, a natural bastion rising six hundred feet above the River Koysu.

Early in 1839 a fresh Russian plan was drawn up for the purpose of subduing Chechnia and Northern Daghestan and finally eliminating Shamyl. Nine thousand men were concentrated in Chechnia and three thousand more in Northern Daghestan. By the middle of June, Shamyl found himself besieged on the rock of Akhulgo by a strong Russian force. Two months later, on 21 August, orders were given for a general assault. The ensuing battle lasted a week and in the end Akhulgo was taken. Anxiously the Russians searched the piles of enemy dead for Shamyl's body. There was no trace of it. Slipping through the Russian lines, the Imam and a few followers had made good their escape into the mountains.

In 1840 a Russian decision to build three more forts as part of a fresh line of defence in Chechnia once again set the country ablaze. In Chechnia, Shamyl showed himself as much a master of forest fighting as of the mountain warfare he had waged hitherto. Avoiding pitched battles, he kept constantly on the move, making sudden raids on enemy outposts, while his subordinate commanders did the same from the borders of Daghestan in the east to the country round Vladikavkaz in the west. In Daghestan, as in Chechnia, thousands flocked to his standards. Within a year of his setback at Akhulgo, Shamyl was again the leader of a people in arms.

Once more the Russian defences were strengthened, new forts built, the troops in the Caucasus reinforced, and large areas of country laid waste. But when, at the end of 1841, the Russians regained their winter quarters, Shamyl's position was stronger than ever. The ensuing year's campaign followed the same pattern. In four years the Russian had lost four hundred officers and eight thousand men.

Shamyl used the first part of 1843 to reorganize his forces. Resuming the offensive in August, he completely out-manoeuvred a strong Russian force. By the end of the year the Russians had lost another twenty-seven guns, ninety-two officers, and two thousand, five hundred and twenty-eight men. By now, the insurrection had spread to the Caspian littoral in the east and to the Moslem tribes both north and south of the main mountain range. To Shamyl, 1843 brought fresh successes; to the Russians, nothing but frustration.

In the spring of 1845 a large-scale expedition was planned, of which the purpose was to penetrate deep into the mountains, pin down Shamyl, capture his new stronghold of Andee in north-west Daghestan, and establish a Russian base there. But, in the event, a strong expeditionary force under a new Commander-in-Chef, Count Michael Vorontsov, until recently Governor-General of Southern Russia, was in its turn disastrously ambushed in the mountains; the Russians suffered another four thousand casualties; and Shamyl again withdrew into the mountains with negligible losses.

During the years that followed the Russians were given no peace, either in Chechnia or Daghestan. In the summer of 1847 they sought to storm Shamyl's stronghold of Ghergebil with ten battalions of infantry, strongly supported by cavalry and artillery, but were again repulsed with heavy losses and forced to withdraw. Shamyl meanwhile had moved his headquarters to Veden in Chechnia, not far from Dargo, near the borders of Daghestan.

Almost twenty years had passed since he had first taken the field against the Russians. During those years his insurrection had prospered and spread; there was no sign of its being quelled; his influence and authority were now stronger than ever before.

The outbreak of the Crimean War in 1853 brought home to the Russians the danger of having such an enemy in their rear and, with the conclusion of peace, they turned all their energies and resources to the final subjugation of the Caucasus. In July 1856, Tsar Alexander II appointed an outstanding soldier, Prince Alexander Baryatinski, to be Viceroy and Commander-in-Chief of the Caucasus. Baryatinski brought to the conduct of the war a new and effective strategy. During the year 1857 three strong columns gradually closed in on the Murid heartland in the wild mountain country between Chechnia and Daghestan, building roads and cutting broad rides through the forest as they advanced.

Shamyl was still at the head of a considerable force. In the wooded mountains enclosing the upper gorges of the Argoun River he possessed a practically impregnable second refuge barely a dozen miles from Veden, on which to fall back in case of need. But now, in mid-winter, three Russian columns secretly converged on the upper valley of the Argoun. By the end of January 1858, both branches of the river were in Russian hands and Shamyl had been deprived of his last refuge. By early July everything was ready for the next phase of the campaign.

The insurgents had lost a guerrilla's greatest advantage: the initiative. Early in February 1859, the Russians laid siege to Veden and on 1 April took it by assault. Shamyl himself escaped into the forest, but the fall of Veden made an immense impression throughout Chechnia. Soon even the most warlike tribes were suing for peace. By mid-July the preparations for the final phase of the campaign were complete and the general advance began. The Russians now had forty thousand men and forty-eight guns. With a few followers, Shamyl fled south into his native Daghestan to make a last stand on the natural stronghold of Gounib, a high mountain plateau surrounded by precipitous escarpments six or seven thousand feet about sea-level. At dawn on 25 August 1859 the Russian assault on Gounib went in. From all sides the Russian infantry swarmed up the escarpment. Soon only a handful of the four hundred defenders were left alive and in the end Shamyl sent emissaries to treat with the Russians. On being told that, if he surrendered, his life and the lives of those with him would be spared, he rode out to make his submission and, with bowed head, handed his sword to Prince Baryatinski.

To this day the Autonomous Soviet Republic of Daghestan is full of memories of Shamyl and his long fight against the Russians. From the capital, Makhach Kala, now a sizeable modern town, an hour's drive brings you to the foothills. Soon you start to climb in earnest, passing through little hill-towns, where mosques and turbaned gravestones show that you are in Moslem country. In spring and early summer the apple-trees are in flower and the green of the poplars stands out vividly against the grey of the rough stone houses and barren, rocky hills. Crossing a first mountain range, you come steeply down on Shamyl's much fought-over stronghold of Ghergebil, where it lies at the junction of the Sulak River and its fast-flowing tributary, the Karakoysu. On the hillsides, men carrying long daggers watch herds of sheep or cattle or horses – Avars, in all probability, but there are no less than forty different races in Daghestan, including what are known as Mountain Jews, a lost tribe who still speak a kind of Hebrew and whose own still very active synagogue I was fascinated to come on in a back street of Baku. Daghestan means Land of Mountains and, as elsewhere in the Caucasus, the tribe in one valley can quite often not communicate with their neighbours in the next, save through an interpreter. 'This mountain', wrote Mas'udi in the tenth century, 'has valleys, gorges and defiles in which live tribes not knowing one another owing to the arduous nature of the mountains which reach to the sky.'

As you turn up the valley of the Karakoysu, the great mountains loom up all round you, their peaks wreathed in mist. Ten miles beyond Ghergebil the valley, emerging from a narrow canyon, widens and you find yourself looking across to where the great rock-fortress of Gounib rises abruptly above the river, its almost perpendicular escarpment presenting a seemingly insuperable barrier to any assailant. From the foot of the escarpment a narrow track brings you to the summit, emerging unexpectedly into a shallow green valley five or six miles long and three or four across, watered by natural springs and enclosed by the rocky rim of the escarpment. Here, half a mile from the original *aul* (village) of Gounib, on a grassy bank beneath a birch tree, is a stone on which, an inscription informs you, Prince Baryatinski sat on that August morning in 1859 to receive the surrender of the Imam Shamyl, thereby to all intents and purposes completing the Russian conquest of the Caucasus.

I first visited Daghestan some years back as the guest of the famous Avar poet Rasul Gamzatov, one of the relatively few people I know who really can be called a legend in his own time. On this occasion, Rasul, a compactly built white-haired man of astounding energy and dynamism, whom I had hitherto only encountered in Moscow, met me at Makhach Kala airport with an outsize bottle of champagne which we finished on the spot. In addition to being his country's national bard, Rasul is a Hero of Socialist Labour, a Lenin Prize winner, a member of the Praesidium of the Supreme Soviet and, to all intents and purposes, the uncrowned king of Daghestan. At the moment, he explained, he was running for election and without further ado swept me off on a lightning tour of his constituency. Just what he was being elected to I never quite made out, probably the Supreme Soviet, but, as we sped from one mountain village to another, it at once became clear that he was winning hands down. Everybody who was anybody, including the Prime Minister, turned out to pay him their respects and, amid the prevailing enthusiasm, the amounts of food and drink consumed were, even by Highland standards, phenomenal. At first sight, the idea of a country being run by its Poet Laureate seemed to have much to commend it, always depending, of course, on his quality as a Poet.

Next morning early, we set out once more for the mountains, following, this time, in the footsteps of Shamyl and indeed of Rasul himself. Rasul, it should be explained, is a bard by birth as well as vocation. In Daghestan, as in the Highlands of Scotland, the office of *ashug* or bard is apt to run in families and Rasul's father, Gamzat Tsadasa, Gamzat of the *aul* of Tsada, had been a famous bard before him. It was therefore only natural that, on our way, we should visit Tsada and the *saklia* or rough stone house where Rasul himself was born in 1923 and which is by now already a house-museum. Speaking of his people's poetry, Rasul explained that the traditional instrument of the Daghestanis, the *kumuz*, has two strings, one for celebrating, at a high pitch, the heroic deeds of their *dzhigits* or warriors, and the other for recounting in dulcet tones tales of love and fair women. I have only read Rasul's poems in Russian or English translation, but to me it seems that, in his own way, he is equally at home in both modes, treating his themes with the directness one would expect from so robust and positive a character, but also with considerable subtlety and depth of feeling.

On my next journey to Daghestan, again for the purpose of visiting Rasul, I travelled by car from Baku, driving this time northwards across the dreary coastal plain which separates the Caspian from the eastern foothills of the Caucasus. A couple of hours out of Baku you cross the Azerbaijani border and enter the Autonomous Republic of Daghestan, officially part of the Russian Federation, though visually and in most other ways, except possibly the increasing number of vineyards along the road, there is little to mark your passage from one former Persian dominion to another.

Twenty or thirty miles beyond the border the gap between sea and mountains suddenly narrows and you come to the ancient city of Derbent, its name directly derived from the Persian *darband* or Gate. It is not difficult to see why it was so called. Here in the sixth century of our era, on the site of some even earlier settlement, Persia's Sasanid rulers built the mighty stronghold of Naryn Kala with its massive line of fortifications reaching from the mountains to the sea and manifestly designed to block the advance of any intruders from north or south or beyond the Caspian.

To this day, Naryn Kala's crumbling ruins dominate Derbent from their hilltop above the town and, with the help of an expert, it is possible to identify amongst them the remains of a mosque, of a fifteenth-century hammam, of the ruler's residence, occupied at one time, or so I was told, by Haroun al Rashid himself, who is said to have had the plumbing repaired, and finally of the Zindan, a thirty-four-foot well, to which, like the Emir of Bokhara, the rulers of Derbent consigned their unfortunate prisoners. Amongst the ruins I found in a corner the elaborately chiselled gravestone of one Iftikhar, who commanded the local garrison in 1446, and near it a more recent guardroom said to have been built by the Russians in General Yermolov's day, when Derbent, after a period as part of Persia, again became Russian territory. Over the centuries visitors to Derbent included, as we know, Marco Polo and the English merchant-adventurer Anthony Jenkinson, as well as that untiring aficionado of things Caucasian, Alexandre Dumas Père. But more significant than any of these was the great Tamerlane himself, who, on his way to administer the *coup de grâce* to Toktamish at Tatartub, stopped off there in 1395, when he was, as can be imagined, received with considerable deference by Sheikh Ibrahim, the Shirvanshah of the day. Immediately beneath Naryn Kala the thousands of headstones of an ancient Moslem graveyard project from the hillside at as many different angles.

The mayor of Derbent, who entertained me to a lavish and much-needed luncheon, has his Council Chambers in a fine early nineteenth-century classical buildings looking out on to the main square of the modern town with its statutory statue of Lenin. Its elegant façade had at some stage, I noticed, been liberally spattered with machine-gun fire, presumably during the Civil War and Allied intervention of nearly seventy years ago. But what struck me most were the two portraits which adorned the mayor's own office: a modern bronze bas-relief of Peter the Great, who first seized Derbent for the Russians in 1722, and a handsome oil painting of a heavily-bearded Karl Marx, whose doctrines, after a good deal of bloodshed, finally found favour there two hundred years later. Just how these two worthies would have regarded their somewhat arbitrary juxtaposition is hard to say, though to any reasonably attentive follower of Soviet form, the underlying reasons for their combined presence must be clear enough.

Continuing on our way to Makhach Kala, I was interested to visit an exemplarily well-ordered Sovkhoz or State Farm, the size of a small town, named for Aliyev, a local school-teacher killed in action in 1943 at the age of twenty-seven and posthumously created a Hero of the Soviet Union. Young Aliyev's bust stands on the village square in front of the club built to commemorate him and across the way from the school where he once taught. After being regaled by the farm authorities with a mass of statistics concerning the admirable medical, educational, recreational, residential and other facilities which the Sovkhoz provided for its workers (including a stable of remarkably nice-looking thorough-breds for eventing), and hearing with interest of its steeply-rising production figures (the Daghestanis claim they produce more grapes than any republic in the Russian Federation), I was amused to notice that in contrast to the rest, there had in the past twelve months been a cut of no less than seventy per cent in the amount of grapes used for wine production, something of which Mikhail Gorbachov disapproves as fervently as did the mullahs and imams who in Moslem Daghestan once set the standards in such matters. Certainly the delicious grape-juice we drank at lunch showed no sign whatever of fermentation.

After spending the night in Makhach Kala's significantly named Hotel Leningrad, of which we were told floors nine and twenty-one had been specially equipped for foreigners (one could not but wonder just how), I once more visited Gounib, the scene of Shamyl's last stand and final surrender on that fateful day in August 1859. There, half-way up the mountain, in a town hall overlooking the valley below, I was again welcomed with true Highland hospitality, this time by the mayor and his deputy, an immense Avar who certainly did credit to his race and in his fine new business suit and large shiny shoes still managed to look every inch a Highlander. As I ate some savoury pancakes or *chudus* drenched in butter and closely resembling drop-scones, together with lavish dollops of *tvorog*, a cottage cheese indistinguishable from our own crowdy, I was once more struck by Daghestan's manifold affinities with the Highlands of Scotland. This, you are constantly reminded, is and always has been a land of warriors (*dzhigits*) and heroes, and, with forty different warlike races in one tiny country, of tribal warfare as well, not to mention the population's unending struggles against successive outside invaders. The local hospitality is likewise compulsive and overwhelming, with home-grown hill mutton predominating. The hills, not as high as those of the Central Caucasus, are in their way even more dramatic and, when it rains (which it often does) take on the same shades of brown and violet and sepia as they do in Scotland. Strangest of all, by some mysterious metempsychosis, if that is the word I want, every other woman you meet is wearing a shawl or skirt of faded tartan. And so in any village you come to, you will be likely to eounter, advancing down the street under a gentle drizzle, first a very Highland-looking shepherd with his stick and his dog and his flock of sheep and then a couple of old wifeys, gossiping and keeping an eye on the bairns and wrapped, as often as not, in a rug bearing the ancient sett and colours of some famous Highland clan.

There is, needless to say, no truer Highlander than Rasul himself, who with his charming and remarkably intelligent wife Fatima, entertained me next morning to a late breakfast of freshly-caught sturgeon and caviar from the Caspian, luscious *chudus* and home-made cherry conserve, liberally washed down with locally-distilled spirits of one kind or another. Listening as he spoke with the fluency and vigour of the born talker, of literature in general and the latest Soviet literary trends in particular and what he hoped was their ultimate significance, I felt encouraged to hear such revolutionary views coming from so prominent, if unconventional, a member of the Soviet Establishment and at the same time irresistibly reminded of the quicksilver discursiveness of some of our own Celtic men of letters.

On visiting Makhach Kala's historical museum after breakfast, I was relieved to find that the great Imam Shamyl, who, more than a century on, still has his periodic ups and downs in the estimation of the powers-that-be, continues to receive the prominence that by any standards he deserves, though possibly with a slight shift of emphasis. A number of large oil-paintings dramatically portray his Murids' bloody encounters with the soldiers of the Tsar. But, however heroic the bayonet and dagger thrusts exchanged by the tribesmen and Russians, the battles depicted were now, I noticed, invariably those from which the Russians had in the end emerged victorious, notably the storming of Ghimri, Akhulgo and Gounib, while in the painting of Shamyl's surrender it is, perhaps quite naturally, not Shamyl, but Prince Baryatinski and his glittering staff who dominate the scene. There was, it is true, a time not long ago when Shamyl was still officially described as leader of a national liberation movement against Russian imperialism. But this time I found prominently displayed in the museum a significant quotation from no less an authority than Karl Marx to the effect that in his day Imperial Russia's role in the East had been a civilizing one, nowhere more than between the Black Sea and the Caspian – a dictum not without its message for our own times.

After Shamyl's capitulation, resistance in the Caucasus quickly came to an end. For another four or five years the Circassians, encouraged by the Turks and by David Urquhart, kept up their fight in the western valleys and on the Black Sea littoral around Sochi. But by 1864 they too had been crushed and their territories occupied by the Russians. Later that year some six hundred thousand of them took refuge in Turkey.

For another half-century Transcaucasia was governed from Tbilisi by a Russian viceroy, various revolutionary and semi-revolutionary movements being repressed with varying degrees of vigour. An active member of the Bolshevik faction of the Georgian Social Democrats at this time was the young Joseb or Soso Djugashvili, later to become famous as Stalin. In 1917 the Russian Revolution threw Transcaucasia into confusion. At the end of November of the same year, power in Transcaucasia passed into the hands of a group of moderate Social Democrats, known as the Transcaucasian Commissariat, and in April 1918, Transcaucasia, having severed its connection with Russia, was proclaimed an Independent Democratic Federative Republic, soon to be replaced by three separate Republics of Georgia, Armenia and Azerbaijan.

They were to be short-lived. Soon the Soviet government felt able to put an end, with the help of native revolutionaries, to what from their point of view was an anomalous state of affairs. In the course of 1920 and 1921 all three republics were invaded by the Red Army and brought under Soviet rule and three years after that duly incorporated in the newly-formed Union of Soviet Socialist Republics.

PART FOUR

LOOKING BACKWARDS WE MOVE FORWARDS

Russia's past is admirable;
her present more than magnificent;
as to her future, it is beyond the grasp
of the most daring imagination.
GENERAL COUNT ALEXANDER BENCKENDORFF,
CHIEF OF POLICE TO TSAR NICHOLAS I
1836

Looking Backwards,
We Move Forwards

'Achieving a greater awareness of the past,' wrote the Russian revolutionary thinker, Alexander Ivanovich Herzen, 'we clarify the present; digging deeper into the significance of what has gone before, we discover the meaning of the future; looking backwards, we move forwards.' Of no country is this truer than of Russia and, by extension, of the Soviet Union. Without some knowledge of Russian history and of the history of the other countries which go to make up the Soviet Union, it is impossible to understand what is happening there today or to form any idea of what is likely to happen there in the future. Everything, you soon find, is deeply rooted in the past. The continuity of Russian history is positively flabbergasting.

The present rulers of Russia are as much the heirs of Ivan the Terrible and Peter the Great as of Lenin and Stalin. Moreover, as the Bolshevik Revolution in its turn recedes into history, they and the Russian people with them are becoming increasingly aware of this. Today in the ideological field, a pride in Russia's national heritage more than holds its own with the precepts of Marxism–Leninism. Mr Gorbachov's recent reference to the Soviet Union as 'Russia' was more than a Freudian slip. Old-fashioned Russian patriotism is as strong a force as ever it was. 'Our motherland', wrote my wartime friend, Konstantin Simonov, many years ago in a now famous poem, 'is not the city of my carefree boyhood, but the hamlets where our forebears dwelt before us, with simple crosses on the Russian graves.' In the Soviet Union the victories and sacrifices of World War II are kept fresh in the memories of successive generations in a way that, for better or for worse, has, passed out of fashion in the West.

Russia never was an easy country to govern. As Count Witte, briefly Prime Minister to the last tsar, once put it: 'The world should be surprised, not that we have a less than perfect government in Russia but that we have a government at all.' The present rulers of the Soviet Union face many of the same problems that faced their immediate and their earlier predecessors, notably how to keep abreast of foreign competition and satisfy an emergent public opinion, while restricting contacts with the outside world and retaining adequate control over every aspect of Soviet life. Nor is their task simplified by the rate at which things are now moving. While some factors remain constant, others are changing at breakneck speed. 'I expect you notice a difference', said the man on the park bench when he heard that I had known the Soviet Union in Stalin's day. 'I will tell you the biggest difference of all; people are beginning to think for themselves.'

Stalin died in 1953. For thirty-five years now human nature has been at work, human nature, which Stalin somehow kept in check, but which, given the chance, can be one of the most disruptive and subversive forces on earth, especially under a system which has hitherto sought to ignore it and, most of all, Russian human nature which, to put it mildly, is more human than most.

Under Stalin there had been total control. Under Khrushchov the pressure was relaxed. Between 1954 and his removal from office in 1964 the lid was taken off Pandora's Box. Even if they had wanted to, his successors could no longer turn the clock right back to where it stood in Stalin's day. Things had gone too far for that. From time to time, there was a tightening up. Purges were undertaken, dissidents disciplined and repressive measures enforced. But the machine-gun could no longer be the answer to everything and the power exercised by Stalin's successors has been quite different in character and quality from the power which he once wielded. As one well-qualified observer has put it, 'Soviet totalitarianism is now often less than total'.

One significant development of the past thirty-five years has been the increasing stratification of Soviet society, in other words, the emergence in the Soviet Union, seventy years after the Bolshevik Revolution, of what amounts to a hereditary ruling class, one might almost say aristocracy. Under Stalin the turnover by terror was too rapid for this to be possible, but now, for thirty-five years, those in positions of power and responsibility in the Party, in government, in the armed forces, in industry and trade and finance, in diplomacy, in the arts and in the academic world, have not only been consolidating their own positions, but ensuring (and what, after all, could be more natural?) that their children and grandchildren have a good start in life. It is still the job you do that matters. But it is much easier to get a good job if your father and grandfather had good jobs before you. In the Soviet Union, as elsewhere, a good start in life makes all the difference, as does the inherited wealth that usually goes with it.

As elsewhere, most top people know each other or at any rate know of each other. The Party serves as a link between them. If, to take just one example, a Marshal's son does not want to go into the army, even into one of the smarter Guards Regiments in which his father's rank would secure him an immediate commission, plenty of other careers will be open to him and a word from his father at a high level in the right quarter will be bound to help. Meanwhile, from childhood he will have been brought up in luxurious circumstances: comfortable flats or houses to live in, orderlies to wait on him, cars to drive around in. 'We have such fun in Daddy's yacht', a top-ranking Admiral's daughter said to me, 'and when he gets leave, we take the car and drive round Europe.' Given thirty years and more in which to crystallize, these processes have produced not three but four generations who take their privileges for granted and who expect without question to be able to pass them on in their turn to their children and grandchildren.

These are the people who earn (and keep) the most money and spend it at special shops, who, like the nobles under Catherine the Great, are authorized to travel abroad, who pay for private tuition for their children, who wear the smartest clothes and jewellery. ('How do you like this evening dress? It comes from Paris', said the grand-daughter of one leading statesman, while even to my untutored eye it was clear that the neat, well-cut coat and skirt worn by the daughter of another could scarcely have come from anywhere else.) These are the people one sees driving in the grandest cars, occupying the best tables at the smartest restaurants and night-spots and the best seats at the theatre. Like their fathers and by now their grandfathers and great-grandfathers before them, they constitute a privileged class who are beginning to wield at least as much power as the old aristocracy ever did under the tsars and who, while undoubtedly adding to the stability of the régime, demand, as of right, due recognition of their special position.

No less important politically than the emergence of an upper class is the appearance, for the first time, it could be said, in Russian history, of a firmly-established middle class. What irony that it should have fallen to the heirs of Lenin to bring into being a genuine bourgeoisie, possessing the social stability and other bourgeois virtues so sadly lacking under the tsars and effectively bridging the dangerous gap that long existed between the highest and the lowest levels of Russian society, between the rulers and those 'dark masses' who, barely a century ago, were still being bought and sold as serfs. Not as elegant or as self-assured or as sophisticated as the upper class, with fewer privileges and less money to spend (four or five hundred roubles a month is a good salary), these new bourgeois nonetheless know what they want, are by and large beginning to get it and, like the upper class, cannot safely be left out of account. Throughout the Soviet Union they can be seen shopping at the big state stores, putting their money on a horse, spending their evenings at the theatre or ballet, driving their medium-sized family cars into the country on their days off, and enjoying their holidays at the better-class resorts. Moreover, as in Victorian Britain, the modest privileges they enjoy clearly serve as a valuable incentive to the working class to work a little harder and so, with time, luck and shrewdness, to climb in their turn a little higher up the social ladder.

What it amounts to is that in the Soviet Union today a complicated social life is in progress, regulated, as elsewhere, by good or bad luck, by prejudice, by every other kind of human motive or emotion, virtue or weakness, by good judgement and bad, by ambition, success or failure, by intrigue or corruption, by poverty or wealth, by hard work, idleness, envy or greed – none of which important human factors seem so far to have been eliminated by a system which used once to aim, in theory at any rate, at the creation of an entirely New Soviet Man unmoved by such mundane considerations.

While in many respects beneficial, this stratification of society inevitably complicates the task of government. There are now any number of people in the Soviet Union who have a considerable stake in society, who know their own minds and whose views and requirements have to be taken into account by those in power, who constitute, in other words, an embryonic public opinion which can no longer be ignored. To anyone who, like myself, knew the Soviet Union of fifty years ago, the improvement that has taken place in the Soviet standard of living, in the availability of consumer goods, in housing conditions and in amenities generally, is positively startling. But this does not prevent all these important people, many of whose families have by now enjoyed power and privilege for three or four generations, from demanding a greater improvement still, and going on demanding it.

Most visits to the Soviet Union begin in Moscow. Here the changes are immediately obvious, especially to anyone who knew Stalin's Russia. The consumer revolution has raised both living and housing standards, widened the choice of both necessities and luxuries in the shops and raised the status of the consumer in relation to the producer – in other words, of the citizen in relation to the State. For in the Soviet Union, the State is by and large the monopoly producer.

Soviet citizens of today, unlike the consumer of fifty years ago, have come to expect a steadily sustained improvement in living conditions. Though still infinitely patient and long-suffering by Western standards (their tribulations are a regular subject for music-hall jokes), Soviet customers have become much harder to please, the women in particular. One has only to notice their attitude when told that something they want is not available to realize that Soviet womanhood's deep-seated desire for consumer goods and in particular for more luxury and glamour is something no Soviet government can afford to ignore. 'It's a shame', they say, when they can't get what they want – tights or bras, for example, using that particularly telling Russian expression, *byezobrazhye*, meaning a shapeless horror. But still there are shortages. Sent by *Nedelya* earlier this year to find out why tights had yet again disappeared from the shops, a Soviet investigative journalist discovered to her dismay that, owing to an interdepartmental muddle and the consequent failure of the Ministry for Chemical Industry to provide the necessary raw material, only two pairs per user per year would be available until, at the earliest, 1990.

Prices on the whole are a secondary consideration compared with availability, except when the government suddenly puts them up and they too become a source of grievance and complaint. Though advances have been made over the last thirty years, the quality and range of goods in the big stores still do not compare with their equivalents in the West. Even so, though distribution is uneven, you can now choose between several makes of cameras, radios, tape recorders or TV sets, some made in the Soviet Union and some imported, most probably from East Germany. Equally there is a much larger range than formerly of clothes, groceries, ornaments, furnishings, footwear and sporting goods, and never any lack of customers buying them.

One immediate effect of this consumer revolution is that goods are now being produced or even imported because there is a demand for them and not just to fulfil some theoretical norm. To meet the ever more insistent demand for a better standard of living, the balance of the Soviet economy is gradually being altered.

Simultaneously, to supply needs so far neglected by the State, a flourishing black or grey market has come into being, *na levo*, on the side, which, in many respects the most efficient branch of the economy, has been calculated by *Izvestia* to generate around 7,000 million roubles a year. Under the new dispensation, current measures of reform, taking account of this, seem likely to legalize a number of practices which, though universal, have hitherto been technically illegal.

Driving along a country road in the Ukraine not long ago, I saw a large number of cars parked by the roadside and asked what was going on, 'It's Sunday', was the reply. On Sundays, it seems, sailors from the Port of Odessa, foreign as well as Russian, head in their hundreds for the nearest peasants' market and sell at several times the cost price whatever foreign cameras, radios, watches, tape-recorders, scent and nylons they have been able to smuggle in. A lot of this the authorities have hitherto winked at. On a street corner not long ago I saw a well-dressed young woman furtively but successfully selling home-made chewing-gum. On the other hand, the Soviet press not long ago reported that two women had been locked up for selling ersatz eye-black made from boot polish. Both Georgians and Armenians have the reputation of getting away with more than most people, and the story is told of the enterprising Georgian who booked all the seats on a Soviet airliner (the single flight costs 37 roubles), filled them with mimosa from the Black Sea, flew them to snow-bound, flower-starved Moscow, and sold them there. For how much? History does not relate, but certainly enough to cover all expenses and leave himself a handsome profit. In such cases, the law of supply and demand operates with all its pristine vigour.

Over the years there has been a noticeable improvement in the quality of both clothing and footwear. A foreigner no longer stands out from a crowd of Russians like a canary among a flock of sparrows. Not only the quality but the range is improving. Red Square or Gorki Street may hardly compare for elegance with Bond Street or the rue de la Paix, but they are beginning to creep up on the less fashionable districts of Birmingham or Lille. For fifty kopeks you can watch a fashion show in one of the new dress-shops on Moscow's American-style Prospekt Kalinina, while on a higher level of both clothes and models, you can attend the much more sophisticated displays put on at the *Dom Modeli* ('House of Fashion') on Kuznetski Most or, at a higher level still, by the prestigious Vladimir Zaitsev, an up-to-the-minute exponent of *haute couture*, who has had the most magnificent display rooms built for him by a grateful government and is said to be patronized by Raisa Gorbachova herself, who certainly sets an outstanding example of elegance and dress-sense. Dress shows are mostly for trade representatives and the dresses shown are not for sale, but cut-out patterns are available from which customers can either make the dresses up themselves or else get them made up by the proverbial little woman round the corner, who will be either a member of the State-controlled Dressmakers' Guild or, more probably, working on her own for what she can get.

Dressmaking or tailoring are only two of many forms of flourishing small-scale private enterprise. Others are plumbing, painting, electrical work, joinery, bricklaying and a number of allied trades. In theory all of these should be officially sanctioned and licensed by the State, coming within the purview of this ministry or that. In practice, the best way to get a job done has long been either to do it yourself or else to employ a moonlighter working either in his spare time or in his employer's time, and using materials which, to judge by newspaper reports, as often as not started life as state property. Meanwhile a class of middle-men or fixers has sprung up in these grey areas of the economy, who make a good thing on the quiet out of marrying supply to demand by cornering desirable goods and cautiously releasing them as and when the opportunity offers. Just how much they make by their often strictly speaking illicit, but nonetheless useful activities is, needless to say, a closely-guarded secret. But one can be quite sure that it takes into account the fact that in general goods and services are in greater demand than money.

With the coming of *glasnost*, Soviet investigative journalists have been picking up and passing on to their readers any number of choice titbits. Why, enquired the man from *Izvestia*, did aircraft landing at Kursk 'brush the tops of the trees with their landing gear?' The answer was illuminating in more senses than one. The essential red filters covering the approach lights on the runway had, it emerged, been removed and used to light the local disco. Clearly, an unusually enterprising fixer had been at work.

Understandably, the shortage of vodka has led to a corresponding demand for eau-de-cologne, to the extent that the cheaper brands are now known by sales assistants as 'drinking cologne'. Some seekers after relief evidently go further still. 'Specialists', reported the influential *Literaturnaya Gazeta* recently, 'say that addicts not only drink toiletries, but eat them as well – some sorts of toothpaste apparently induce oblivion.' Sad, too, is the case of the 'New Dawn' perfume factory, whose management, in the hope of saving addicts from themselves, loyally halved production of their cheaper brands of eau-de-cologne and tripled the output of their top quality, Charlie, at twelve roubles a bottle, only to find themselves promptly denounced for profiteering.

But worst of all, surely, with its ideological undertones, was the story, picked up by the ever-vigilant *Ogonyok*, of Second Officer Ivan Brunovski, who, while serving on a tanker plying between Finland and the Soviet Union, made a practice of smuggling not only car radios 'by the hundred', but even two complete cars 'disguised as spare parts'. Indeed it was only after his ship had gone right off course that he was finally unmasked, when a convenient cavity in the steering-gear was found to have been stuffed with four Orders of Lenin, three Orders of the Red Star, one Order of Glory, and a selection of lesser medals, which enterprising Ivan was proposing to sell to foreign collectors for a handsome amount of hard currency.

One most important and relatively recent development is the advent in large numbers of the private automobile. Over twelve million Russians now own cars. This still scarcely compares with the West, but the number is increasing all the time at the rate of more than a million cars a year. Anyone who is anyone now has a car. Suddenly a growing number of Soviet citizens have become more mobile, more independent and more status-conscious, a big change in such a controlled society. Inevitably the internal combustion engine brings trouble in its train; road accidents, pollution, congestion, meter-maids and various kinds of crime. There is already a flourishing Soviet secondhand car market, with all that that implies, and you need only look at the photographs of 'wanted men' outside any Soviet police station to see how frequently their crimes are stealing vehicles, switching number-plates, forging licences, etc. Several makes of Soviet car are now in production, notably the sturdy Zhiguli, based on the Fiat 124, the Volga, which is larger and more powerful, and the Chaika, the standard ministerial car. Then there is the Zil, a Cadillac-type car used by the topmost people of all. This comes with the job but, if some rich bandleader or popular novelist were to want one, and had the right contacts, it could cost him 50,000 or 60,000 roubles.

In the Soviet Union, cars are not marketed by slick, fast-talking salesmen. Demand still so greatly exceeds supply that there is no need for advertisement. Nor are they glossily displayed behind gleaming shop-windows. With, in practice, only two or three makes to choose from, a potential customer should have no difficulty in making up his mind by inspecting the cars of his friends and acquaintances. Then he simply puts his name down for a car at the appropriate office and waits for a year or two to be notified that it is ready for collection from a depot. After which he pays cash down and drives it triumphantly away. A friend of mine, a medium-level official with exceptionally good connections, is the proud possessor of a Zhiguli station-wagon and is delighted with it. 'The only trouble', he says, 'is getting it serviced and getting spare parts for it when I need them.' Spares are in permanently short supply and garages overburdened, but Russians are of necessity immensely ingenious and, here again, a fixer with friends among the drivers of official cars can be useful. As for secondhand cars, the difficulty of getting a new car means that, once you have one, you can quite easily sell it for a good deal more than you paid in the first place. Most deals of this kind are transacted privately, but there are now also government-sponsored depots where secondhand cars are sold on a commission basis.

Nothing is more confusing than to try to compare Soviet prices and earnings with prices and earnings elsewhere or, for that matter, to form an accurate idea of the true standard of living of various categories of Soviet citizens. The official rate of exchange for the rouble is at present fixed at around one pound sterling, whereas a more realistic rate would be 5 or 10 roubles to the pound, which in effect is what you are offered by the currency touts who accost you in the street. ('Wouldn't you rather pay in dollars?' an enterprising salesman said to me recently in one of the state shops, admittedly in Armenia.)

But even if, in an attempt to find a more valid standard of comparison, you base your calculation on relative prices and earnings, there are still a number of other factors to be taken into account. A rather poor quality man's suit costs at least 100 roubles, a greatcoat 120 roubles and a pair of shoes 50. A couple with two children, earning, say, 400 roubles a month, will probably spend 200 roubles a month on food. The average industrial wage is around 180 roubles a month. The average earnings of an agricultural worker are rather less. Most wives go out to work. (In theory there is equal pay for women, though, as elsewhere, women seem to gravitate to lower-paid jobs.)

So far, so good. But this is only a beginning. In the Soviet Union the state is the producer, importer and retailer of practically all goods and services and also the universal landlord and universal employer and is therefore is a position to fix all prices, rents and wages quite arbitrarily and also to regulate at will the availability of all goods to meet the requirements of government policy. Thus, for social reasons, rents and rail fares are deliberately kept low (around 8 or 10 roubles a month for a two- or three-roomed flat and 33 roubles for a 2,000-kilometre rail journey), while the price of vodka is deliberately kept high (10 roubles a bottle) and supplies limited. The state, it may be added, also controls the trade unions, whose function is to increase, not the wage rates or living standards, but the productivity of the workers, who are constantly reminded that it is their duty to the Soviet Fatherland to work harder and produce more. The emergence some years back of an unofficial, dissident trade union movement, if significant, was, not surprisingly, short-lived.

The prices of state-manufactured goods in state shops are, like most other things, state-controlled nationwide. In principle, a bath-towel, if you can find one, costs the same in Soviet Central Asia as it does in Moscow. There is thus no such thing as bargain-hunting in the ordinary sense of the word. What there is, under a system where both production and distribution are apt to be capricious, is the enormous satisfaction, after a long chase, of finding something you really want to buy. The price (and money generally), once you have found what you want, is apt to be a secondary consideration. This of course was even truer when consumer goods were in shorter supply. With more to spend it on, money gains in attraction.

In country regions, choice is necessarily limited to one or more fairly rough-and-ready village shops. In the cities, most women do their basic shopping locally in the stores which form part of most big housing developments and only make expeditions to the big department stores in the centre of the city on special occasions. In Moscow, the most spectacular of these is GUM, the great State Universal Store across the Red Square from the Kremlin. Built about a hundred years ago, it is like nothing else in the world and is visited by several hundred thousand potential customers a day. Here, according to whim, you can buy food, clothes, linen, grand pianos, jewellery, fur hats and television sets, always queuing three times: once to identify your purchase, once to pay for it, and once to collect it. You can also buy (rather more expeditiously) an ice-cream and eat it, dangling your legs from the rim of an ornate fountain.

All shops, large and small, come under this ministry or that and the employees, from the manager in his well-appointed office to the lady who sweeps the floor, are all government servants of varying grades, drawing salaries in accordance with their rank. Just how they or other government functionaries achieve their respective ranks is, as everywhere, a question of seniority, ability, favouritism and luck. As in the government service elsewhere, pay is on a generally applicable nationwide scale, additional bonuses being sometimes paid according to conditions of work or results, which are usually measured in terms of fulfilment or, better still, over-fulfilment of an overall plan. Training in, say, salesmanship, is basically no different from such training anywhere else and, as elsewhere, a watch is kept on the honesty, punctuality and general efficiency of employees, both by their immediate superiors and by visiting inspectors. (Shades of Gogol's *Government Inspector*!) Political reliability also counts for a lot, all government appointments being in a sense Party appointments, especially at a higher level. As everywhere else in the world, there are nice but also less nice ways of getting ahead.

For children with reasonably prosperous parents a whole department store is set aside, the *Detski Mir*, or Children's World, a fine new building just across the way from the notorious Lubianka, where the KGB still have their headquarters. Russians adore children and here, wandering from floor to floor, they can buy them anything from cuddly dolls and Micky Mice to sailor suits and plastic machine guns, while on special occasions a spectacular illuminated space missile shuttles merrily between the floors.

For the committed shopper, even GUM and *Detski Mir* are not the whole picture. On a higher level, the prime aim of every status-conscious Soviet citizen must be somehow to obtain access to a whole range of special stores reserved for specially privileged members of the ruling class and carrying all kinds of goods otherwise in short supply, including imported and home-produced goods not readily available elsewhere. To take one example, anyone having such access goes automatically to the top of the waiting-list for a car and obtains it at a greatly reduced price. Access is by official pass only, issued by the holder's branch of the Party or government service. The nearest equivalents in the West are, I suppose, our own NAAFI stores for British Forces serving overseas or American PX facilities to which access is also by official pass, or the directors' dining-rooms of our big firms. To use them, you need to be a member of some specific body or organization, such as the Council of Ministers or the Central Committee of the Party or the Supreme Soviet or the Judiciary or the General Staff. Similar facilities are available to top industrialists, top newspaper men, Lenin Prize-winners, People's Artists, People's Heroes. In this extremely rank-conscious society, the advantages you enjoy vary according to your rank. A Colonel will not do as well as a Marshal, nor will a Deputy Minister have the same privileges as his boss, while at a lower level still middling functionaries will enjoy middling facilities. Nominally, those possessing these privileges cannot share them with outsiders, but, human nature being what it is, one can be sure that the aides, personal assistants and relatives of these great men reap many of the privileges of hangers-on the world over.

No less desirable is a supply of foreign currency which can either be spent in the special foreign currency stores provided for tourists or, in certain circumstances, used to buy goods from abroad such, for example, as a bottle of Chivas Regal, the ultimate status symbol for those who know. More valuable still is the right to travel abroad and shop there, still, as it was under Catherine the Great, a jealously-guarded privilege of the ruling class. At all levels of the hierarchy, special perquisites go with special jobs, official rations, official houses, official cars and the services of official personnel – all far more desirable than mere money. Instead of queuing for admission to some restaurant, where everything is apt to be 'off, Comrade', it is far more agreeable to be a member of a select club, such as the House of Writers, belonging to the Writers' Union, where one can lunch or dine in congenial company and where service and food are, in the present author's experience, both excellent.

In the Soviet Union, wages and earnings vary widely. In industry, as we have seen, the average wage is about 180 roubles a month; on the land, rather less. A senior teacher or official or newspaper man might get 400 roubles a month. But at a higher level rewards are many times larger, as are the accompanying perquisites. A Marshal of the Soviet Union or senior defence scientist will get as much as 2,000 roubles a month as well as many other advantages. In the arts and sciences and in industry too, large sums of money can be earned. A successful writer may make 100,000 roubles from the sale of a single book or play and, with luck, foreign currency as well.

Having noted the wide differentiation in wages and earnings and grasped that there is nothing to prevent a Soviet citizen from investing his money in state bonds or leaving it to his children, the first question most Westerners will ask is: what about taxation? The short answer is that taxes do not have the same importance or serve the same purpose in the Soviet Union as in capitalist countries. Most people, by our standards, pay practically no tax at all. Even the highest rates of income tax and death duties are only in the region of twelve per cent, though in theory private earnings, if declared, attract a higher rate. Thus a leading scientist or a general or a writer or a ballet dancer who earns tens of thousands of roubles a year from the state will keep around ninety per cent of it and a Soviet millionaire will, when he dies, be able to leave some nine-tenths of his fortune to his family, thus enabling them to continue to live in approximately the style to which they are accustomed. Rigid egalitarianism is something with which the Russians, seventy years after the Revolution, are not unduly concerned. In the Soviet Union the idea that hard work, skill and initiative merit higher rewards or that incentives boost production is not regarded as in any way shocking. 'He does a good job', a Soviet friend of mine said recently. 'Why shouldn't he be properly paid for it?' The argument struck me, a life-long Conservative, as sound. As to raising funds for the exchequer, this can be done in any number of ways in a country where the state really does control the means of production, distribution and exchange. Nor is mere money, as such, as useful in the Soviet Union as elsewhere. Privilege, position, access to goods and services are all much more important.

Sometimes, of course, practice does not accord with theory. Such things as attendance and hours of work are officially regulated in accordance with carefully laid-down rules, norms and plans. But this does not mean that people keep to them. However all-encompassing, the system is there to be beaten. 'They pretend to pay us and we pretend to work', runs an old Russian joke. Absenteeism is a problem, so is alcoholism, both now heavily under attack. In the Soviet Union as elsewhere, some people work longer and harder than others. Moreover a great many people in all walks of life take time off to supplement their income on the side. The fixer, the wangler, the skrimshanker, the moonlighter and the pilferer all exist under Communism as they do under Capitalism. In practice, hours of work in Soviet factories are apt to be erratic. In theory there is a forty-hour week. But everything depends on the Plan and if, towards the end of the month, the Plan is not running to schedule, weekends go by the board and double shifts are worked in a final burst of energy which, once the crisis has passed, is usually made up for by an all-round easing off of pressure. By Western standards, too, manpower is used over-lavishly. Nor, when every citizen is guaranteed a job by law, is it easy to get rid of a bad worker.

In the Soviet Union things are certainly not standing still, least of all during the past three years. On the contrary, they are evolving and developing at varying rates and in a number of different directions, not always in accordance with the hopes and aspirations of the founding fathers. Though it has had its setbacks and its reverses, there can be no doubt that the consumer revolution has come to stay. Better living accommodation, the resulting increase in privacy, a wider choice of goods and other amenities, more contact with the outside world, all make it easier for the Soviet citizen to escape from the centralization, standardization and collectivization of the system.

Under Stalin, there was no 'internal emigration'. Dangerous thoughts were dealt with summarily before they had time to take shape. Only the utterly reckless risked poor-taste jokes. The intelligentsia, like every other section of Soviet society, were kept strictly under control. For some time this has no longer been so. With much the same attachment to abstract ideals as their nineteenth-century predecessors, the intelligentsia reverted, to a limited extent, to their historic role as critics of the system. Poor-taste jokes proliferated. People listened to foreign broadcasts, protests were made, books and poetry written, pictures painted, ideas expressed and plays put on, which, if not openly subversive, did not strictly conform to the precepts of the Party Line. It was true of course that, if this or that intellectual overstepped the mark, he was as often as not severely disciplined. But, to put it brutally, there is all the difference in the world between a couple of years in a lunatic asylum and a bullet in the back of the neck. For some time already policy has had to be delicately balanced between what could be safely withheld and what must be grudgingly granted. Indeed it has long seemed probable that change, when it came, would in the long run spring first and foremost from reforms initiated at a high level and from sectional and other interests vigorously pursued.

In this context, recent changes at the top are highly relevant. In Russia, change is apt to come from above and it is becoming every day clearer that Mikhail Sergeyevich Gorbachov, having once consolidated his own position, is determined to put through, under the guise of *perestroika* or restructuring a wide range of far-reaching reforms. Conscious of the need for urgent measures to stimulate a flagging economy and of the importance of anticipating social and political change which might otherwise come spontaneously, it now seems certain that, while stamping out the abuses which over the years have become part of the system and combating the perennial curse of bureaucracy, he will at the same time set out to stimulate competition and provide more effective incentives than hitherto in industry, commerce and agriculture. This clearly is the purpose of his decision to authorize a measure of private enterprise in certain sectors of the economy. At the same time, there is every indication that he intends to allow, indeed encourage, far more freedom of expression in literature and in the arts.

That, like Khruschchov before him, he will encounter stubborn opposition from strongly-entrenched conservative elements in Party and government seems certain. But it should be remembered that, in their day, neither Ivan the Terrible nor Peter the Great let themselves be deterred by reactionary boyars and, as anyone who has met him must realize, Mikhail Sergeyevich is clearly also a man with a gift for getting what he wants. He will, however, have to contend in a big way with the dead hand of bureaucracy and the deep-seated inertia of the system, both, I would say, harder to overcome than any boyar.

Soon after he came to power there were already signs of a new attitude to literature and the creative arts, and of greater *glasnost* or openness in such matters. For example, the poet Yevgeni Yevtushenko, who, while treading carefully, has over the past twenty-five years or more courageously upheld the cause of literary and cultural freedom and who by now well knows when to speak up and when to lie low, has of late been more than usually active and, what is more, has received marked encouragement from above, as has the less flamboyant Andrei Vosnesenski. At the Writers' Union five-yearly Congress in June 1986, the discussion was already infinitely livelier than at any period since Khrushchov's day, being marked by fierce attacks on censorship and bureaucratic control, and by many derogatory references to the poor quality of officially sponsored literature. There were also proposals (since brought to fruition) that Boris Pasternak's long-banned *Dr Zhivago* and various other hitherto forbidden works should now at last be published, while Yevtushenko successfully carried a motion that Pasternak's former dacha at Peredelkino should be turned into a museum. No less important, the septuagenarian Georgi Markov, a notorious conservative, was replaced as head of the Writers' Union by Vladimir Karpov, the talented and remarkably liberal-minded novelist and editor of *Novy Mir*, who, while serving on account of political misdemeanours in a penal battalion as a teenager in World War II, performed acts of such outstanding gallantry as to be made a Hero of the Soviet Union. Meanwhile the magazine *Ogonyok*, now generally accepted as the flagship of *glasnost*, has actually published some of the poems of Nikolai Gumilov, executed as a counter-revolutionary in 1921 and said to be one of Raisa Gorbachova's favourite poets, and at long last a handsome monument and a measure of official recognition have been posthumously accorded to Vladimir Vysotski, an earthy, outspoken and immensely popular ballad-writer and actor who died in 1980 at the age of forty-two.

No less significant than those of the Writers' Union were the proceedings of the Film Workers' Union in May of the same year when, amid noisy scenes, defenders of existing standards, were howled down and the Union's reactionary First Secretary Lev Kulidzhanov removed after twenty years in office and replaced by Elem Klimov, whose remarkable film *Agonia*, concerning Rasputin, Tsar Nicholas II and the Revolution, had for the past ten years been kept from the public by the censors. Now, not only *Agonia*, but a large number of other more or less controversial films were, after years on the shelf, at long last released to a public profoundly bored by decades of rubbish and avid for something new and better. Of these recent releases perhaps the most sensational was the Georgian director Tenghiz Abuladze's *Repentance*, with its biting attacks not only on Stalin and Stalinism but on neo-Stalinism as well.

To anyone who happened to be in Moscow in the summer of 1986, yet another sign of the times was the remarkable exhibition of the works of Ilya Glazunov, who, while admired by many as a painter, had until recently been regarded with suspicion by the cultural establishment. For the past thirty years (he is in his fifties), Glazunov's main theme has been the greater glorification of Holy Russia, her history, her saints and her heroes, with no little emphasis on the positive role in all this of the Orthodox Church. Though the cultural climate in official circles has admittedly been changing of recent years (particularly in regard to Russia's historical heritage), one of Glazunov's pictures, a large canvas entitled *The Return of the Prodigal Son*, was long considered to go much too far. It depicts a young man, naked to the waist and in jeans, humbly kneeling before a bearded, Christ-like figure, behind whom are ranged in glory all Russia's great saints, heroes and thinkers. Below them in the foreground two gigantic and highly symbolic hogs wallow in filth and blood, while beyond them, under a blood-red moon, there stretches away into the distance a long table littered with wine-glasses, naked women and a corpse or two, against a bleak landscape of barbed wire, concentration camps and wrecked churches. Hitherto *The Return of the Prodigal Son* had only been grudgingly exhibited or not at all. This time it was deliberately made the central feature of a mammoth display of six hundred of Glazunov's paintings, held across the road from the Kremlin in the vast Manège or Imperial Riding School. Outside the Manège, from morning to night, tens of thousands of Muscovites jostled each other to secure a sight of *The Return*, with its strident cultural and political message.

Even more explicit and no less indicative of a changing attitude towards the past was the chief attraction at the 1987 Exhibition of the official Soviet Academy of Art – a huge canvas by Academician Dmitri Zhilinski, depicting the artist's father being arrested in his underclothes by three NKVD men in uniform, entitled simply but sufficiently *1937* and dedicated to 'those who perished innocently at the time of the repression'.

How to handle the history of the Stalin era, indeed the history of the last seventy years, remains a delicate question. Following Khrushchov's denunciation of the *Vozhd* (Leader) there was a good deal of backtracking under Brezhnev. With the advent of *glasnost* historians have again become bolder. One recently put the number of political prisoners who passed through Stalin's camps at the time of the purges at seventeen millions, of whom half probably died. A number of the *Vozhd*'s more distinguished victims have by now been posthumously rehabilitated, but to demolish the Stalin legend completely could detract to an unacceptable extent from what rightly or wrongly have been recognized as Stalin's personal achievements, namely Russia's economic transformation in the 1930s and her hard-won victories in the war. Nor could it conveniently be forgotten that Stalin succeeded Lenin and that it was Lenin who laid the foundations of the present system, which in all too many respects is now found wanting.

That in the Soviet Union far-reaching change is urgently needed is indisputable. Of this no one is more aware than Mikhail Gorbachov. Seventy years after the Revolution, the Soviet Union, like many other countries, has serious economic difficulties to contend with. In practice, State Socialism has not proved a success. Economic growth, bedevilled by the side-effects of what, for want of a better word, is popularly known as bureaucratic centralism, is apt to be disappointing. And, despite much loose talk by Khrushchov and others of overtaking America in the economic field, an American industrial worker still produces twice as much and an American farm-hand ten times as much as his Soviet counterpart.

Soviet agriculture, owing partly to collectivization, partly to old-fashioned farming methods, partly to climatic conditions and partly to the perennial problem of keeping the peasants on the land, is all too often in trouble. Year after year the government has had to spend valuable currency on importing grain. On collective and even more so on state farms, the individual peasant is in practice no more than an employee. There is, however, a brighter side to the picture. After Stalin's enforced collectivization and nationalization of all land in the early 1930s, it was decided to meet the average peasant's deep-seated yearning to work his own land by allocating approximately one acre to every peasant, for him to work on his own account in his spare time. These single-acre, part-time allotments amount to less than three per cent of all the agricultural land in the Soviet Union. Yet such is the loving care lavished on them that they produce over thirty per cent of all the foodstuffs produced in the Soviet Union – a truly remarkable tribute to the efficiency of private enterprise. In short, they have become an indispensable part of the Soviet economy, a fact which the government have long recognized by building in every town vast peasants' markets, where the foodstuffs thus produced are sold by the peasants for what they will fetch. Equally significant is the fact that the goods for sale there are of better quality and offer a wider choice than those in the state food shops, which depend for their supplies on produce from state or collective farms. This is where the freshest eggs and poultry, the thickest cream, the best honey, fruit and vegetables are to be found. As for the prices, they are considerably higher, being arrived at after a lot of hard bargaining between customer and producer.

For the enterprising farm-worker the opportunities are considerable. One smallholder I visited in Western Georgia somehow managed to be farming on his own account not one but what I reckoned to be three or four acres of land, carrying a fine crop of Indian corn, some fruit trees and vegetables, two cows and a dozen sheep. He lived in his own neat little house in the middle of it. 'Who does all this belong to?' I asked him. 'Who do you think?' was his reply. His son, who helped part-time, had another regular job nearby. It may not be good Marxism, but it certainly seems to work and to the satisfaction of all concerned. Even in the towns, where meat is usually in short supply, one often encounters private and personal sheep grazing by the roadside.

Though for more than half a century the Soviet countryside has been divided up into state farms and collective farms, this has not altered its appearance as much as one might have expected. Here and there, special housing has been provided for farm workers and every state or collective farm has its headquarters with the chairman's office and appropriate displays of statistics and propaganda material. But normally workers on a state or collective farm live in their own houses in villages which have changed very little in appearance since tsarist days. In Georgia or Armenia, these are not so very different from mountain villages in the Balkans or across the border in Turkey or Iran. Stone or plaster-built houses cluster on a hillside or nestle in a sheltered valley. In Russian villages, two rows of traditional wooden houses or *izbas*, often elaborately carved, face each other across a wide village street, snowbound in winter, dusty in summer, muddy in spring and autumn. Usually there is a church, occasionally still in use, and sometimes, in Moslem villages, a mosque. A village shop offers a limited range of groceries, basic clothing, such as dungarees, soap and detergents and formerly if you were lucky, vodka, but this is now in short supply, if available at all. For further supplies you would make your way to the nearest town, taking the train or, if you have done well enough from the sale of the produce from your private plot to possess one, your own car, probably combining a shopping expedition with a trip to the market to sell your produce.

In the average Soviet village, there is no real equivalent of the English village pub, least of all since the recent drive against alcohol. This does not mean that the Russians (or for that matter the Georgians) do not enjoy drinking with their friends, relatives and neighbours; there is nothing they like better. But they do it with their meals and on special occasions, such as a wedding or to welcome visitors or delegations from the city or another farm. Then feasts are laid on which can last for hours and at which, until recently, quite phenomenal quantities of vodka, beer, wine and brandy were consumed, but always (and very sensibly) as an accompaniment to food. In the same way in both town and country, three or four friends will often go to the nearest hotel or restaurant together, order a meal and sit over it, drinking, until the place closes and they have to go home. Most villages have some kind of village hall or community centre, where meetings and functions can be held, probably under Party auspices.

The prosperity of what can fairly be called the private sector of Soviet agriculture naturally depends, as it does elsewhere, on soil and climate. A rich, sun-soaked, well-watered acre of cherries or strawberries or carnations will clearly bring in a bigger return than an acre of mouldy worm-eaten turnips on a patch of barren hillside. Honey is something that sells well (8 or 10 roubles a kilo) and you will often see groups of private enterprise beehives along the side of the road. The peasants' markets in the bleak frozen north do not compare with the lavish exuberance of their counterparts in the south and this difference is of course reflected in the lifestyle of the peasants concerned. And so, once more, with the tacit acceptance of the Party and government, an alternate economy is in operation, which again, by any standards, represents a concession, if not to capitalism, at any rate to a more elastic brand of socialism. With time, other such concessions seem bound to follow.

Until the advent of Mikhail Gorbachov it would probably have been possible to spend two or three years in the Soviet Union and still take the view that no progress was being made or even that things were getting worse. But, looking back over a much longer period and allowing for periodic setbacks and reversals, it was hard to resist the conclusion that, long term, a gradual evolution was taking place, even though, to paraphrase Lenin, it was often a case of three steps forward and two back. What is more, the primary motive force behind this evolution (or should one perhaps call it revolution?) was, once again, the pursuit not of vague abstract ideals, but of solid material advantages for those concerned. That sooner, rather than later, further far-reaching reforms will be required is certain. But again change, as it comes, is likely to come slowly, within the existing system and from the top, rather than as the result of any sudden upheaval or explosion. To my mind, Western observers who over the years have seriously predicted the early collapse of the Soviet economy and the consequent disruption by one means or another of the Soviet system, greatly underestimate its basic stability or, to put it in another way, inertia.

For some time past the emergence of a class structure and the accompanying consumer revolution have been changing the face of Soviet society. The Soviet scene now presents infinitely more variety than it did even twenty years ago. There is no longer the same dreary uniformity about it. Not only are there now several different social classes, there are any number of different lifestyles to go with them. All kinds of cracks are beginning to appear in the monolith. Outward appearances are changing. The people you meet walking down the street in any Soviet town now look different and you can be reasonably sure that, within limits, their lifestyles are also different. Some are shabby. Some are smart. Some are on the trendy side. Others favour more conservative styles. Some, with long hair and way-out clothes, are deliberately Bohemian or intellectual in appearance. Others, in track-suits and gym shoes, in waders, crash-helmets or ski-pants, proclaim their enthusiasm for some sport or other. Some lead enormous dogs, others tiny ones. The total standardization of Stalin's day and the even more total control that went with it have become a thing of the past. Human nature, which Stalin by one means or another managed to keep under control, is continually asserting itself and the results are becoming more noticeable every year.

Complete freedom of thought and expression is, of course, another matter. This is something that has never existed in Russia and is not likely to be introduced suddenly there, even by Mikhail Gorbachov. Controls, it is true, are no longer anything like as complete or as far-reaching as they were. But they are still there, ready to be put into effect as and when needed, and seem likely to remain so for the foreseeable future.

Even the dissidents have in a sense been over the years a manifestation of the loosening-up process, of the gradual relaxation of tension, which marked the end of the Stalin era. In Stalin's day there were no dissidents, for the simple reason that any potential dissident was shot out of hand before he had time to become one (a policy to which Stalin's ghost, if consulted, would undoubtedly recommend an immediate return). During the years that followed, despite harassment, dissidents somehow managed to stage occasional demonstrations, to hold press conferences, to circulate banned books and secret news-sheets, and to communicate with the outside world, which continued to take a keen interest in their affairs. More recently still their situation has been radically changed.

What of the younger generation? Where do they fit in? As elsewhere, they present a problem. 'What cannot help alarming us', remarked the late Mr Chernenko plaintively during his brief tenure of office, 'is the desire on the part of our youth to make themselves noticeable, not by their knowledge or industry, but by expensive things bought with their parents' money.' To most of us his words had a familiar ring.

In a Park of Rest and Culture at Ferghana in deepest Turkestan I interrupted an after-dinner stroll to read a notice. 'Punk Rock,' it said, 'Hard Rock, Country Rock', and finally 'Black Humour Rock.' 'Led Zeppelin' was scrawled on a nearby wall. In jeans and printed T-shirts what seemed like the entire juvenile population were rocking under the stars to a variety of rhythms emanating from several brightly illuminated bandstands. 'What magazine do you represent?' asked a juvenile bandleader, eagerly eyeing my cameras. 'Shall I get them to turn up the lighting? How do you like our playing?'

The Park, like many Parks of Rest and Culture, was dedicated to Maxim Gorki. What that old-time pillar of Soviet literature and of the Soviet régime would have made of punk rock, and whether it would have corresponded to his own ideas of culture or rest, is hard to say. But it is certainly what the rising generation in the Soviet Union wants to hear and, despite prolonged official disapproval, has long been determined to get. Already the passion for rock and pop and for everything else American has reached a scarcely believable pitch and cries out to be satisfied.

Not long ago I asked a Russian friend which was the best rock group in Moscow. 'We will go there tonight', he said. That evening we drove through the darkness for three-quarters of an hour into the outer suburbs of Moscow, finally arriving at a brand-new high-rise concrete building, apparently one of the new hotels put up for the Moscow Olympics. Passing through revolving-doors into a dark, deserted lobby and then down two flights of stairs and through another pair of doors, we suddenly found ourselves in a large and brilliantly lit restaurant, crowded with cheerful well-dressed customers eating and drinking for all they were worth and shouting merrily at the waiters and at each other above the deafening beat of the band which, to be fair, fully justified its reputation. On the narrow dance floor twenty couples jerked and gyrated rhythmically. I would not be able to find my way back there unaided, but the noise was unforgettable and the faultlessly served dinner we had that night has stuck in my memory as one of the best I have ever eaten in Moscow.

The passion for American-style jeans, long regarded by the Soviet authorities as a secret weapon of the CIA, is equally compulsive. 'How nice', I said to a girl I met in Turkmenistan who was wearing the British Royal Arms emblazoned across her bosom. 'Yes', she replied coyly. 'It's something American.' And when I pointed out that it wasn't, 'Well,' she said a trifle ruefully, 'anyhow my *jeans* are real.'

The first *dzhinnzi* or blue jeans made their appearance in the Soviet Union twenty-five or thirty years ago. Sold secondhand by enterprising foreign tourists for large sums in roubles, they soon became a status symbol, a mark of extreme sophistication. Next came local imitations produced by private enterprise in something approximating to blue denim. Then better jeans made in Hungary and Poland. And now, yielding at long last to teenage pressure, the Soviet government find themselves manufacturing jeans of such remarkable quality as to be indistinguishable from actual American ones. But still the *cognoscenti* demand the genuine article. Indeed only the other day, *Pravda* reported the sad case of a Soviet air hostess who, having bought a couple of dozen pairs for 30 roubles a pair in Moscow, sewed on smuggled foreign labels and flew them to Georgia, where, when picked up by the police, she was reselling them as imports for 220 roubles a pair. But what could be called the ultimate apotheosis of *dzhinnzi* occurred at Ilya Glazunov's sensational exhibition at the Manège in the summer of 1986, where one of the biggest crowds gathered to gape at a picture entitled simply *Dzhinnzi*, depicting an exceptionally well-built blonde topless in a pair of the tightest possible jeans.

T-shirts are a different matter. It is surely inconceivable that a Soviet government department should countenance the manufacture and distribution of T-shirts bearing the national emblem of a capitalist imperialist power. And yet suddenly three or four years ago the Stars and Stripes and the American Eagle were everywhere, the product, presumably, of private presses turning them out by the score in little back rooms. Foreign gramophone records, too, change hands all over the country for surprising sums. 'You can't *give* me that', said an Uzbek youth whom I had presented with a very ordinary pop record (his mother and sister had entertained us to tea, jam and then, suddenly, soup). 'Why, it's worth 50 roubles!' (about £50). And he insisted on presenting me with a piece of local pottery in exchange. In one shop in Tbilisi I even found punk necklaces for sale, complete with replica razor-blades.

One commodity that for years was in perpetually short supply in the Soviet Union was any book that the ordinary person could possibly want to read for pleasure or amusement. Of late there has been a big change for the better. Now, if you walk into a bookshop and try to buy a novel by Tolstoi or Turgenyev, by Gogol, Chekhov or Dostoyevski, you stand a good chance of finding one, a good deal better produced than formerly, as well as a much wider range of translations of books by Western authors. Moreover in the Library of Foreign Literature in Moscow, long presided over by the late Mr Kosygin's capable daughter Ludmila Gvishiani, an encouragingly wide range of foreign books of all kinds are now available. Which of course means access, for those who find their way there, not only to the books themselves, but to the ideas they contain, often no doubt at variance with the current Party line.

Something that never fails to impress me is the enviable eagerness of Soviet children and young people generally for knowledge and their consequent enthusiasm for education as such. Historically, education came late to the Russians. Now they have it, they want all they can get. At a school I visited, which concentrated on English, I found plenty of twelve- and fourteen-year-olds who not only had a good grasp of the language but also knew a lot about Great Britain and America, and wanted more than anything to go there. All the teachers spoke good English and had at their disposal well-equipped language laboratories. Education – good, old-fashioned no-nonsense, Victorian-style education, to match the prim pre-Revolutionary uniforms still worn by the children – is something the Soviet government have wisely concentrated on ever since the Revolution and there can be no doubt that this has paid abundant dividends by reducing illiteracy and raising the general standards of education. At the moment some fifty million children attend ordinary ten-year schools, bracketing primary and secondary education, while in the last thirty-five years the number of university students has risen from just over one million to over five million. Any exceptionally gifted children are given every encouragement and opportunity to develop their special talents. The same, it appears, applies to upper-class children, who, whether gifted or not, are daily whisked to their special schools or *spetsshkoli* in their parents' chauffeur-driven limousines. Indeed, according to an indignant article in *Moskovskaya Pravda*, no more than six per cent of the first-year children in Moscow's ninety special schools had working-class parents and there were even fewer in the higher grades.

Even so, the existing arrangements do not seem to satisfy the thirst for improvement of the Soviet élite, who spend substantial sums supplementing their children's education with expensive private tuition. Nor, quite certainly, do they have any difficulty in finding suitable tutors, who are only too glad to increase their earnings and, incidentally, make valuable contacts among the rich and influential. A good language teacher, it appears, can earn as much as six or seven hundred roubles a month in his spare time, probably doubling his regular salary.

Another area in which there have been enormous advances is housing. Before the War, housing conditions in the Soviet Union were indescribably bad, little fresh living accommodation having been built in the twenty years that followed the Revolution. Whole families had no more than a share of a room in some tumbledown old house, separated from their immediate neighbours by a curtain or blanket on a clothes-line. Kitchen and bathroom, if they existed, were shared with neighbouring tenants. Only people of great consequence had small self-contained flats to themselves. During the War little new housing could be built and much existing accommodation was destroyed, leaving things worse than ever. Over the last forty years, however, a tremendous effort has been made to improve housing conditions.

Each year for the last thirty years or more, two or three million new flats have been completed. Moscow, to take the most obvious example, is expanding in every direction, covering vast new areas of countryside with whole new suburbs of high-rise buildings, and the same is happening elsewhere. In addition to state housing, apartment blocks are being built by cooperative groups under the auspices of one government department or another, in which individuals can actually buy their own flats by means of a down-payment and instalments spread over a number of years. Even so, housing is still short, but it is no great exaggeration to say that by now the average family either has somewhere adequate to live or else has a reasonably good prospect of finding somewhere in the foreseeable future.

Meanwhile, despite determined efforts to keep the peasants on the land, the movement of population from the country to the towns and in particular to Moscow still continues, regulated, as far as possible, by the issue of official residence permits and the expulsion, when caught, of illegal residents who have moved to Moscow without proper documents. 'Your documents, please', is the first thing a militiaman asks you for. 'Documents' mean first and foremost your internal passport (a feature of life in Russia since long before the Revolution). This gives particulars of your birth, parentage, nationality (i.e. Russian, Georgian, Uzbek, Jewish, etc.) and marital status, and also includes a *propiska* or residence permit, showing where you are officially domiciled. To move from one area to another for more than a short time you need, in theory at any rate, official permission. Should the move be permanent, you are required to re-register and apply for a fresh *propiska*. For an official trip or *komandirovka* you are issued with a *spravka* or movement-order to show all concerned that you are not just joy-riding. You are equally given an appropriate document when you go on holiday. In this way, any militiaman or other official you meet can, again in theory, see at a glance who you are, where you belong and what you are supposed to be doing, and it will be up to you to explain any discrepancies. Other important documents are your *kharakteristika* or character reference, which you have to produce every time you change jobs, and your work-book, which gives a list of all the jobs you have ever held. This is kept by your employer and only returned when you change jobs.

Residence permits for Moscow and Leningrad, where there is still overcrowding, are notoriously hard to get. If, on the other hand, you want to move to an area with plenty of vacancies which the government are trying to fill or, better still, if you have a job and a flat waiting for you, a move should present no difficulties. Indeed a graduate, on first getting his degree, could easily find himself appointed to a region remote from his home and family. These controls are designed to discourage too much haphazard drifting from one job and one area to another with resulting loss of productivity. But, like other regulations, they are not a hundred per cent effective. To quote one somewhat cynical observer of the Soviet scene, 'proliferation of rules makes for proliferation of loopholes'. All an industrial worker who wants to move needs do is to hand in his notice and apply to the appropriate labour exchange for another job which, owing to shortage of skilled labour, he should, if he has the necessary qualifications, have little difficulty in finding. As a rule, the time spent looking for and finding jobs (which are prominently advertised in the press) seems not to exceed three or four weeks and factories which are short of workers often offer valuable perquisites such as new flats to attract the labour they need. But, even when a worker signs on for, say, three years, there is in practice nothing to stop him leaving at the end of just one, sometimes simply because he has heard the canteen facilities are better somewhere else. Once again, it is not too difficult to beat the system if you really set your mind to it.

In the rural areas in particular, a surprising number of houses are privately owned. Having gained possession of a patch of land (which in theory at any rate continues to belong to the state much as, under a feudal system, it belonged to the monarch), an intending householder builds himself or gets himself built a house which then becomes his personal property. Russians love the country and most Muscovites who can afford it have a dacha, a country cottage, or at any rate a share in one, as well as a flat in Moscow.

A house can be built in several ways. If you possess the necessary skills, you can build it yourself, calling on your friends and relations to help you (Russians are always ready to give a friend a hand) and accumulating the materials required by whatever method comes handiest. This in theory is done, once you have the necessary permits, by buying them for cash direct from the state factory or from some kind of intermediate depot or store. Equally, if you can't build it yourself and aren't in too much of a hurry, you can have it built by a state-controlled building guild. In practice, however, you would be more likely to enlist the services of a moonlighter, who would do the job for you in his spare time and as likely as not provide the materials from sources of his own, into which you would be well advised not to enquire too closely. Motoring through the mountains of Armenia recently, I stopped to ask the way of a cheerful-looking party eating an al fresco lunch in a charming roadside pavilion. 'Come and join us', said a dark-eyed lady, thrusting a mug of wine and a plateful of meat into my hand. 'Isn't it a beautiful pavilion?' she said. 'When my husband was killed here in a crash some years back, his workmates put it up in his memory, "borrowing" everything they needed for it from the factory where he worked. Wasn't it sweet of them? And now we meet here every year to commemorate the anniversary of his death.' And she refilled my mug. Clearly the cost of building in the

Soviet Union varies according to circumstances. Luxury dachas with all mod. cons are said to change hands for a hundred thousand roubles or more. But, if you are clever and lucky and well-placed, you might manage to put one up for very much less.

Another way of finding accommodation is by exchange. One feature of every Soviet city is some kind of housing exchange where people can let it be known by displaying advertisements of one kind or another or even verbally that they have houses or apartments or rooms to let or exchange. Thus young marrieds and their in-laws living temporarily together might be offering one big flat in exchange for two smaller ones. Some people might well prefer a small flat in Moscow to a large flat in the provinces, or vice versa. A family finding themselves with one room more than they needed would almost certainly let it, preferably to a respectable tenant from the right walk of life and with his papers in order. What is more, they would probably ask (and get) two or three times the rate for equivalent local authority housing.

In the cities the landlord of most of the big apartment blocks is the city council. Rents are low. Flats vary in size, the larger, more commodious and more conveniently situated being allocated to the more important people. Most new flats now provide adequate kitchens and bathroom facilities. Furniture and fittings, either bought or inherited, vary in style and quality. A whole range of household goods and furniture now being imported from Eastern Europe lend a new dimension to gracious living in the Soviet Union, while those in a position to do so proudly display the result of forays still further afield. 'How do you like this wallpaper?' a Georgian friend asked me recently while having dinner at her daughter's apartment. 'I got it for my daughter in Paris.'

Everywhere taste in such things is improving by leaps and bounds. Dining not long ago with some well-connected young intellectuals in their two-roomed apartment in a new high-rise building a long taxi-ride from the centre of Moscow, I was as much struck by the simple but charming way in which their small but well-equipped flat was furnished and decorated as by the tender loving care which had gone into the preparation of dinner. I was pleased and surprised, too, by the ready humour and frankness of their conversation which, coming from staunch supporters of the régime, showed a new and welcome open-mindedness and readiness to discuss any question on its merits. Altogether it would have been hard to spend a more agreeable evening anywhere in more attractive surroundings. The party was completed by my host and hostess's baby son and his grandmother or *babushka*.

Although immediately after the Revolution there was much talk of free love and communal kindergartens, and though, as in the West, many marriages end in divorce, the deep-rooted Russian idea of the family as the basis of society has persisted and for many years now has enjoyed the whole-hearted support of the government. Today the typical Soviet household consists not only of father, mother and one or two children (large families are rare) but also of a grandmother or other elderly relative to give a hand with the cooking and housework and help look after the children. The famous Russian *babushka* remains a pillar of Soviet society. Usually both parents go out to work and it is she who is left in supreme charge of the children.

LOOKING BACKWARDS, WE MOVE FORWARDS

When there is a family wedding, especially in the country, all the relations turn up and a good number of neighbours as well. Invariably the ceremony, whether civil or religious, is followed by a feast which, like all feasts in the Soviet Union, is apt to last for several hours. In the Ukraine I became involved not long ago in a wedding which was attended by practically the whole village. Long tables, laden with enormous quantities of food and drink – roast meat, cheeses, chickens, fruit, wine, beer and, above all, home-made vodka – had been laid out in the village hall, specially draped with tapestries for the occasion. A local pop group, complete with dark glasses, long hair and jeans, were playing jazz. The bride was in white and the bridegroom was wearing his best dark suit. The best man and bridesmaid were equally smart and seemed equally in love with each other. Both young men wore broad ceremonial sashes. Round them clustered their families and their work-mates from the local collective farm, all in their best clothes.

At the Sioni Cathedral in Tbilisi in Georgia, I recently attended a full-scale Christian wedding, beginning with beautifully sung High Mass in the body of the cathedral and concluding with the actual wedding ceremony in a side-chapel tightly packed with relatives and friends. All concerned were fashionably dressed and the cars that swept them away afterwards were sleek and shiny. The ensuing wedding reception, held in a relative's large and luxurious apartment, was well up to even Georgian standards of hospitality and speech-making. At Zagorsk, too, church weddings have of late become extremely popular.

To meet the keen competition of church weddings, the Soviet authorities have done their best to brighten up the civil ceremonies which now take place amid pastel shades and soft lighting in resplendent Wedding Palaces, often the ornate former mansions of rich merchants, to the accompaniment of Mendelssohn's Wedding March and much fizzy champagne. In Moscow it is usual for the newly wedded couple to drive straight from the wedding ceremony either to Lenin's Mausoleum on the Red Square or to the nearby Tomb of the Unknown Soldier, where the bride solemnly deposits her bouquet. Whether a wedding (or a funeral) is held in church or not, it has to be registered with the local registrar of births, deaths and marriages and noted on the personal documents of the bride and bridegroom.

The exact place of religion in Soviet life is not easy to define. The Russians have always been an intensely religious people. Officially Marxism–Leninism has superseded Orthodoxy as the state religion. Portraits of Marx and Lenin have replaced the old icons as its outward and visible manifestation, while Lenin's Tomb has become an official place of pilgrimage. On the other hand, there are still millions of Christian believers in the Soviet Union, the figure claimed by the Orthodox Church being thirty million, not to mention other denominations, including some thirty million or so Moslems. Though a number of churches have been turned into cinemas or museums, those that are still working are filled on Sundays and feast days by large and devout congregations. As elsewhere, many, though by no means all of the worshippers, belong to the older generation. But then it is now seventy years since the Revolution, which means that any sixty-year-old must have been born into a country which had already been subjected to intensive atheist propaganda for a full ten years. In Moscow, several Orthodox priests have a considerable reputation as preachers and it has become fashionable for the younger intelligentsia to listen to their sermons. In some country churches, heavily bearded village priests carry on the tradition of their pre-Revolutionary predecessors; in other villages the church has long stood derelict. At an old lady's funeral I attended at a village in north-west Russia, the open coffin was followed from the little church to the grave by what must have been the whole population. No less characteristic was a Mohammedan funeral which I found making its noisy way to a Moslem cemetery far away in the foothills of the Pamirs.

For more than twenty years after the Revolution, a determined effort was made to root out religion altogether, often by the most brutal means. The first major change came in 1941 when Stalin, in his effort to mobilize all available national resources, spiritual as well as material, in support of the war effort, decided as a matter of policy to reach an accommodation with the Orthodox Church which he rightly considered was still a force to be reckoned with. The accommodation, based on a measure of mutual forbearance, has continued ever since, one of its conditions being that, in their public utterances, especially on international problems, the Orthodox leaders never deviate from the official Soviet line. This year's celebration of the thousandth anniversary of Russia's conversion to Christianity will give an interesting indication of the current relationship between Church and State.

Later, Russia's forward policy in the Middle East led to a comparable *modus vivendi* with Islam and in particular with the Grand Mufti of Central Asia in Tashkent. Recent developments in Afghanistan and the emergence of Islamic fundamentalism in Iran and elsewhere have however brought a fresh awareness of possible dangers in this field. That it would be a mistake to dismiss such dangers too lightly was made abundantly clear during the winter of 1986-7 by an outbreak of rioting at Kurgantepe in Tajikstan, some thirty miles from the Afghan border, where angry crowds marched on the local headquarters of the Ministry of the Interior, clamouring for the release of Mullah Abdullah Saidov, a popular Moslem preacher with nationalist tendencies and a big local following. 'The news of Abdullah Saidov's arrest soon spread', reported the local paper, *Tajikstan-i-Sovieti*, 'and quickly brought the Mullah's fellow-believers, who had sworn loyalty to him, out on the streets.' Worse still, it went on, the demonstrators included intellectuals and actual Party members. Mikhail Gorbachov promptly made his own views on the subject abundantly clear. Speaking to Party officials in Tashkent in November 1986, he called for a 'firm and uncompromising struggle against religious phenomena'. 'We must', he declared, 'be strict, above all with Communists and senior officials, particularly those who claim to defend our morality and themselves actually take part in religious ceremonies.'

Considerable influence in religious matters is exercised in Russia by the ever-present *babushka*. If a believer, she may well have her grandchildren christened and continue to take them to church, whatever their parents may think. She will likewise use her very considerable influence in the family in favour of church weddings and funerals. If, on the other hand, she is a keen Party member, the children will appear in the white shirts and scarlet neckties of the Pioneers or Communist Scouts and Guides. While relations between government and churches are now on the whole correct, no conscientious Party member would make a habit of going to church himself, whatever his mother or grandmother said, though he might possibly attend a friend's wedding or funeral.

What part do politics as such play today in the life of the average Soviet citizen? It is no exaggeration to say that Marxism–Leninism and the Party pervade every aspect of life in the Soviet Union in much the same way that Christianity and the Church pervaded every aspect of life in mediaeval Europe. Party and state (with the Party predominant) are Marxist–Leninist, and everything is state-owned and state- or Party-controlled. In government, in industry, in the armed forces, in education, in science, literature and the arts, the Party is the directing force, the ultimate authority. At the top of the pyramid, the Politburo of the Party reigns supreme and lays down the Party line which, through all its chops and changes, is gospel for everyone.

Thus the average Soviet citizen lives and dies under the aegis of the Party and under a system which, if it has not yet officially attained Communism, is confidently expected to do so in the foreseeable future. From earliest youth, at school, and as a member of the Communist Youth Organization, he will have been exposed to incessant Communist indoctrination and everything he sees or reads or listens to will be tinged with Marxism–Leninism. Whether or not he himself takes an active part in politics depends very largely on his personal inclinations. But one thing is certain, if he wants to get on, the surest way to advancement in any walk of life is membership of the Party which, incidentally, can also offer a worthwhile full-time career for those so inclined.

There are of course exceptions that prove the rule, but in general top people and people who hope to become top people will be found on enquiry to belong to the Party, which simultaneously provides a convenient old-boy network. On the other hand, while a successful career in the Party is synonymous with a successful political career, and while leading public figures outside actual politics are expected to attend Party functions, much as their equivalents in Victorian England were expected to attend church, the enormous majority of Soviet citizens are not Party members and, though they frequently join in functions organized by the Party, do not attend the meetings of its members. The Party, in other words, is an élite with a membership of around nineteen million out of a total population of over two hundred and eighty million. In the Soviet Union much the same sort of people join the Communist Party as in England might join the Conservative Party – straightforward, active, ambitious, public-spirited, patriotic, conservative-minded members of the public, upholders of the establishment and admirers of the leadership, deeply suspicious of all long-haired, subversive, dissident or anti-social elements, and prepared to work energetically through the Party for the greater glory of the Soviet Fatherland.

A Party function I inadvertently attended in the old town of Pskov provided a good illustration of this. While strolling through a public park by the river, we suddenly heard the sound of a piano and an accordion being played with a good deal more enthusiasm than skill. Catching sight through the trees of some red bunting, we made our way to where a rather shaky-looking small stage had been erected. On this, half-a-dozen plump fourteen-year-old girls in neat white blouses and red neckties were doing a little song-and-dance act, while a middle-aged lady played the piano and the slightly seedy equivalent of a scoutmaster or curate helped out on the squeeze-box. Thump, thump, thump, squeak, squeak, squeak, went the little girls, tinkling their tambourines, while six small boys nudged each other and sucked sweets, waiting for their turn to go on. Sitting in rows on some very hard-looking benches were several dozen proud parents, grandparents, aunts, uncles, brothers and sisters, all in their Sunday best, watching the infant prodigies perform. Nothing could have been more like a church fête at home. Only the inscription on a red banner draped across the stage reminded us that this was a Revolutionary meeting, but in aid of a Revolution, one soon realized, that was already almost seventy years away. 'If only the Americans wouldn't go on so about *ideology*', a senior Soviet official remarked to me recently. 'Who started that?' was my reply. But I could see what he meant.

As for the two hundred and sixty million Soviet citizens who are not Party members, it is a reasonable assumption that, human nature being what it is, they take neither more nor less interest in politics than do the mass of the population in most other countries. What primarily concerns them are their families, their jobs, their homes, their way of life and standard of living. In all these respects, they will notice, especially if they are over forty, a marked improvement over the years which will be a cause of satisfaction to them. When called upon to vote, just on one hundred per cent of them will vote the same way, there being in effect no choice, and, when at their place of work they are invited to take part in some demonstration or other, they will obediently take part in it. For the rest, they will no doubt grumble from time to time, as most of us grumble, not about any abstract political principle or aspect of Soviet policy, but about working or housing conditions, the personality of the works foreman or chairman of the collective farm, the absence of whatever commodities happen at that moment to be in short supply or the shortcomings of their wives and children.

If over the past twenty years you asked anyone connected with the Party or government about an aspect of the Soviet political scene which particularly preoccupies Western opinion, namely the dissidents, you would have been told that their numbers were very small and that they did not count for much. This, in a sense, was true. For the most part intellectuals, their appeal was restricted and, outside Moscow, the enormous majority of people had never heard of them. The Party and government, on the other hand, being themselves heirs to the dissidents of seventy-odd years ago, remained acutely conscious of them. But here, too, things are now changing fast.

By comparison with the thirties and forties, the celebrated Soviet Secret Police, though readily available when needed, are less in evidence than they once were. This reflects greater self-confidence on the part of the régime and, in this respect at any rate, a continuation of the limited liberalization begun by Khrushchov, though here progress has been anything but constant. Undoubtedly the average Russian is still very much aware of the KGB and, unless he himself happens to have a connection with it, anxious to keep out of its way. He will also naturally be extremely conscious of the Party hierarchy and in particular of the Party secretary or organizer at his place of work and where he lives. Well aware too that any openly subversive activity on his part would immediately be reported to the 'competent authorities' and that he would then be in trouble (though not quite the sort of trouble he would have been in in Stalin's day). If, on the other hand, a man keeps quiet, avoids what are known as 'dubious connections', gives no trouble and does a good job of work, he should have nothing much to worry about.

Until quite recently interest in politics was certainly not stimulated by the Soviet Press, which by Western standards was almost incredibly boring, containing nothing but long, dreary, repetitive articles and speeches hammering home the Party line, together with a bare minimum of heavily angled domestic and foreign news and none of the sensational stories of sex, violence and mawkish human interest which find such favour with Western readers.

Of late, however, there has, in this field, too, been a big change. With the coming of *glasnost*, even *Pravda* and *Izvestia*, the organs of the Party and government respectively, now quite often carry news and stories with general appeal in addition to occasional sharp criticism of government institutions, while in style and content Mikhail Gorbachov's speeches could hardly fail to arouse the interest of any intelligent Soviet citizen – a change for the better already clearly reflected in improved circulation figures. 'For years', said one middle-aged Soviet intellectual, 'our papers were not only dull. They were not even believable. Now you actually look forward to reading them. You never know what they are going to dig up next.' One off-beat joke going the rounds points up recent developments and has a special appeal for the older generation. '*Have* you read the latest article in *Pravda*?' asks one elderly citizen. 'No', replies his friend. 'What does it say?' 'Oh, I couldn't tell you *that* over the telephone', comes the cautious reply.

A lead in this loosening-up process has been given by the two magazines, *Ogonyok* and *Novi Mir*, both of which, in addition to publishing a good deal of material that had hitherto been banned, have of late not been afraid to print news of beatings and other excesses by the KGB. For the readers of *Literaturnaya Gazeta* it must likewise have been an entirely novel experience suddenly to come on a full-page interview with no less a person than Cardinal Glemp, the Roman Catholic Primate of Poland, accompanied by an article stressing the strength of the Church in Poland and its profound influence on patriotic Poles, revealing that the Polish State Radio regularly broadcasts the mass, and concluding that 'this is a reality we have to reckon with'. To the Russian people the Cardinal sent a message the meaning of which, in their present receptive frame of mind, can scarcely have escaped them. 'When one people has dealings with another', it ran, 'it must know the whole truth about that people. Sometimes propaganda only gives part of the truth. Which is harmful.'

In some sections of the press correspondents still express grave doubts as to the validity or indeed desirability of *perestroika* and *glasnost*. 'I'm fed to the teeth with it', wrote one. 'We won't see justice or reform in a hundred years. It's all just another campaign - words!' Others doubt whether it will last, fearing that it is too fragile a phenomenon to withstand the crushing weight of the Soviet state and indeed of Russian history and that before long it will simply 'go pop like a soap bubble'. 'Up to the age of twenty', he reminisced, 'I never suspected anything was wrong. We were always being told *truth* was the most valuable thing in life. Perhaps that was why they were so careful to keep it from us. And so we got used to leading a double life. And now I'm afraid someone will suddenly decide there has been too much truth and that this campaign has been going on too long.'

Meanwhile to existing titles has been added an entirely new magazine, cheekily named *Glasnost*, edited by a former political prisoner and containing articles by a number of well-known dissidents including Andrei Sakharov. At the time of writing it is still in circulation.

Nine out of ten of the families in the Soviet Union now own television sets. Like the newspapers, Soviet television programmes are limited in scope and the regular news broadcasts still consist very largely of Marxist–Leninist uplift, though here again there has of late been a marked improvement in the quality of the programmes shown and an increase in the amount of light entertainment. Moreover, now that jamming has ceased or at any rate lessened, an ever-increasing number of people throughout the Soviet Union listen to foreign radio broadcasts and pass on anything they hear to a wide circle of friends – another link with the outside world and, in its way, another intellectual stimulus.

To me the most extraordinary and in some ways the most encouraging thing about the Soviet Union after seventy years of standardization, of socialist planning, of mass education, mass production and mass control, of ceaseless efforts to eliminate all deviations and divergences from a firmly imposed and all-embracing Party line, to impose *poryadok*, the semblance of order, as beloved by Party planners as it was by tsarist officialdom before them, of seeking by all possible means to produce a stereotyped Soviet Man, is still the ever-increasing diversity of it all, the new and different trends and ideas which, in spite of everything, still keep breaking through, the social, natural, economic, intellectual and physical differences and eccentricities which, to the despair of the powers-that-be, keep emerging and re-emerging at every level of society and in every field of activity and, finally, the part played in all this by human nature, which socialist planners so regularly leave out of account and which no less regularly bounces back notwithstanding.

All this applies at least as much to the non-Russian parts of the Soviet Union where, overall, the national minorities now actually outnumber the ethnic Russians. A century-and-half ago, the Russian poet Lermontov, who himself fought in the Caucasus, predicted that, with time, the conquered Caucasians would come to say with pride: 'We may truly be slaves, but enslaved by Russia, the Ruler of the Universe'. How does this look today? Is the Kremlin tightening or relaxing its grip on its non-Russian dominions? In theory, each of the fifteen Soviet Socialist Republics has the right to secede from the Union. Each has its own president and government, mainly recruited from its own nationals. Each has its own national flag. Over the years there has been a measure of genuine decentralization and quite important decisions are now taken locally, without reference to Moscow. But, if a Georgian or an Armenian or an Uzbek or a Tajik were silly enough to suggest that his country should make use of its constitutional right to secede from the Soviet Union, he would at once be in trouble. On the other hand, no one can deny that life in Tbilisi or Tashkent, like life in Moscow, is very much freer and more agreeable than it was fifty years ago. The standard of living has improved and there is no longer the same fear of the secret police. People speak their own language and, within limits, practise their own religion.

One reason for this is that their rulers feel more secure than they did. As each generation grows up, the process of Sovietization is carried a stage further. Everywhere millions and millions of Soviet citizens, whatever their nationality, are being taught in identical schools, are reading identical books and newspapers, listening to identical broadcasts and speeches. Everywhere the Party exercises ultimate control. The mills of Communism grind small. National usages are dying out and national differences becoming less marked. And, as Lermontov predicted a century-and-half-ago, Russians and non-Russians alike take a genuine pride in the great empire to which they belong. But, nonetheless, even under Communism, nationalism, like religion, remains a force to be reckoned with.

Beyond the frontiers of the Soviet Union, the ring of Communist satellite states, established in 1945 to protect the Soviet Union from capitalist encroachment, have instead proved over the years a cause for serious concern, culminating in the continuing, if partially contained, crisis in Poland. Here again state Socialism has not been a success and there have also been recurrent signs of nationalism, liberalism and other unwelcome and disturbing trends, including the emergence of a strong independent trade-union movement and clear evidence that the power of the Catholic Church is at least as strong as it was fifty years ago. Indeed the problem of the Soviet Union's future relationship with its neighbours of the Eastern Bloc is one for which it will take Mikhail Gorbachov's tact, ingenuity and skill to find a solution, on the lines, one might surmise, of the existing and astonishingly successful Soviet *modus vivendi* with Finland. Meanwhile, ironically enough, Gorbachov's own unsettling moves in the direction of 'democratization' have in more ways than one been a cause of embarrassment to the hard-pressed rulers of Russia's own satellites.

In the Far East, meanwhile, China, from a close ally has over the years become a potential menace. Of this particular preoccupation I have more than once been conscious when visiting Siberia. Several times the size of Western Europe, Siberia has a population of not much more than thirty millions. It also possesses vast scarcely tapped natural resources. Across the frontier, which they still dispute, over a thousand million not particularly friendly Chinese are looking for somewhere to expand into. And beyond them are the Japanese. Little wonder that the Russians are concentrating as hard as they can on the province's development, which, whatever the state of their relations with China or Japan, or, for the matter of that, with the USA, is bound to be of immense importance for their country's future and play an essential part in its emergence as a Pacific power.

Inevitably, Siberia must bulk large in any attempt to assess the future of the Soviet Union. Its significance for Russia dates back to the days of Ivan the Terrible. Following their arrival there from further east in the first half of the thirteenth century, the Mongols or Tartars were to hold sway over much of Siberia for the next two or three hundred years and by the end of the fifteenth century had established a Tartar khanate on the Irtysh River with its capital at Sibir, which eventually gave its name to the region as a whole.

But by the mid-sixteenth century Ivan the Terrible's victories over the Tartars at Kazan and Astrakhan had opened up the whole area to Russian colonization and soon, as the Russians began to move relentlessly into Tartar territory, the former roles of Russians and Tartars were reversed. As early as the beginning of the sixteenth century, the Tsar's forces had reached the River Ob. By the middle of the century they had made contact with the Siberian Tartars and already in 1555 we find Yadiger, Khan of Siberia, sending envoys to Moscow and paying a tribute of a thousand sable-skins a year to Ivan the Terrible, on the strength of which the latter felt able to describe himself, in a letter to King Edward VI of England, as Ruler of Siberia.

Three years later, in 1558, Ivan authorized Grigori Stroganov, a member of the famous family of merchant-adventurers from Novgorod, to establish a first settlement on the Upper Kama River, just to the west of the Urals, and in 1574 he gave the Stroganovs a twenty-year lease to 'Siberia', with authority to wage war there on his behalf and establish *ostrogs* or fortresses beyond the Urals. Six years after this, in September 1581, encouraged by the Stroganovs, who were themselves by now well aware of Siberia's economic potential, the Cossack Hetman Yermak, a former Volga pirate, set out with eight hundred and forty of his men to cross the Urals and conquer fresh territories for the Tsar. Barely twelve months later, after defeating the Tartars, he occupied Sibir. The Tartars now counter-attacked and Yermak was drowned while hastily crossing the Irtysh. But in the years that followed other leaders were found to take his place. Boris Godunov, himself of Tartar origin, showed as much interest in Siberia as Ivan had done and during his reign fresh bands of frontiersmen, actively supported by Moscow, continued their forays across the Urals. By the end of the century a whole series of *ostrogs* had been built in strategic positions and the year 1604 saw the foundation of the town of Tomsk on the River Ob. Not long after, the Russias reached the River Yenisei. They were to make as good use of the great rivers of Siberia as earlier generations had of the rivers of European Russia.

Russia's colonization of Siberia continued all through the seventeenth century. Subduing the nomad tribes they encountered beyond the Yenisei, her settlers now pushed on another thousand miles to the River Lena, building more forts as they went and in 1639, just fifty-seven years after Yermak's capture of Sibir, the first Russians reached the Sea of Okhotsk, thus establishing a foothold on the Pacific.

Over the next half-century, Russian colonists further consolidated and extended their conquests, subduing the Buryat Mongols in the region of Lake Baikal, founding Irkutsk in 1652 and pressing on northwards and eastwards towards the Arctic Ocean and the Bering Straits. In 1653, the Cossack Hetman Yerofei Khabarov, a man of much the same stamp as Yermak, reached the Amur River. Hitherto the Russians had only encountered occasional Tartar khans and roving tribes of nomads. By now they were beginning to encroach on actual Chinese territory. In the end they were obliged to return the territory they had occupied to the Emperor of China, but the Amur River remained their long-term goal.

In their search for natural resources, Russian explorers and men of science continued during the eighteenth and early nineteenth centuries to range far and wide over Siberia. In

1803 the whole region was organized as a single *Guberniya* with a governor-general residing at Irkutsk and a population of not much more than a million, consisting partly of voluntary settlers, but partly also of convicts and political deportees. Not long after this, Russia, looking still further east, had reached out across the Bering Straits and established a base in Alaska. Then in 1847 came the appointment of the diminutive Count N. N. Muravyev, a hero of the war in the Caucasus, as Governor-General of Eastern Siberia, with his headquarters at Irkutsk in a handsome white mansion overlooking the Angara River which he liked to call the White House.

This marked the beginning of a new phase in Siberian history. Control of the Amur River with the access it gave to the Pacific now became as openly declared and essential aim of Russian Far Eastern policy. 'It seems natural for Russia', Muravyev explained in a memorandum to Nicholas I, 'if not to own all Asia, at any rate to control the whole Far Eastern coast' – from which the need to control the Amur followed automatically.

Muravyev, for his part, continued to promote this point of view as strongly as he could and early in 1854, just as Russia was embarking on the Crimean War, the Tsar, despite objections from his harassed Minister of War, agreed to send some troops down the Amur, while at the same time prudently stipulating that there should be 'no smell of powder'. In May 1854, after Muravyev had stopped off in Moscow on his way back to Siberia to receive the personal blessing of the Orthodox Metropolitan, an expeditionary force of about a thousand men set out from Chita. The Chinese offered no resistance. An attempt at off-shore intervention by British and French naval forces (both now at war with Russia in the Crimea) failed miserably; the British admiral subsequently shot himself and the French admiral died on his way back to France.

A year later, a second, larger Russian expeditionary force followed the first and in May 1858 a treaty was concluded at Aigun with the Chinese (by now under pressure from other quarters) under which the Amur became the frontier between their two countries. Muravyev, meanwhile, had consolidated his gains by securing the formation of an immense new province to be known as the Maritime Territory and embracing Kamchatka, the Okhotsk coast and the Amur region. More Russian troops and settlers were now despatched to the Amur, a line of forts built, and an Amur Company formed. Already increasing numbers of Russian and foreign steamers were using the river and an American commercial agent, the heavily-bearded Major Perry McDonough Collins, had actually opened an office in Irkutsk.

Following the signature of the Treaty of Aigun, the magnificently bewhiskered little Governor-General, dapper in his white tunic, raised a glass of champagne as he dictated his Order of the Day to the Russian Army and Navy in the Far East. 'Comrades,' he proudly declared, 'our efforts have not been in vain. The Amur belongs to Russia. The Holy Orthodox Church prays for you. Russia thanks you.' Next day he laid the foundation stone of the Cathedral of the Assumption at Blagoveshchensk and shortly after founded the new town of Khabarovsk at the confluence of the Amur and the Ussuri Rivers, thus commemorating Russia's first Amur expedition two hundred years earlier and paying due tribute to its leader, Yerofei Khabarov. In 1860 the Treaty of Aigun was formally confirmed;

A Siberian Grandmother

A Siberian

OPPOSITE His Holiness the Most Venerable Bandido Khambo Lama

Ulan-Ude, Buryat Mongolia

A Political Meeting, Pskov

OPPOSITE A Hunter, Siberia

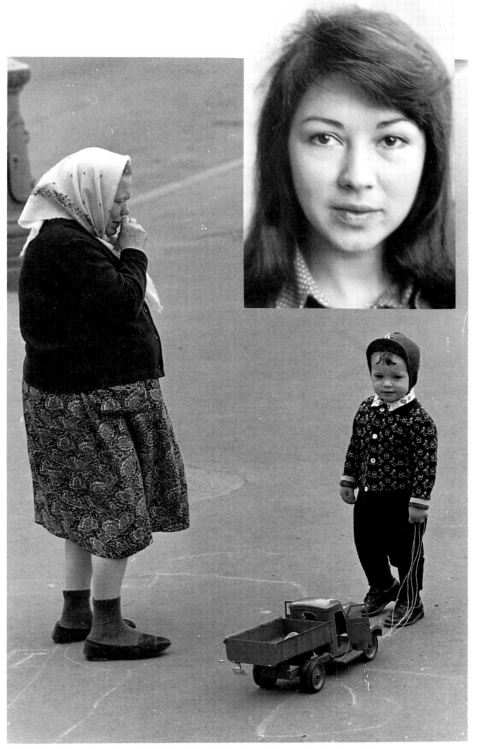

ABOVE The Eternal Babushka   TOP RIGHT A Tartar Girl, Moscow

OPPOSITE Acadmgorodok, Siberia

Young Georgians, Kutaisi

the Ussuri Region became Russian and Muravyev, sailing down the coast, picked a site at its southern end for the Future city of Vladivostok or Ruler of the East, a potential naval base which, with the help of ice-breakers, could be kept open all the year round. Within months the first Russian settlers were moving in.

In Irkutsk at this time a constant guest at Government House was Muravyev's nephew, the anarchist Mikhail Bakunin, recently deported to Siberia as a dangerous revolutionary, but made none the less welcome by the Tsar's Governor-General. Though a revolutionary, a personal friend of Karl Marx, and a founder-member of the First International, Mikhail Bakunin was in complete and enthusiastic agreement with his uncle the Governor-General as far as the future for Siberia was concerned. 'What need one say', he wrote to his friend and fellow-revolutionary, Alexander Herzen, 'about the political significance of a huge newly acquired territory which has a mild climate and fertile soil, is enclosed by two mighty, navigable rivers, and is connected to the Pacific, the Mediterranean of the future? Through the Amur, Siberia has for the first time acquired a meaning. For through the Amur it is linked to the Pacific and is no longer a wilderness without an outlet.' 'The Slav Russian Empire', he continued enthusiastically, 'now stands on the Pacific, and an alliance with the United States, previously a Platonic idea, has become a reality. . . . Thanks to the Amur, we can now maintain a powerful fleet in the Pacific instead of toys in the Black Sea and the Baltic: Muravyev has transplanted Siberia to another site; it is now closer to America and Europe than to Russia, it has been ennobled and humanized – a blessed country of the future, a land of renewal.' Nor was Alexander Herzen, who had himself also done time in Siberia, any less enthusiastic, writing of the need to 'drive Siberia ahead with American speed'. 'We shall see', he noted gleefully in his memoirs, 'what will happen when the mouths of the Amur are opened to navigation and America meets Siberia on the borders of China.'

The idea of an alliance with the United States was a popular one and Major Perry Collins, the American commercial agent, a picturesque New Yorker, reputed to have played an active part in the Gold Rush of 1849 and in winning the West for the United States, was a frequent and welcome visitor at Irkutsk's White House. Nor did he believe in letting the grass grow under his feet. He had not been in Siberia long when he presented to Count Muravyev-Amurski, as he now was, a detailed plan for the construction of a railway line from Chita to Irkutsk, which the Governor-General at once submitted to St Petersburg, strongly recommending it to the government's attention. Meanwhile, a Mr Dull, an enterprising Englishman, had put forward a scarcely less imaginative though possibly less practical scheme for a horse-tramway all the way from Nizhni Novgorod to the Sea of Okhotsk. But for the time being, nothing came of these ideas. In the end Count Muravyev-Amurski retired and went to live in Paris. Russia's energies were fully occupied elsewhere, in the Caucasus, in Central Asia and in the Balkans. Siberia ceased to be a focus of attention and for a time was once again mainly regarded as a repository for exiled convicts and revolutionaries.

It was not until towards the end of the century that the idea of a Trans-Siberian railway was seriously revived. This time the driving force behind the project was Sergei Yulyevich

Witte, a truly remarkable man who, having himself worked as a station-master in order to study the railways at first hand, became in 1892 Minister of Transport, then Minister of Finance and, in 1905, though only briefly, Prime Minister. For Siberia, communications have obviously always been (and still are) of paramount importance. Witte understood this. When completed, the railway would not only link European Russia with Siberia but, by providing a direct connection between Europe and the Pacific, would make Russia a Far Eastern power in the fullest sense of the word, enabling her to move her troops rapidly from one part of her empire to another, opening up to her merchants the markets of China and Japan and, it was hoped, improving her communications with North America, already considered of great importance. There were even at one stage serious talks in which the great E. H. Harriman himself was actively involved, of a tunnel under the Bering Straits, providing a direct railroad link between Paris and New York.

Hitherto, Siberia's principal, if not only, line of communication besides her rivers had been the *Trakt*, a rough post road for sledges or carts which meandered for thousands of miles across most of two continents. In March 1891 it was officially announced that Tsar Alexander III, whose imagination had been caught by the project, had decided to build a railway from the Urals to Vladivostok and the first sleeper was formally laid in the latter town by his son Nicholas, who subsequently travelled back to St Petersburg across Siberia in order to familiarize himself with the region. Construction started from Chelyabinsk in the Urals in 1891. By 1894, the stretch from Vladivostok to Khabarovsk had been completed; in 1895, Omsk was linked to the existing Russian railway system and by 1898 the two-thousand-mile line reached from Chelyabinsk to Irkutsk. Not long after Vladivostok was, by agreement with the Chinese, directly connected with Chita by the construction of the Chinese Eastern Railway across Manchuria, by this time partly occupied by Russian troops – a contributory cause of the Russo–Japanese War, which broke out early in 1904 and was shortly to end so disastrously for Russia. Once peace had been signed with Japan, however, work began again on the missing section of the railway, directly linking Chita with Khabarovsk on Russian territory by way of the Amur River, which was ultimately completed in 1916.

Thereafter, Siberia endured its full share of Revolution, Civil War and Allied intervention. For over a year, from 1918 to 1919, Omsk was the seat of a White counter-revolutionary government under Admiral Kolchak, which enjoyed the support of Great Britain, France, Japan and the United States. Only in November 1919, two years after the Revolution, was the city retaken by the Bolsheviks and Admiral Kolchak tried and shot.

Even before the outbreak of World War I, Siberia had begun to feel the economic benefits of the Trans-Siberian Railway and, after the Revolution, the economic development of Siberia not unnaturally became a high priority for the new Soviet government who, like Bakunin, rightly regarded it as 'the land of the future'. Ever since then, the population has continued to increase, some of the settlers being volunteers, though, as under the tsars, by no means all went there of their own free will. In the 1930s, victims of Stalin's great purges and millions of peasants who resisted collectivization were despatched there and in 1934 the notorious Gulag or *Glavnoye Upravlenye Lagherev* (Main Administration of Camps) was set up to accommodate them. Already in 1931, the Turksib line, linking the Trans-Siberian with Alma Ata and Tashkent, had opened up new areas to development and other branch lines followed. More recently BAM, the Baikal-Amur Railway, has provided an alternative Trans-Siberian line with a branch line to Yakutsk. Better communications remain the key to Siberia's future. River shipping and the northern sea route between Archangel and Vladivostok have also been actively developed, while Aeroflot, the Soviet state airline, operating under difficult conditions, serves a surprising number of useful purposes.

'You are coming in to land at Tomsk', said the air-hostess unconcernedly on my last visit to Siberia, adding with equal unconcern, that the ground temperature there was 40 degrees under zero. Her announcement came as a not altogether agreeable surprise, as we were bound, not for Tomsk but for Novosibirsk, a good many hundred miles to the south and by now, it appeared, completely blizzard-bound. It also served as a timely reminder of the hazards of travel, indeed of existence, in Siberia in mid-January. There was yet another complication. Tomsk, unlike Omsk, is, no doubt for excellent reasons, closed to foreigners, so that the mere fact of our presence there confronted the long-suffering authorities with one more burdensome problem. Later, after some hours of uncertainty and a surprisingly good dinner at Tomsk airport, a different, smaller, ice-cold aircraft was suddenly made available, apparently ready to take us to Novosibirsk whatever the weather conditions. After we had sat shivering in it alone on the frozen tarmac for half an hour, this filled, equally suddenly, with a hundred or so passengers (in the Soviet Union there are always passengers waiting to go anywhere); the temperature in the aircraft rose by a welcome degree or two and we took off abruptly, landing in Novosibirsk shortly before midnight under a clear starlit sky, slightly confused by the vagaries of our journey, but glad, on the whole, to be there, though I, for my part, still hankered after the hot sun and balmy breezes of Central Asia we had left behind us that morning.

Novosibirsk is now to all intents and purposes the capital of Siberia and next day I called on the mayor, an energetic-looking man in early middle age. On earlier visits to Novosibirsk, I had found the local authorities friendly and overwhelmingly hospitable (Siberian-brewed vodka, like Siberian black bread and Siberian caviar, is famous). This time, as, conforming to the latest rules, we sipped our mineral water, I was at once struck by the new mayor's youth, by his frankness and by his dynamic approach to the formidable problems which confronted him. The city's population, which had been a mere three hundred thousand when I first visited it in 1938, was, he said, now almost a million and a half and, with every inducement from the government was still growing fast. Siberian families, he explained, were getting bigger all the time. It might well reach the two million mark before they celebrated the city's centenary in 1993. For all these people, despite a continuing shortage of trained labour, the city had to provide – and provide quickly – more and more dwellings, schools, hospitals, shops, entertainment and transport facilities. Only the week before, he had himself opened Siberia's first underground railway. What is more, all this had to be achieved under Siberian conditions, notably a ferocious climate, immense distances, appalling difficulties of transport and communication and, though this seemed to worry him least of all, a built-in remoteness from Moscow. Building costs were thirty per cent higher than in Central Russia and they had to spend three million roubles a year on keeping the city's streets reasonably clear of snow. Clearly, despite generous subsidies from the central government, the city Soviet had any number of formidable problems on their hands. But I could not help being impressed with the openness with which the mayor discussed these, by his utter determination to solve them, and by his confidence in his own ability to do so.

When I first went there in 1938, Novosibirsk, which, as Novonikolayevsk, had at the turn of the century been little more than a village, was already a bustling modern city, boasting a number of what then seemed daringly modernistic public buildings. This tradition has continued. A massive modern opera house, along with some startling modern statues, now adorns the principal square and more and more skyscrapers and high-rise buildings are going up on every side, while new factories and industrial plants match them on the outskirts of the city and acres and acres of glass, regularly patrolled by a single, highly competent cat, house the collective farm which furnishes the city with what it needs in the way of fresh vegetables, for the most part, I noticed, cucumbers and tomatoes. Amid all these startling improvements, the town's very first stone building (a modest late nineteenth-century office building and shop, used by the Bolsheviks as their headquarters during the Civil War) is still proudly pointed out, while numerous streets of finely carved wooden houses of the same period are also, I am glad to say, still carefully preserved.

After seeing the mayor, I visited, for the third or fourth time, Akademgorodok, the Academic Township established by the central government some thirty years ago for the purpose of studying in depth the natural potentialities and resources of Siberia with a view to their intensive and urgent development. With its faculty buildings, its up-to-date research establishments, its well-equipped lecture rooms, its halls of residence and the neat houses and gardens of its senior faculty members, it resembles nothing so much as the campus of an American university. Indeed, eating an unusually good and well-served lunch in one of its select restaurants (or should one say private clubs), amid a number of faculty members, both male and female, dressed in the elaborately casual manner affected by academics the world over, one could easily have imagined oneself at Princeton or Yale.

No less memorable was a visit to the senior class of one of the children's schools in Akademgorodok, specializing in English. On a previous occasion I had visited a junior class, where the girls in their early teens wore the demure nineteenth-century school uniforms and lace aprons which somehow survived the Revolution (though the bolder had successfully adjusted them to mini-skirt length). This time, the seniors, having left uniforms behind them, were, within reason, wearing what they chose, favouring a broadly collegiate style. The juniors, when I visited them, had been studying England and the English. Now the maps and wall-displays showed that the seniors were concentrating on America. Practically all the pupils, it appeared, were themselves the children of academics and practically all intended to follow in their parents' footsteps as geographers, geologists, botanists, chemists, nuclear scientists, physicists, economists or ecologists, as the case might be. All, clearly, were of above-average intelligence and all clearly appreciated the advantages of an assured career offered by this style of education. 'What is so special about this school?' I asked one of them. 'We have such wonderful teachers', he replied without hesitation, bringing a gratified smirk to the teacher's face and no doubt an additional good mark to his own end-of-term report.

There can be no doubt that the Soviet government rightly attach great importance to Akademgorodok and consequently go out of their way to provide for every one of its human and material needs. With the same object in view, they go out of their way to make life in Siberia as attractive as possible to potential pioneers. Wages are high. Development of all kinds is lavishly subsidized. The roads are excellent. Consumer goods are in generous supply. ('There's far more to buy in the shops here than in Moscow. And better bargains!' said one high Siberian official.) Rents, if demanded at all, are low. Housing is of the highest quality. And the all-important younger generation are provided with every kind of high-quality entertainment of which they take the fullest advantage. Young Siberians, the mayor told me proudly, prefer to stay in Siberia. And I heard the same story wherever I went. Though built thirty years ago and, in the mayor's view, slightly substandard, the principal hotel in Novosibirsk has a dance-band which plays not only rock and pop, but the latest and purest American jazz and attracts as lively and sophisticated a crowd as you could find anywhere. Meanwhile a bigger, better and up-to-the-minute hotel is in the process of construction with the help of Polish architects and builders.

As a result of all this, and, it must be added, of the Siberians' own native qualities and ingrained pioneering spirit, Siberia is fast becoming a success story comparable to what happened in Texas in the first half of this century. There has long been a Siberian myth not all that different from the Texan saga and, as in Texas, actively promoted by the proud inhabitants who see themselves, with some reason, as larger-than-life characters, bigger, tougher, richer, more generous, more cultured and, in general, higher, wider and handsomer than their fellows.

Quite apart from government policy, the challenge of Siberia itself has a lot to do with this. The fact that the forces of nature, the savage climate, the tremendous distances, mean that life is bound to be a struggle and, on top of this, the knowledge that their country's immense natural resources have scarcely been tapped, that its ultimate potential is still unknown, in itself helps to produce a self-confident breed of men and women, well fitted to meet the challenge. No one is prouder of his roots than the *Sibiriak*, Siberian born and bred, and it is a safe guess that most of the new settlers, attracted by the opportunities Siberia has to offer, will quickly develop the same characteristics as their predecessors over past centuries. Nor is the way in which they rise to the occasion or the pride they take in being Siberians at all surprising when you consider the immense importance Siberia is bound to have for the future of the Soviet Union as a whole.

The size of Siberia is in itself astounding. When you reach Novosibirsk, you soon realize that, although you are by now some one thousand seven hundred and fifty miles from Moscow, you have still not penetrated very far. Flying another nine hundred miles on to Irkutsk on the borders of Mongolia and looking down on the snowy waste below and remembering that, when you arrive, you will still be over a thousand miles from the Pacific coast, you begin to get some idea of Siberia's extent, not to mention that of the Soviet Far Eastern Territories that lie beyond it.

Though there are geographical and other differences between Eastern and Western Siberia, you quickly realize, when you land in Irkutsk, that you are still in Siberia and among Siberians. The spirit is still the same. If you ask a citizen of Irkutsk (seven hours' flying time from Moscow), if he doesn't sometimes feel rather removed from the centre of things, he will no more understand what you are talking about than would a native Texan or a Californian if asked whether he minded being so far from Washington DC or New York. Nor was I at all surprised to find the mayor of Irkutsk to be as young, as confident, as energetic and as forward-looking as his opposite number back in Novosibirsk. Like him, he impressed me by telling me not only of his city's material achievements and industrial development, but of its cultural life and also, to my mind, quite significantly, what was being done in his city to prevent industrial pollution, something from which many other Soviet cities still suffer most severely.

But though the two cities share many of the same problems, climate, remoteness and the need for rapid expansion, Irkutsk is in many ways a very different town from Novosibirsk. For one thing, though, with a population of 600,000, it is considerably smaller, its recorded history goes back very much further, beginning in the seventeenth century when, some years after a first far-flung *ostrog* or citadel had been built there, it was accorded the status of city and eventually became the seat of the governor-general of Eastern Siberia. On the little hill which marks the site of the original citadel stand two handsome eighteenth-century churches, the Church of the Redeemer and the Cathedral of the Epiphany.

Although Irkutsk has suffered at least two disastrous fires, which wiped out much of the town, a number of other pleasant eighteenth- and nineteenth-century buildings still survive as well as whole streets of typical Siberian wooden houses which somehow escaped destruction. Among these, at no distance from each other, are the houses of two famous Decembrist conspirators exiled to Siberia in 1826, Prince Sergei Volkonski and Prince Trubetskoi. Of particular interest is Prince Volkonski's sizeable mansion, bought from a rich fur merchant by his beautiful and utterly determined young wife, Maria, who followed him into exile and before long had, despite her husband's criminal status, achieved a remarkable position locally, remaining there for the best part of thirty years. This, together with the smaller house of Prince Trubetskoi and some adjoining buildings, including the Church of the Transfiguration, where the exiles worshipped, has recently been carefully restored and furnished as a kind of memorial to the Decembrists who, despite their aristocratic origins and liberal ideas, are seen by the powers-that-be as forerunners of the Bolshevik Revolution of 1917.

In the days of the indomitable Princess Volkonska who, following her husband's arrest, travelled to Siberia to join him at high speed in mid-winter with a piano on the back of her sledge, her house served as a social, musical and cultural centre for the local community, which then possessed no opera house or theatre. This need was, however, supplied in 1897 when a handsome opera house was built, which now attracts some of the best opera, theatre and ballet companies in the Soviet Union, for in Siberia the strongest possible emphasis continues to be laid on cultural activity of every kind. Indeed, while in Irkutsk, I observed that Tennessee Williams' *Rose Tattoo* was advertised as coming shortly.

Irkutsk lies on both sides of the Angara River, some forty miles from the point where it enters Lake Baikal which, incidentally, provides the city with an unlimited and, one is assured, singularly pure water supply. Driving through forests of familiar Scots pine (originally brought there from Scotland by some nineteenth-century forestry enthusiast), you suddenly emerge to find yourself looking out over one of the biggest expanses of fresh water in the world. Here at Listvianka the road ends and if you want to explore further, you must either walk or go by water. In summer you can take a boat. In mid-winter, when Baikal is frozen hard, you can drive over its surface in a truck. Spring and autumn are the problem periods, when Baikal is frozen but, as some people have found to their cost, not always hard enough to support a vehicle. The experts will tell you that, as a general rule, it is then safer to travel in a horse-drawn sledge, as in an emergency a good Siberian horse will jump the crevasse as soon as it appears, while a truck goes straight to the bottom and takes you with it. In January, however, in a Soviet jeep, we could with reasonable confidence pick our way across the rugged surface of the lake for fifteen miles as far as Bolshie Koti, the little lakeside hamlet where Nikolai, the local trapper, has his headquarters and whence he plies his trade, furs being one of the mainstays of the Siberian economy.

Meanwhile new cities are springing up all over Siberia. About 400 miles from Irkutsk you come to the entirely new town of Ust-Ilimsk, built quite recently in a dozen years in the middle of the *taiga*, with its huge hydro-electric dam, aluminium smelter and timber-processing complex, not to mention the inevitable Palace of Culture, where, if you are lucky enough to get a ticket, you can watch an impeccable performance of *Swan Lake*.

Having in the past used Irkutsk as a jumping-off place for trips to Outer Mongolia and Peking, I have always been conscious of its proximity to what we usually think of as the Far East. Without venturing across the frontier, however, one can, by simply joining the Trans-Siberian Railway for a few hours, travel in reasonable comfort along the shore of Lake Baikal to Ulan Ude (formerly Verkhneudinsk), capital of the Autonomous Soviet Socialist Republic of Buryat Mongolia, which has for two or three hundred years been part of Russia.

Though Ulan Ude with its fine new concrete public buildings in most ways resembles any other small town in Siberia, you quickly notice the Mongol cast of countenance of its inhabitants, especially if, as when I was last there, a Party Conference is in progress, attended by numerous delegates from the outback. What is more, after driving for forty miles or so from Ulan Ude through rolling country strongly reminiscent of Outer Mongolia, you can, if you wish, visit at Datsan a genuine Lamaist Buddhist monastery, presided over by His Holiness the Most Venerable Bandido Khambo Lama, Chief Lama of all the Buddhists in the Soviet Union. Over an excellent lunch of *pilmeni* (savoury Mongolian dumplings), some delicious, if slightly weird, sweetmeats and milky tea, His Holiness, who keeps in close touch with the exiled Dalai Lama of Tibet, as well as with his co-religionists in Outer Mongolia, explained that the monastery, founded as recently as 1946 and extended in 1976, contained some thirty or forty monks, a number of whom we found at their devotions in a brightly painted temple, busily thumping drums, beating gongs and turning prayer-wheels amid clouds of incense.

Back in Irkutsk, in the bar of the surprisingly good Hotel Intourist, a highly sophisticated young Siberian friend pointed out to me that a touch of Mongol blood often made girls in Siberia prettier than other Russians. Looking round me, I could see what he meant. In Irkutsk the Hotel Intourist is the smart place to go and its restaurant and bars are regularly filled with a good-looking, well-dressed local clientèle. One side of Siberia, the enterprise, self-confidence and outgoing character of its people, was, I found to my relief, clearly and refreshingly reflected in its management. A modern concrete building looking out across the Angara River, it seems at first sight no different from other Intourist hotels. It is only when you get inside that you notice the difference. In marked contrast to all too many other Intourist hotels, you are warmly welcomed by the reception clerk, by the smiling *dezhurnaya* on your floor and, most important of all, in the restaurant, where a neatly dressed waiter or waitress immediately brings you the menu and even makes helpful suggestions as to what to try and what to avoid. The rooms are well-furnished; the plumbing works; the service is excellent and the food good. In short, with not too great a stretch of the imagination, you might fancy yourself in a provincial hotel in the United States or Western Europe.

On the long flight back to Moscow we only touched down briefly at Omsk. As we were coming in to land, the air-hostess, who clearly came from Omsk herself and knew its history, gave us a thumb-nail sketch of the city which, in addition to a million inhabitants, clearly possessed every virtue under the sun. It was for this reason, she said, that during the Allied Intervention of 1918, the British, French, Americans, Japanese and Czechs had all tried to grab it for themselves; but, thanks to the timely intervention of the heroic Red Army, had happily been repulsed.

One leaves Siberia with the clear impression that for the Soviet Union this is indeed what Mikhail Bakunin called 'the land of the future', containing vast potential riches and offering infinite scope for their development and exploitation. Just what the future will hold for Russia and the rest of the world and how the pattern of international relations in the Far East is likely to develop is anyone's guess. Inevitably much will depend on the course of events in China. A measure of economic cooperation between a less than one hundred per cent Marxist–Leninist China and a technologically booming Japan could easily change the balance of power world-wide and cause both the Soviet Union and the United States to reconsider their present policies. Equally, a complete reconciliation between the Soviet Union and China or indeed Japan, both of which now seem quite possible, could have no less far-reaching results for all concerned. Of one thing we can be quite sure: the Pacific's significance for Russia is something of which Mikhail Gorbachov is most profoundly aware.

For the time being Russia's relations with the West, while now improving, continue variable. Over the years détente, coexistence and confrontation have followed each other in bewildering succession, the difference between them not always being very clear. As the Soviet Marshal Shaposhnikov aptly and authoritatively put it, 'If war is a continuation of policies by other means, so also peace is a continuation of conflict by other means'. But there is a brighter side to the picture. With the years, Soviet contacts with the outside world have slowly increased. There is more trade between East and West. There are more cultural and other exchanges. Each year more foreigners visit the Soviet Union, more Soviet citizens travel abroad, read foreign books, and listen to foreign broadcasts. The Soviet Union is no longer anything like as completely closed to outside influences and ideas as it used to be. This is in itself a step forward.

In Russia there have for centuries been two competing trends: the resolutely inward-looking Easterners or Muscovites and the more outward-looking Westerners, who, like Ivan the Terrible and Peter the Great in their time, feel that Russia has something to gain from more contacts with the West. After the Revolution the removal of the capital to Moscow seemed to mark a return to Muscovy and a slamming of Russia's Window on the West. Seventy years later it still remains to be seen how enduring this original shift of emphasis will prove. There are still a number of ways in which Russia needs the West and it is clear that there are those in Russia who, to a greater or lesser extent, realize this and recognize the disadvantages of perpetual isolation and confrontation. There is at present every indication that Mikhail Gorbachov is one of them.

Moscow today is well on its way to becoming a fitting capital for a Superpower, with an urban sprawl reaching even further into the countryside and all the other standard accompaniments of big city life, high-rise buildings, vast hotels, a racecourse, discos, rival gangs of trendy teenagers roughing each other up, fashion shows, traffic jams, parking problems, pollution and more and more families living, like those in the West, in modern flats with modern plumbing, refrigerators, washing-machines, telephones and television. To anyone who, like myself, knew it in pre-War days, it is barely recognizable.

How deep does all this go and what difference does it make? It is hard to say. In the Soviet Union, you are still constantly reminded in all kinds of ways that you are in a different world, a world as different from the West as China. And yet, for over thirty years now, imperceptibly, more and more similarities, more and more outside, indeed universal, influences and trends have been creeping in. For an optimist like myself it still seems possible to conclude, in spite of everything, that Peter the Great's Window on the West has at least remained ajar – a conclusion still further strengthened by the events of the past couple of years.

EPILOGUE

You are blind like little kittens.
You cannot recognize an enemy when you see one.
What will become of Russia when I am gone?
STALIN TO THE POLITBURO
1953

In the spring of 1988 Mikhail Sergeyevich Gorbachov completed three full years as Party Secretary. By this time it was already abundantly clear that, whatever the ultimate outcome, a new era in Soviet history had begun, an era, as Gorbachov himself put it, of 'revolutionary change'. 'Objectively,' said Andrei Sakharov a couple of months after his return from years of exile, 'something real is happening. How far it is going to go is a complicated question, but I myself have come to the conclusion that the situation has changed.'

That such a change should have come when it did was, with the benefit of hindsight, not surprising. With the advent of Mikhail Gorbachov, power has passed to a new generation, a generation separated from its predecessors by a gap of twenty all-important years and differing from them markedly in experience and outlook. Born fourteen years after the Revolution, the new Party Secretary could fairly be regarded as a product of the system. Here, sprung, like Minerva, fully armed from the collective matrix of the Revolution, was *Homo Sovieticus,* the New Soviet Man, of whom the Founding Fathers had dreamt seventy years earlier.

A little child at the time of the notorious treason trials and purges, Mikhail Sergeyevich had barely come to manhood when Stalin died and, having listened to Khrushchov's scathing denunciation of the *Vozhd* in 1956, could in 1961, as First Secretary of the Stavropol Komsomol, vote without a qualm for his removal from the glass-topped coffin which for the past eight years he had rightly or wrongly shared with Lenin. Having thus been lucky enough to escape the traumas of the thirties and forties, he had reached maturity

217

in Khrushchov's time, in a self-confident, newly victorious country, with an increasingly relaxed atmosphere, an improving standard of living and by this time every claim to be regarded as a Superpower. Ambitious, free of inhibitions, the son and grandson of respected and influential Party members, himself endowed with exceptional energy and intelligence, he had had an excellent start in life. With Raisa, his wife, he had also had the benefit of a university education, an advantage enjoyed by none of his predecessors in office since Lenin.

All of which distinguished him sharply from his immediate predecessors, every one of whom had spent his formative years under Stalin, an experience bound to scar him for life. For the whole of that generation it was utterly impossible to forget those nightmare years, when the slightest error of judgement, any minor deviation from a continually changing Party line, any contact with foreigners, even in the course of official business, and any dubious or inadvisable connections (*somnitelnie sviazi*) could (and often did) lead to immediate 'liquidation'. Years when it was far wiser to avoid accepting any responsibility, taking any initiative or indeed doing anything which could possibly attract unwanted attention and when, worst of all, it was profoundly unwise to trust any friend, relative or associate, in case he or she might, for reasons of their own, denounce you to what were all too justly known as 'the competent authorities'. With such traumatic memories and such a background to their lives, these aged survivors were scarcely the men to give their country a new look, however badly it might need one.

If Stalin left his mark on individuals, he left it no less surely on the state. 'Under Stalin', said Khrushchov, 'the whole machine was fast seizing up.' For a decade after Stalin's death Khrushchov himself had, with some courage, tried to change things, indeed had achieved a surprising amount in the time vouchsafed him. But after ten years he had been eliminated and, though his successors failed to force the lid right back on the Pandora's box he had opened, for the next twenty years they steadfastly did what they could to restore the Stalinist *status quo*. As a result, the Brezhnev years and those that followed were by and large a period of stagnation, drift and, alarmingly, of ever-growing financial and moral corruption.

The social, political, economic and above all psychological legacy which Gorbachov inherited was thus by any standards a daunting one. Despite the Soviet Union's immense potentialities, despite its rich human and natural resources, despite undoubted successes achieved in a whole range of different fields, despite, some might say because of, close on seventy years of Building Socialism, the fact was that the system as a whole was not working. Of this Mikhail Sergeyevich was well aware, indeed had been well aware long before he came to power. The question was how to put things right. It was not just a matter of new policies and new measures. What was needed nationwide was a new attitude and a new frame of mind, an end to the hang-ups and hang-overs of the past, an end to what Yevtushenko has aptly called taboos. As Gorbachov himself put it, 'The process must be made irreversible. If not us, then who? If not now, when?'

From the start Gorbachov showed himself a skilful tactician. His first step along the road to reform was to get rid, as quickly as he conveniently could, of any potential opponents and replace them by trusted supporters. While most people would welcome an improvement in the economy if and when it came, even at the cost of a tot or two of vodka, and would in the main approve of a greater degree of *glasnost*, there were without doubt a considerable number, notably in the middle and higher ranks of an all-encompassing bureaucracy, who, whether from inertia or self-interest, liked things the way they were and would do their level best to keep them that way. Obstruction, *résistance molle*, is, as we all know, the classical weapon of the bureaucrat.

In deciding how far and above all how fast to go, Gorbachov could not but recall the instructive example of Khrushchov, who, after ten years of pushing through badly-needed reforms, had been pulled down from within by his own closest colleagues. Nor could recent developments in China be without their message for him, where there were signs that the reformers had been in too great a hurry and had consequently allowed things to get out of hand. Least of all could Mikhail Sergeyevich afford to ignore events in his own country.

Here, where anything approaching a public disturbance was supposedly a thing of the remote past, the spontaneous, large-scale nationalist rioting in Kazakhstan which had followed the dismissal of Breshnev's corrupt old crony Kunayev had come as an unpleasant shock. No less disturbing were the Moslem riots in Tajikstan. Then, in Moscow itself, in February 1987, a demonstration on behalf of the imprisoned Jewish dissident Josef Begun had provoked an altogether disproportionate reaction from the security authorities who had promptly given their own angle on *glasnost* by beating up Jewish demonstrators and Western newsmen alike with all the old-fashioned gusto of Cossacks at a pogrom. This at a time when it was of the utmost importance to make a favourable impression on close on a thousand distinguished foreign intellectuals, including Claudia Cardinale, Yoko Ono and Graham Greene, then assembled in Moscow for a well promoted Peace Forum at the Kremlin, with an important speech from Gorbachov himself and, as, in a sense, the guest of honour, Dr Andrei Sakharov, who, for his part, duly contributed a few unkind words about President Reagan's Strategic Defence Initiative.

But Gorbachov, while playing his hand with due care, did not let any of this deter him or divert him from a programme which by now presumably had the support of a comfortable majority of like-minded colleagues. Despite administrative and other hitches and setbacks, despite the mixed reactions of the world press and an uneasy feeling in many quarters that he might be going too far too fast, more dissidents, including Josef Begun and the famous psychiatrist Anatoli Koryagin, were released and there were numerous fresh manifestations of *glasnost*. As for the released dissidents, they mostly followed Sakharov's example by freely declaring their intention to carry on their campaign for human rights.

As time went by, even political demonstrations came to be tolerated. In July 1987 over a thousand Crimean Tartars, the victims of mass deportation by Stalin in 1944, were allowed, under strong police supervision, to assemble in Red Square and there protest against their continued banishment from the Crimea, while in August in the three Baltic Republics, where previous manifestations of nationalism had been quickly broken up, demonstrations to mark the anniversary of the Soviet–German pact, which deprived them of their independence forty-eight years ago, passed off peacefully. They were to be followed later in the year by further nationalist demonstrations this time on a rather larger scale, particularly in Latvia.

Glasnost has also brought in its train demonstrations of a different character. One ostensibly conservationist group of self-declared Russian patriots, known as *Pamyat* or Memory, while loudly celebrating Russia's glorious past, has also taken to preaching anti-semitism, seeking to revive the unsavoury traditions of the notorious Black Hundreds, who organized pogroms under the tsars, and, it may be said, drawing big crowds in the process.

There were meanwhile many indications that Gorbachov, as a skilled tactician, knew precisely what he was doing. From the first he had not attempted to disguise the fact that his policies were encountering a measure of opposition; indeed at times he even seemed to go out of his way to emphasize this. Before eventually being held in January 1987, the Plenum of the all important 307-member Central Committee of the Party (the body which a score of years earlier had deposed Khrushchov) had, he later admitted, had to be postponed no less than three times.

But, when it finally met, it accepted, apparently without a murmur, every one of the far-reaching and in some ways revolutionary proposals put before it. It was only then that Gorbachov let it be known that, had he failed to get his way, he would have been forced to resign (by Soviet standards an entirely novel political gambit). 'The broad democratization' of society, he added, was now 'irreversible'. 'There is', he declared, 'no other way.'

After their fashion, the proceedings of the Central Committee, nearly half of whose members had by now been replaced by new men, were of paramount importance, marking as they did another important step forward in Gorbachov's programme of *glasnost* and *perestroika* and the consolidation of all that he had so far achieved. As Gorbachov knew better than anyone, the role of the Party was central to all this. Whatever he did had of a necessity to be done through the Party. In his key speech (immediately published in full), he declared for all to hear that the blame for everything that had gone wrong over the past two decades and more must lie fairly and squarely with the Party and that it was equally through the Party that reform must now come. Equally in a handbook on *perestroika* published later in the year he went out of his way to provide his brainchild with an impeccably Leninist pedigree and to emphasize yet again that its purpose was not to replace Socialism, but to strengthen it. The only question, of course, being just what he or, for that matter, anyone else meant by Socialism.

In denouncing the Party's shortcomings to a Party audience, Gorbachov pulled no punches, emphasizing first and foremost the dangerous inertia which over the years had crept in everywhere, and its corrupting and demoralizing effect. There had, he said (and his listeners knew exactly what he was talking about), been 'a tendency to brush aside anything that did not fit into a conventional pattern, a reluctance to come to grips with outstanding social and economic problems'. The moral atmosphere, he went on, had been poisoned by disregard for the law, by report-padding, bribery, sycophancy and toadyism.

Rule by decree, a show of efficiency, mountains of paperwork had taken the place of practical day-to-day work. Alcoholism, drug abuse and an increase in crime were clear indications of a decline in social standards. No effective obstacles had been placed in the way of ambitious, greedy people, determined to exploit their Party membership for all it was worth.

But, while calling for an end to these abuses and, no less sensationally, for an end to the present self-perpetuating Party hierarchy by the introduction of multiple candidates and secret ballots at Party elections and the election of factory managers by the workforce, Gorbachov made it absolutely clear that these reforms would in no way interfere with strict Party control, which he emphasized, would remain 'unshakable'. 'The point at issue', he concluded reassuringly, 'is most certainly not any break-up of our political system.' Meanwhile, though a few old Brezhnevites still kept their seats on the Politburo, several more of the new leader's close adherents now joined its ranks.

To a second plenary meeting of the Central Committee held in June, Gorbachov presented an even further-reaching instalment of his programme, calling for what he described as 'a major breakthrough on the theoretical front'. A 'pre-crisis situation' necessitated, he declared, a revolutionary solution. What was needed was a drastic reduction in central, in other words bureaucratic, control, a marked extension of decision-making at factory level and a radical reform of the pricing mechanism. At the same time he demanded wider differentials in wages, profit-sharing for workers and greatly enhanced rewards for good work. 'It is vital', he said, 'that the actual pay of every worker should be closely linked to his performance and that no limits should be set.'

In effect, this meant that, while factories would in future be freer to take their own decisions, they would also be required to pay their own way and wages would vary according to profitability. Clearly, under such a system, prices and unemployment could well go up, while wages went down. In other words the survival of the unfittest would in future no longer be automatically guaranteed – for many a deeply disturbing innovation.

While obediently endorsing the General Secretary's proposals, which were then unanimously passed by the Supreme Soviet in the shape of a Law on State Enterprise, the Central Committee obligingly strengthened his political position by promoting a couple more of his most active supporters to full membership of the now fourteen-strong Politburo, notably Alexander Yakovlev, his propaganda chief, and Dmitri Yazov, his new Minister of Defence.

Despite repeated protestations to the contrary, there were moments when Gorbachov and some of his supporters seemed to be moving some distance from orthodox Marxist–Leninism. 'We intend to make socialism stronger, not replace it with another system', he said to a gathering of influential newspaper editors in July. *Glasnost*, he assured them, 'is not an attempt to undermine socialism'. Meanwhile, in *Novi Mir*, Nikolai Shmelyev, by now a jump ahead of Gorbachov himself, was, in a bold assault on what he called Russia's 'ideological virginity', openly urging the introduction of free-market mechanisms, even if this meant accepting a measure of unemployment. Over the centuries, he declared, mankind had found 'no more effective measure of work than profit', while Abel Aganbegyan, a leading Armenian economist, was urging that prices should be allowed to rise to market levels and that thousands of unprofitable enterprises should simply be shut down. At the same time, Gorbachov was advocating the application of the profit-motive to Soviet agriculture and an important increase in small-scale private farming, to supplement the altogether inadequate output of the state and collective farms. 'Competition', he said bluntly, 'is needed to activate the motive forces of socialism.'

The big question was what impact all of this would have on the bureaucrats and indeed on a nation unfamiliar with market mechanisms, by nature uncompetitive and unambitious and in many respects temperamentally not yet ready for change. As one eminent observer of the Soviet scene has put it, 'It's a vicious circle. For workers to produce more, Gorbachov needs to offer them more consumer goods and services. Yet, in order to offer them more goods and services, he needs more productive workers.' Meanwhile Soviet workers are being required to work harder for no additional reward and with vodka in short supply. 'We are', Gorbachov complained, 'being hampered by encrusted bureaucratic layers. . . . It is a matter of antiquated approaches, the inertia of old habits, a fear of anything new, of actually accepting responsibility.'

But he was nevertheless determined not to be put off. As the months went by, restrictions on small-scale free enterprise continued to be relaxed and the profit-motive introduced in more and more state industries. Soon hundreds of state firms had been put on a self-financing basis, foreign trade increasingly freed from bureaucratic controls and literally hundreds of thousands of small-scale enterprises licensed under the new Individual Labour Law. Finally, a no less significant innovation, provision was being made for more and more joint ventures, *sovmestniye predpriyatiya*, lavishly advertised in the *Wall Street Journal*, under which Western capitalists could actually own a forty-nine per cent interest in a Soviet enterprise, a measure which would give welcome access to western technology and bring in badly-needed hard currency, while at the same time helping to open up the Soviet Union to outside influences. The key question continued to be: how far and how fast? But, while exercising reasonable precautions, Gorbachov was certainly not letting the grass grow under his feet. Nor, in fact, could he afford to do so.

In the West, inevitably, there was much speculation as to the precise meaning of what was happening. Was the whole thing merely a propaganda exercise, a more than usually advanced display of the old Russian art of *pokazhuka* or window-dressing? Or had the Soviet Union suddenly gone Liberal? Opinions varied. In fact, the true answer was not far to seek. To a patriot and a realist, which is what Gorbachov most definitely was, it could in this day and age no longer make sense for the Soviet Union to go on behaving like a benighted mediaeval theocracy. What he was trying to do, within limits, was to rationalize Russia, to normalize it, to put an end to practices and attitudes which since the time of the Tartars had held it back under tsars and commissars alike and, more recently, in a fast-shrinking, fast-moving world, had, greatly to its own detriment, isolated it from other countries and from the main stream of human progress. The myth that everything was perfect, had always been perfect, and would quite soon be even more perfect no longer held water. It was time to face up to reality. *'Ot vranya vsya beda'*, says a character in a recent Soviet television play: 'All our troubles come from lying'.

On the other hand there could be no greater mistake than to suppose that Gorbachov's intended reforms sprang from a sudden conversion on his part to Liberalism (as dirty a word in the Soviet Union as it ever was in tsarist Russia) or from any new-found feelings of benevolence towards humanity as a whole. They sprang, rather, from plain common sense and from an equally keen sense of where his country's real interests lay – never a bad basis for national policy.

Considered in this light, it was only logical that, having made a start by releasing Sakharov, Gorbachov should have followed this by freeing a number of other dissidents. To keep them under restraint would have served no useful purpose, while giving the Soviet Union a bad name. That after their release some might publicly abuse their former jailers and declare their intention of carrying on their fight for human rights was a risk that had to be taken, but no worse than the odium incurred worldwide by keeping them in jail any longer.

The same applied equally to *glasnost* in its various other manifestations. Logically there could no longer be any real reason for the obsessive, all-inhibiting secrecy which still permeated the whole system or for the censorship arbitrarily imposed on any source of information and on every form of creative activity. Offered nothing but good news, the public were bound to assume that the bad news was even worse than in fact it was. As to the no less stringent censorship imposed since Stalin's day on all works of literature and art, it recalled all too tellingly Count Uvarov's old saying that only when literature ceased to be written would he be able to sleep soundly. Nor had it in effect ever prevented the continuing circulation of *samizdat* editions, of banned books which, human nature being what it is, inevitably gained in popularity from the mere fact of being prohibited.

Glasnost had other important advantages. Besides providing a means of putting pressure on the idle, the corrupt and the inefficient, it won for Gorbachov the almost universal support of the intelligentsia, traditionally a thorn in the side of any Russian government, but now glad to find Party and government at long last doing what they themselves had been fighting for for years. A fact which lent substance to the poet Yevtushenko's proud claim that much of what was now happening had come from below rather than from above.

There could, on the other hand, be no greater mistake than to assume that Gorbachov's new *glasnost* meant that complete freedom of speech was just around the corner or to suppose that provision for secret ballots and multiple candidates (belonging to the same party and supporting the same programme) in certain elections heralded the early intro-duction of Western-style democracy any more than the latest economic adjustments and innovations signified a sudden return to capitalism. All three are simply indications of an increasing degree of relaxation and reform which, if the trend continues, may lead to further evolution in due course. It should moreover be remembered, as Gorbachov certainly remembers, that there are few more delicate or precarious tasks in politics than to liberalize or even marginally relax a totalitarian system of government.

Without doubt, the underlying reason for most of Gorbachov's reforms is the urgent need to improve the performance of the Soviet economy. As Andrei Sakharov said a couple of months after his return from exile, 'I don't know what Gorbachov wants personally, but there are a number of people at the top who understand that without democratization none of his goals in the economic and international spheres are attainable', while Yevtushenko has declared that without a spiritual *perestroika* there can be no economic *perestroika*. No doubt the term 'democratization' requires closer definition, but clearly the closer the attention paid in all this to what Gorbachov likes to call the human element, the greater the incentives offered to workers at all levels and the more say they are given in the running of their own industry, the better the job they will do. Which, as he himself has emphasized, is something the system (and the trade unions in particular) have not always taken sufficiently into account. Economic considerations are likewise an added reason for breaking down barriers and in general improving contacts with the outside world and thus enabling Soviet scientists, technicians and industrialists to keep abreast of the latest developments in their respective fields.

While it is by now clear enough that a new era in Soviet history has begun, it is still hard to say what its ultimate outcome is likely to be. As Andrei Sakharov has said, 'How far it is going to go is a complicated question'. In the early stages Gorbachov evidently encountered a measure of resistance to his reforms but no less evidently managed to overcome it. Which, providing the trend continues, bodes well for the future. What is less clear is just what the long-term effect of the reforms is likely to be. Having once released the genie from the bottle, Gorbachov can clearly not afford to stand still. He must justify himself and justify himself soon. Events, it should be remembered, generate their own momentum. Change has its own dynamic. That the evolutionary process which began under Khrushchov and has, with some difficulty, persisted ever since, will continue seems certain, though at what rate is less clear. If Stalin were brought back from the dead and his opinion asked, he would, with his vast experience of running Russia, undoubtedly prophesy disaster. One thing is for sure. To transform the USSR into something entirely different, if that is what Mikhail Gorbachov is trying to do, will take time and demand all his very considerable energy and determination. One is therefore hardly surprised to find him announcing in his own little handbook on *perestroika* that this is not all. Inevitably there is more to come.

In the seventeenth century the Tsar was still in the habit of cleansing himself ceremonially after any contact with a foreign ambassador. The tradition of Holy Russia, set apart from other countries by her inherent sanctity and sense of mission, did not die with the Revolution, but was if anything strengthened and intensified by it, the myth of Holy Russia, set in an unregenerate world, being promptly superseded by that of the Country of the Revolution, hemmed in by a hostile Capitalist Encirclement. As the philosopher Nikolai Berdyayev so perceptively put it, 'the spirit of the people could very easily pass from one integrated faith, to another integrated faith, from one orthodoxy to another orthodoxy embracing the whole of life'. Which is by an large what happened seventy years ago.

As part of his programme of rationalization and reform, of his attempt, two decades after the unfortunate Dubcek, to give Communism a human face, Mikhail Gorbachov is already seeking to break down barriers and put his country's relations with the rest of the world on a more rational footing. In view of the massive backlog of mutual suspicion and distrust, this is not likely to prove an easy process, but is nonetheless essential if the Soviet Union is to play its proper part in the world.

Just what this proper part will turn out to be is still to seek. It is of course possible to argue that the Soviet Union has no further territorial ambitions; that the vast territories acquired during and after the last war were simply a part of Russia irredenta. That the establishment of a ring of satellite states and its maintenance, when necessary by force of arms, were purely defensive measures; the occupation of Afghanistan likewise. Equally that in other parts of the world Russia is doing no more than further her own legitimate national interests – if in a somewhat nineteenth-century manner. And finally that, as a fellow Superpower, the Soviet Union is fully entitled to at least the same level of armaments as the United States.

On the other hand, a considerably less reassuring interpretation can quite easily be put on the same set of facts, especially if current Soviet activities in Africa, Central America and the Middle East are taken into account, not to mention the old doctrines of world revolution and the inevitability of an armed clash between the Communist and capitalist worlds, though of late Gorbachov has admittedly gone out of his way to play these down.

Which leads inevitably to the conclusion that things will need to go a good deal further before the members of the Western Alliance can afford to lower their guard to any serious degree. On the other hand, it seems probable that, given the chance (and there is no reason why they should not be given it), the Soviet government would welcome a measure of mutual disarmament and, on purely economic grounds, the consequent reduction in their own defence expenditure. But this, in turn, seems likely to depend on a genuine improvement in East-West relations and mutual understanding, which, with the best will in the world, may take some time to achieve.

THE RULERS OF RUSSIA 862–1917

862	Rurik in Novgorod
879–912	Oleg, regent during the minority of Rurik's son Igor
912–945	Igor
945–957	Olga, widow of Igor and regent for her son Svyatoslav
957–972	Svyatoslav I, Igorevich
980–1015	Vladimir I
1019–1054	Yaroslav I
1113–1125	Vladímir II, Monomákh
1125–1132	Mstislav I, Grand Prince of Kiev
1224	First invasion of the Tartars under Jenghiz Khan
1237–1242	Second Tartar invasion under Batu Khan
1238–1246	Yaroslav II Vsevolodovich, Grand Prince of Vladimir. Russia under Tartar suzerainty
1252–1263	Alexander Nevski, Grand Prince of Vladimir. His son Daniel, Prince of Moscow
1328–1340	Ivan I, Danilovich Kalita, Grand Prince of Moscow, Vladimir and Novgorod
1363–1389	Demetrius of the Don (Dmitri Donskoi)
1425–1462	Vasili II
1462–1505	Ivan III, Grand Prince of Moscow
1505–1533	Vasili III, Ivanovich
1533–1584	Ivan IV Grozni (the Terrible)
1584–1598	Fyodor I Ivanovich, last of the line of Rurik
1598–1605	Boris Godunov
1606	The boyar Vasili Shuiski (1606–10) elected Tsar
1610–1613	Interregnum. Kuzma Minin and Prince Pozharski; the Poles driven from Russia
1613–1645	Mikhaíl Romanov, kinsman of Theodore I, elected Tsar
1645–1676	Aleksei I, Mikhailovich
1676–1682	Fyodor Alekseyevich
1682	On the death of Fyodor, Grand Duchess Sophia Alekseyevna (1682–9) became regent on behalf of her half-brothers, the Tsars Ivan and Peter (b. 1672)
1689–1725	Peter I, the Great
1725–1727	Catherine I, widow of Peter I
1727–1730	Peter II, grandson of Peter the Great
1730–1740	Anna Ivanovna
1740–1741	Ivan VI
1741–1761	Elizabeth Petrovna
1761–1762	Peter III
1762–1796	Catherine II, the Great
1796–1801	Paul I
1801–1825	Alexander I
1825–1855	Nicholas I
1855–1881	Alexander II
1881–1894	Alexander III
1894–1917	Nicholas II

INDEX